INTRODUCTION TO SYRIAC

An Elementary Grammar with Readings from Syriac Literature

Wheeler M. Thackston

IBEX Publishers
Bethesda, Maryland

Introduction to Syriac
An Elementary Grammar with
Readings from Syriac Literature
by Wheeler M. Thackston

Manufactured in the United States of America

The paper used in this book meets the minimum requirements of the American National Standard for Information Services—Permanence of Paper for Printed Library Materials, ANSI Z39.48-1984

IBEX Publishers
Post Office Box 30087
Bethesda, Maryland 20824 U.S.A.
Telephone: 301-718-8188
Facsimile: 301-907-8707
www.ibexpub.com

LIBRARY OF CONGRESS CATALOGING-IN-PUBLICATION DATA

Thackston, W.M. (Wheeler McIntosh), 1944-
Introduction to Syriac : an elementary grammar with readings from Syriac literature / by W. M. Thackston.
p. cm.
Includes bibliographical references and index.
ISBN 0-936347-98-8
1. Syriac language --Grammar. I. Title.
PJ5423T53 1999
492'.382421--dc21 99-39576
CIP

1 3 5 7 9 8 6 4 2

Contents

Preface

SYRIAC IS THE ARAMAIC DIALECT of Edessa, now Urfa in Eastern Turkey, an important center of early Christianity in Mesopotamia. Edessene Syriac was rapidly accepted as the literary language of all non-Greek eastern Christianity and was the primary vehicle for the Christianization of large parts of central and south-central Asia. Even after the rupture in the fifth century between the monophysitic Jacobite church of Syria and the Nestorian Church of the East, which coincided geographically with the Persian Empire, Syriac remained the liturgical and theological language of both these "national" churches. Today it is the classical tongue of the Nestorians and Chaldeans of Iran and Iraq and the liturgical language of the Jacobites of Eastern Anatolia and the Maronites of Greater Syria. As a result of the far-reaching missionary activity of Syriac speakers, the script of Mongolian even today is a version of the Syriac alphabet written vertically *à la chinoise* instead of horizontally. Syriac is also the language of the Church of St. Thomas on the Malabar Coast of India.

Syriac belongs to the Levantine (northwest) group of the central branch of the West Semitic languages together with all other forms of Aramaic (Babylonian Aramaic, Imperial Aramaic, Palestinian Aramaic, Samaritan, Mandaean) and Canaanite (Ugaritic, Hebrew, and Phoenician). Also to the central branch belongs the North Arabian group, which comprises all forms of Arabic. Classical Ethiopic (Ge'ez) and many modern Ethiopian and South Arabian languages fall into the south branch of West Semitic. More distantly related are the East Semitic Akkadian (Assyrian and Babylonian) and Eblaite.

Syriac literature flourished from the third century on and boasts of writers like Ephraem Syrus, Aphraates, Jacob of Sarug, John of Ephesus, Jacob of Edessa, and Barhebraeus. After the Arab conquests and the advent of Islam in the seventh century to the area over which eastern Christianity held sway, Syriac became the language of a tolerated but disenfranchised and diminishing community and began a long, slow decline both as a spoken tongue and as a literary medium in favor of the dominant Arabic. Although there are a few scattered pockets of Aramaic speakers left in remote areas of the Near East, there are no immediate descendants of Syriac spoken today.

Of major importance is the role Syriac played as the intermediary through which Greek learning and thought passed to the Islamic world, for it was Syriac-speaking translators who first turned the corpus of late Hellenistic science and philosophy from Syriac into Arabic at the Dār al-Ḥikma in caliphal Baghdad. Syriac translations also preserve much Middle Iranian wisdom literature that has been lost in the original Persian.

In this text the language is presented both in the Syriac script, as it will always be seen, and in transcription, which is given so that the pronunciation of individual words and the structure of the language as a whole may be represented as clearly as possible. As is the case with most Semitic languages, Syriac leaves so much of a word unwritten that to read an unvocalized text requires a good deal of decipherment on the part of the reader. It is essential therefore for the learner to become accustomed as early as possible to recognizing words, along with all their potential readings, from the written consonantal skeleton.

After the first few lessons, the majority of the sentences in the exercises—and all of the readings in later lessons—are taken directly from the *Pšiṭṭā,* the standard Syriac translation of the Bible. It is recognized on the one hand that most students learn Syriac as an adjunct to biblical or theological studies and will be interested primarily in this text; it is difficult, on the other hand, to overestimate the stylistic influence of the Bible on Syriac authors in general. Biblical passages also have the advantage of being familiar, to some degree or other, to most English-speaking students.

Sections II and V of Preliminary Matters must be studied thoroughly before proceeding to the grammar because an understanding of the principles of *begadkepat* and the schwa, as well as vocalic reduction, is mandatory before any substantial grammatical explanations can be given. There is a preliminary exercise on p. xxvi; it should be done after one has become familiar with the contents of section II of Preliminary Matters (pp. xxii–xiv). The answers to the exercise are given on p. 224, as are transcriptions of the exercises for lessons one through five. These are intended not as a crutch but as a check for readings and spirantizations. After the twenty lessons of grammar have been finished, the learner should proceed to the section of Readings beginning on page 151, where a few biblical passages and some specimens of religious and secular literature are given. All words that occur in the reading section are contained in the Vocabulary.

For many of those whose interest in Syriac stems from biblical studies or from the history of eastern Christianity, Syriac may be their first Semitic language. Every effort has been made in the presentation of the grammar to keep the Semitic structure of the language in the forefront and as clear as possible for those who have no previous experience with languages of that family. Syriac is structurally perhaps the simplest of all the Semitic languages. It is free of the complexities of classical Arabic, has little of the unpredictability of Biblical Hebrew, and is not subject to the great dialectal and regional differences of Jewish and Imperial Aramaic.

A chart of correspondences among Arabic, Hebrew, and Syriac is given on p. xxv for the benefit of those who are approaching Syriac with a knowledge of one or more of the Semitic languages. Those who have not studied Hebrew or Arabic may safely ignore this section.

Preliminary Matters

I. The Sounds of Syriac

Consonants. The consonants of Syriac are as follows.

STOPS

p the *p* in 'pit'

b the *b* in 'bit'

t the *t* in 'ten'

d the *d* in 'den'

k the *c* in 'cave'

g the *g* in 'gave'

SPIRANTS

p̱ the *f* in 'fan'

ḇ the *v* in 'van'

ṯ the *th* in 'thing'

ḏ the *th* in 'then'

ḵ the *ch* of German *Bach*, Scottish 'loch,' and the Arabic خ, a voiceless velar fricative, pronounced like a scraped *k* but slightly further back in the throat; the point of articulation is against the soft palate [x].

g̱ the voiced counterpart to the spirantized *ḵ* above, a voiced velar fricative, the Arabic غ, rather like a gargle [γ].

VELARIZED CONSONANTS

ṭ articulated like *t* but with the tongue raised high against the velar ridge; accompanied by a constriction in the throat as a secondary articulation, like the Arabic ط, [ṭ]

ṣ articulated like *s* but, as with *ṭ* above, the tongue is raised toward the velar ridge; *ṣ* also has a constriction in the throat as a secondary articulation, like the Arabic ص, [s̴]. The European tradition mispronounces as "ts."

FRICATIVES

s the *s* in 'sip'

z the *z* in 'zip'

š the *sh* in 'ship'

GLOTTO-PHARYNGEALS

h the *h* in 'hat'

ʾ the glottal stop, as in the dialect pronunciation of "bo'l" for "bottle" and "li'l" for "little." Although glottal stop is usually lost in Syriac unless it is doubled or intervocalic, it is an integral feature of the language's morphophonemic system.

ḥ a voiceless pharyngeal fricative [ħ], articulated like *h* but father forward in the throat with the throat muscles severely constricted to produce a low hissing sound with no trace of scraping (the Arabic ح).

ʿ the voiced pharyngeal fricative, in which the vocal cords vibrate with the muscles of the throat tightly constricted; correct pronunciation is something approximating a gag (the Arabic ع).

NASALS, CONTINUANTS, SEMIVOWELS

m the *m* in 'moon'

n the *n* in 'noon'

l the *l* in 'leaf'

r the flap of the Spanish and Italian *r*, not the constriction of American English

w the *w* in 'wet'

y the *y* in 'yet'

Vowels. Syriac has the following vowels:

- *a* short *ă,* like the *o* in 'dot'
- *ā* long *ā:* in the Eastern Syriac tradition *ā* is pronounced like the *a* in 'father'; in the Western tradition it is pronounced like the *o* in 'bone'
- *e* short *ĕ,* like the *e* of 'debt'
- *ē* long *e,* like the *ay* of 'day'
- *ey* also long *ē,* used to show certain morphological forms
- *ê* in Eastern Syriac this vowel is pronounced exactly like *ē;* in Western Syriac this vowel merged with *i* everywhere and is pronounced like the *ee* in 'see'
- *i* long *ī,* like the *ee* in 'see'
- *o* both short and long *o* are pronounced in East Syriac like the *o* in 'bone'; in West Syriac *o* merged with *u* everywhere. The long *ō* is used to indicate an irreducible *o.*
- *u* long *ū,* like the *oo* in 'moon'

II. *BEGADKEPAT* AND THE SCHWA

The stops *p, b, t, d, k* and *g* and their spirantized counterparts *(p̱, ḇ, ṯ, ḏ, ḵ, g̱)*, known collectively as the *begadkepat* letters, occur in mutually exclusive environments.

(a) Only stops occur doubled, never spirants, i.e., *-pp-*, *-bb-*, etc., not *-p̱p̱-*, *-ḇḇ-*, etc., as in *ne**pp**el* 'he falls,' *sa**gg**i* 'much,' and *me**dd**em* 'thing.'

(b) The stops occur word-initially when preceded by a word ending in a consonant. The stops occur within a word at the beginning of a syllable (see section III) that is immediately preceded by one other consonant that is preceded by a vowel, as in *mal**k**ā* 'king,' *men **b**er* 'from my son,' and *lwāṯ **g**aḇrā* 'unto the man.'

(c) When preceded by any vowel, even across word boundaries, the stops are spirantized, as in *neplet (nep̱leṯ)* 'I fell,' *hāpek-nā (hāp̱eḵ-nā)* 'I am returning,' *ebad (eḇaḏ)* 'he perished,' *bnā baytā (bnā ḇaytā)* 'he built a house,' and *nektob (neḵtoḇ)* 'he writes.'

"Any vowel" in the above definition includes the schwa (ə), an unpronounced "relic," the position of which is almost entirely predictable:

(1) In any word-initial cluster of two consonants, a schwa is assumed between the two, e.g., *ktab* → *kəṯaḇ* 'he wrote,' *^{c}bad* → *^{c}əḇaḏ* 'he made,' and *tpalleg* → *təp̱alleg̱* 'you divide.'

The addition of a proclitic to such words spirantizes the first letter. The second letter, already spirantized, remains spirantized. For example, *ktab* 'he wrote' begins with two consonants; therefore, a schwa falls between the *k* and the *t*, spirantizing the *t,* and the *b* is spirantized by the vowel that precedes it: *kəṯaḇ*. The addition of a proclitic like *da- (da-ktab* 'he who wrote') results in the spirantization of the *k*, and the *t* and *b* remain spirantized as before: *da-ḵṯaḇ*. If another proclitic like *w-* is added *(w-da-ktab* 'and he who wrote'), a schwa is assumed between the *w* and the *d*, spirantizing the *d: wə-ḏa-ḵṯaḇ*.

(2) In any cluster of three consonants, a schwa is assumed between the second and third consonants, e.g., *madbrā* → *maḏbərā* 'wilderness,' *hallket* → *halləḵeṯ* 'I walked,' *atttā* → *attəṯā* 'woman,' and *makkkat* → *makkəḵaṯ* 'she humbled.'

The existence of the schwa is so entirely predictable that its use will be dispensed with in this book. The few exceptions that occur, mainly for historical reasons, will be noted.

Rule (a) does not apply across morphological boundaries. For instance, in the word *baytā* 'house,' the initial *b-* is a stop when the word is sentence-initial or preceded immediately by a word that ends in a consonant. When a proclitic like the preposition *b-* is added, the second *b* is spirantized by applying rule c(1), giving *b-ḇaytā* 'in the house.' If another proclitic, such as *da-,* is added, the resulting *da-ḇ-*

ḇaytā will have the first *b* spirantized by the vowel of *da-*. Doubled spirants occur only across morphological boundaries or as a result of vocalic reduction—never word-internally.

There are two important and constant exceptions to the *begadkepat* rules:

(1) The *-t-* of the feminine termination *-ṯā* (see §1.2) is always spirantized, whether it conforms to the *begadkepat* rules or not—for instance *amṯā* 'maidservant.' The only exception to this rule occurs when the feminine *-tā* is preceded immediately by *t*, as in *mḏittā* (with nonspirantized doubled *t*).

(2) The pronominal enclitics of the second-person plural, masculine *-ḵon* and feminine *-ḵēn*, always have spirantized *-ḵ-*.

In addition, certain verb-forms have endings not conditioned by the *begadkepat* rules. These will be noted as they occur.

III. Syllabification

Every syllable in Syriac begins with one and only one consonant, which is necessarily followed by a vowel (long, short, or schwa). Any two-consonant cluster is then broken between the two because no syllable may begin with more than one consonant. Clusters of three consonants have an implied schwa between the second and third consonants (see c(2) above) and are therefore treated as two-consonant clusters. In words that begin with a vowel, the initial vowel is reckoned a glottal stop plus vowel; where it occurs, the glottal stop is treated like any other consonant. Examples: *malkā (mal-kā), ṭurā (ṭu-rā), šmayyā (šə-may-yā), emar ('e-mar), malktā (mal-kə-tā), madbrā (mad-bə-rā, sleqt (sə-leqt), ḥakkim (ḥak-kim).* Syllables ending in a vowel are called "open"; those that end in a consonant are called "closed."

IV. STRESS

Stress may fall on any of the final three syllables in a word.

(1) Ultimate stress. Any final syllable (ultima) that is closed and contains a long vowel is stressed, as in *ḥakkim (ḥak-kim´), nebnōn (neb-nōn´), bāneyn (bā-neyn´), šaddarnāk (šad-dar-nāk´), bnāt (bə-nāt´), ḥzayt (ḥə-zayt´), qaṭluh (qaṭ-luh´), šappirān (šap-pi-rān´).*

(2) Penultimate stress. If the final syllable is not stressed, then the next to last syllable (penultima) receives stress if it contains a long vowel or is closed, e.g., *malkā (mal´-kā), bānē (bā´-nē), emret (em´-ret), qaṭleh (qaṭ´-leh), qṭalton (qə-ṭal´-ton), attat (at´-tat).*

(3) Antepenultimate stress. If the criteria set forth in (1) and (2) above are not met, then stress recedes to the syllable before the penultimate, the antepenultimate, e.g., *madbrā (mad´-bə-rā), atttā (at´-tə-tā), malktā (mal´-kə-tā), etqṭel (et´-qə-ṭel).*

In no instance may an open syllable with a short vowel be stressed. In such a situation stress falls forward to the next stressable syllable, as *emar (e-mar´), ḥzā (ḥə-zā´), enā (e-nā´), qṭal (qə-ṭal´).*

V. VOCALIC REDUCTION AND PROSTHESIS

An important element of Syriac phonology is the principle of retrogressive vocalic reduction. Simply stated, any short vowel *(a, e, o)* in an open syllable is reduced to zero or schwa (|Cv̆| → |Cꝟ| → |C|). Such reduction is always calculated retrogressively, i.e., from the end of the word back toward the beginning. Examples: *qāṭel + -in* → **qā-ṭe-lin* → *qāṭlin; nektob + -un* → **nek-to-bun* → *nektbun; šaddar + -āk* → **šad-da-rāk* → *šaddrāk; ta^{cc}el + -an* → **ta^{c}-^{c}e-lan* → *ta^{cc}lan.*

Words are immune to vocalic reduction in the following cases:

(1) with the optional third-person plural perfect endings *-un*

and *-ēn* (see §1.3);

(2) with the singular copulas *-u* and *-i* (see §6.2);

(3) in syllables resulting from the loss of glottal stop, e.g., *še'let* → *šelet.*

The principle of prosthesis is as follows: wherever vocalic reduction would give a glottal stop a schwa, the schwa is replaced with the vowel *e* and the glottal stop is then dropped *(C'C* → *C'eC* → *CeC).* For example, *neš'al* + *-un* → **neš-'a-lun* → **neš'lun* → **neš'elun* → *nešelun,* and **'amar* → **'mar* → **'emar* → *emar.*

Similarly when the two "weak" consonants *w* and *y* occur in a position that would require them to take schwa, they become the full vowels *u* and *i* respectively, e.g., **ḥadwtā* → **ḥadwətā* → *ḥadutā,* **yda^c* → **yəda^c* → *ida^c*, **etyled* → **etyəled* → *etiled.* Syllables resulting from such changes are immune to vocalic reduction.

VI. THE SYRIAC ALPHABET

The Syriac alphabet, written from right to left, was developed from the Aramaic alphabet and, like Arabic, is basically a cursive script, i.e., most letters are joined one to another within a word. All letters connect from the right, and all but eight letters (indicated by asterisks below) connect forward to the left. Most of the various forms of a given letter are quite similar; only *kāp* and *nun* have wildly divergent forms.

There are three varieties of Syriac script in use, Estrangela, Nestorian and Jacobite. Because of its linear simplicity and elegance, Estrangela has much to recommend it and has been chosen as the basic script for this book.

The Estrangela letters are as follows:

ARAMAIC EQUIVALENT	FINAL/ALONE FORM	INITIAL/MEDIAL FORM	NAME OF LETTER	VALUE
א		ܐ	*ālap**	*', -ā, -ē*
ב	ܒ	ܒ	*bēt*	*b*
ג	ܓ	ܓ	*gāmal*	*g*
ד		ܕ	*dālat**	*d*
ה		ܗ	*hēt**	*h*
ו		ܘ	*wāw**	*w, o, u*
ז		ܙ	*zayn**	*z*
ח	ܚ	ܚ	*ḥēt*	*ḥ*
ט	ܛ	ܛ	*ṭēt*	*ṭ*
י	ܝ	ܝ	*yod*	*y, i, ē*
כ	ܟ	ܟ	*kāp*	*k*
ל	ܠ	ܠ	*lāmad*	*l*
מ	ܡ	ܡ	*mim*	*m*
נ	ܢ	ܢ	*nun*	*n*
ס	ܣ	ܣ	*semkat*	*s*

ע	ܥ	ܥ	*ᶜē*	ᶜ
פ	ܦ	ܦ	*pē*	*p*
צ		ܨ	*ṣādē**	*ṣ*
ק	ܩ	ܩ	*qop*	*q*
ר		ܪ	*rēš**	*r*
ש	ܫ	ܫ	*šin*	*š*
ת		ܬ	*taw**	*t*

Plus one optional digraph:

תא		ܬܐ	*taw-ālap**	*tā*

The Nestorian (East Syriac) letters are as follows. Note particularly the *ālap* and the various forms of *kāp*.

ALONE	FINAL	MEDIAL	INITIAL	NAME
	ـܐ		ܐ	*ālap*
ܒ	ـܒ	ـܒـ	ܒـ	*bēt*
ܓ	ـܓ	ـܓـ	ܓـ	*gāmal*
	ـܕ		ܕ	*dālat*
	ـܗ		ܗ	*hēt*
	ـܘ		ܘ	*wāw*
	ـܙ		ܙ	*zayn*
ܚ	ـܚ	ـܚـ	ܚـ	*ḥēt*
ܛ	ـܛ	ـܛـ	ܛـ	*ṭēt*
ܝ	ـܝ	ـܝـ	ܝـ	*yod*
ܟ	ـܟ	ـܟـ	ܟـ	*kāp*
ܠ	ـܠ	ـܠـ	ܠـ	*lāmad*
ܡ	ـܡ	ـܡـ	ܡـ	*mim*
ܢ	ـܢ	ـܢـ	ܢـ	*nun*
ܣ	ـܣ	ـܣـ	ܣـ	*semkat*
ܥ	ـܥ	ـܥـ	ܥـ	*ᶜē*
ܦ	ـܦ	ـܦـ	ܦـ	*pē*
	ـܨ		ܨ	*ṣādē*

ܩ	ـܩ	ـܩـ	ܩـ	*qop*
	ـܪ		ܪ	*rēš*
ܫ	ـܫ	ـܫـ	ܫـ	*šin*
	ـܬ		ܬ	*taw*
	ـܬ			*taw* (alternative[1])
	ـܠܐ		ܠܐ	*lāmad-ālap*

The Jacobite (West Syriac) letters are as follows. Note particularly the various forms of *dālat, rēš, kāp,* and *taw* and the double lines of the final ^{c}*ē* and *lāmad.*

ALONE	FINAL	MEDIAL	INITIAL	NAME
	ـܐ		ܐ	*ālap*
ܒ	ـܒ	ـܒـ	ܒـ	*bēt*
ܓ	ـܓ	ـܓـ	ܓـ	*gāmal*
	ـܕ		ܕ	*dālat*
	ـܗ		ܗ	*hēt*
	ـܘ		ܘ	*wāw*
	ـܙ		ܙ	*zayn*
ܚ	ـܚ	ـܚـ	ܚـ	*ḥēt*
ܛ	ـܛ	ـܛـ	ܛـ	*ṭēt*
ܝ	ـܝ	ـܝـ	ܝـ	*yod*
ܟ	ـܟ	ـܟـ	ܟـ	*kāp*
ܠ	ـܠ	ـܠـ	ܠـ	*lāmad*
ܡ	ـܡ	ـܡـ	ܡـ	*mim*
ܢ	ـܢ	ـܢـ	ܢـ	*nun*
ܣ	ـܣ	ـܣـ	ܣـ	*semkat*
ܥ	ـܥ	ـܥـ	ܥـ	^{c}*ē*
ܦ	ـܦ	ـܦـ	ܦـ	*pē*
	ـܨ		ܨ	*ṣādē*

[1]Only when word final and connected to preceding letter.

ܩ	ܩـ	ـܩـ	ܩ	*qop*
	ـܪ		ܪ	*rēš*
ܫ	ܫـ	ـܫـ	ܫ	*šin*
	ـܬ		ܬ	*taw*

and the special digraph for an initial *ālap-lāmad:*

ܐܠ *ālap-lāmad*

As in most Semitic alphabets, the graphic system basically represents the consonants. The short vowels *a* and *e* are not at all represented graphically.

Ālap represents (1) all initial vowels, as in ܐܪܥܐ *ar*^{c}*ā* 'earth,' ܐܕܡ *ādam* 'Adam,' and ܐܡܪ *emar* 'he said,' (2) final *-ā* and final *-ē,* as in ܟܬܒܐ *ktābā* 'book' and ܓܒܪܐ *gabrē* 'men,' as well as (3) original glottal stop, as in ܢܫܐܠ *nešal* (originally *neš'al*—even though the glottal stop was dropped from pronunciation in Syriac, the *ālap* remained as a historical spelling).

Yod is used (1) as the consonant *y* as in ܝܕܥ *yāda*^{c} and ܡܠܝܐ *malyā,* and (2) to represent the vowels *i* and internal *ē* as in ܣܝܡ *sim* and ܒܝܬ *bēt.* The vowel *ê* is sometimes spelled with *yod* and sometimes not, as in ܗܘܝܬ *hwêt* 'I was' but ܥܕܬܐ ^{c}*êdtā* 'church.'[1] Initial *i* and *ē* are spelled *ālap-yod,* as in ܐܝܙܓܕܐ *izgaddā* 'envoy.'

Wāw serves (1) as the consonant *w* as in ܘܠܐ *wālē* and ܝܘܡܐ *yawmā,* and (2) to indicate the vowels *o, ō* and *u* as in ܝܘܡ *yom,* ܢܒܢܘܢ *nebnōn* and ܩܘܡ *qum.* Initial *o* and *u* are spelled *ālap-wāw,* as in ܐܘܪܝܐ *oryā* 'manger' and ܐܘܪܚܐ *urḥā* 'road.'

For representing the vowels there are two orthographic conventions, neither of which will be used in this book. The East Syriac (Nestorian) convention is as follows.

ـܲ *a*, as in ܗܲ *ha*

[1]In a few words *ê* is spelled with *ālap,* as ܚܐܪܐ *ḥêrā* 'nobleman' and ܫܐܕܐ *šêdā* 'demon.' These must simply be learned as items of spelling.

ـܵ *ā,* as in ܗܵ *hā* (also represents Greek *α*)

ـܸ *e,* as in ܗܸ *he* (also Greek *ϵ*)

ـܹܝ *ē* and *ey,* as in ܗܹܝ *hē* and *hey* (also Greek *ϵι*)

ـܹ *ê,*[1] as in ܗܹ and ܗܹܝ *hê* (also Greek *η*)

ـܝܼ *i,* as in ܗܝܼ *hi* (also Greek *ι*)

ܘܿ *o,* as in ܗܘܿ *ho, hō* (also Greek *ο* and *ω*)

ܘܼ *u,* as in ܗܘܼ *hu* (also Greek *υ* and *ου*)

In some fully vocalized Nestorian texts the diphthong *aw* is consistently pointed *āw,* as ܝܵܘܡܵܐ for *yawmā.*

The West Syrian (Jacobite) convention uses the "Greek" vowels as follows. In general, the vowels are written over short letters and upside down under tall letters, but they can be placed in either position with any letter.

ـܰ *a (ptāḥā),* as in ܗܰ *ha* and ܛܱ *ta*

ـܳ *ā (zqāpā),* as in ܗܳ *hā* and ܛܴ *tā* (pronounced *ho* and *to)*

ـܶ *e (rbāṣā),* as in ܗܶ *he* and ܛܷ *te*

ـܺܝ *i (ḥbāṣā),* as in ܗܺܝ *hi* and ܛܻܝ *ti*

ܘܽ *u (ᶜṣāṣā),* as in ܗܽܘ *hu* and ܛܾܘ *tu*

In the Jacobite/West Syriac tradition, original *o*-vowels are marked with a dot above the *wāw,* and original *u*-vowels with a dot below, even though the two vowels merged as *u.* For example, ܢܩܽܘܡ *nqum* (originally *nqum),* but ܢܶܥܽܘܿܠ *neᶜᶜul* (originally *neᶜᶜol).*

VII. Other Orthographic Devices

(1) Linea occultans, a line drawn over or under a letter to indicate

---

[1] *ê* is usually, but not always, spelled with a *yod;* some words omit the *yod.*

(a) assimilation of that letter to the following or preceding letter, as in ܡܕܝܢ̱ܬܐ *mdittā* 'city' and ܐܙܠ̱ܬ *ezzet* 'I went.'

(b) the loss of initial *ālap* and *hē* in pronunciation, as in ܐ̱ܚܪܝܐ *ḥrāyā* 'last' and ܗ̱ܘܐ *wā* 'was.'

(2) *Syāmē,* two dots placed over all plural nouns and adjectives (except the masculine plural absolute participle, see §8.1) and certain feminine plural verbs. Although the *syāmē* dots may occur over any letter, they tend to combine with the dot of *rēš* (ܪ̈) when a word contains that letter; otherwise they are usually placed over one of the shorter letters. Unlike other orthographic devices, the *syāmē* dots are not optional; without them it is impossible to distinguish the plural of most nouns and adjectives from the singular.

ܢܦܩ̈ܢ ܗ̱ܘ̈ܝ ܢܫ̈ܐ ܫܦܝܪ̈ܬܐ.	*nāpqān-way neššē šappirātā.*	The beautiful women went out.

(3) Verb and homograph dots: one dot is placed beneath all perfect verbs except the first-person singular, which is distinguished by one dot above, as in ܢܦܩ̣ܬ *nepqat* 'she went out' but ܢܦܩܬ̇ *nepqet* 'I went out.' In fully pointed Nestorian texts, the perfect dot is dispensed with in the third-person feminine singular perfect, and the *taw* ending is marked with two underdots, as in ܢܦܩܬ̤ *nepqat* 'she went out.'

One dot is placed over all active participles to distinguish them from orthographically similar forms, as ܟ̇ܬܒ *kāteb* 'writing' versus ܟܬ̣ܒ *ktab* 'he wrote.' These dots may occur anywhere in the word.

Since Syriac abounds in homographs, dots are sometimes used to distinguish words that are written identically but pronounced differently, e.g.

ܗ̇ܘ	*haw* 'that'	ܗ̣ܘ	*hu* 'he'
ܡ̇ܠܟܐ	*malkā* 'king'	ܡ̣ܠܟܐ	*melkā* 'counsel'
ܡ̇ܢ	*man* 'who?'	ܡ̣ܢ	*men* 'from'

In this book the verbal and participial dots will be fairly consistently shown; other distinguishing dots will be used occasionally, but not with consistency.

(4) Gemination of Consonants. There is no device in Syriac orthography to indicate gemination (doubling) of consonants. In West Syriac true consonantal gemination was probably lost long ago; in East Syriac, on the other hand, gemination is traditionally retained and will be so indicated in the present transcription.

There does exist a device for marking the spirantization and non-spirantization of the *begadkepat* consonants, and this may incidentally indicate the doubling of one of these consonants.

(a) *quššāyā,* in West Syriac a small dot above the letter, and in East Syriac a small oblique line above the letter (ܒ݁ *b*). It indicates that the *begadkepat* consonants are stops.

(b) *rukkākā,* in West Syriac a small dot beneath the letter, and in East Syriac a small oblique line beneath the letter (ܒ݂ *b̲*). It indicates the spirantization of the *begadkepat* consonants, as in ܟܬܒ݂ *kt̲ab̲* 'he wrote' and ܬܟܬܘܒ݂ *tek̲tob̲* 'she writes.'

Neither *quššāyā* nor *rukkākā* will be used in this book.

VIII. Alphabetic Numerals

In Syriac, as in most other Semitic languages, the letters of the alphabet are also used as numerals, as follows:

LETTER	NUMERICAL VALUE
ܐ	1
ܒ	2
ܓ	3
ܕ	4
ܗ	5

ܘ	6
ܙ	7
ܚ	8
ܛ	9
ܝ	10
ܟ	20
ܠ	30
ܡ	40
ܢ	50
ܣ	60
ܥ	70
ܦ	80
ܨ	90
ܩ	100
ܪ	200
ܫ	300
ܬ	400

Compound numbers are expressed decimally from right to left as ܝܒ for 12 and ܪܠܘ for 236. Numbers over 400 use ܢ and ܣ as 500 and 600, &c. ܐ is used for 1000. Therefore, 1999 is expressed as ܐܨܨܛ.

IX. Comparative Chart of Semitic Consonants

The following chart gives the consonants of Arabic, Hebrew, and Syriac as they normally occur in cognate roots. There are, of course, exceptions.

ا	ب	ت	ث	ج	ح	خ	د	ذ	ر	ز	س	س	ش	ص	ض
א	ב	ת	שׁ	ג	ח	ח	ד	ז	ר	ז	ס	שׁ	שׂ	צ	צ
ܐ	ܒ	ܬ	ܬ	ܓ	ܚ	ܚ	ܕ	ܕ	ܪ	ܙ	ܣ	ܫ	ܣ	ܨ	ܥ

ط	ظ	ع	غ	ف	ق	ك	ل	م	ن	ه	و	ى
ט	צ	ע	ע	פ	ק	כ	ל	מ	נ	ה	ו	י
ܛ	ܛ	ܥ	ܥ	ܦ	ܩ	ܟ	ܠ	ܡ	ܢ	ܗ	ܘ	ܝ

The Syriac ܣ that is ס in Hebrew is س in Arabic: Syriac ܣܓܕ *sge͟d* = Hebrew סָגַד *sāg̱ad̲* = Arabic سجد *sajada* 'bow down' (Ethiopic ሰገደ *sagada)*; Syr. ܐܣܝܪܐ *asirā* = Heb. אָסִיר *āsīr* = Ar. اسير *asīr-* 'prisoner, captive' (Eth. አሱር *əsur)*, while the Syriac ܣ that is שׂ in Hebrew is ش in Arabic: Syr. ܣܥܪܐ *sa^{c}rā* = Heb. שֵׂעָר *śē^{c}ār* = Ar. شعر *ša^{c}r-* 'hair' (Akkadian *šārtam,* Eth. ሥዕርት *śə^{c}ərt);* Syr. ܣܒܥ *sb̲a^c* = Heb. שָׂבֵעַ *śāb̲ēa^c* = Ar. شبع *šabi^{c}a* 'be satiated' (Akk. *še-bûm)*; Syr. ܥܣܪ *^{c}sar* = Heb. עֶשֶׂר *^{c}eśer* = Ar. عشر *^{c}ašr-* 'ten' (Akk. *ešer,* Eth. ዐሥሩ *^{c}aśru).* All Syriac ܫ's are س in Arabic: Syr. ܫܡܐ *šmā* = Ar. اسم *ism-* 'name' (Heb. שֵׁם *šēm,* Eth. ስም *səm,* Akk. *šu-mum*); Syr. ܫܒܥ *šb̲a^c* = Ar. سبع *sab^c-* 'seven' (Heb. שֶׁבַע *šeb̲a^c*, Eth. ሰብዑ *sab^{c}u,* Akk. *sebe).*

The Arabic ض is צ in Hebrew but ܥ in Syriac: Ar. ارض *arḍ-* = Heb. אֶרֶץ *ereṣ* = Syr. ܐܪܥܐ *ar^{c}ā* 'land' (Akk. *erṣetum)*; Ar. ضأن *ḍa'n-* = Heb. צֹאן *ṣōn* = Syr. ܥܢܐ *^{c}ānā* 'sheep.'

The Arabic ت and ث are ת and שׁ respectively in Hebrew, but they are both ܬ in Syriac: Ar. تسع *tis^c-* = Heb. תֵּשַׁע *tēša^c* = Syr. ܬܫܥ *tša^c* 'nine' (Eth. ተስዑ *təs^{c}u,* Akk. *tiše);* Ar. ثلاث *thalāth-* = Heb. שָׁלֹשׁ *šāloš* = Syr. ܬܠܬ *tlāt̲* 'three' (Eth. ሠላስ *śalās,* Akk. *ša-lāš);* Ar. حدث *ḥadath-* = Heb. חָדָשׁ *ḥād̲āš* = Syr. ܚܕܬ *ḥd̲et̲* 'new' (Eth. ሐዲስ *ḥaddis,* Akk. *eššum).* Similarly the Arabic د and ذ, which are ד and ז respectively in Hebrew, are both ܕ in Syriac: Ar. يد *yad-* = Heb. יָד *yād̲* = Syr. ܐܝܕܐ *id̲ā* 'hand' (Eth. እድ *əd);* Ar. ذهب *dhahab-* = Heb. זָהָב *zāhāb̲* = Syr. ܕܗܒܐ *dahb̲ā* 'gold'; Ar. ذئب

dhi'b- = Heb. זְאֵב *zə'ēb̲* = Syr. ܕܐܒܐ *dêb̲ā* 'wolf'; Ar. أذن *udhn-* = = Heb. אֹזֶן *ózen* = Syr. ܐܕܢܐ *ed̲nā* 'ear' (Eth. እዝን *əzn,* Akk. *uznum).* So also Arabic ط and ظ, which are ט and צ respectively in Hebrew, are both ܛ in Syriac: Ar. طلا *ṭalā* = Heb. טָלֶה *ṭāleh* = Syr. ܛܠܝܐ *ṭalyā* 'kid' (Eth. ጠሊ *ṭali);* Ar. ظفر *ẓufur-* = Heb. צִפֹּרֶן *ṣipporen* = Syr. ܛܦܪܐ *ṭep̲rā* 'fingernail'; Ar. نظر *naẓara* = Heb. נָצַר *nāṣar* = Syr. ܢܛܪ *nṭar* 'to look, look after, guard' (Eth. ነጸረ *naṣṣara*, Akk. *naṣārum).*

Arabic ح and خ are both ܚ in Syriac and ח in Hebrew: Ar. خمس *khams-* = Syr. ܚܡܫ *ḥammeš* = Heb. חָמֵשׁ *ḥāmēš* 'five' (Eth. ኀምስ *khams,* Akk. *ḫamiš);* Ar. حسب *ḥasaba* = Syr. ܚܫܒ *ḥšab̲* = Heb. חָשַׁב *ḥāšab̲* 'reckon' (Eth. ሐሰበ *ḥasaba).* Arabic ع and غ are both ܥ in Syriac and ע in Hebrew: Ar. عبد *ᶜabd-* = Syr. ܥܒܕܐ *ᶜab̲dā* = Heb. עֶבֶד *ᶜeb̲ed̲* 'slave, servant'; Ar. مغرب *maghrib-* = Syr. ܡܥܪܒܐ *maᶜrb̲ā* = Heb. מַעֲרָב *maᶜărāb̲* 'west' (Eth. ምዕራብ *məᶜrāb);* Ar. غلام *ghulām-* = Heb. עֶלֶם *ᶜelem* = Syr. ܥܠܝܡܐ *ᶜlaymā* 'lad.'

The remaining consonants have one-to-one correspondences.

X. Preliminary Exercise

In the following text (The Lord's Prayer, Matthew 6:9–13), the *begadkepat* consonants are given in boldface. Mark all the spirantized consonants with an underline. Treat the entire passage as continuous, i.e. with no significant pauses that would affect spirantization. (Answer given on p. 224.)

ܐܒܘܢ ܕܒܫܡܝܐ ܢܬܩܕܫ ܫܡܟ ܬܐܬܐ ܡܠܟܘܬܟ ܢܗܘܐ ܨܒܝܢܟ
ܐܝܟܢܐ ܕܒܫܡܝܐ ܐܦ ܒܐܪܥܐ: ܗܒ ܠܢ ܠܚܡܐ ܕܣܘܢܩܢܢ
ܝܘܡܢܐ: ܘܫܒܘܩ ܠܢ ܚܘܒܝܢ: ܐܝܟܢܐ ܕܐܦ ܚܢܢ ܫܒܩܢ ܠܚܝܒܝܢ:
ܘܠܐ ܬܥܠܢ ܠܢܣܝܘܢܐ: ܐܠܐ ܦܨܢ ܡܢ ܒܝܫܐ: ܡܛܠ ܕܕܝܠܟ
ܗܝ ܡܠܟܘܬܐ ܘܚܝܠܐ ܘܬܫܒܘܚܬܐ ܠܥܠܡ ܥܠܡܝܢ ※

*a**b**un **d**-**b**a-šmayyā, ne**t**qa**dd**aš šmā**k**, **t**ê**t**ē mal**k**u**t**ā**k**, nehwē ṣe**b**-yānā**k** ay**k**annā **d**-**b**a-šmayyā ā**p** **b**-arᶜā. ha**b** lan laḥmā **d**-sunqā-*

*nan yawmānā. wa-š**b**oq lan ḥaw**b**ayn. ay**k**annā **d**-ā**p** ḥnan š**b**aqn l-ḥayyā**b**ayn. w-lā **t**a^{cc}lan l-nesyōnā. ellā **p**aṣṣān men **b**išā. meṭṭul **d**-**d**ilā**k**-i mal**k**u**t**ā w-ḥaylā w-**t**eš**b**oḥ**t**ā l-^{c}ālam-^{c}ālmin.*

The Grammar of Syriac

ܪܫܐ ܩܕܡܝܐ
Lesson One

§ 1.1 The Emphatic State. All Syriac nouns occur in a basic lexical form, with the termination *-ā,* known traditionally as the emphatic state. Two other states of the noun occur, and these will be taken up later. For the moment, suffice it to say that the emphatic state may mean both the indefinite and the definite in English (e.g., *gabrā* 'a man' or 'the man,' and *ktābā* 'a book' or 'the book'). For translation, context should be the guide to which of the two fits a given occurrence.

§ 1.2 Gender. There are two grammatical genders in Syriac, masculine and feminine. As far as persons and things have natural gender ('father, mother, son, daughter, ram, ewe,' etc.), grammatical gender follows natural gender; otherwise there is no clear or consistent relationship between grammatical gender and meaning. There is, however, a correspondence between form and gender: almost all feminine nouns are marked by the ending *-tā* in the emphatic state, whereas masculine nouns have no special ending other than the *-ā* termination of the emphatic state.

MASCULINE		FEMININE	
ܡܠܟܐ	*malkā* king	ܡܠܟܬܐ	*malktā* queen
ܓܒܪܐ	*gabrā* man	ܐܢ̄ܬܬܐ	*atttā* woman
ܟܬܒܐ	*ktābā* book	ܡܕܝܢ̄ܬܐ	*mdittā* city
ܛܘܪܐ	*ṭurā* mountain	ܩܪܝܬܐ	*qritā* village

The only class of exceptions consists of nouns that are feminine in gender but do not have the *-tā* ending, like ܐܝܕܐ *idā* 'hand,' ܐܡܐ *emmā* 'mother,' and ܐܪܥܐ *ar^{c}ā* 'earth.' The few nouns that do not show their gender will be marked in the vocabularies.

§ 1.3 The Perfect of the Simple (G) Verb. The basic lexical form of the perfect verb consists of the verbal root, usually triconsonantal, with an appropriate vowel pattern, either *CCaC,* as in ܟܬܒ *ktab* 'he wrote, he has written,' or *CCeC,* as in ܣܠܩ *sleq* 'he went forth, he has gone forth.' This form *(ktab, sleq)* is the third-person masculine singular ('he') of the perfect, which usually translates into English as the simple past ('he wrote') or, according to context, the present perfect ('he has written'). It represents the unaugmented base, or ground, form of the verb and has the Semitic designation G (for *Grundstamm).*

The third-person feminine singular adds an ending *-at* to the verbal root. Concurrently all verbs undergo a pattern change from *CCaC* or *CCeC* to *CeCC-*, giving the invariable 3rd-pers. fem. form *CeCCat,* e.g., ܟܬܒܬ *ketbat* 'she wrote, she has written' and ܣܠܩܬ *selqat* 'she went out, she has gone out.'

The third-person masculine plural ('they') has two forms, in more or less free variation, (1) with an unpronounced *-w* added to the 3rd masc. sing., as in ܟܬܒܘ *ktab* 'they wrote' and ܣܠܩܘ *sleq* 'they went out,' and (2) with the ending *-un* added to the singular, as in ܟܬܒܘܢ *ktabun* 'they wrote' and ܣܠܩܘܢ *slequn* 'they went out.' There is no discernible difference in meaning between the two forms.

The third-person feminine plural ('they') has three alternative forms: (1) identical to the 3rd masc. sing. (ܟܬܒ *ktab* 'they [f] wrote'), (2) with an unpronounced *-y* added to the masc. sing. form (ܟܬ̈ܒܝ *ktab* 'they [f] wrote'), and (3) with the ending *-ēn* added to the masculine singular (ܟܬ̈ܒܝܢ *ktabēn* 'they [f] wrote'). In the two latter cases, the *syāmē* dots are placed above the verb to mark plurality.

Note that all these forms of the perfect have a dot beneath the verb; this distinguishes the perfect verb from other orthographically similar forms.

The full 3rd-person inflection of a perfect verb will then be either on the patterns of *ktab:*

3 m	ܟܬܒ	*ktab*	ܟܬܒ(ܘܢ)	*ktab(un)*
f	ܟܬܒܬ	*ketbat*	ܟܬܒ(̈ܝܢ)	*ktab(ēn)*

or on the patterns of *sleq:*

3 m	ܣܠܩ	*sleq*	ܣܠܩ(ܘܢ)	*sleq(un)*
f	ܣܠܩܬ	*selqat*	ܣܠܩ(̈ܝܢ)	*sleq(ēn)*

Verbs agree with their noun subjects in number and gender and may precede or follow the subject indiscriminately:

ܣܠܩ ܡܠܟܐ	*sleq malkā.*	The king went forth.
ܡܠܟ̈ܐ ܣܠܩܘ	*malkē sleq.*	The kings went forth.
ܡܠܟܬܐ ܣܠܩܬ	*malktā selqat.*	The queen went forth.
ܣܠܩ̈ ܡܠܟ̈ܬܐ	*sleq malkātā.*	The queens went forth.

The negative of the perfect is made by *lā,* which precedes the verb:

ܠܐ ܟܬܒ ܡܠܟܐ	*lā ktab malkā.*	The king did not write.
ܠܐ ܣܠܩܬ ܡܠܟܬܐ	*lā selqat malktā.*	The queen did not go forth.

§ 1.4 The Proclitics. The prepositions *l-* ('to, for' a person, 'to' a place) and *b-* ('in, at') and the conjunction *w-* ('and') are proclitic, i.e., they are added orthographically directly to the beginning of the next word.

(1) When added to a word that begins with a consonant followed by a vowel, these proclitics are added as they are (i.e., without vowel), as in ܠܡܠܟܐ *l-malkā* 'to/for the king,' ܒܛܘܪܐ *b-ṭurā* 'at/on the mountain,' and ܘܥܡܐ *w-'ammā* 'and the people.' The addition of any such proclitic to a word that begins with a stop results in spirantization of the stop, as ܓܒܪܐ *gaḇrā* 'the man' > ܠܓܒܪܐ *l-gaḇrā* 'for the man.' For spirantization, see Preliminary Matters, II. *Begadkepat*

and the *Schwa*, p. xii.

(2) When added to a word that begins with two consonants, these proclitics are read *la-*, *ba-* and *wa-*, as in ܒܡܕܝܢ̄ܬܐ *ba-mdittā* 'in the city,' ܘܡܕܝܢ̄ܬܐ *wa-mdittā* 'and the city,' and ܠܩܪܝܬܐ *la-qritā* 'to/for the village.' The addition of any such proclitic to a word beginning with a stop results in the spirantization of the stop, as ܟܬܒܐ *kṯāḇā* 'the book' > ܒܟܬܒܐ *ba-kṯāḇā* 'in the book.'

(3) When added to a word that begins with *ālap,* these proclitics assume the vowel of the *ālap,* as in ܘܐܡܐ *w-emmā* (pronounced *wemmā)* 'and the mother' and ܠܐܢ̄ܬܬܐ *l-atttā* (pronounced *lattṯā)* 'to/for the woman.'

Vocabulary 1

NOUNS

- ܐܢ̄ܬܬܐ *atttā* woman, wife
- ܓܒܪܐ *gabrā* man
- ܛܘܪܐ *ṭurā* mountain
- ܡܕܝܢ̄ܬܐ *mdittā* city
- ܡܠܟܐ *malkā* king
- ܡܠܟܬܐ *malktā* queen
- ܥܡܐ ^{c}*ammā* people

VERBS[1]

- ܟܬܒ *ktab* to write
- ܢܦܠ *npal* to fall
- ܣܠܩ *sleq* to go up/out
- ܥܪܩ ^{c}*raq* to flee
- ܫܡܥ *šma*^{c} to hear

[1] Verbs in all Semitic languages are traditionally quoted lexically in the 3rd-person masc. sing., the simplest form in which the verb occurs. Only for purposes of vocabulary lists is this form equivalent to the English infinitive.

OTHERS

ܒ *b- (ba-)* in, at, with[1]
ܗܪܟܐ *hārkā* here
ܘ *w- (wa-)* and
ܠ *l- (la-)* to, for
ܠܐ *lā* not (negative)
ܡܢ *men (menn-*[2]*)* from
ܬܡܢ *tammān* there

Exercise 1

(a) Read and translate the following:

1 ܦܠܛ ܡܢ ܡܕܝܢ̈ܬܐ
2 ܪܗܛܬ ܠܛܘܪܐ
3 ܪܗܛܘ ܡܢ ܡܕܝܢ̈ܬܐ
4 ܦܠܛ̈ܝ ܠܛܘܪܐ
5 ܢܦܠ ܓܒܪܐ
6 ܟܬܒܬ ܐܢ̈ܬܬܐ
7 ܪܗܛܘ ܥܡܐ ܡܢ ܗܪܟܐ
8 ܟܬܒ ܡܠܟܐ ܠܥܡܐ
9 ܪܗܛܝ ܡܢ ܬܡܢ
10 ܥܒܕܬ ܡܠܟܬܐ
11 ܪܗܛܬ ܐܢ̈ܬܬܐ ܡܢ ܡܕܝܢ̈ܬܐ
12 ܪܗܛ ܓܒܪܐ ܡܢ ܡܠܟܐ
13 ܦܠܛܬ ܐܢ̈ܬܬܐ ܡܢ ܬܡܢ
14 ܢܦܠ ܓܒܪܐ ܡܢ ܛܘܪܐ

---

[1] *B* means ‘with’ only for instrumentals, as ‘he hit me *with* a stick.’

[2] I.e., *men* before nouns; *menn-* before enclitic pronouns (§3.1).

15 ܠܐ ܥܪܩ ܡܠܟܐ ܡܢ ܡܕܝܢ̈ܬܐ

16 ܠܐ ܣܠܩܬ ܐܢ̈ܬܬܐ ܡܢ ܛܘܪܐ

17 ܠܐ ܫܡܥ ܥܡܐ

18 ܠܐ ܟܬܒܬ ܠܡܠܟܐ

19 ܣܠܩܬ ܡܠܟܬܐ ܡܢ ܥܡܐ

20 ܠܐ ܥܪܩ ܓܒܪܐ ܠܬܡܢ

21 ܣܠܩܬ ܐܢ̈ܬܬܐ ܠܡܕܝܢ̈ܬܐ

(b) Translate the following into Syriac:

1. The woman fled from the man.
2. The mountain fell.
3. The man did not write to the king.
4. The people did not hear.
5. The man went out from the city to the mountain.
6. The people fled from here.
7. The people wrote to the king and queen.
8. They (m) went out from there.
9. They (f) wrote to the man.
10. The city fell to the king.

ܪܫܐ ܕܬܪܝܢ
Lesson Two

§ 2.1 The Perfect: Full Inflection. Following is the full inflection of the perfect. The masculine-feminine distinction is maintained in both the second and third persons; the first persons are of common gender. Because the third-person masculine singular form is the basic lexical form of the verb, all paradigms begin with that form, in accord with general Semitic usage.

	SINGULAR		PLURAL	
3 m	ܟܬܰܒ	*kṯaḇ*	ܟܬܰܒܘ	*kṯaḇ* or
			ܟܬܰܒܘܢ	*kṯaḇun*
f	ܟܶܬܒܰܬ	*keṯbaṯ*	ܟܬܰ̈ܒ / ܟܬܰܒ	*kṯaḇ* or
			ܟܬܰ̈ܒܶܢ	*kṯaḇēn*
2 m	ܟܬܰܒܬ	*kṯaḇt*	ܟܬܰܒܬܘܢ	*kṯaḇton*
f	ܟܬܰܒܬܝ	*kṯaḇt*	ܟܬܰܒܬܶܝܢ	*kṯaḇtēn*
1 c	ܟܶܬܒܶ̇ܬ	*keṯbeṯ*	ܟܬܰܒܢ	*kṯaḇn* or
			ܟܬܰܒܢܢ	*kṯaḇnan*

Perfect verbs with sound roots are inflected either on the pattern of *ktab* or on the pattern of *sleq,* the inflection of which is like that of *ktab* but the vowel *e* replaces *a* in the stem wherever it occurs *(sleq, selqat, sleqt, selqet, &c.).* The first-person singular form has the dot above the verb to distinguish it from the other forms that are written the same.

Verbs with initial *ālap* have the vowel *e-* initially (see Preliminary Matters, V); otherwise the inflection is absolutely regular, like that of *emar* 'to say':

3 m	ܐܡܪ	*emar*	ܐܡܪܘ(ܢ)	*emar(un)*
f	ܐܡܪܬ	*emrat*	ܐܡܪ(ܝ̈ܢ)	*emar(ēn)*
2 m	ܐܡܪܬ	*emart*	ܐܡܪܬܘܢ	*emarton*
f	ܐܡܪܬܝ	*emart*	ܐܡܪܬܝܢ	*emartēn*
1 c	ܐܡܪܬ	*emret*	ܐܡܪܢ	*emarn(an)*

§ 2.2 Direct Objects. The direct object of a transitive verb may optionally be indicated by the particle *l-* (exactly like the preposition) when the object is definite.

ܥܒܪ ܠܢܗܪܐ	*ᶜbar l-nahrā.*	He crossed the river.
ܩܛܠܘ ܠܡܪܢ ܝܫܘܥ ܡܫܝܚܐ	*qṭal l-māran išoᶜ mšiḥā.*	They killed our Lord Jesus Christ.

The *l*-marker is more consistently found when the object precedes the verb, e.g.,

ܠܡܠܟܐ ܩܛܠܘ	*l-malkā qṭal*	They killed the king,

but there is no consistency when the object follows the verb and is unambiguously the object.

Vocabulary 2

NOUNS

ܐܪܥܐ *arᶜā* (f) earth, land
ܟܬܒܐ *ktābā* book
ܢܗܪܐ *nahrā* river
ܢܡܘܣܐ *nāmōsā* law
ܨܦܪܐ *ṣaprā* morning
ܩܪܝܬܐ *qritā* village
ܪܡܫܐ *ramšā* evening

VERBS

ܐܒܕ *ebad* to perish
ܐܚܕ *eḥad* to seize, take

ܐܙܠ *ezal* to go[1]
ܐܡܪ *emar* to say, tell (*ᶜal* about something)
ܢܛܪ *nṭar* to keep
ܢܦܩ *npaq* to go forth[2]
ܥܒܪ *ᶜbar* to cross; (with *ᶜal)* to transgress (the law, a commandment, etc.)
ܩܛܠ *qṭal* to kill

OTHERS

ܐܝܟܐ *aykā* where?
ܥܠ *ᶜal* on, over; against; about
ܠ *l- (la-)* direct object marker (nonobligatory)
ܠܡܢܐ *l-mānā* why?, what for?
ܡܐ *mā* }
ܡܢ *mān* } what?
ܡܢܐ *mānā* }

Exercise 2

Read in Syriac and translate into English:

1 ܐܒܕ ܓܒܪܐ ܒܐܪܥܐ.
2 ܠܡܢܐ ܠܐ ܢܛܪܬ ܠܢܡܘܣܐ؟
3 ܫܠܒܢ ܒܓܦܪܐ.
4 ܢܦܩܬ ܘܐܙܠܬ ܠܢܗܪܐ.
5 ܥܒܪܘ ܥܠ ܢܡܘܣܐ.
6 ܟܬܒ ܠܟܬܒܐ ܡܠܟܐ.
7 ܒܪܡܫܐ ܥܒܪ ܠܢܗܪܐ.

---

[1]The *l* of *ezal* assimilates to the *z* wherever they occur together in the perfect inflection. Assimilation is marked with the linea occultans, e.g., ܐܙܠ *ezal,* ܐܙܠܬ *ezzat,* ܐܙܠܬ *ezalt,* ܐܙܠܬ *ezzet.*

[2]When it precedes other verbs of motion, *npaq* is often otiose, e.g., *npaq wa-ᶜbar* "he got up and crossed" or simply "he crossed."

8 ܡܢܐ ܐܡܪܬ ܠܓܒܪܐ ܐܢ̈ܬܬܐ؟
9 ܐܙܠܬ ܡܢ ܡܕܝܢܬܐ ܒܪܓܠܐ.
10 ܢܦܩܬܘܢ ܡܢ ܡܕܝܢ̈ܬܐ ܠܛܘܪܐ.
11 ܥܪܩܘ ܥܡܐ ܡܢ ܩܪܝܬܐ ܘܐܙܠܘ ܠܡܕܝܢ̈ܬܐ.
12 ܓܒܪܐ ܩܛܠ ܠܡܠܟܐ.
13 ܠܐ ܥܒܪܢ ܥܠ ܢܡܘܣܐ.
14 ܡܢ ܐܒܕ ܓܒܪܐ ܡܢ ܩܪܝܬܐ؟
15 ܣܠܩܘ ܠܛܘܪܐ ܘܬܡܢ ܐܒܕܘ.
16 ܡܢܐ ܐܡܪܬ ܠܥܡܐ؟
17 ܐܒܕܬ ܒܩܪܝܬܐ ܐܢ̈ܬܬܐ.
18 ܠܡܢܐ ܠܐ ܫܐܠܬ ܠܡܠܟܐ ܘܠܡܠܟܬܐ؟
19 ܠܐ ܫܡܥܬ ܠܓܒܪܐ.
20 ܐܚܕܬ ܟܬܒܐ ܘܐܙܠܬ ܠܫܘܩܐ.
21 ܠܐ ܥܒܪܢ ܡܢ ܩܪܝܬܐ ܒܪܡܫܐ.
22 ܠܐ ܫܐܠܘ ܠܐܢ̈ܬܬܐ.
23 ܟܬܒܬ ܠܡܠܟܐ ܟܬܒܐ.
24 ܥܪܩܬ ܡܢ ܬܡܢ ܘܐܙܠܬ ܠܫܘܩܐ.
25 ܐܡܪܬ ܠܡܠܟܐ ܥܠ ܐܢܬܬܐ.
26 ܠܐ ܐܡܪܢ ܠܥܡܐ ܥܠ ܡܠܟܐ.
27 ܠܡܢܐ ܠܐ ܐܡܪܬܘܢ ܠܡܠܟܐ ܥܠ ܢܡܘܣܐ؟
28 ܠܡܠܟܐ ܘܠܡܠܟܬܐ ܫܐܠ.

(b) Translate into Syriac:

1. Where did they perish?
2. Why did you not keep the law?
3. We crossed the river in the evening.

4. I told the woman about the village.
5. Why did you (m pl) go to the city?
6. They killed the king in the village.
7. The king crossed the river and seized the city.
8. We went forth and up to the mountain in the morning.
9. What did you say to the man?
10. I told the people about the law.

ܪܫܐ ܕܬܠܬܐ

Lesson Three

§ 3.1 Pronominal Enclitics. Following is the set of pronominal enclitics used with most (but not all) prepositions:

3 m	ܗ	*-eh*	ܗܘܢ	*-hon*
f	ܗ̇	*-āh*	ܗܝܢ	*-hēn*
2 m	ܟ	*-āk*	ܟܘܢ	*-k̲on*
f	ܟܝ	*-ek*	ܟܝܢ	*-k̲ēn*
1 c	ܝ	*-#/-i*	ܢ	*-an*

These enclitics serve as the complements to the majority of prepositions, for instance *b-* 'in, at' and *l-* 'to, for':

3 m	ܒܗ	*beh*	ܒܗܘܢ	*bhon*	ܠܗ	*leh*	ܠܗܘܢ	*lhon*
f	ܒܗ̇	*bāh*	ܒܗܝܢ	*bhēn*	ܠܗ̇	*lāh*	ܠܗܝܢ	*lhēn*
2 m	ܒܟ	*bāk*	ܒܟܘܢ	*bkon*	ܠܟ	*lāk*	ܠܟܘܢ	*lkon*
f	ܒܟܝ	*bek*	ܒܟܝܢ	*bkēn*	ܠܟܝ	*lek*	ܠܟܝܢ	*lkēn*
1 c	ܒܝ	*bi*	ܒܢ	*ban*	ܠܝ	*li*	ܠܢ	*lan*

The *-i* of the first-person singular enclitic is pronounced only when there is no other vowel in the word, as in ܒܝ *bi* and ܠܝ *li;* otherwise the *yod* is silent, as in ܡܢܝ *menn* 'from me' and ܠܘܬܝ *lwāt* 'unto me.'

So also with the following prepositions: ܠܘܬ *lwāt* 'unto,' ܥܡ *^{c}am (^{c}amm-)* 'with,' ܡܢ *men (menn-)* 'from,' and ܐܟܘܬ *akwāt* 'like.' All of these take the -# pronunciation with the first-person singular enclitic; otherwise they are regular (ܠܘܬܗ *lwāteh,* ܥܡܗ *^{c}ammeh,* ܡܢܗ *menneh,* ܐܟܘܬܗ *akwāteh,* etc.).

§ 3.2 Predication of Existence and Expression of Possession.

For the predication of existence (English 'there is, there are'), ܐܝܬ *it* and the negative ܠܝܬ *layt* ('there is/are not') are used. Note in the examples below that the order of sentences in which *it* and *layt* are used for the predication of existence is fixed as *it/layt* + prepositional phrase + subject.

ܐܝܬ ܒܝܡܐ ܡܝܐ	*it b-yammā mayyā.*	There is water in the sea.
ܠܝܬ ܒܒܝܬܐ ܠܚܡܐ	*layt b-baytā laḥmā.*	There is not any bread in the house.

As there is no verb 'to have' in Syriac, the construction *it/layt l-* ('to be to') is used, for instance:

ܐܝܬ ܠܝ ܒܝܬܐ	*it li baytā.*	I have a house.
ܠܝܬ ܠܗ ܐܢܬܬܐ	*layt leh atttā.*	He does not have a wife.

§ 3.3 Relative Clauses. The relative pronoun is *d-*, the vocalic patterning of which is exactly like that of *l-* (see §1.4). The relative pronoun always stands next (or as close as possible) to its antecedent and is invariably the first element in the relative clause.

ܓܒܪܐ ܕܐܙܠ	*gabrā d-ezal*	the man who came
ܐܢܬܬܐ ܕܣܠܩܬ	*atttā d-selqat*	the woman who went forth
ܡܠܟܐ ܕܒܡܕܝܢܬܐ	*malkā d-ba-mdittā*	the king who is in the city

Prepositional relationships ('in which, from which, of whom, whose,' etc.) are expressed by resumptive pronouns within the relative clause. The relative pronoun *d-* still stands at the head of the relative clause and its proper place within the clause is marked by an appropriate pronoun.

ܓܒܪܐ ܕܝܗܒܬ ܠܗ ܟܣܦܐ	*gabrā* ***d****-yehbet* ***leh*** *kespā*	the man **to whom** I gave money

ܡܕܝܢܬܐ ܕܣܠܩܬ ܡܢܗ	*mdittā ḏ-selqet* ***mennâh***	the city **from which** I went out
ܥܝܢܐ ܕܐܝܬ ܒܗ ܡܝܐ	*ʿaynā* ***d**-it* ***bâh*** *mayyā*	a spring **in which** there is/was water
ܓܒܪܐ ܕܢܣܒܬ ܟܣܦܗ	*gabrā* ***d**-nesbet kesp**eh***	the man **whose** money I took

Prepositional phrases do not function adjectivally; instead, such phrases are turned into relative constructions, as the following examples show:

ܒܝܬܐ ܕܒܡܕܝܢܬܐ	*baytā d-ba-mdittā*	the house in the city (lit., "the house that is in the city")
ܡܝܐ ܕܒܝܡܐ	*mayyā da-b-yammā*	the water in the sea

Vocabulary 3

NOUNS

- ܒܝܬܐ *baytā* (m) house, home
- ܝܡܐ *yammā* sea
- ܠܚܡܐ *laḥmā* bread, food (in general)
- ܡ̈ܝܐ *mayyā* (pl) water
- ܢܒܝܐ *nbiyā* prophet
- ܟܣܦܐ *kespā* money
- ܦܘܩܕܢܐ *puqdānā* commandment
- ܫܠܝܚܐ *šliḥā* messenger, apostle

VERBS

- ܐܟܠ *ekal* to eat
- ܢܚܬ *nḥet* to go down, descend, dismount; (with *ʿal)* to march against
- ܢܣܒ *nsab* to take, receive
- ܥܒܕ *ʿbad* to do, make
- ܫܠܚ *šlaḥ* to send, dispatch

OTHERS

- ܐܝܬ *it* there is/are
- ܕ *d(a)-* who, which, that (relative pronoun)

ܠܘܬ *lwāt* to, unto, into the presence of (someone)
ܠܝܬ *layt* there is/are not
ܡ̇ܢ *man* who? (distinguished from *mān* and *men* by a dot on top)
ܥܕ *ʿad* up to, as far as, until
ܥܡ *ʿam (ʿamm-)* with

Exercise 3

Read and translate:

1 ܡ̇ܢ ܐܢ̱ܬ ܒܟܘܢ؟
2 ܢܚܬܬ ܡܠܟܬܐ ܠܡܕܝܢ̈ܬܐ ܥܡ ܥܡܐ.
3 ܢܦܩܬ ܠܫܘܩܐ ܡܢܟ
4 ܐܬܠܗ ܒܡ̇ܢ
5 ܢܚܬܬܘܢ ܥܕ ܝܡܐ
6 ܒܪܬ ܡܢܘ
7 ܫܠܚܗ ܠܘܬ ܡܠܟܐ ܫܠܝܚܐ
8 ܢܦܩ ܓܒܪܐ ܠܦܘܩܕܢܐ ܡܢܗܘܢ.
9 ܐܙܠ ܥܕ ܩܪܝܬܐ.
10 ܡ̇ܢ ܥܒܕ ܠܠܚܡܐ؟
11 ܠܝܬ ܠܓܒܪܐ ܟܣܦܐ.
12 ܫܕܪܗ ܠܘܬ ܓܒܪܐ ܕܐܬܐ ܡܢ ܡܕܝܢ̈ܬܐ ܕܠܝܬ ܒܗ̇ ܡܝܐ.
13 ܠܝܬ ܒܐܪܥܐ ܢܒܝܐ.
14 ܠܝܬ ܠܝ ܠܚܡܐ ܒܒܝܬܐ.
15 ܠܐ ܢܛܪܘ ܦܘܩܕܢܐ ܕܢܦܩ ܢܒܝܐ ܡܢ ܛܘܪܐ.
16 ܢܚܬܬ ܡܢ ܛܘܪܐ ܘܐܙܠܬ ܥܕ ܝܡܐ.
17 ܡ̇ܢ ܫܠܚ ܠܝ ܠܘܬܟ؟
18 ܐܢ̈ܬܬܐ ܕܥܒܕܬ ܠܚܡܐ ܢܦܩܬ ܘܫܠܚܬ ܠܒܥܠ ܘܠܒܢܝܗ̇.
19 ܐܝܬ ܒܐܪܥܐ ܢܗܪܐ ܕܐܝܬ ܒܗ ܡܝܐ.
20 ܐܝܬ ܒܡܕܝܢ̈ܬܐ ܡܠܟܐ ܘܡܠܟܬܐ.
21 ܫܠܚܗ ܟܣܦܐ ܠܡܕܝܢ̈ܬܐ ܥܡ ܫܠܝܚܐ.
22 ܡܢܐ ܐܓܪ̈ܬܗ ܠܫܠܝܚܐ ܕܐܬܐ ܡܢ ܬܡܢ؟

23 ܠܝܬ ܠܗ̇ ܒܝܬܐ ܒܡܕܝܢܬܐ.
24 ܐܙܠ ܢܒܝܐ ܠܘܬ ܥܡܐ ܘܐܡܪ ܠܗܘܢ ܠܡܢܐ ܠܐ ܢܛܪܬܘܢ
ܠܢܡܘܣܐ؟
25 ܓܢܒ ܥܒܕܐ ܡܢܢ.
26 ܐܟܠܬ ܥܡܗ̇ ܠܚܡܐ.
27 ܫܩܠܬ ܡܢ ܡܝܐ.
28 ܢܦܩܢ ܡܢܗ.
29 ܡܢ ܐܡܪ ܠܟ ܥܠ ܟܣܦܐ ܕܐܚܕ ܡܠܟܐ ܡܢ ܥܡܐ؟
30 ܫܕܪܬ ܠܡܕܝܢܬܐ ܘܢܣܒܬ ܠܟܣܦܐ ܡܢ ܥܠܝܡܐ.

Translate into Syriac:

1. There is a man in the house.
2. Who sent them the messenger who went to the city?
3. I went down to the river with her in the morning.
4. We have no money.
5. She took water from the man.
6. They told me about the food they ate.
7. They killed the man who transgressed the law.
8. The prophet received the law on the mountain.
9. She did not eat the food we made.
10. Do you have any money in the house?

ܪܫܐ ܕܐܪܒܥܐ

Lesson Four

§ 4.1 Possessive Pronouns. The pronominal enclitics given in §3.1 are also attached to singular nouns to indicate possession. The stem of the noun to which they are attached is obtained by dropping the final *-ā* of the lexical (emphatic) form. Thus, from *baytā:*

ܒܝܬܗ *bayteh* his house	ܒܝܬܗܘܢ *baython* their house
ܒܝܬܗ̇ *baytāh* her house	ܒܝܬܗܝܢ *baythēn* their house
ܒܝܬܟ *baytāk̲* your house	ܒܝܬܟܘܢ *baytk̲on* your house
ܒܝܬܟܝ *baytek̲* your house	ܒܝܬܟܝܢ *baytk̲ēn* your house
ܒܝܬܝ *bayt* my house	ܒܝܬܢ *baytan* our house

There are, however, a few complications involved in the suffixation of the first-person singular zero enclitic and the second- and third-person plurals, *-kon/-kēn* and *-hon/-hēn*. Stems that end in three consonants *(-CCC-)* or in two consonants preceded by a long vowel *(-āCC-, -êCC-, -iCC-* or *-uCC-)* restore a full vowel to the stem between the last two consonants before the enclitics are added. Most such nouns restore *a* as the vowel, but this is not entirely predictable. For example, ܗܝܟܠܐ *haykla* 'temple' > ܗܝܟܠܗܘܢ *hayk**a**lhon* 'their temple,' ܡܐܡܪܐ *mêmrā* 'word' > ܡܐܡܪܝ *mêm**a**r* 'my word,' and ܪܚܡܐ *rāḥmā* 'friend' > ܪܚܡܟܘܢ *rāḥemk̲on* 'your friend.'

Many feminine singular nouns in *-tā* fall under this rule, restoring the vowel *a* before the *t,* as ܡܠܟܬܐ *malktā* > ܡܠܟܬܗܘܢ *malk**a**thon* 'their queen,' ܡܕܝܢܬܐ *mdittā* > ܡܕܝܢܬܟܘܢ *mdin**a**tkon* 'your city,' and ܐܢܬܬܐ *atttā* > ܐܢܬܬܝ *att**a**t* 'my wife.'

§ 4.2 Noun–Noun Possession. There are three ways to express possession involving two or more nouns in Syriac.

(1) The first, the construct, involves changes in the stem of the first noun. As its use is limited, it will be dealt with later (§10.3).

(2) In the second, the first noun, the thing possessed or limited, is in the emphatic state, and the second, the possessor or limiter, follows *d-*, as in the following:

ܒܝܬܐ ܕܓܒܪܐ	*baytā d-gabrā*	the man's house
ܫܠܝܚܐ ܕܡܠܟܐ	*šliḥā d-malkā*	the king's messenger
ܦܘܩܕܢܐ ܕܢܒܝܐ	*puqdānā da-nbiyā*	the prophet's commandment
ܡܠܟܬܐ ܕܡܕܝܢܬܐ	*malktā da-mdittā*	the queen of the city
ܟܣܦܐ ܕܓܒܪ̈ܐ	*kespā d-gabrē*	the men's money

(3) In the third construction, an anticipatory pronoun, agreeing in number and gender with the second noun, is attached to the first noun, and the second noun is introduced by *d-*, as in the following:

ܒܝܬܗ ܕܓܒܪܐ	*bayteh d-gabrā*	the man's house
ܫܠܝܚܗ ܕܡܠܟܐ	*šliḥeh d-malkā*	the king's messenger
ܦܘܩܕܢܗ ܕܢܒܝܐ	*puqdāneh da-nbiyā*	the prophet's commandment
ܡܠܟܬܗ̇ ܕܡܕܝܢܬܐ	*malktāh da-mdittā*	the queen of the city
ܟܣܦܗܘܢ ܕܓܒܪ̈ܐ	*kesphon d-gabrē*	the men's money

§ 4.3 The Pronoun *Koll.* The pronoun *koll,* usually spelled without *wāw,* means 'all' when it is followed by a noun in the emphatic state or by an enclitic pronoun, as ܟܠܗ *kolleh* 'all of it (m)' and ܟܠܗܘܢ *kollhon* 'all of them.' With noun complements, *koll* is commonly followed by an anticipatory pronoun that agrees in gender and number with the following noun, as

ܟܠܗ ܟܬܒܐ	*kolleh ktābā*	all of the book, the whole book

ܟܠܗ̇ ܡܕܝܢܬܐ	*kollāh mdittā*	all of the city, the whole city

Such constructions are also rendered by placing *koll* with its enclitic pronoun in apposition following a noun in the emphatic state, as

ܟܬܒܐ ܟܠܗ	*ktābā kolleh*	all of the book, the whole book
ܒܡܕܝܢܬܐ ܟܠܗ̇	*ba-mdittā kollāh*	in the whole city, throughout the city
ܐܪܥܐ ܟܠܗ̇	*ar^{c}ā kollāh*	the whole land, all of the earth

When followed by a noun in the absolute state (to be introduced in §13.1), *koll* means 'every.'

ܟܠܡܕܡ	*koll-meddem*	everything
ܟܠܢܫ	*koll-nāš*	everybody
ܟܠ ܝܘܡ	*koll yom*	every day

§4.4 Pronominal Anticipation with Prepositions. Prepositions with noun complements are often anticipated by a redundant preposition with a pronominal enclitic complement agreeing with the noun complement of the following, "real" prepositional phrase. Thus, either ܒܡܕܝܢܬܐ *ba-mdittā* or ܒܗ̇ ܒܡܕܝܢܬܐ *bāh ba-mdittā* for 'in the city,' and either ܐܡܪܬ ܠܓܒܪܐ *emret l-gabrā* or ܐܡܪܬ ܠܗ ܠܓܒܪܐ *emret leh l-gabrā* for 'I said to the man.' These constructions are extremely frequent in Syriac narrative prose.

Vocabulary 4

NOUNS

ܕܗܒܐ *dahbā* gold
ܒܥܠܕܒܒܐ *b^{c}eldbābā* enemy
ܗܝܟܠܐ *hayklā (haykal-)* temple
ܥܒܕܐ *^{c}abdā* servant, slave

VERBS

ܥܕܪ *ᶜdar* to help

ܦܩܕ *pqad* to command, order

ܪܕܦ *rdap* to drive on, persecute; (with *bātar)* to pursue

ܪܗܛ *rheṭ* to run

ܫܒܩ *šbaq* to leave, abandon; (with *l-)* to forgive

OTHERS

ܐܝܟܢܐ *aykannā* how?

ܐܝܟܢܐ ܕ *aykannā d-* as, just as

ܒܬܪ *bātar* after, behind (often *men bātar);* the short *a* in the second syllable is reduced when enclitics beginning with vowels are added, e.g. ܒܬܪܗ *bātreh* 'after him,' but ܒܬܪܗܘܢ *bātarhon* 'after them'

ܕܝܠ *dil-* belonging to

ܟܠ *koll* all, every

ܟܠܡܕܡ *kollmeddem* everything

Exercise 4

Read and translate:

1 ܪܕܦ ܡܠܟܐ ܒܬܪ ܒܥܠܕܒܒܗ.
2 ܫܒܩܬ ܠܥܒܕܐ ܕܗܝܟܠܐ.
3 ܐܚܕ ܠܕܗܒܐ ܒܥܠܕܒܒܐ ܘܥܒܕ ܠܡܕܝܢܬܐ.
4 ܠܝܬ ܗܪܟܐ ܟܣܦܐ ܕܕܝܠܟ.
5 ܠܐ ܥܕܪ ܠܝ ܥܒܕܢ.
6 ܪܕܦ ܓܒܪܐ ܠܥܒܕܗ.
7 ܪܗܛ ܥܒܕܐ ܕܗܝܟܠܐ ܒܬܪ ܓܒܪܐ ܕܐܚܕ ܠܕܗܒܐ ܕܕܝܠܗ.
8 ܐܙܠܬ ܠܩܪܝܬܐ ܕܥܒܕܐ.
9 ܫܒܩ ܠܥܒܕܗ ܓܒܪܐ.
10 ܠܐ ܥܕܪ ܠܢ ܕܗܒܟ.
11 ܫܠܚ ܡܠܟܐ ܠܥܠܝܡܗ ܠܘܬܟ.
12 ܢܣܒ ܓܒܪܐ ܟܣܦܐ ܡܢܗܘܢ.
13 ܥܒܕܘ ܐܝܟܢܐ ܕܦܩܕ ܠܗܘܢ ܡܠܟܐ ܕܡܕܝܢܬܐ.
14 ܐܡܪܬ ܠܗ ܐܝܟܢܐ ܕܐܡܪܬ ܠܝ.

15 ܪܗܛܬ ܒܬܪܗܘܢ.
16 ܪܕܦ ܒܬܪܗ ܒܥܠܕܒܒܐ ܥܕ ܝܡܐ ܘܬܡܢ ܐܒܕ.
17 ܩܛܠܗ ܠܒܥܠܕܒܒܗ ܕܡܠܟܐ.
18 ܢܦܩ ܥܒܕܐ ܡܢ ܒܝܬܗ ܒܨܦܪܐ ܘܣܠܩ ܠܛܘܪܐ.
19 ܪܕܦܬ ܠܒܥܠܕܒܒܝ ܒܡܕܝܢܬܐ ܟܠܗ̇.
20 ܥܕܪܘ ܠܝ ܥܡܐ ܟܠܗܘܢ.
21 ܐܡܪ ܠܝ ܓܒܪܐ ܟܠܡܕܡ ܕܐܡܪܬ ܠܗ ܐܢܬܬܗ.
22 ܫܒܩܘ ܟܠܡܕܡ ܕܐܚܕܘ ܡܢ ܗܝܟܠܐ ܘܥܪܩܘ.
23 ܐܚܕܬ ܟܠܡܕܡ ܕܝܠܝ ܘܐܙܠܬ ܠܒܝܬܝ.
24 ܪܗܛܢ ܒܬܪ ܥܒܕܐ ܕܓܒܪܐ ܐܝܟܢܐ ܕܦܩܕ ܠܝ
25 ܐܟܠܬ ܟܠܗ ܠܚܡܐ ܕܝܗܒܬ ܠܟܝ ܐܢܬܬܝ؟
26 ܠܡܢܐ ܠܐ ܝܗܒܬ ܟܠܡܕܡ ܕܦܩܕܬ ܠܗ̇؟
27 ܠܡܢܐ ܫܒܩܘ ܠܒܬܝܗܘܢ ܕܒܩܪܝܬܐ ܘܐܙܠܘ ܠܡܕܝܢܬܐ؟

Translate into Syriac:

1. We left our servant in the village.
2. I ran from my enemy's village.
3. The king pursued the enemy of his people throughout the land.
4. The servant took his king's gold and fled from the land.
5. You took everything from me.
6. The man took everything from his house and went down to the sea.

ܪܫܐ ܕܚܡܫܐ

Lesson Five

§ 5.1 Noun Plurals: Emphatic State. The plural of a noun in the emphatic state is made by (1) changing the *-ā* termination of a masculine-type noun to *-ē,* or (2) by changing the *-tā* termination of feminine-type nouns to *-ātā. Syāmē* dots are placed over all plural nouns, most of which could not otherwise be distinguished orthographically from the singular. *Syāmē* dots may come anywhere in the word, but if there is a *rēš* in the word, the dots combine with the dot of the *rēš* as ܪ̈.

	SINGULAR	PLURAL
masc.	ܫܠܝܚܐ *šliḥā* apostle	ܫܠܝ̈ܚܐ *šliḥē* apostles
fem.	ܡܠܟܬܐ *malktā* queen	ܡܠܟ̈ܬܐ *malkātā* queens

Although most nouns form their plurals as described above, there are exceptions to regular formation of the following types:

(a) Some words have a feminine form in the singular and a masculine form in the plural.

ܡܠܬܐ *melltā* word	ܡ̈ܠܐ *mellē* words
ܒܝܥܬܐ *bêᶜtā* egg	ܒܝ̈ܥܐ *bêᶜē* eggs

(b) Some words have a masculine form in the singular and a feminine form in the plural.

ܢܦܫܐ *napšā* (f) soul	ܢܦ̈ܫܬܐ *napšātā* souls
ܐܒܐ *abā* father	ܐܒ̈ܗܬܐ *abāhātā* fathers

Note that the gender of words in categories (a) and (b) does not change from the singular. *Mellē* is feminine plural even though its form is that of a masculine plural; *abāhātā,* regardless of its form, is masculine plural.

(c) Other, unpredictable irregularities are exemplified by the following:

ܩܪܝܬܐ	*qritā* village	ܩܘܪܝܐ	*quryā* villages
ܐܢܬܬܐ	*atttā* woman	ܢܫ̈ܐ	*neššē* women
ܒܝܬܐ	*baytā* house	ܒ̈ܬܐ	*bāttē* houses
ܨܦܪܐ	*ṣaprā* morning	ܨܦܪ̈ܘܬܐ	*ṣaprwātā* mornings

Regular plurals are formed for the following words, which have already been introduced:

MASCULINE

ܒܥܠܕܒ̈ܒܐ *b*^c^*eldbābē*
ܓܒܪ̈ܐ *gabrē*
ܕܗܒ̈ܐ *dahb̲ē*
ܗܝܟ̈ܠܐ *hayklē*
ܛܘܪ̈ܐ *ṭurē*
ܝܡ̈ܡܐ *yammē*
ܟܣ̈ܦܐ *kespē*
ܟܬ̈ܒܐ *ktābē*
ܠܚ̈ܡܐ *laḥmē*
ܡܠܟ̈ܐ *malkē*
ܢܒܝ̈ܐ *nbiyē*
ܢܗܪ̈ܐ *nahrē*
ܢܡܘ̈ܣܐ *nāmosē*
ܥܒ̈ܕܐ *^c^abdē*
ܥܡ̈ܡܐ *^c^ammē*
ܦܘܩܕ̈ܢܐ *puqdānē*
ܪܡ̈ܫܐ *ramšē*
ܫܠܝ̈ܚܐ *šliḥē*

FEMININE

ܐܪ̈ܥܬܐ *ar*^c^*ātā*
ܡܕܝ̈ܢܬܐ *mdinātā*
ܡܠܟ̈ܬܐ *malkātā*
ܩܪ̈ܝܬܐ *qeryātā*

Note particularly the spelling of *yammē* and *^c^ammē.*

Vocabulary 5

NOUNS

ܐܠܗܐ *alāhā* God
ܐܡܐ *emmā* pl ܐܡܗ̈ܬܐ *emmhātā* mother
ܡܠܐܟܐ *malakā* pl *malakē* angel
ܡܠܟܘܬܐ *malkutā* pl *-kwātā* kingdom

ܢܦܫܐ *napšā* (f) pl ܢܦܫ̈ܬܐ *napšātā* soul, breath of life; (with pronominal enclitics) -self, as ܢܦܫܗ *napšeh* himself, ܢܦܫܗܘܢ *napšhon* themselves

ܢ̈ܫܐ *neššē* (fem pl) women

ܫܡ̈ܝܐ *šmayyā* (plural, no singular) heaven

VERBS

ܩܪܒ *qreb* to draw near *(l-* to), approach

ܥܡܪ *ᶜmar* to live

OTHERS

ܗܐ *hā* lo, behold

ܗܟܢܐ *hākannā* thus, so, in this way

ܟܕ *kad* when, while, as

Exercise 5

Read and translate:

1 ܪ̈ܕܦܘ ܡܠܟ̈ܐ ܒܬܪ ܒܥܠܕܒ̈ܒܐ ܟܕ ܡܕܝܢܬܗܘܢ.
2 ܠܐ ܫܒܩܘܢ ܒ̈ܢܝܐ ܒܗܝܟܠܐ.
3 ܠܒܗܡܢ ܐܒܕܘ ܝ̈ܗܘܕܝܐ ܘܒܙܘ ܠܡܕܝܢܬܐ.
4 ܪ̈ܕܦܘ ܠܒ̈ܢܝܐ ܝ̈ܗܘܕܝܐ
5 ܢܦܠܘ ܒ̈ܢܝܐ ܒܬܪ ܝ̈ܗܘܕܝܐ ܕܐܒܕܘ ܠܒ̈ܗܡܬܗܘܢ ܕܠܗܘܢ.
6 ܐܙܠܬ ܠܩܘܪ̈ܝܐ ܕܢ̈ܫܐ.
7 ܠܐ ܫܒܩܘ ܠܒ̈ܢܝܐ.
8 ܠܐ ܓܙܪܘ ܠܟܝ ܕܗ̈ܒܐ.
9 ܫܠܚܘ ܡܠܟ̈ܐ ܠܫܠܝ̈ܚܐ ܠܘܬܢ.
10 ܢܦܩܘ ܝ̈ܗܘܕܝܐ ܠܫܘܩܐ ܡܢ.
11 ܚܙܘ ܒ̈ܢܝܐ ܐܢܫܐ ܕܦܩܕܘ ܠܗܘܢ ܡܠܟ̈ܐ.
12 ܐܡܪܬ ܠܗ ܐܢܬܬܐ ܐܚܪܢܐ ܕܐܡܪ̈ܝ ܠܗ̇ ܢ̈ܫܐ.
13 ܢܦܠ ܒܬܪܗܝܢ ܢ̈ܫܐ.
14 ܪܕܦ ܒܬܪܗ ܒܥܠܕܒ̈ܒܐ ܟܕ ܚܙܐ ܘܩܛܠܗ ܠܗ ܒܚܝܠ.
15 ܟܕ ܡܠܠܗ ܠܡܪܢܐ ܫܠܡܬ ܢܦܫܗ ܠܫܡ̈ܝܐ.
16 ܗܐ ܡܠܐܟ̈ܐ ܕܐܠܗܐ ܩܪܒܘ ܠܗ ܠܒܝܬܐ.
17 ܫܒܩ ܠܡܕܝܢܬܐ ܘܥܡܪ ܒܩܪܝܬܐ.

18 ܡܪܕܘ ܠܒܝܬܗ̇ ܕܐܠܗܗܘܢ.
19 ܡܢ ܫܩܠ ܒܥܠܕܒܒܝܗܘܢ ܕܡܠܟ̈ܐ؟
20 ܡܪܕܬ ܡܠܟܘܬܐ ܕܥܡܡ̈ܐ.
21 ܠܡܢܐ ܪܕܦܘ ܠܢܒܝ̈ܐ؟
22 ܟܕ ܢܚܬ ܡܢ ܛܘܪܐ ܢܦܩ ܘܐܙܠ ܠܒܝܬܗ.
23 ܫܩܠ ܠܢܦܫܗ.
24 ܠܐ ܫܩܠܘ ܠܢܦܫܗܘܢ.
25 ܢܦܩܘ ܒܢ̈ܝܐ ܡܢ ܒܝܬܗ̇ ܕܐܢܬܬܐ.
26 ܪܕܦܘ ܥܡܐ ܟܠܗܘܢ ܠܒܥܠܕܒܒܗ ܕܡܠܟܐ.
27 ܥܡܪ̈ܝ ܢܫ̈ܐ ܒܩܘܪ̈ܝܐ.
28 ܟܕ ܡܪܕ ܒܥܠܕܒܒܐ ܪܕܦܘ ܟܠܗܘܢ ܓܒܪ̈ܐ.
29 ܠܢܡܘܣܐ ܕܐܠܗܐ ܢܛܪ ܓܒܪܐ.
30 ܢܚܬܘ ܡܠܐܟ̈ܐ ܡܢ ܫܡܝܐ.
31 ܐܫܕܪܬ ܠܢܫ̈ܐ ܟܠܗܝܢ ܡܢ ܒܝܬܐ ܘܫܠܚܬ ܠܛܘܪܐ ܟܕ
ܐܡܪ.
32 ܗܟܢܐ ܐܡܪ ܢܒܝܐ ܟܕ ܢܦܩ ܦܘܩܕܢܐ ܕܐܠܗܐ.

Translate into Syriac:

1. The men lived in the villages of the kingdom.
2. The angels descended from heaven.
3. There is no water in the rivers of the land.
4. The women transgressed the laws of the kings of the kingdom.
5. We drove the servants of the enemies from all the temples of our land.

ܪܫܐ ܕܐܫܬܬܐ
Lesson Six

§ 6.1 Independent Pronouns. Following is the set of independent pronouns. These are used as sentence subjects of verbless sentences and for stressing the pronominal subject of a verb.

3 m	ܗܘ	*hu*	ܗܢܘܢ	*hennon*
f	ܗܝ	*hi*	ܗܢܝܢ	*hennēn*
2 m	ܐܢܬ	*att*	ܐܢܬܘܢ	*atton*
f	ܐܢܬܝ	*att*	ܐܢܬܝܢ	*attēn*
1 c	ܐܢܐ	*enā*	ܐܚܢܢ	*naḥnan* and
			ܚܢܢ	*ḥnan*

§ 6.2 The Short Pronouns as Copulas. The following shortened pronouns are used as copulas ('is, are'):

3 m	ܗܘ	*-u (-w)*	ܐܢܘܢ	*-ennon*
f	ܗܝ	*-i (-y)*	ܐܢܝܢ	*-ennēn*
2 m	ܐܢܬ	*-(a)tt*	ܐܢܬܘܢ	*-(a)tton*
f	ܐܢܬܝ	*-(a)tt*	ܐܢܬܝܢ	*-(a)ttēn*
1 c	ܐܢܐ	*-nā*	ܢܢ	*-nan*

The third-person copulas are used with both the first- and the second-person pronouns, although the corresponding first- and second-person copulas also occur.

ܐܢܬ ܗܘ ܡܠܟܐ	*att-u malkā.*	You are the king.
ܐܢܬ ܡܠܟܐ ܐܢܬ	*att malka-tt.*	You are the king
ܐܢܬܘܢ ܐܢܘܢ ܬܡܢ	*atton-ennon tammān.*	You are there.

ܐܢܬܘܢ ܬܡܢ ܐܢܬܘܢ	*atton tammān-atton.*	You are there.

The copulas may occur anywhere in the sentence, after subject or predicate.

ܐܢܐ ܐܢܐ ܫܠܝܚܐ ܕܐܠܗܐ.	*enā-nā šliḥā d-alāhā.*	I am an apostle of God.
ܚܢܢ ܫܠܝ̈ܚܐ ܚܢܢ ܕܡܠܟܐ.	*ḥnan šliḥē-nan d-malkā.*	We are messengers of the king.

When the masculine copula *-u* is preceded by *-ā,* the *-ā* is shortened to *-a-* and forms a diphthong *-aw:*

ܗܘ ܡܠܟܐ ܗ̣ܘ	*hu malka-w.*	He is the king.

But when it is preceded by a consonant, the copula is read as enclitic *-u,* as in

ܓܒܪܐ ܬܡܢ ܗ̣ܘ.	*gabrā tammān-u.*	The man is there.

The feminine enclitic copula preceded by a consonant is read as *-i:*

ܐܢܬܬܐ ܬܡܢ ܗ̇ܝ.	*atttā tammān-i.*	The woman is there.

But when the feminine copula is preceded by a vowel, it is read as *-y:*

ܗ̇ܝ ܡܠܟܬܐ ܗ̇ܝ.	*hi malktā-y.*	She is the queen.

§ 6.3 Third-Person Plural Pronouns as Direct Objects. The third-person plural short pronouns, and only they of the independent pronouns, are used as direct objects of verbs. Although they are written separate, they should be considered as quasi-enclitic.

ܫܠܚ ܐܢܘܢ.	*šlaḥ-ennon.*	He sent them.
ܩܛܠܬ ܐܢܘܢ.	*qeṭlet-ennon.*	I killed them.
ܕܒܪ ܐܢܝܢ.	*dbar-ennēn.*	He led them (f).

The other direct-object pronouns will be taken up in §7.3.

§ 6.4 Demonstratives. The same words are used as both demonstrative adjectives and demonstrative pronouns. They are as follows.

	SINGULAR	PLURAL
this (m)	ܗܢܐ *hānā*	ܗܠܝܢ *hālēn*
this (f)	ܗܕܐ *hādē*	ܗܠܝܢ *hālēn*
that (m)	ܗܘ *haw*	ܗܢܘܢ *hānon*
that (f)	ܗܝ *hay*	ܗܢܝܢ *hānēn*

As adjectives, these words may either precede or follow the words they modify. Thus, both ܡܠܟܐ ܗܢܐ *malkā hānā* and ܗܢܐ ܡܠܟܐ *hānā malkā* mean 'this king,' and both ܡܕܝܢܬܐ ܗܕܐ *mdittā hādē* and ܗܕܐ ܡܕܝܢܬܐ *hādē mdittā* mean 'this city.'

Hādē followed immediately by the feminine enclitic copula *-i* is pronounced *hādā-y. Hānā* followed by the masculine singular enclitic copula *-u* may be written as one word, ܗܢܘ *hāna-w.*

Vocabulary 6

NOUNS

ܟܢܘܫܬܐ *knuštā* assembly, synagogue
ܡܕܒܪܐ *madbrā* wilderness
ܡܠܚܐ *melḥā* (f) salt
ܦܓܪܐ *pagrā* body
ܪܘܚܐ *ruḥā* (f) spirit[1]

VERB

ܕܒܪ *dbar* to lead, guide

OTHERS

ܐܦ *āp* so, so also
ܕ *d(a)-* that (subordinating conjunction)
ܗܢܐ *hānā* (m sing), ܗܕܐ *hādē* (f sing), ܗܠܝܢ *hālēn* (c pl) this
ܗܘ *haw* (m sing), ܗܝ *hay* (f sing), ܗܢܘܢ *hānon* (m pl), ܗܢܝܢ

---

[1] *Ruḥā* is feminine except in the phrases ܪܘܚܐ ܕܩܘܕܫܐ *ruḥā d-qudšā* and ܪܘܚܐ ܩܕܝܫܐ *ruḥā qaddišā* 'Holy Ghost,' in which *ruḥā* is usually construed as masculine.

hānēn (f pl) that
ܡܚܕܐ *meḥdā* at once, immediately
ܡܢܘ *manu* (for *man-*[*h*]*u)* who is (he/it)?
ܡܢܘ *māna-w* (for *mānā-*[*h*]*u)* what is he/it?

PROPER NAME

ܝܫܘܥ ܡܫܝܚܐ *išo*[c] *mšiḥā* Jesus Christ

Exercise 6

Read and translate:

1 ܡܿܢ ܗܿܝ ܗܕܐ ܘܡܢܘ ܗܿܘ؟
2 ܡܚܕܐ ܢܦܩܘ ܡܢ ܟܢܘܫܬܐ ܘܐܙܠܘ ܠܒܝܬܗ̇ ܕܐܡܗܘܢ.
3 ܐܡܪܘ ܠܗ ܟܠ ܐܢܬܬܐ ܕܗܿܝ ܫܠܝܚܬ ܐܢܝܢ
4 ܠܡܢܐ ܠܐ ܐܡܪܬ ܠܝ ܐܢ̄ܬ ܟܠ ܗܕܐ ܟܠܗ̇؟
5 ܐܢܬܘܢ ܐܢܘܢ ܡܠܟܐ ܕܐܪܥܐ.
6 ܗܕܐ ܗ̇ܝ ܡܕܝܢܬܐ ܗܿܝ ܕܡܠܟܐ ܕܗܕܐ ܐܪܥܐ.
7 ܗ̇ܘ ܗܘ ܡܠܟܗ̇ ܗܿܘ ܕܡܕܝܢܬܐ.
8 ܡܢܘ ܕܕܝܠܗ ܗܿܝ ܡܠܟܘܬܐ ܕܫܡ̈ܝܐ؟
9 ܐܝܟܢܐ ܕܐܡܪܘ ܠܝ ܐܦ ܐܢܐ ܐܡܪܬ ܠܗܘܢ.
10 ܡܚܕܐ ܕܝܢ ܫܡܥܬ ܗܕܐ ܢܦܩܬ ܘܪܗܛܬ ܠܒܝܬܐ.
11 ܐܢܐ ܫܠܝܚܗ ܐܢܐ ܕܐܠܗܐ.
12 ܢܚܬ ܡܢ ܫܡ̈ܝܐ ܡܠܐܟܐ ܕܗܘ ܫܠܝܚܗ ܕܐܠܗܐ ܘܕܒܪ
ܠܒܝܬܐ ܠܡܕܒܪܐ.
13 ܗܕܐ ܗܿܝ ܐܡܐ ܕܥܒܕܬ ܠܝ ܠܫܡܥܐ ܗܢܐ.
14 ܠܡܢܐ ܐܚܕܬ ܐܡܟܝ ܒܗܦܟܐ ܗܢܐ ܡܢܝ؟
15 ܕܒܪܘܢ ܐܢܘܢ ܠܫܡ̈ܝܐ ܡܠܐܟ̈ܐ.
16 ܒܪܡܫܐ ܢܦܩܘ ܘܐܙܠܘ ܠܟܢܘܫܬܐ.
17 ܐܡܪ ܝܫܘܥ ܡܫܝܚܐ ܕܐܢܫ ܡܠܟܐ ܚܝ ܕܐܪܥܐ.
18 ܡܢܘ ܓܒܪܐ ܕܠܟܘܢ ܕܒܪ ܠܗܬܢ؟
19 ܠܡܢܐ ܠܐ ܐܙܠܘ ܠܡܠܟܐ ܗܢܘܢ ܕܢܦܩܘ ܡܢ ܡܕܝܢܬܐ؟
20 ܗܕܐ ܗܿܝ ܡܠܟܘܬܗ ܕܐܪܥܐ ܗܕܐ
21 ܐܝܟܢܐ ܕܫܡܥܬ ܢܦܫܐ ܠܦܓܪܐ ܫܠܝܚܬ ܪܘܚܐ ܠܫܡ̈ܝܐ.
22 ܪܕܦܬ ܠܒܥܠܕܒܒ ܠܡܕܒܪܐ ܘܬܡܢ ܩܛܠܬ ܠܗ.

23 ܒܗ̇ ܫܒܩܘ ܠܢܫ̈ܐ ܡܨܪ̈ܝܐ ܢܦܩܘ ܘܐܙܠܘ ܒܬܪܗ.
24 ܗܕܐ ܐܢܬܬܐ ܐܡܗܘܢ ܗ̄ܝ ܕܗܠܝܢ ܓܒܪ̈ܐ
25 ܗ̄ܘ ܕܐܒܪ ܠܟ ܟܠܗ̇ ܗܕܐ ܥܠܝܡܗ ܗ̄ܘ ܕܡܠܟܐ
ܕܡܕܝܢܬܐ
26 ܡܢܘ ܕܕܒܪ ܐܢܘܢ ܠܡܕܒܪܐ؟
27 ܡܢܘ ܕܫܡܥܬ ܗ̇ܢܝܢ ܦܬ̈ܓܡܐ ܡܢܗ؟
28 ܐܝܟܐ ܐܒܕܘ ܒܡܕܒܪܐ ܗ̇ܢܘܢ؟

Translate into Syriac:

1. This is the assembly of all the peoples of the land.
2. Those men are in the wilderness.
3. Are you the man whose wife killed herself?
4. There is no salt in our house.
5. The angels went up into heaven.
6. These messengers led them to the kings' cities.
7. Who is it that pursued the enemy as far as the river?
8. This man abandoned his wife in the village.

ܪܫܐ ܕܫܒܥܐ
Lesson Seven

§ 7.1 Inflection of III-Weak Verbs. Most verbs whose third radical consonant is weak, i.e., originally *w* or *y*, have slightly modified inflections in the perfect. The vast majority of these verbs appear in the 3rd masculine singular with the ending *-ā*, as *bnā* 'to build.' The inflection is as follows.

3 m	ܒܢܐ	*bnā*	ܒܢܘ	*bnaw*
f	ܒܢܬ	*bnāṯ*	ܒܢܝ	*bnay*
2 m	ܒܢܝܬ	*bnayt*	ܒܢܝܬܘܢ	*bnayton*
f	ܒܢܝܬܝ	*bnayt*	ܒܢܝܬܝܢ	*bnaytēn*
1 c	ܒܢܝܬ	*bnêṯ*	ܒܢܝܢ	*bnayn*

Note especially the pattern of the first-person singular.

The second inflectional pattern of III-weak verbs—much less common—is like that of *ḥdi* 'to be glad.' The inflection is as follows.

3 m	ܚܕܝ	*ḥḏi*	ܚܕܝܘ	*ḥḏi*
f	ܚܕܝܬ	*ḥeḏyaṯ*	ܚܕܝ	*ḥḏi*
2 m	ܚܕܝܬ	*ḥḏiyt*	ܚܕܝܬܘܢ	*ḥḏiyton*
f	ܚܕܝܬܝ	*ḥḏiyt*	ܚܕܝܬܝܢ	*ḥḏiytēn*
1 c	ܚܕܝܬ	*ḥḏiṯ*	ܚܕܝܢ	*ḥḏiyn*

Note that the 3rd-person feminine singular is absolutely regularly formed, while the 1st-person singular is like *bnêṯ,* but with the vowel *-i-*. As the transcription shows, the *-t* of the 2nd persons is not spirantized; the *-ṯ* of the 1st-person singular is spirantized.

§ 7.2 The Perfect of *Hwâ*. The perfect inflection of *hwā* 'to be' is exactly like that of *bnā.*

3 m	ܗܘܐ	*hwā*	ܗܘܘ	*hwaw*
f	ܗܘܬ	*hwāt*	ܗܘܝ	*hway*
2 m	ܗܘܝܬ	*hwayt*	ܗܘܝܬܘܢ	*hwayton*
f	ܗܘܝܬܝ	*hwayt*	ܗܘܝܬܝܢ	*hwaytēn*
1 c	ܗܘܝܬ	*hwêt*	ܗܘܝܢ	*hwayn*

However, when this verb is used as the past copula, the initial *h-* is silenced with the linea occultans throughout the inflection. As a copula, *-wā* is treated as an enclitic.

ܓܒܪܐ ܒܒܝܬܗ ܗܘܐ.	*gabrā b-bayteh-wā.*	The man was in his house.
ܫܠܝܚܐ ܒܡܕܝܢܬܐ ܗܘܘ.	*šliḥē ba-mdittā-waw.*	The apostles were in the city.

§ 7.3 The Perfect with Object Suffixes. The objective pronominal enclitics, which are suffixed directly onto a verb, are basically the same as the set of enclitics I given in §4.1; an important exception is the first-person singular objective enclitic *-an* (with otiose *yod).* The 3rd-person plural enclitics are not used as object suffixes (see §6.2).

With the vowel-initial enclitics (3 masc. sing. *-eh,* 3 fem. sing. *-āh,* 2 masc. sing. *-āk,* 2 fem sing. *-ek,* 1 sing. and pl. *-an)* the verbal stem of the 3rd masc. sing. verb *(CCaC, CCeC)* undergoes a change in pattern to *CaCC-*, the third radical consonant remaining spirantized. The 1st sing. *(CeCCet)* and the 3rd fem. sing. *(CeCCat)* both change to *CCaCt-* before vowel-initial suffixes. All revert to their original patterns with the 2nd pl. suffixes *(-kon, -kēn)*, which are consonant-initial. Thus, from *rdap* 'to drive':

	ܪܕܦ	*RDAP*	ܪܕܦܬ	*REDPAT/REDPET*
+ 3 masc. sing.	ܪܕܦܗ	*radpeh*	ܪܕܦܬܗ	*rdapteh*
+ 3 fem. sing.	ܪܕܦܗ̇	*radpāh*	ܪܕܦܬܗ̇	*rdaptāh*
+ 2 masc. sing	ܪܕܦܟ	*radpāk*	ܪܕܦܬܟ	*rdaptāk*

+ 2 fem. sing.	ܪܕܦܟܝ	*rad̲p̲ek̲*	ܪܕܦܬܟܝ	*rd̲ap̲tek̲*
+ 1 sing.	ܪܕܦܢܝ	*rad̲p̲an*	ܪܕܦܬܢܝ	*rd̲ap̲tan*
+ 3 masc. pl.	ܪܕܦ ܐܢܘܢ	*rd̲ap̲-ennon*	ܪܕܦܬ ܐܢܘܢ	*red̲paṯ/red̲peṯ-ennon*
+ 3 fem. pl.	ܪܕܦ ܐܢܝܢ	*rd̲ap̲-ennēn*	ܪܕܦܬ ܐܢܝܢ	*red̲paṯ/red̲peṯ-ennēn*
+ 2 masc. pl.	ܪܕܦܟܘܢ	*rd̲ap̲k̲on*	ܪܕܦܬܟܘܢ	*red̲paṯk̲on/ red̲peṯk̲on*
+ 2 fem. pl.	ܪܕܦܟܝܢ	*rd̲ap̲k̲ēn*	ܪܕܦܬܟܝܢ	*red̲paṯk̲ēn/ red̲peṯk̲ēn*
+ 1 pl.	ܪܕܦܢ	*rad̲p̲an*	ܪܕܦܬܢ	*rd̲ap̲tan*

As in the possessive construction, the use of anticipatory object pronouns is quite common, e.g.,

ܩܛܠܗ ܠܡܠܟܐ.	*qaṭleh l-malkā.*	He killed the king.
ܩܛܠܬܗ ܠܡܠܟܬܐ.	*qṭaltāh l-malktā.*	She/I killed the queen.

Vocabulary 7

NOUNS

ܐܬܪܐ *atrā* pl *-ē* place

ܒܪܢܫܐ *barnāšā* pl ܒܢܝܢܫܐ *bnaynāšā* man, person, human, (pl) people

ܒܪܐ *brā* pl ܒܢܝܐ *bnayyā* son (+ 1st sing. possessive enclitic, ܒܪܝ *ber* 'my son')

ܒܪܬܐ *bartā* pl ܒܢܬܐ *bnātā* daughter

ܝܗܘܕܝܐ *yudāyā* pl *-ē* Jew (*h* silent except after proclitics, as *da-yhudāyē* 'of the Jews')

ܝܘܡܐ *yawmā* pl *-ē/-ātā* (m) day

ܡܣܟܢܐ *meskênā* pl *-ē* poor, poor person, unfortunate

ܥܕܬܐ *ᶜêdtā* pl *-ātā* church, assembly

VERBS

ܐܬܐ *etā* to come

ܒܢܐ *bnā* to build

ܒܥܐ *bᶜā* to seek, search for

ܗܘܐ *hwā* to be
ܚܕܝ *ḥdi* to rejoice
ܚܙܐ *ḥzā* to see

OTHERS

ܐܠܐ *ellā* but
ܒܟܠܙܒܢ *b-koll-zban* always
ܕܝܢ *dēn*[1] but, however, for, then

Exercise 7

Read and translate:

1 ܚܙܝ ܠܒܪܬܐ ܕܒܝܬ ܒܗܘ̇ ܐܬܪܐ.
2 ܠܐ ܐܬܬ݂ ܠܘܬܗܘܢ.
3 ܓܒܪܐ ܢܟܪܝܐ ܠܢܒܝܐ ܒܟܠܗ̇ ܡܕܝܢܬܐ.
4 ܠܡܢܐ ܐܬܝܬܘܢ ܠܗܪܟܐ؟
5 ܡܢܘ ܕܝܬܒ ܬܡܢ؟
6 ܒܬܪ ܗܕܐ ܫܠܡܘ ܡܢ ܒܪܬܐ ܠܟܠܗܘܢ ܕܗܘܘ ܒܗ̇.
7 ܐܡܪ ܝܫܘܥ ܕܒܟܠܙܒܢ ܡܣܟܢܐ ܐܝܬ ܠܟܘܢ ܥܡܟܘܢ. ܠܝ ܕܝܢ
ܠܐ ܒܟܠܙܒܢ ܐܝܬ ܠܟܘܢ.
8 ܕܒܪܗ ܠܬܡܢ.
9 ܡܢܘ ܕܡܠܠܗ ܠܗܢܐ؟
10 ܒܢܬܐ ܕܗܘ̇ ܢܟܪܝܐ ܠܐ ܐܬܝ̈.
11 ܗܢܐ ܦܘܩܕܢ ܡܠܟܬܐ.
12 ܟܕ ܚܙܐ ܐܢܘܢ ܚܕܝ ܒܗܘܢ.
13 ܗܘܐ ܒܒܝܬܗ ܕܓܒܪܐ.
14 ܠܡܢܐ ܠܐ ܥܒܕܬܘܢ؟
15 ܗܘ̇ ܢܛܪܗ ܠܦܘܩܕܢܐ ܐܠܐ ܗܝ̇ ܠܐ ܢܛܪܬܗ.
16 ܐܟܠܘ ܠܠܚܡܐ ܟܠܗ.

[1]Like the Greek postpositive particle δέ, with which this word has been confused, *dēn* may not stand first in a sentence but must be preceded by another word; it is often best left untranslated.

17 ܫܒܩ ܒܢ ܒܟܠܙܒܢ.

18 ܙܕܩܬܗ ܐܬܬܐ ܠܒܢܝܗ̇ ܡܢ ܠܘܬܗ̇.

19 ܫܠܝܚܗ ܠܫܠܝܚܐ ܠܗܕܐ ܡܕܝܢܬܐ ܡܠܟܐ.

20 ܕܗܒܐ ܕܐܚܕܗ ܠܝܬ ܒܒܝܬܗ.

21 ܒܗ̇ ܚܕܘ ܒܥܕܬܐ ܕܒܢܐ ܠܗܘܢ ܡܠܟܐ ܕܡܕܝܢܬܐ ܚܕܘ ܒܗ̇.

22 ܗܢܐ ܓܒܪܐ ܒܪܗ ܗ̄ܘܐ ܕܐܠܗܐ.

23 ܒܗ̇ ܪܡܫܐ ܗ̄ܘܐ ܒܒܪܬܗ ܠܢܗܪܐ.

24 ܐܢܐ ܫܒܩܬܗ ܠܟܣܦܐ ܡܢܗ.

25 ܒܗ̇ܘ ܐܬܪܐ ܒܢܘ ܒܥܕܬܐ ܠܡܫܝ̈ܚܐ.

26 ܒܗܘܢ ܡ̈ܕܝܢܬܐ ܠܝܬ ܗ̄ܘܐ ܠܝ ܠܚܡܐ.

Translate into Syriac:

1. He said that we always have the poor with us.

2. And in those days they rejoiced in the church the king had built for them in that place.

3. The sons of this man killed the enemy of their city.

4. Why did he abandon you in a village in which there was no water?

5. I led him from the wilderness to his daughter's house.

6. He perished on the mountain with the money had had seized from the poor people.

7. He and the men of his village marched against the king who had killed his son.

ܪܫܐ ܕܬܡܢܝܐ
Lesson Eight

§ 8.1 The Active Participles. The masculine singular active participle for all sound verbs of the G-form (i.e., verbs with no weakness on the pattern *CCaC* or *CCeC)* is made on the pattern *CāCeC,* as *kāteb* 'writing' from *ktab, sāleq* 'leaving' from *sleq,* and *rāheṭ* 'running' from *rheṭ.* The active participles occur mainly in the absolute state as predicates; following are the masculine and feminine singular and plural forms of the absolute state for the three types of verbs introduced so far. All active participles are distinguished orthographically by a dot on top of the word.

TYPE	MASC. SING.		FEM. SING.		MASC. PL.		FEM. PL.	
Sound	ܟܬܒ	*kāteb*	ܟܬܒܐ	*kātbā*	ܟܬܒܝܢ	*kātbin*	ܟܬܒܢ	*kātbān*
III-gutt.	ܐܡܪ	*āmar*	ܐܡܪܐ	*āmrā*	ܐܡܪܝܢ	*āmrin*	ܐܡܪܢ	*āmrān*
III-weak	ܒܢܐ	*bānē*	ܒܢܝܐ	*bānyā*	ܒܢܝܢ	*bāneyn*	ܒܢܝܢ	*bānyān*

Note that a 3rd guttural radical *(h, ḥ, ', ᶜ, r)* changes the stem vowel from *-e-* to *-a-;* otherwise formation is regular.

§ 8.2 Uses of the Participle. The active participle is used with the short pronominal enclitics (3rd-person enclitics optional and rarely used) to form a participial inflection used for the present habitual ("he goes"), the present progressive ("he is going") and occasionally the future ("he will go"). The full inflection is as follows.

3 m	ܟܬܒ	*kāteb(-u)*	ܟܬܒܝܢ	*kātbin(-ennon)*
f	ܟܬܒܐ	*kātbā(-y)*	ܟܬܒܢ	*kātbān(-ennēn)*
2 m	ܟܬܒ ܐܢܬ	*kāteb-att*	ܟܬܒܝܢ ܐܢܬܘܢ	*kātbi-tton*

f	ܟܳܬܒܳܐ ܐܢ̄ܬܝ	*kātbā-att*	ܟܳܬܒ̈ܳܢ ܐܢ̄ܬܶܝܢ	*kātbā-ttēn*
1 m	ܟܳܬܶܒ ܐ̱ܢܐ	*kāteb-nā*	ܟܳܬܒܺܝܢ ܚ̄ܢܢ	*kātbin-nan*
f	ܟܳܬܒܳܐ ܐ̱ܢܐ	*kātbā-nā*	ܟܳܬܒ̈ܳܢ ܚ̄ܢܢ	*kātbān-nan*

Note reduction of the stem vowel *-e-* where it occurs. Note also that the *n* of the 2nd pl. participles assimilates to the *t* of the enclitic. Because this inflection is participial/adjectival, all persons have both masculine and feminine forms.

The participial inflection of the 1st and 2nd persons occasionally appears in the following contracted forms:

2 m	ܥܳܒܕܰܬ	*ᶜābdatt*	ܥܳܒܕܺܝܬܘܢ	*ᶜābditton*
2 f	ܥܳܒܕܰܬܝ	*ᶜābdatt*	ܥܳܒܕ̈ܳܬܶܝܢ	*ᶜābdattēn*
1 m	ܥܳܒܶܕܢܐ	*ᶜābednā*	ܥܳܒܕܺܝܢܰܢ	*ᶜābdinnan*

The past habitual/progressive ("he used to go, he was going, would go") is formed with the participles and the past copula *(kāteb-wā, kātbā-wāt, kāteb-wayt, kātbā-wayt, kāteb-wêt, kātbā-wêt,* etc.).

ܗܘ ܣܳܠܶܩ ܠܛܘܪܐ.	*hu sāleq l-ṭurā.*	He's going (he goes) up to the mountain.
ܗܘ ܣܳܠܶܩ ܗܘܳܐ ܠܛܘܪܐ.	*hu sāleq-wā l-ṭurā.*	He was going (used to go) up to the mountain.
ܥܳܡܰܪ ܐ̱ܢܐ ܒܩܪܺܝܬܐ ܗܝ..	*ᶜāmar-nā ba-qritā hay.*	I live in that village.
ܥܳܡܰܪ ܗܘܺܝܬ ܬܰܡܳܢ.	*ᶜāmar-wêt tammān.*	I used to live there.

The past copula often occurs along with the perfect, especially in narrative prose; in such uses the past copula is generally superfluous and should be disregarded in translation, although in specific contexts it may render the English past perfect, as *ezal-wā* 'he went' or, according to context, 'he had gone.'

Attributive uses of the participle are almost always turned into relative constructions with *d-*, e.g.

ܓܒܪܐ ܕܒܥܐ ܠܒܪܗ	*gabrā d-bā^{c}ē la-breh*	the man (who is/was) searching for his son
ܡܠܐܟܐ ܕܢܚܬܝܢ ܠܐܪܥܐ ܘܣܠܩܝܢ ܠܫܡܝܐ	*malakē d-nāḥtin l-ar^{c}ā w-sālqin la-šmayyā*	angels descending to earth and ascending to heaven

The active participle is often used adverbially (even redundantly) to express the manner in which something is done, e.g.

ܐܡܪ ܠܝ ܐܡܪ ܕ...	*emar li āmar d-...*	he said to me, saying...
ܢܦܩܬ ܡܢ ܠܘܬܢ ܒܥܝܐ ܡܕܡ.	*nepqat men lwātan bā^{c}yā meddem.*	She went out from our presence, looking for something.

Such adverbial uses, especially when complementary to a verbal object, are frequently introduced by *kad,* e.g.

ܐܫܟܚܘܗܝ ܟܕ ܝܬܒ ܒܒܝܬܐ.	*eškḥu kad yāteb b-baytā*	They found him sitting in the house.

In general the participles do not take enclitic objects as finite verbs do; rather, they take pronominal objects through *l-*. The exception is the 3rd-person plural short pronouns *ennon* and *ennēn*, which do follow a participle as direct object.

ܗܘ ܕܕܒܪ ܗܘܐ ܠܟ	*haw d-dābar-wā lāk*	he who was guiding you
ܗܘ ܕܕܒܪ ܐܢܘܢ	*haw d-dābar-ennon*	he who was guiding them

§ 8.3 Object Suffixes with Third-Person Plural Verbs. Just as the verbal stem of the 3rd sing. perfect verb undergoes changes before the addition of the object suffixes, so also do 3rd-person plural verbs. The 3rd masc. pl. verb assumes the pattern *Ca<u>CC</u>u-;* the 3rd-person fem. pl. verb takes the pattern *Ca<u>CC</u>ā-* before the enclitics that are originally vowel-initial.

	ܪܕܦܘ	*rd̲ap̲*	ܪܕܦ	*rd̲ap̲*
+ 3 m s	ܪܕܦܘܗܝ	*rad̲p̲u*	ܪܕܦܗܝ	*rad̲p̲āy*
+ 3 f s	ܪܕܦܘܗ̇	*rad̲p̲uh*	ܪܕܦܗ̇	*rad̲p̲āh*
+ 2 m s	ܪܕܦܘܟ	*rad̲p̲uk*	ܪܕܦܟ	*rad̲p̲āk*
+ 2 f s	ܪܕܦܘܟܝ	*rad̲p̲uk*	ܪܕܦܟܝ	*rad̲p̲ek*
+ 1 c s	ܪܕܦܘܢܝ	*rad̲p̲un*	ܪܕܦܢܝ	*rad̲p̲ān*
+ 2 m pl	ܪܕܦܘܟܘܢ	*rad̲p̲uk̲on*	ܪܕܦܟܘܢ	*rd̲ap̲k̲on*
+ 2 f pl	ܪܕܦܘܟܝܢ	*rad̲p̲uk̲ēn*	ܪܕܦܟܝܢ	*rd̲ap̲k̲ēn*
+ 1 c pl	ܪܕܦܘܢ	*rad̲p̲un*	ܪܕܦܢ	*rad̲p̲ān*

Note especially the form and spelling of the 3rd masc. sing. enclitic on each of these two persons. The original form of this enclitic was *-ohi* (Aramaic והי) which explains the historical spelling in Syriac orthography.

With the 3rd masc. pl. verb, the vowel-initial enclitics all lose their initial vowels. With the 3rd fem. pl. verb, the vowel-initial enclitics similarly lose their vowels, with the exception of the 2nd fem. sing. enclitic *-ek,* which takes precedence over the inflectional vowel.

Vocabulary 8

NOUNS

ܟܪܘܙܘܬܐ *kārōzutā* pl *-zwātā* gospel, preaching
ܡܪܚܡܢܘܬܐ *mraḥḥmānutā* pl *-nwātā* mercy, loving kindness
ܦܘܪܩܢܐ *purqānā* pl *-ē* salvation
ܦܪܘܩܐ *pārōqa* pl *-ē* savior
ܩܢܛܪܘܢܐ *qenṭrōnā* pl *-ē* centurion
ܪܚܡܐ *rāḥmā* pl *-ē* friend
ܪܚܡܬܐ *rāḥemtā* pl *-ātā* friend (f)
ܩܫܝܫܐ *qaššišā* pl *-ē* elder

ADJECTIVES (given in the absolute state)

ܚܕ / ܚܕܐ *ḥad* (m), *ḥdā* (f) one, a

ܩܫܝܫ *qaššiš* old, elder

ܩܪܝܒ *qarrib* near, close (*l-* to)

ܪܚܝܩ *raḥḥiq* far, distant

VERBS

ܐܫܟܚ *eškaḥ* to find

ܚܝܐ *ḥyā* to live, be alive

ܦܪܣ *pras* to spread

ܪܚܡ *rḥem* to love

ܫܕܪ *šaddar* to send

OTHERS

ܒܝܕ *b-yad* by, through, by means of, via

ܒܠܚܘܕ *balḥōd* alone (also takes pron. encl. II [see §9.2], e.g., *balḥōdaw* 'by himself')

ܩܪܝܒ ܠܡܡܬ *qarrib la-mmāt* near death

ܓܝܪ *gēr* but, however, indeed (a causal conjunction; like *dēn* and the Greek postpositive *γαρ*, *gēr* does not stand at the head of a sentence)

ܣܓܝ *saggi* very

PROPER NAMES

ܝܘܚܢܢ *yōḥannān* John

ܠܘܩܐ *luqā* Luke

ܡܪܩܘܣ *marqōs* Mark

ܡܬܝ *mattay* Matthew

Exercise 8

Read and translate:

1 ܚܕܝܢ ܚܝܢ ܒܦܘܪܣܝܢ ܒܝܕ ܦܪܘܣܐ.
2 ܠܐ ܗܘܐ ܒܠܚܡܐ ܒܠܚܘܕ ܚܝܐ ܒܪܢܫܐ.
3 ܐܢܐ ܠܐ ܫܠܡ ܐܢܐ ܡܢ ܒܫܬܐ.
4 ܚܕܐ ܐܢܬܬܐ ܒܒܪܗ̇ ܕܠܐ ܚܙܪ ܠܡܡܘܬܐ.
5 ܐܫܟܚܘܗ̇ ܒܗ ܚܡܪܐ ܒܡܪܬܐ ܗܝ.
6 ܡܢܘ ܕܒܟܐ ܐܢܬ ܠܗ؟

7 ܒܗ̇ ܗܘܳܐ ܪܡܫܐ ܪܳܟܒܺܝܢ ܠܢܗܪܐ.

8 ܐܢܐ ܫܳܠܰܚ ܐ̱ܢܐ ܠܗ ܠܗܢܐ ܟܬܒܐ ܠܘܬܟܘܢ ܒܝܕ ܗܢܐ
ܫܠܝܚܐ.

9 ܚܙܝܢ ܐܢܬܘܢ ܠܗܘܢ.

10 ܐܚܘܝܬ ܠܝ ܐܬܪܐ ܕܒܳܢܶܐ ܐ̱ܢܐ ܒܗ ܒܝܬܐ.

11 ܗܽܘ ܕܕܰܒܰܪ ܠܝ ܒܥܠܕܒܒܝ ܗ̱ܘ.

12 ܐܢܐ ܐܡܪ ܐ̱ܢܐ ܠܟܘܢ ܕܗܽܘ ܕܡܛܠܘܗ̱ܝ ܦܪܘܩ ܗ̱ܘ.

13 ܚܙܘ ܠܝ ܒܗ̇ ܢܦܩ ܡܢ ܒܝܬܝ.

14 ܒܨܦܪܐ ܕܝܢ ܐܙܠܝܢ ܗ̱ܘܘ ܠܒܪܝܬܐ.

15 ܡܛܠܝ ܚܳܣ ܠܗܘܢ ܟܠܗܘܢ.

16 ܐܠܗܐ ܦܪܩ ܡܫܥܒܕܘܬܗ ܟܠ ܐܪܥܐ ܟܠܗ̇.

17 ܥܒܕܗ ܕܝܢ ܕܩܢܛܪܘܢܐ ܚܕ ܡܪܝܥ ܗ̱ܘܐ ܠܡܡܬ. ܘܫܡܥ
ܥܠ ܝܫܘܥ. ܘܫܕܪ ܠܘܬܗ ܩܫܝܫܐ ܕܝܗܘܕܝܐ. ܗܢܘܢ ܕܝܢ ܟܕ
ܐܬܘ ܠܘܬ ܝܫܘܥ ܒܥܝܢ ܗ̱ܘܘ ܡܢܗ ܘܐܡܪܝܢ. ܪܚܡ ܓܝܪ
ܠܥܡܢ. ܘܐܦ ܒܝܬ ܟܢܘܫܬܐ ܗܘ ܒܢܐ ܠܢ. ܝܫܘܥ ܕܝܢ ܐܙܠ
ܗ̱ܘܐ ܥܡܗܘܢ. ܟܕ ܕܝܢ ܠܐ ܣܓܝ ܪܚܝܩ ܡܢ ܒܝܬܐ. ܫܕܪ
ܠܘܬܗ ܩܢܛܪܘܢܐ ܪ̈ܚܡܘܗܝ.[1] ※

Translate into Syriac:

1. A centurion whose servant was near death sent the elders of the Jews, who had heard of Jesus, unto him.

2. In this place the apostle built a church for the men and women who live in the city.

3. He is sending a messenger to the king of whom he has heard.

4. He abandoned us with our enemy.

5. Thus the king commanded, and thus he did.

6. After that, they all went out from the city to the mountains.

7. Have you (pl) seen the woman who went out in the morning to the house of her friend (f)?

8. I have heard of the prophet's preaching from the elders.

[1] *Rāḥmaw* 'his friends.'

ܪܫܐ ܬܫܝܥܝܐ
Lesson Nine

§ 9.1 Adjectives. Adjectives occur as masculine and feminine, singular and plural. The regular endings for the emphatic and absolute states are given below (example *ṭāb* 'good').

	MASCULINE				FEMININE			
	SINGULAR		PLURAL		SINGULAR		PLURAL	
emph.	ܛܒܐ	*ṭābā*	ܛܒ̈ܐ	*ṭābē*	ܛܒܬܐ	*ṭābtā*	ܛܒ̈ܬܐ	*ṭābātā*
abs.	ܛܒ	*ṭāb*	ܛܒ̈ܝܢ	*ṭābin*	ܛܒܐ	*ṭābā*	ܛܒ̈ܢ	*ṭābān*

An attributive adjective follows the noun it modifies and agrees in number, gender, and state. Examples:

ܡܠܟܐ ܒܝܫܐ	*malkā bišā*	wicked king
ܐܢܬܬܐ ܫܦܝܪܬܐ	*atttā šappirtā*	beautiful woman
ܫܠܝ̈ܚܐ ܚܟܝ̈ܡܐ	*šliḥē ḥakkimē*	wise apostles
ܢܫ̈ܐ ܥܬܝܪ̈ܬܐ	*neššē ᶜattirātā*	rich women

An attributive adjective modifying a noun qualified by a possessive pronoun is also in the emphatic state, e.g.

ܒܪܗ̇ ܚܟܝܡܐ	*brāh ḥakkimā*	her wise son
ܐܢܬܬܗ ܥܬܝܪܬܐ	*attteh ᶜattirtā*	his rich wife
ܒܝܬܟ ܪܒܐ	*baytāk rabbā*	your large house

Predicate adjectives stand in the absolute state—and they tend to come first in the sentence—while agreeing with the subject in number and gender, e.g.

ܒܝܫ ܗܘ ܡܠܟܐ.	*biš-u malkā.*	The king is wicked.
ܫܦܝܪܐ ܗܝ ܐܢܬܬܐ.	*šappirā-y atttā.*	The woman is beautiful.
ܚܟܝܡܝܢ ܗܘܘ ܫܠܝܚܐ.	*ḥakkimin-waw šliḥē.*	The apostles were wise.
ܥܬܝܪܢ ܐܢܝܢ ܢܫܐ.	*ᶜattirān-ennēn neššē.*	The women are rich.

There is no comparative or superlative degree of the adjective. The comparative sense is conveyed by the use of *men*, e.g.

ܐܢܐ ܐܢܐ ܥܬܝܪ ܡܢܟ.	*enā-nā ᶜattir mennāk.*	I am richer than you.
ܫܠܝܚܐ ܚܟܝܡ ܗܘ ܡܢ ܗܠܝܢ ܓܒܪܐ.	*šliḥā ḥakkim-u men hālēn gabrē.*	The apostle is wiser than these men.

The superlative sense is achieved by the adjective with *men koll-* or simply by sense.

ܓܒܪܐ ܗܘ ܪܒ ܗܘܐ ܡܢ ܟܠܗܘܢ ܒܢܝ ܡܕܢܚܐ.	*gabrā haw rabb-wā men kollhon bnay-madnḥā.*	This man was the greatest of all the men of the east.
ܡܢܘ ܪܒ ܒܡܠܟܘܬܐ ܕܫܡܝܐ؟	*man-u rabb b-malkutā da-šmayyā?*	Who is the greatest in the kingdom of heaven?

§ 9.2 Pronominal Enclitics II. The second set of pronominal enclitics is as follows.

3 m	ܘܗܝ	*-aw*	ܝܗܘܢ	*-ayhon*
f	ܗ̇	*-ēh*	ܝܗܝܢ	*-ayhēn*
2 m	ܟ	*-ayk*	ܝܟܘܢ	*-ayk̲on*
f	ܟܝ	*-ayk*	ܝܟܝܢ	*-ayk̲ēn*
1 c	ܝ	*-ay*	ܝܢ	*-ayn*

These pronominals are attached to certain prepositions, such as *ᶜal* (combining form, *ᶜl-)*, to give the following inflection:

3 m	ܥܠܘܗܝ	*ᶜlaw*	ܥܠܝܗܘܢ	*ᶜlayhon*
f	ܥܠܝܗ̇	*ᶜlēh*	ܥܠܝܗܝܢ	*ᶜlayhēn*

2 m	ܥܠܝܟ	*ʿlayk*	ܥܠܝܟܘܢ	*ʿlaykon*
f	ܥܠܝܟܝ	*ʿlayk*	ܥܠܝܟܝܢ	*ʿlaykēn*
1 c	ܥܠܝ	*ʿlay*	ܥܠܝܢ	*ʿlayn*

Other common prepositions that take this set of pronominals are ܨܝܕ *ṣēd* 'beside, at' *(ṣēdaw, ṣēdēh, &c.)*, ܚܠܦ *ḥlāp* 'on behalf of' *(ḥlāpaw, ḥlapēh, &c.)*, ܚܕܪ *ḥdār* 'around' *(ḥdāraw, ḥdārēh, &c.)*, and ܩܕܡ *qdām* 'before' *(qdāmaw, qdāmēh, &c.)*.

The particle of existential predication, *it,* also takes this set of pronominals *(itaw, itēh, itayk, &c.)*. When the enclitics are attached to *it,* it ceases to function as an existential predicator and becomes merely a subject carrier, e.g.

ܟܕ ܗܘ ܐܝܬܘܗܝ ܗܘܐ ܒܒܝܬܗ ܕܫܡܥܘܢ ܐܬܬ ܐܢܬܬܐ.	*kad hu itaw-wā b-bayteh d-šemʿōn, etāt atttā.*	While he was at Simon's house, a woman came.
ܐܢܐ ܕܝܢ ܠܐ ܒܟܠܙܒܢ ܐܝܬܝ ܠܘܬܟܘܢ.	*enā dēn lā b-koll-zban itay lwātkon.*	for I will not always be amongst you.

§ 9.3 Possessive Suffixes with Plural Nouns. The pronominal possessive enclitics are attached to plural nouns as follows.

(a) plurals in *-ātā:* the final *-ā* is dropped and the enclitic suffixes I (§4.1) are added, as from *bnātā* 'daughters' > ܒܢܬܗ *bnāteh* 'his daughters,' ܒܢܬܗ *bnātāh* 'her daughters,' ܒܢܬܟ *bnātāk* 'your daughters.'

(b) plurals in *-ē* and *-ayyā:* final *-ē/-ayyā* is dropped and the enclitic suffixes II (§9.2) are added, e.g., ܫܠܝܚܘܗܝ *šliḥaw* 'his apostles,' ܒܢܝܗ *bnēh* 'her sons,' ܢܫܝܟܝ *neššayk* 'your women,' and ܒܬܝ *bāttay* 'my houses.'

§ 9.4 Paradigm of *y(h)ab* 'To Give.' The verb *y(h)ab* 'to give,' used only in the perfect and imperative, is regularly inflected insofar as the personal endings are concerned. With the exception of the 3rd fem. sing. and 1st sing., whose patterns are absolutely regular, in all other forms the *h* is unpronounced and its vowel falls back to the *y.*

3 m	ܝܗܒ	*yab*	ܝܗܒܘ(ܢ)	*yab(un)*
f	ܝܗܒܬ	*yehbat*	ܝܗܒ(ܝ̈)	*yab(ēn)*
2 m	ܝܗܒܬ	*yabt*	ܝܗܒܬܘܢ	*yabton*
f	ܝܗܒܬܝ	*yabt*	ܝܗܒܬܝܢ	*yabtēn*
1 c	ܝܗܒܬ	*yehbet*	ܝܗܒܢ	*yabn(an)*

Vocabulary 9

NOUNS

ܡܠܬܐ *melltā* pl ܡ̈ܠܐ *mellē* (f) word[1]

ܦܪܕܝܣܐ *pardisā/pardaysā* paradise

ADJECTIVES

ܒܝܫ *biš* bad, evil, wicked

ܚܕܬ *ḥdet* (m) *ḥadtā* (f) pl *ḥadtin/ḥadtān* (emph *ḥadtā/ ḥdattā*[2] pl *ḥadtē/ ḥadtātā)* new

ܚܟܝܡ *ḥakkim* wise

ܛܒ *ṭāb* good

ܣܓܝ *saggi* (m) ܣܓܝܐܐ *saggi'ā* (f) pl ܣܓܝܐܝܢ *saggi'in* (m) ܣ̈ܓܝܐܢ (f) *saggi'ān*[3] many, much

ܥܬܝܪ *ᶜattir* rich

ܩܕܝܫ *qaddiš* holy, sacred

ܪܒ *rabb* pl ܪ̈ܘܪܒܝܢ *rawrbin/*ܪ̈ܘܪܒܢ *rawrbān* big, great

ܫܦܝܪ *šappir* beautiful

VERB

ܝܗܒ *yab* to give (perfect and imperative only)

OTHER

ܚܠܦ *ḥlāp* for the sake of, instead of (+ pron. encl. II: ܚܠܦܘܗܝ *ḥlāpaw* 'for his sake')

ܨܝܕ/ܨܐܕ *ṣêd*[4] beside, next to, at (+ pron. encl. II: ܨܐܕܘܗܝ *ṣêdaw*

---

[1]*Melltā* is normally feminine; however, when it translates ὁ λόγος, it is masculine.

[2]The doubled *-tt-* in *ḥdattā* is spelled with one *tāw;* two *tāws* only in the fem. pl. ܚܕ̈ܬܬܐ *ḥadtātā.*

[3]Note that *ālap* appears in all forms except the masc. sing. absolute.

[4]Generally *ṣêd* is spelled with *yod* when followed by a noun and with *ālap*

'next to him')

PROPER NAMES

ܐܕܡ *ādām* Adam

ܚܘܐ *ḥawwā* Eve

ܡܘܫܐ *mušē* Moses

Exercise 9

(a) Read and translate the following phrases:

1 ܓܒܪܐ ܚܟܝܡܐ
2 ܢ̈ܫܐ ܛܒ̈ܬܐ ܕܐܟܕܝ
3 ܡܠܟܘܬܐ ܚܕܬܐ
4 ܒܢ̈ܬܗ ܦ̈ܬܝܐܬܐ ܕܕܝܠܗ
5 ܒܪܬܐ ܩܕܝܫܬܐ
6 ܡܠܟ̈ܐ ܪ̈ܘܪܒܐ
7 ܐܡ̈ܗܬܐ ܫܦܝܪ̈ܐ
8 ܒܝ̈ܫܐ ܒܬ̈ܠܐ
9 ܡܠܟܐ ܒܝܫܬܐ
10 ܦܓܪܗ ܩܕܝܫܐ
11 ܪܘܚܐ ܩܕܝܫܐ
12 ܒܝ̈ܫܬܐ ܦ̈ܬܝܐܬܐ
13 ܒܢ̈ܬܐ ܪ̈ܘܪܒܬܐ
14 ܡܕܒܪܐ ܪܒܐ
15 ܐܡܝ ܚܟܝܡܬܐ
16 ܡܠܐܟ̈ܐ ܩܕܝ̈ܫܐ
17 ܒܥܠܕܒ̈ܒܐ ܒܝ̈ܫܐ
18 ܒܢ̈ܝܐ ܛܒ̈ܐ ܕܐܟܕܘ̇
19 ܒ̈ܬܐ ܦܬ̈ܝܐܐ
20 ܦܘܩܕܢܗܘܢ ܪܒܐ
21 ܪܚܡܐ ܚܕܬܐ ܕܫܠܦܘܗ̄ܝ

---

when followed by a pronominal enclitic.

22 ܐܪܒܥ ܪܒܬܐ

23 ܡܪܬܐ ܒܬܘܠܬܐ

24 ܡܪ̈ܬܐ ܩܫ̈ܝܐܬܐ

25 ܠܫܢܐ ܩܫܝܐ ܐܟܕܝܢ

26 ܡܕܝܢܬܐ ܡܫܒܚܬܐ

27 ܪ̈ܚܡܐ ܒܬܘ̈ܠܐ

28 ܡܫܝܚܐ ܝܗܘܕܝܐ

29 ܡܕ̈ܝܢܬܐ ܪ̈ܚܝܩܬܐ

30 ܒܝܬܐ ܡܪܒܐ

(b) Turn the phrases in exercise A into sentences, e.g., ܒܝܬܐ ܚܕܬܐ *baytā ḥadtā* 'new house' → ܚܕܬ ܗܘ ܒܝܬܐ *ḥdet-u baytā* 'the house is new.'

(c) Read and translate:

1 ܒܢܘ ܠܗܘܢ ܒܝܬܐ ܚܕܬܐ ܒܗܘ ܐܬܪܐ.

2 ܝܫܘܥ ܡܫܝܚܐ ܦܪܘܩܐ ܗܘ ܕܒܪܝܬܐ ܡܫܒܚܬܐ.

3 ܒܢ̈ܬܢ ܐܚܝ ܗܠܝܢ ܢܫ̈ܐ.

4 ܚܟܝܡ ܗܘ ܗܘ ܕܠܐ ܒܥܐ ܠܦܘܪܫܢܐ ܕܐܠܗܐ.

5 ܟܕ ܚܙܐ ܐܕܡ ܠܚܘܐ ܚܕܝ ܒܗ ܣܓܝ.

6 ܒܝܫ ܗܘ ܕܠܐ ܢܛܪ ܠܦܘܩܕܢܐ ܕܐܠܗܐ ܕܢܦܩܝܢ ܒܢܝ̈ܢܫܐ
ܡܢ ܡܘܫܐ ܢܒܝܐ.

7 ܠܐ ܚܟܝܡܝܢ ܐܢܬܘܢ ܒܢ̈ܝܗ ܕܐܢܬܬܐ ܒܬܘܠܬܐ.

8 ܠܒܢ̈ܝ ܡܠܟܗܘܢ ܕܢܫ̈ܐ.

9 ܪܒ ܗܘܐ ܡܠܟܐ ܕܡܕ̈ܝܢܬܐ ܗܢܝܢ.

10 ܡܕ̈ܝܢܬܐ ܕܡܠܟܐ ܗܢܐ ܪܘܪ̈ܒܢ ܐܚܝ.

11 ܫܠܝܛ ܗܘܐ ܡܠ̈ܟܐ ܥܠܝܗܘܢ ܒܥܠܕܒܒ̈ܝܗܘܢ.

12 ܠܒ ܐܬܘܗܝ ܗܘܐ ܠܫܢܐ ܕܐܟܠ ܒܒ̈ܬܝܗܘܢ.

13 ܒܟܠܝܘܡ ܕܝܢ ܐܬܝܢ ܥܠܝܢܘܗܝ ܕܐܠܗܐ ܠܘܬܗܘܢ ܒܢܝ̈ܢܫܐ.

14 ܐܝܟܐ ܝܫܘܥ ܡܫܝܚܐ ܫܠܝܡ.

15 ܣܓܝܐܝܢ ܐܢܬܘܢ ܒܢܝ̈ܢܫܐ ܒܡܕܝܢܬܐ ܪܒܬܐ ܕܡܠܟܘܬܐ.

16 ܒܢ̈ܝܐ ܠܝ ܦܪܘܣܐ ܡܠܟܘܬܐ ܚܕܬܐ ܒܥܡ̈ܡܐ.
17 ܚܙܐ ܐܠܗܐ ܦܪܕܝܣܐ ܠܟܠܗܘܢ ܒܢ̈ܝܢܫܐ ܘܙܕܝ̈ܩܐ.
18 ܚܕ ܡܢܗܘ ܠܡܕܝܢܬܐ ܠܐ ܢܦܩ ܠܗ ܠܒܪܐ ܗܘ̇.
19 ܠܡܢܐ ܫܠܠܬܘܢ ܠܒ̈ܢܝܐ?
20 ܕܒܪܘܢ ܠܡܕܒܪܐ.
21 ܒܕܪܘ ܠܗ ܒܒܕ̈ܪܘ.
22 ܢܦܩ ܠܝ ܚܕ ܡܠܟ ܐܝܬ ܠܗ̇ ܠܐܝܬܘܬܗ.

Translate into Syriac:

1. Our enemy was evil.
2. The new churches that they built were large.
3. His sons were many.
4. Their houses in the city are new.
5. I gave her the books that you gave me.
6. My sons were the greatest in the kingdom.
7. That new city is larger than the one in which we live.

ܪܫܐ ܕܥܣܪܐ
Lesson Ten

§ 10.1 Paradigm of I-*y* Verbs. Verbs whose first radical is *y* are pronounced with an initial *i-* in all persons of the inflection except for the fixed 3rd fem. sing. and 1st sing. Thus, from *iled:*

3 m	ܝܠܕ	*iled*	ܝܠܕܘ(ܢ)	*iled(un)*
f	ܝܠܕܬ	*yeldat*	ܝܠܕ(ܝ̈ܢ)	*iled(ēn)*
2 m	ܝܠܕܬ	*iledt*	ܝܠܕܬܘܢ	*iledton*
f	ܝܠܕܬܝ	*iledt*	ܝܠܕܬܝܢ	*iledtēn*
1 c	ܝܠܕܬ	*yeldet*	ܝܠܕܢ	*iledn*

I-*y* verbs of the P^{c}AL *(CCaC)* type exhibit the same initial change, e.g., *ida^c* 'to know' *(ida^c, yed^{c}at, ida^{c}t, yed^{c}et,* &c.). Active participles are regularly formed, as ܝܬܒ *iteb* 'to sit' > ܝܬܒ *yāteb* 'sitting' and ܝܕܥ *ida^c* 'to know' > ܝܕܥ *yāda^c* 'knowing.'

§ 10.2 Object Suffixes with the Remaining Persons of the Perfect. The verbal stem of the first-person plural and the second persons undergoes no vocalic shift before the enclitic object pronouns; changes are made, however, in the endings: the 2nd masc. sing. becomes *CCaCtā-*, the 2nd fem. sing. becomes *CCaCti-*, the 2nd masc. pl. becomes *CCaCtonā-*, and the 1st pl. becomes *CCaCnā-*. The enclitic objects added to the forms that end in *-ā* are identical to those added to the 3rd fem. pl. (see §8.3).

	ܪܕܦܬ	*RDAPT*	ܪܕܦܬܝ	*RDAPT*
+ 3 m s	ܪܕܦܬܗܝ	*rdaptāy*	ܪܕܦܬܝܗܝ	*rdaptiw*
+ 3 f s	ܪܕܦܬܗ	*rdaptāh*	ܪܕܦܬܝܗ	*rdaptih*

+ 1 c s	ܪܕܦܬܢܝ	*rdaptān*	ܪܕܦܬܝܢܝ	*rdaptin*
+ 1 c pl	ܪܕܦܬܢ	*rdaptān*	ܪܕܦܬܝܢ	*rdaptin*
	ܪܕܦܬܘܢ	*RDAPTON*	ܪܕܦܢ	*RDAPN*
+ 3 m s	ܪܕܦܬܘܢܝܗܝ	*rdaptonāy*	ܪܕܦܢܝܗܝ	*rdapnāy*
+ 3 f s	ܪܕܦܬܘܢܗ	*rdaptonāh*	ܪܕܦܢܗ	*rdapnāh*
+ 1 c s	ܪܕܦܬܘܢܝ	*rdaptonān*		
+ 1 c pl	ܪܕܦܬܘܢ	*rdaptonān*		

The 2nd fem. pl. takes the enclitic pronouns in the same manner as the masculine: *rdaptēnāy, rdaptēnāh,* &c.

§ 10.3 The Construct Singular. The construct is the second state of the noun to be introduced. It is used when two nouns or a noun and a descriptive phrase are put together in a genitive or limiting relationship, i.e., the first noun is put into the construct state and is followed immediately by the second noun (usually emphatic) or by the limiting term (prepositional phrase, e.g.).

For many nouns the construct state is formed by dropping the *-ā* termination of the emphatic state, as *pārōqā* (emph) > *pārōq-* (const) and *ktābā* (emph) > *ktāb-* (const). Adjustments must be made, however, in the stems of the following types of noun:

(a) stems that consist of only two consonants, stems that end in three consonants, and stems ending in two consonants preceded by a long vowel restore a full vowel, usually *-a-*, as *brā* > *bar-*, *hayklā* > *haykal-*, *madnḥā* > *madnaḥ-*, *šmā* > *šem-* and *ᶜālmā* > *ᶜālam-*. This category includes most feminines that end in *-tā*, e.g., *atttā* > *attat-*, *malktā* > *malkat-*, *mdittā* > *mdinat-* and *briktā* > *brikat-*.

(b) stems ending in two consonants (where there is no implied schwa and where the two consonants are different) exhibit a variety of forms, either *CCvC-* or *Cv̄C-* in shape. These are not predictable from the emphatic state. Examples are: *baytā* > *bēt-*, *gabrā* > *gbar-*, ^{c}*abdā* > ^{c}*bed-*, *laḥmā* > *lḥem-*, *ar*^{c}*ā* > *ara*^{c}- and *tar*^{c}*ā* > *tra*^{c}-.

Nouns that have been adjusted for the construct state may then be placed in construct with another noun (generally emphatic in state) or with a prepositional phrase, e.g.

ܬܪܥ ܡܠܟܘܬܐ	*tra*^{c}*-malkutā*	palace (lit., "gate of kingship")
ܒܪ ܐܢܫܐ	*bar-nāšā*	person (lit., "son of man")
ܥܒܕ ܝܫܘܥ	^{c}*bed-išō*^{c}	Ebedjesus ("servant of Jesus")
ܡܠܟ ܡܠܟ̈ܐ	*mlek-malkē*	king of kings
ܒܪܝܟܬ ܒܢܫ̈ܐ	*brikat-b-neššē*	blessed among women

The construct state, or "chain" as it is sometimes called, cannot be considered free in Syriac, i.e., it generally occurs in set phrases and idiomatic constructions. The possessive constructions with *d-*, on the other hand, are quite free in formation. For example, ܒܝܬܐ ܕܐܒܗ̈ܬܐ *baytā d-abāhātā* and ܒܝܬܗܘܢ ܕܐܒܗ̈ܬܐ *baython d-abāhātā* both mean 'the (spiritual) fathers' house,' while the construct chain ܒܝܬ ܐܒܗ̈ܬܐ *bēt-abāhātā* is a set phrase with a particularized meaning, 'patriarchal see.' Both ܒܪܐ ܕܝܥܩܘܒ *brā d-ya*^{c}*qōb* and ܒܪܗ ܕܝܥܩܘܒ *breh d-ya*^{c}*qōb* mean 'Jacob's son, a son of Jacob,' while ܒܪܝܥܩܘܒ *bar-ya*^{c}*qōb* is a proper name, Barjacobus.

§ 10.4 The Construct Plural. The construct plural for masculine-type nouns replaces the emphatic plural ending *-ē* with *-ay-*. In feminine-type nouns the final *-ā* of *-ātā* is dropped, giving a construct ending *-āt-*.

ܬܪ̈ܥܝ ܡܠܟܘܬܐ	*tar*^{c}*ay-malkutā*	courts, palaces
ܒܝܘܡ̈ܝ ܗܪܘܕܣ ܡܠܟܐ	*b-yawmay-hêrōdes malkā*	in the days of Herod the king
ܥܒ̈ܕܝ ܡܠܟܐ	^{c}*abday-malkā*	servants of the king

ܡܠܟܬ ܐܪܥܐ	*malkāt-arᶜā*	queens of the earth
ܒܢܝ̈ ܐܢܫܐ	*bnay-nāšā*	people ("sons of man")
ܥܒܕ̈ܝ ܫܠܡܐ	*ᶜābday-šlāmā*	peacemakers ("makers of peace")
ܐܢܬܘܢ ܙܥܘܪ̈ܝ ܗܝܡܢܘܬܐ	*atton zᶜōray-haymānutā*	ye of little faith ("little of faith")

§ 10.5 Adjectives in the Construct State. Adjectives occur in the construct state only when they are further limited by another word or phrase bound to them by the construct, as the following examples show.

ܡܕܝܢܬܐ ܣܓܝܐܬ ܒܥܡ̈ܡܐ	*mdittā saggi'at-b-ᶜammā*	a city numerous in people, a populous city
ܐܢܬܬܐ ܡܠܝܬ ܛܝܒܘܬܐ	*atttā malyat-ṭaybutā*	a woman full of grace
ܒܢܝ̈ܢܫܐ ܣܓܝܐ̈ܝ ܒܝܘ̈ܡܬܗܘܢ	*bnaynāšā saggi'ay-b-yawmāthon*	aged people ("people many in their days")

§ 10.6 Adverbs. Adverbs are normally made from adjectives in the feminine singular absolute with the adverbial suffix *-'it,* for example ܫܪܝܪ *šarrir* 'true' > ܫܪܝܪܐܝܬ *šarrirā'it* 'truly,' and ܚܟܝܡ *ḥakkim* 'wise' > ܚܟܝܡܐܝܬ *ḥakkimā'it* 'wisely.'

Other adverbs are simply adjectives in the absolute state, as *saggi* 'very' and *ṭāb* 'quite.'

ܣܓܝ ܥܬܝܪ ܗܘܐ.	*saggi ᶜattir-wā.*	He was very rich.
ܚܕܝ ܛܒ ܒܗܕܐ.	*ḥdi ṭāb b-hādē.*	He was quite glad of that.

ܚܙܐ ܐܠܗܐ ܟܠ ܕܥܒܕ. ܘܗܐ ܛܒ ܫܦܝܪ.	*ḥzā alāhā koll da-^{c}bad w-hā ṭāb šappir.*	God saw all that he had made and, behold, it was very good.

Vocabulary 10

NOUNS

ܐܝܕܐ *idā* (const *id-,* abs *yad)* pl *idē/idayyā* hand

ܟܗܢܐ *kāhnā* pl *-ē* priest

ܡܪܐ *mārā* (const *mārē)* pl ܡܪ̈ܝܐ *mārayyā*/ ܡܪ̈ܘܬܐ *mārawwātā* lord, master

ܡܪܝܐ *māryā* The Lord (used only of God and Christ)

ܢܘܗܪܐ *nuhrā* light

ܥܠܡܐ *^{c}ālmā* (const *^{c}ālam)* the world

ܪܒ ܟܗ̈ܢܐ *rabb-kāhnē* pl *rabbay-kāhnē* chief priest

ܪܫܐ *rêšā* head (often in construct, e.g., *rêš-abāhātā* patriarch, bishop; *rêš-malakē* archangel); heading, chapter

ܬܠܡܝܕܐ *talmidā* disciple

ܬܪܥܐ *tar^{c}ā* (constr *tra^c)* gate; chapter

ܬܪܥ ܡܠܟܘܬܐ *tra^c-malkutā* pl *tar^{c}ay-malkutā* palace, court

ADJECTIVES

ܙܥܘܪ *z^{c}ōr* little, small

ܫܪܝܪ *šarrir* true, trusty, faithful

VERBS

ܕܡܟ *dmek* to sleep, go to sleep

ܗܦܟ *hpak* to return, go back

ܝܕܥ *ida^c* to know

ܝܠܕ *iled* to give birth, bear, beget

ܝܩܕ *iqed* to burn (intr.), catch fire

ܝܬܒ *iteb* to sit, sit down

ܢܗܪ *nhar* to be light, bright, to shine

OTHER

ܒܪܫܝܬ *b-rāšit* in the beginning (< בראשית)

PROPER NAME

ܐܘܪܫܠܡ *ōrêšlem* Jerusalem

Exercise 10

Read and translate:

1 ܐܢܬܘܢ ܐܝܟ ܢܘܗܪܐ ܕܥܠܡܐ.
2 ܟܕ ܢܗܪ ܗܘܐ ܨܦܪܐ ܕܝܘܡܐ.
3 ܟܪܟ ܟܘܟܒܐ ܒܫܡܝܐ ܘܠܐ ܝܕܥ ܡܪܘܗ ܕܐܝܟܢܐ ܗܘ.
4 ܗܕܐ ܗܝ ܡܠܬܐ ܫܪܝܪܬܐ ܕܢܒܝ̈ܐ.
5 ܒܬܪ ܗܕܐ ܗܦܟ ܒܗܝܐ ܠܗܝܟܠܐ ܥܡ ܬܠܡܝ̈ܕܘܗܝ.
6 ܐܫܟܚܘܗܝ ܟܕ ܝܬܒ ܥܡ ܬ̈ܪܝܢ ܟܗ̈ܢܐ.
7 ܟܕ ܗܦܟܬ ܠܒܝܬܐ ܫܬܩܬ.
8 ܫܪܝܪܐܝܬ ܠܐ ܝܕܥܝܢ ܚܢܢ.
9 ܕܝܘܡܐ ܒܥܕ̈ܢܐ ܡܠܟܐ ܒܗܝܟܠܐ.
10 ܟܕ ܗܦܟܬ ܚܙܬ ܢܘܗܪܐ ܕܢܗܪ ܒܐܦܘܗܝ ܕܡܪܢܐ ܒܥܕܬܐ.
11 ܠܡܢܐ ܙܕܩܬܘܢ ܡܢ ܠܘܬܟ؟
12 ܗܫܐ ܚܙܝܢ ܗܘܝܢ ܐܠܐ ܠܐ ܐܫܟܚܢܝ ܠܡܪܢ.
13 ܡܫܡܫܢܐ ܚܕ ܐܝܬ ܗܘܐ ܕܝܬܒ ܗܘܐ ܠܘܬ ܬܪܥܗ ܕܗܘ
ܒܝܬܐ.
14 ܒܪܫܝܬ ܐܝܬܘܗܝ ܗܘܐ ܡܠܬܐ. ܘܗܘ ܡܠܬܐ ܐܝܬܘܗܝ
ܗܘܐ ܠܘܬ ܐܠܗܐ. ܘܐܠܗܐ ܐܝܬܘܗܝ ܗܘܐ ܗܘ ܡܠܬܐ.
ܗܢܐ ܐܝܬܘܗܝ ܗܘܐ ܒܪܫܝܬ ܠܘܬ ܐܠܗܐ. ܟܠ ܒܐܝܕܗ
ܗܘܐ...※

Translate into Syriac:

1. Did you see me going down to the little village near the city?
2. We sat down with our disciples near the palace.
3. In the days of the king our kingdom was great.
4. You (f s) drove him from my presence.
5. I know that people are not always wise.
6. We found him in the temple.
7. While the bishop was sitting with his disciples and trusty friends, the church caught fire.

ܪܫܐ ܕܚܕܥܣܪ

Lesson Eleven

§ 11.1 Paradigm of ‘Hollow’ Verbs: The Perfect. Verbs with an original second radical *w* or *y* are known as “hollow” verbs. The paradigm for the common type, *CāC* in the perfect, is as follows with an example from *qām* ‘to rise up.’

3 m	ܩܡ	*qām*	ܩܡܘ(ܢ)	*qām(un)*
f	ܩܡܬ	*qāmat*	ܩܡ(ܝ̈ܢ)	*qām(ēn)*
2 m	ܩܡܬ	*qāmt*	ܩܡܬܘܢ	*qāmton*
f	ܩܡܬܝ	*qāmt*	ܩܡܬܝܢ	*qāmtēn*
1 c	ܩܡܬ	*qāmet*	ܩܡܢ	*qāmn(an)*

Active participles (note that *ālap*/glottal stop represents the second radical in the masc. sing.; *y* serves as the second radical in all others):

masc.	ܩܐܡ	*qā’em*	ܩܝܡܝܢ	*qāymin*
fem.	ܩܝܡܐ	*qāymā*	ܩܝ̈ܡܢ	*qāymān*

A much rarer type is represented by *mit,* regularly inflected like *qām* but with the *-i-* vowel in the stem throughout *(*ܡܝܬ *mit,* ܡܝܬܬ *mitat,* ܡܝܬܬ *mitt,* ܡܝܬܬ *mitet,* &c., act. part.: ܡܐܬ *mā’et,* ܡܝܬܐ *māytā,* &c.).

§ 11.2 Paradigm of Geminate Verbs: The Perfect. Verbs whose second and third radical consonants are identical are known as geminate, or doubled, verbs; they are inflected similarly to the hollow verbs, the only differences being the length of the stem vowel and the 3rd fem. sing. and 1st sing., both of which are regularly formed with the doubled consonant of the second and third radicals; gemination is lost in all other persons of the inflection. An example is from *ᶜal* (root √*ᶜLL)* 'to go in, enter':

3 m	ܥܠ	*ᶜal*	ܥܠܘ(ܢ)	*ᶜal(un)*
f	ܥܠܬ	*ᶜellat*	ܥܠ(ܝ̈ܢ)	*ᶜal(ēn)*
2 m	ܥܠܬ	*ᶜalt*	ܥܠܬܘܢ	*ᶜalton*
f	ܥܠܬܝ	*ᶜalt*	ܥܠܬܝܢ	*ᶜaltēn*
1 c	ܥܠܬ	*ᶜellet*	ܥܠܢ	*ᶜaln(an)*

Active participles:

masc.	ܥܐܠ	*ᶜā'el*	ܥܐܠܝܢ	*ᶜāllin*
fem.	ܥܐܠܐ	*ᶜāllā*	ܥܐܠܢ̈	*ᶜāllān*

Note that the masc. sing. participle is formed as though from a hollow root; others are predictably formed. The *ālap* is retained by convention in all forms of *ᶜal*, which is by far the most common geminate G verb; with other geminates *ālap* appears consistently only in the masc. sing. participle (e.g. √*QṢṢ* > ܩܐܨ *qā'eṣ,* ܩܨܐ *qāṣṣā,* ܩܨܝܢ *qāṣṣīn,* ܩܨܢ *qāṣṣān).*

§ 11.3 Paradigm of II-*Âlap* Verbs. The vocalic patterning of the perfect of all II-*ālap* verbs is similar. The *ālap,* which originally carried the glottal stop, is only vestigial, and the vowel that would have been carried by the glottal stop falls back onto the first radical consonant. An example is from *šel* (originally *š'el* √*Š'L)* 'to ask':

3 m	ܫܐܠ	*šel*	ܫܐܠܘ(ܢ)	*šel(un)*
f	ܫܐܠܬ	*šelat*	ܫܐܠ(ܝ̈ܢ)	*šel(ēn)*
2 m	ܫܐܠܬ	*šelt*	ܫܐܠܬܘܢ	*šelton*
f	ܫܐܠܬܝ	*šelt*	ܫܐܠܬܝܢ	*šeltēn*
1 c	ܫܐܠܬ	*šelet*	ܫܐܠܢ	*šeln(an)*

Active participles:

masc.	ܫܐܠ	*šā'el*	ܫܐܠܝܢ	*šālin*
fem.	ܫܐܠܐ	*šālā*	ܫܐܠܢ̈	*šālān*

§ 11.4 The Pleonastic Dative. Fairly common in Syriac is the pronominal repetition of a verbal subject after the verb with the preposition *l-* as a type of reflexive dative ("to do something for oneself"). Most such pronominal constructions have no translational value whatsoever.

ܩܪܒܬ ܠܗ ܓܝܪ ܡܠܟܘܬܐ ܕܫܡܝܐ.	*qerbat-lāh gēr malkutā da-šmayyā.*	The kingdom of heaven has drawn nigh.
ܩܡ ܠܗ ܓܝܪ ܐܝܟܢܐ ܕܐܡܪ.	*qām leh gēr aykannā d-emar.*	He has risen as he said (he would).
ܗܦܟܘ ܠܗܘܢ ܬܘܒ ܠܐܘܪܫܠܡ.	*hpak lhon tub l-ōrêš-lem.*	They turned back once more to Jerusalem.

This construction is especially common with verbs of motion, as can be seen in the above examples.

Vocabulary 11

NOUNS

ܐܟܠܩܪܨܐ *ākel-qarṣā* the Devil
ܗܓܡܘܢܐ *hegmōnā* governor
ܛܠܝܐ *ṭalyā* pl *ṭlāyē* (m) child
ܛܠܝܬܐ *ṭlitā* pl *ṭalyātā* child (female)
ܟܘܟܒܐ *kawkbā* (abs/const *kawkab-)* pl *-ē* star, heavenly body
ܡܓܘܫܐ *mgušā* pl *-ē* magus
ܡܕܢܚܐ *madnḥā* (const *madnaḥ-)* orient, east
ܥܢܐ *ᶜānā* sheep (a collective, singular in form but plural in meaning, hence *syāmē;* generally construed as fem. sing.)
ܨܠܘܬܐ *ṣlōtā* pl *ṣlawwātā* prayer
ܪܥܝܐ *rāᶜyā* pl *rāᶜawwātā* shepherd

VERBS

ܡܝܬ *mit* to die
ܣܡ *sām* to put, place
ܥܠ *ᶜal* to go in, enter

ܩܡ *qām* to rise, arise, stand up, stop
ܫܐܠ *šel* to ask, demand

OTHERS

ܠܥܠ *l*ᶜ*el* above (as a preposition, *l*ᶜ*el men)*
ܥܙܝܙܐܝܬ ᶜ*azzizā'it* strongly, vehemently
ܥܕܡܐ ܕ ᶜ*dammā d-* until
ܩܕܡ *qdām* before, in front of (takes pron. encl. II: ܩܕܡܘܗܝ *qdāmaw* 'before him')

IDIOMS

ܐܟܠ ܩܪܨܐ *ekal qarṣā* to backbite, slander

PROPER NAME

ܗܪܘܕܣ *hêrodes* Herod

Exercise 11

Read and translate:

1 ܐܢܐ ܐܢ̄ܐ ܪܥܝܐ ܛܒܐ. ܪܥܝܐ ܛܒܐ ܢܦܫܗ ܣܐܡ ܚܠܦ ܥܢ̈ܗ.

2 ܗܘ̇ ܕܝܢ ܝܫܘܥ ܩܡ ܩܕܡ ܗܓܡܘܢܐ ܘܫܐܠܗ ܗܓܡܘܢܐ ܘܐܡ̇ܪ ܠܗ: ܐܢܬ ܗܘ̇ ܡܠܟܐ ܕܝܗܘ̈ܕܝܐ؟ ܐܡ̇ܪ ܠܗ ܝܫܘܥ: ܐܢ̄ܬ ܐܡ̇ܪܬ.

3 ܩܝܡܝܢ ܗ̄ܘܘ ܕܝܢ ܪ̈ܒܝ ܟܗ̈ܢܐ ܘܥܙܝܙܐܝܬ ܐܟܠܝܢ ܗ̄ܘܘ ܩܪ̈ܨܘܗܝ.

4 ܩܡ ܡܢ ܨܠܘܬܗ ܘܐܬ̇ܐ ܠܘܬ ܬܠܡܝ̈ܕܘܗܝ ܘܐܫܟܚ ܐܢܘܢ ܟܕ ܕܡܟܝܢ.

5 ܘܥܠ ܝܫܘܥ ܠܐܘܪܫܠܡ ܠܗܝܟܠܐ ܘܚܙܐ ܟܠܡܕܡ.

6 ܒܝܘ̈ܡܝ ܗܪܘܕܣ ܡܠܟܐ ܐܬܘ ܡܓܘ̈ܫܐ ܡܢ ܡܕܢܚܐ ܠܐܘܪܫܠܡ ܘܐܡ̇ܪܝܢ: ܐܝܟܐ ܡܠܟܐ ܕܝܗܘ̈ܕܝܐ ... ܚܙܝܢ ܓܝܪ ܟܘܟܒܗ ܒܡܕܢܚܐ.

7 ܗܢܘܢ ܕܝܢ ܟܕ ܫܡܥܘ ܡܢ ܡܠܟܐ ܐܙܠܘ ܘܗܐ ܩܕܡܝܗܘܢ

ܒܥܕܢܐ ܕܐܬܐ ܝܫܟܚ ܠܟܠ ܡܢ ܐܝܟܐ ܕܐܝܬܘܗ̄ܝ ܛܠܝܐ.

8 ܡܢܘ ܕܢܫܟܚ ܠܡܥܒܕܐ ܒܥܒ̈ܕܐ؟

9 ܟܕ ܚܙܐ ܗܝܡܢܘܬܐ ܛܠܠܘܗ ܢܫܟܚ ܘܫܐܠ ܕܡܢ ܕܒܪܐ ܠܗ؟

10 ܚܙܘ ܬܒܘܬܐ ܕܡܫܡܫܬܗ ܒܢ̈ܝܗܘܢ ܟܠܗ ܕܕܠܝܗܘܢ.

11 ܢܫܟܚ ܢܚܬܐ ܡܢܕܡܘܗ̄ܝ ܡܠܟܐ ܘܐܡܪ ܕܢܐܬܐ ܐܢܐ ܠܒܝܬܗ
ܕܐܝܬܝܟ.

12 ܟܕ ܚܙܘ ܒܢ̈ܝܐ ܢܘܗܪܐ ܕܡܕܢܚܐ ܢܦܩܘ ܕܢܐܡܪ ܦܪܘܩܐ
ܕܗܘ ܢܘܗܪܐ ܕܥܠܡܐ.

Translate into Syriac:

1. I stood before him until he sat dawn.
2. We entered the man's house, seeking our enemies.
3. They know that the prophet's words are true.
4. They found me sitting in the wilderness with shepherds.
5. Truly I do not know where he is.
6. After that, the bishop returned to his churches with his disciples.
7. The magi came seeking a child whose star they had seen in the sky.
8. We were sitting on a mountain above the city.
9. Where is the city of the king of this land?
10. I pursued my enemies into the wilderness, and there I killed them.

ܪܫܐ ܬܪܬܥܣܪ
Lesson Twelve

§ 12.1 Passive Participles. The passive participles of all sound transitive G-form (Peal) verbs are patterned on *p*^{c}*il (CCiC)* in the absolute, e.g.

ܩܛܠ *qṭal* > ܩܛܝܠ *qṭil* 'killed'

ܫܠܚ *šlaḥ* > ܫܠܝܚ *šliḥ* 'sent, dispatched'

ܟܬܒ *ktab* > ܟܬܝܒ *ktib* 'written'

The passive participle behaves in every respect like a regular adjective:

	SINGULAR	PLURAL
ABSOLUTE		
masc.	ܩܛܝܠ *qṭil*	ܩܛܝܠܝܢ *qṭilin*
fem.	ܩܛܝܠܐ *qṭilā*	ܩܛܝܠܢ̈ *qṭilān*
EMPHATIC		
masc.	ܩܛܝܠܐ *qṭilā*	ܩܛܝ̈ܠܐ *qṭilē*
fem.	ܩܛܝܠܬܐ *qṭiltā*	ܩܛܝ̈ܠܬܐ *qṭilātā*

Orthographically similar to the passive participle is the adjectival pattern *pa*^{cc}*il (CaCCiC)*, like ܥܬܝܪ ^{c}*attir* and ܚܟܝܡ *ḥakkim*. Care must be taken not to confuse the two, even though some roots produce both the passive participle and the adjective with similar meanings, e.g., ܢܛܝܠ *nṭil* and *naṭṭil*, both meaning 'heavy.'

Passive participles of various verb types:

(a) I-*ālap:* as in the perfect, because the *ālap* cannot have the schwa the pattern would call for, it takes the vowel *a,* as ܐܟܠ *ekal* > ܐܟܝܠ *akil* 'eaten' and ܐܣܪ *esar* > ܐܣܝܪ *asir* 'captured.'

(b) II-*ālap:* as in the perfect, the *ālap* is only an orthographic vestige, as ܫܐܠ *šel* > ܫܐܝܠ *šil* (for original *š'il)* 'demanded, asked for.'

(c) I-*y:* as in the perfect, where the pattern would give *y* a schwa, it is pronounced *i,* as ܝܠܕ *iled* > ܝܠܝܕ *ilid* 'born' (not, however, following a proclitic, as *da-ylid).*

(d) hollow: as in the perfect, the original middle radical is lost, as ܣܡ *sām* > ܣܝܡ *sim* 'placed, put.'

(e) geminate: the passive participle is regularly and predictably formed, as ܒܙ *baz* > ܒܙܝܙ *bziz* 'robbed.'

(f) III-weak: the passive participles differ from all other types; they all conform to the following patterns exemplified by *bnā:*

masc.	ܒܢܐ *bnē*	ܒܢܝܢ *bneyn*
fem.	ܒܢܝܐ *banyā*	ܒܢܝ̈ܢ *banyān*

The passive-participial form from many intransitive verbs, particularly III-weak verbs, is used adjectivally, e.g., ܡܨܐ *mṣā* 'to be able' > ܡܨܐ *mṣē* 'able,' ܨܗܝ *ṣhi* 'to be thirsty' > ܨܗܐ *ṣhē* 'thirsty.'

Agents with passive constructions are usually indicated by the preposition *l-* or *men.*

ܛܠܝܐ ܕܪܚܝܡ ܠܐܒܘܗܝ	*ṭalyā da-rḥim l-abu*	a child loved by its father
ܫܠܝܚܐ ܕܫܠܝܚ ܡܢ ܡܠܟܐ	*šliḥā da-šliḥ men malkā*	a messenger sent by the king

Note also in the above examples that passive participles are not usually used as attributive adjectives but occur in relative-clause constructions.

§ 12.2 III-Weak Verbs with Pronominal Objects. Of the III-weak verbs with the pronominal objects, only the 3rd masc. sing. and the

3rd masc. pl. need special attention. The stem of the 3rd masc. sing. remains unchanged (as *ḥzā* 'he saw'); to this stem are added the pronominal endings given for the forms in *-ā-* (§8.3). The 3rd masc. pl. verb changes in pattern from *CCaw* to *CCa'u-* with *ālap* throughout the inflection.

		ḤZĀ		*ḤZAW*
	ܚܙܐ		ܚܙܘ	
+ 3 m s	ܚܙܝܗܝ	*ḥzāy*	ܚܙܐܘܗܝ	*ḥza'u*
+ 3 f s	ܚܙܗ	*ḥzāh*	ܚܙܐܘܗ	*ḥza'uh*
+ 2 m s	ܚܙܟ	*ḥzāk*	ܚܙܐܘܟ	*ḥza'uk*
+ 2 f s	ܚܙܟܝ	*ḥzāk*	ܚܙܐܘܟܝ	*ḥza'uk*
+ 1 c s	ܚܙܢܝ	*ḥzān*	ܚܙܐܘܢܝ	*ḥza'un*
+ 2 m pl	ܚܙܟܘܢ	*ḥzākon*	ܚܙܐܘܟܘܢ	*ḥza'ukon*
+ 2 f pl	ܚܙܟܝܢ	*ḥzākēn*	ܚܙܐܘܟܝܢ	*ḥza'ukēn*
+ 1 c pl	ܚܙܢ	*ḥzān*	ܚܙܐܘܢ	*ḥza'un*

The pronominal enclitics added to all other persons of the III-weak verb are identical to those given previously (§10.2), as 3rd fem. sing. ܚܙܬ *ḥzāt (*ܚܙܬܗ *ḥzāteh,* ܚܙܬܗ *ḥzātāh,* &c.), 2nd masc. sing. ܚܙܝܬ *ḥzayt (*ܚܙܝܬܗܝ *ḥzaytāy,* ܚܙܝܬܗ *ḥzaytāh,* &c.), 2nd fem. sing. ܚܙܝܬܝ *ḥzayt (*ܚܙܝܬܝܘܗܝ *ḥzaytiw,* ܚܙܝܬܝܗ *ḥzaytih,* &c.), 1st sing. ܚܙܝܬ *ḥzêt (*ܚܙܝܬܗ *ḥzêteh,* ܚܙܝܬܗ *ḥzêtāh,* &c.), 2nd masc. pl. ܚܙܝܬܘܢ *ḥzayton (*ܚܙܝܬܘܢܝܗܝ *ḥzaytonāy,* ܚܙܝܬܘܢܗ *ḥzaytonāh,* &c.), 2nd fem. pl. ܚܙܝܬܝܢ *ḥzaytēn (*ܚܙܝܬܝܢܝܗܝ *ḥzaytēnāy,* ܚܙܝܬܝܢܗ *ḥzaytēnāh,* &c.), and 1st pl. ܚܙܝܢ *ḥzayn (*ܚܙܝܢܝܗܝ *ḥzaynāy,* ܚܙܝܢܗ *ḥzaynāh,* &c.).

§ 12.3 *Abâ, Aḥâ,* and *Ḥmâ* with Pronominal Possessives. The nouns *abā* 'father,' *aḥā* 'brother,' and *ḥmā* 'father-in-law' have the following singular forms with the pronominal suffixes:

	ܐܒܐ	*ABĀ*	ܐܚܐ	*AḤĀ*	ܚܡܐ	*ḤMĀ*
his	ܐܒܘܗܝ	*abu*	ܐܚܘܗܝ	*aḥu*	ܚܡܘܗܝ	*ḥmu*
her	ܐܒܘܗ	*abuh*	ܐܚܘܗ	*aḥuh*	ܚܡܘܗ	*ḥmuh*
your (m)	ܐܒܘܟ	*abuk*	ܐܚܘܟ	*aḥuk*	ܚܡܘܟ	*ḥmuk*
your (f)	ܐܒܘܟܝ	*abuk*	ܐܚܘܟܝ	*aḥuk*	ܚܡܘܟܝ	*ḥmuk*
my	ܐܒܝ	*āb*	ܐܚܝ	*āḥ*	ܚܡܝ	*ḥem*

their (m)	ܐܒܘܗܘܢ	*abuhon*	ܐܚܘܗܘܢ	*aḥuhon*	ܚܡܘܗܘܢ	*ḥmuhon*
their (f)	ܐܒܘܗܝܢ	*abuhēn*	ܐܚܘܗܝܢ	*aḥuhēn*	ܚܡܘܗܝܢ	*ḥmuhēn*
your (m)	ܐܒܘܟܘܢ	*abukon*	ܐܚܘܟܘܢ	*aḥukon*	ܚܡܘܟܘܢ	*ḥmukon*
your (f)	ܐܒܘܟܝܢ	*abukēn*	ܐܚܘܟܝܢ	*aḥukēn*	ܚܡܘܟܝܢ	*ḥmukēn*
our	ܐܒܘܢ	*abun*	ܐܚܘܢ	*aḥun*	ܚܡܘܢ	*ḥmun*

Note especially the lengthened vowel with the first-person singular enclitic in *āb* and *āḥ,* and the form *ḥem.*

The construct state of *abā, aḥā,* and *ḥmā* is wanting.

Abā has two plurals, (1) *abāhē (abāhaw, abāhēh,* &c.) for 'fathers, progenitors' and (2) *abāhātā (abāhāteh, abāhātāh,* &c.) for 'spiritual fathers, ministers.' This is a common phenomenon among nouns that have more than one plural: the first plural, which is usually formed along regular lines, has a more concrete sense than the secondary plural, which is usually formed on a pattern that does not match the singular (i.e. a fem.-type plural like *abāhātā* from a masc. sing.) and has a more metaphorical sense.

Vocabulary 12

NOUNS

ܐܒܐ *abā* pl ܐܒܗ̈ܐ *abāhē*/ ܐܒܗ̈ܬܐ *abāhātā* father
ܐܘܢܐ *awwānā* pl *-ē* abode, lodging
ܐܚܐ *aḥā* pl *aḥē* brother
ܐܚܪܢܐ *ḥrênā* (m) / ܐܚܪܬܐ *ḥrētā* (f) / pl ܐܚܪ̈ܢܐ *ḥrānē*/ ܐܚܪ̈ܢܝܬܐ *ḥranyātā* other, another, someone else
ܓܠܝܠܝܐ *glilāyā* Galilean
ܕܪܬܐ *dārtā* pl *-ātā* courtyard
ܚܡܐ *ḥmā* pl ܚܡܗ̈ܐ *ḥmāhē* father-in-law
ܢܘܪܐ *nurā* (f) fire
ܡܨܥܬܐ *mṣaᶜtā* (const *meṣᶜat)* midst, middle
ܥܠܝܡܐ *ᶜlaymā* pl *-ē* youth, young man, lad
ܥܠܝܡܬܐ *ᶜlaymtā* young woman, maiden

ADJECTIVE

ܩܠܝܠ *qallil* little, little bit; swift

VERBS

ܐܝܬܝ *ayti* to bring, take, lead

ܚܳܪ *ḥār* to look, gaze (*l-* at), pay heed (*b-* to)

ܟܦܪ *kpar b-* to deny, renounce

ܪܥܐ *r^cā* to tend, keep (flocks)

OTHERS

ܒܝܢܬ *baynāt* among, between

ܒܡܨܥܬ *b-meṣ^cat* in the middle/midst of

ܫܥܐ ܚܕܐ *šā^cā ḥdā* one hour

ܚܕܪ *ḥdār* around (+ pron. encl. II: ܚܕܪܘܗܝ *ḥdāraw* 'around him')

ܡܢ ܪܘܚܩܐ *men ruḥqā* from afar

PROPER NAMES

ܫܡܥܘܢ ܟܐܦܐ *šem^cōn kêpā* Simon Peter

ܦܝܠܛܘܣ *pilāṭos* Pilate

Exercise 12

Read and translate the following phrases:

1 ܡ̈ܠܬܐ ܕܟܬܒܐ
2 ܦܘܩܕ̈ܢܐ ܕܦܩܕܢ ܠܥܒܕܘ̈ܗܝ
3 ܠܚܡܐ ܕܐܟܠ
4 ܡܠܐܟܐ ܕܫܠܚ ܠܐܠܗܐ
5 ܕܗܒܐ ܕܐܚܕ ܡܢ ܗܝܟܠܐ
6 ܐܬܝܬܐ ܕܡܛܠܠܐ ܠܐܚ
7 ܬ̈ܠܐ ܕܫܡ̈ܥܝܢ ܗ̄ܘܘ
8 ܛܠܝܐ ܕܝܠܕ
9 ܒܬ̈ܐ ܕܫܡܥܝܢ ܠܘܬ ܐܒܘܟ
10 ܒܢ̈ܬ ܕܒܢܐ ܗ̄ܘܐ ܠܐܚ̈ܘܗܝ
11 ܒܥܒ̈ܕܐ ܕܣܝܡ ܒܥܡ̈ܡܐ
12 ܒ̈ܢܐ ܕܒܒܢܐ ܠܒܢܝܐ
13 ܡܪܚܡܘܬܐ ܕܦܪܘܩܐ ܥܠ ܒܢܝ̈ܢܫܐ
14 ܒܢ̈ܝܐ ܕܪܚܡܝܢ ܠܐܒܗ̈ܝܗܘܢ

Read and translate (beginning with this lesson, an occasional reading will be given in a different script for practice):

1 ܘܐܚܕܘ ܐܝܬܝܘܗ̄ܝ ܠܒܝܬܗ ܕܪܒ ܟܗܢ̈ܐ. ܘܫܡܥܘܢ ܐܬܐ
ܗ̄ܘܐ ܒܬܪܗ ܡܢ ܪܘܚܩܐ. ܘܫܓܪܘ ܕܝܢ ܢܘܪܐ ܒܡܨܥܬܗ ܕܕܪܬܐ.
ܘܝܬܒܝܢ ܗ̄ܘܘ ܚܕܪ̈ܝܗ̇. ܘܝܬܒ ܗ̄ܘܐ ܐܦ ܗܘ ܫܡܥܘܢ
ܒܝܢܬܗܘܢ. ܘܚܙܬܗ ܥܠܝܡܬܐ ܚܕܐ ܕܝܬܒ ܠܘܬ ܢܘܪܐ.
ܘܚܪܬ ܒܗ ܘܐܡܪܐ: ܐܦ ܗܢܐ ܥܡܗ ܗ̄ܘܐ. ܗܘ̇ ܕܝܢ ܟܦ̇ܪ
ܘܐܡܪ: ܐܢ̄ܬܬܐ ܠܐ ܝܕܥ ܐ̄ܢܐ ܠܗ. ܘܒܬܪ ܩܠܝܠ ܚܙܝܗ̄ܝ
ܐܚܪܢܐ ܘܐܡܪ ܠܗ: ܐܦ ܐܢܬ ܡܢܗܘܢ ܐܢܬ. ܟܐܦܐ ܕܝܢ
ܐܡܪ: ܠܐ ܗܘܝܬ. ܘܒܬܪ ܫܥܐ ܚܕܐ ܐܚܪܢܐ ܐܡܪ:
ܫܪܝܪܐܝܬ ܐܦ ܗܢܐ ܥܡܗ ܗ̄ܘܐ. ܐܦ ܓܠܝܠܝܐ ܗ̄ܘ ܓܝܪ.
ܐܡܪ ܟܐܦܐ: ܓܒܪܐ ܠܐ ܝܕܥ ܐܢܐ ܡܢܐ ܕܐܡܪ ܐܢܬ ※

2 ܐܡܪ ܠܗ ܦܝܠܛܘܣ: ܡܠܟܐ ܐܢܬ؟ ܐܡܪ ܠܗ ܝܫܘܥ: ܐܢܬ
ܐܡܪܬ ܕܡܠܟܐ ܐܢܐ. ܐܢܐ ܠܗܕܐ ܝܠܝܕ ܐܢܐ. ܘܠܗܕܐ ܐܬܝܬ ܠܥܠܡܐ ※

3 ܣܒܝܟ̈ܬܐ ܐܝܟ ܐܘ̈ܢܐ ܒܝܬ ܐܟܒ ※

Translate into Syriac:

1. When I arose I found my disciples asleep.
2. They went to where the child was whose star was seen by them in the east.
3. His brothers saw him sitting in the middle of the courtyard with his father.
4. When the governor said to him, "Are you king of the Jews?" he said, "I didn't say that I am king. You said it."
5. Where are the children who were born there?
6. The young man looked at the maiden who was tending her father's sheep.
7. Jesus said, "You always have the poor with you."
8. When they saw the new church the king had built for them, they rejoiced greatly over it.
9. Thus did the king command us.
10. Why did you (pl) not come to me?

ܪܫܐ ܬܠܬܥܣܪ
Lesson Thirteen

§ 13.1 The Absolute State. The third state of the Syriac substantive is the absolute state (emphatic and construct have already been introduced). Although the absolute pertains primarily to predicate adjectives, nouns also occur in the absolute, the forms for which are as follows, e.g., for *malkā* 'king' and for *malktā* 'queen':

masc.	ܡܠܟ *mlek*	ܡܠܟܝܢ *malkin*
fem.	ܡܠܟܐ *malkā*	ܡܠܟܢ *malkān*

Masculine nouns drop the *-ā* termination of the emphatic state; for masculine nouns that do not end in two or more consonants, the absolute singular is identical to the construct singular. The same constraints on stems ending in two or more consonants given for the construct apply to the absolute singular, e.g., *madnḥā* > *madna**ḥ*** and *ᶜālmā* > *ᶜā**la**m*. The same unpredictability that was seen for the construct singular exists for many of these nouns, e.g., *malkā* > *mlek, baytā* > *bēt, yawmā* > *yōm, brā* > *bar* and *zabnā* > *zban.*

Feminine singulars in *-tā* drop the *-tā* and replace it with *-ā,* as *malktā* > *malkā* and *melltā* > *mellā.* This may cause changes in the stem, e.g., *mṣaᶜtā* > *meṣᶜā.*

Nouns on the emphatic pattern *CuCCā* form the absolute on the pattern *CCuC,* as ܓܘܫܡܐ *gušmā* 'body' > ܓܫܘܡ *gšum* and ܫܘܒܚܐ *šubḥā* 'glory' > ܫܒܘܚ *šbuḥ.*

The absolute state occurs infrequently in unbound forms. Common, however, is ܐܢܫ *nāš* (absolute of ܐܢܫܐ *nāšā* 'people') for 'somebody, anybody' and the negative ܠܐ ܐܢܫ *lā-nāš* 'nobody.'

The absolute singular occurs with *koll* when it means 'every,' as in ܟܠ ܝܘܡ *koll yōm* 'every day,' ܟܠ ܙܒܢ *koll zban* 'every time, always,' ܟܠ ܐܢܫ *koll nāš* 'everybody,' ܟܠ ܡܠܬܐ *koll mellā* 'every word,' and ܟܠ ܡܕܝܢܐ *koll mdinā* 'every city.'

The absolute singular also occurs in many compounds such as ܕܠܐܢܡܘܣ *d-lā-nāmōs* 'lawless,' ܡܣܟܢܐ ܒܪܘܚ *meskênē b-ruḥ* 'poor in spirit' and ܚܝܐ ܕܠܥܠܡ *ḥayyē da-l-*^{c}*ālam* 'life eternal.'

The absolute is the normal state with numbers (see following paragraph), as in ܬܠܬܐ ܝܘܡܝܢ *tlātā yawmin* 'three days' and ܫܥܐ ܚܕܐ *šā*^{c}*ā ḥdā* 'one hour.'

The typical endings of all three states of the noun are as follows:

	SINGULAR		PLURAL	
	MASCULINE	FEMININE	MASCULINE	FEMININE
ABSOLUTE	—	*-ā*	*-in*	*-ān*
EMPHATIC	*-ā*	*-tā*	*-ē*	*-ātā*
CONSTRUCT	—	*-at-*	*-ay-*	*-āt-*

§ 13.2 Numbers. In common with other Semitic languages, Syriac uses a feminine-appearing number with masculine nouns and a masculine-appearing number with feminine nouns. This phenomenon, known as chiastic concord, applies to the numbers from 'three' through 'ten' and to the units '-three' through '-nine' in all compound numbers. 'One' and 'two' are irregular adjectives, and the tens from twenty on are invariable.

	WITH MASCULINE NOUNS		WITH FEMININE NOUNS	
1	ܚܕ	*ḥad*	ܚܕܐ	*ḥdā*
2	ܬܪܝܢ	*trēn*	ܬܪܬܝܢ	*tartēn*
3	ܬܠܬܐ	*tlātā*	ܬܠܬ	*tlāt*
4	ܐܪܒܥܐ	*arb*^{c}*ā*	ܐܪܒܥ	*arba*^{c}
5	ܚܡܫܐ	*ḥammšā*	ܚܡܫ	*ḥammeš*

6	(ܐ)ܫܬܐ	*(e)štā*	ܫܬ	*šet*
7	ܫܒܥܐ	*šab^cā*	ܫܒܥ	*šba^c*
8	ܬܡܢܝܐ	*tmānyā*	ܬܡܢܐ	*tmānē*
9	ܬܫܥܐ	*teš^cā*	ܬܫܥ	*tša^c*
10	ܥܣܪܐ	*^cesrā*	ܥܣܪ	*^csar*

Above ten, the 'teen element *(-^csar/-^csrē)* is invariable:

11	ܚܕܥܣܪ	*ḥda^csar*	ܚܕܥܣܪܐ	*ḥda^csrē*
12	ܬܪܥܣܪ	*tre^csar*	ܬܪܬܥܣܪܐ	*tarta^csrē*
13	ܬܠܬܬܥܣܪ	*tlātta^csar*	ܬܠܬܥܣܪܐ	*tlāta^csrē*
14	ܐܪܒܥܬܥܣܪ	*arba^cta^csar*	ܐܪܒܥܣܪܐ	*arba^csrē*
15	ܚܡܫܬܥܣܪ	*ḥammešta^csar*	ܚܡܫܥܣܪܐ	*ḥammša^csrē*
16	ܫܬܥܣܪ	*šetta^csar*	ܫܬܬܥܣܪܐ	*šetta^csrē*
17	ܫܒܥܬܥܣܪ	*šba^cta^csar*	ܫܒܥܣܪܐ	*šba^csrē*
18	ܬܡܢܬܥܣܪ	*tmānta^csar*	ܬܡܢܥܣܪܐ	*tmāna^csrē*
19	ܬܫܥܬܥܣܪ	*tša^cta^csar*	ܬܫܥܣܪܐ	*tša^csrē*

The feminines 'teens all have alternative pronunciations: *ḥda^cesrē, tarta^cesrē, tlāta^cesrē, arb^cesrē, ḥammša^cesrē, šett^cesrē, šba^cesrē, tmāna^cesrē, tša^cesrē.*

The higher numbers are invariable and are as follows:

ܥܣܪܝܢ	*^cesrin* 20
ܬܠܬܝܢ	*tlātin* 30
ܐܪܒܥܝܢ	*arb^cin* 40
ܚܡܫܝܢ	*ḥammšin* 50
(ܐ)ܫܬܝܢ	*(e)štin* 60
ܫܒܥܝܢ	*šab^cin* 70
ܬܡܢܝܢ	*tmānin* 80
ܬܫܥܝܢ	*teš^cin* 90
ܡܐܐ	*mā* (emph ܡܐܬܐ *matā,* pl ܡܐܘܬܐ *mawwātā)* 100
ܡܐܬܝܢ	*mateyn* 200
ܬܠܬܡܐܐ	*tlātmā* 300, &c.
ܐܠܦ	*ālep* pl *alpin* (emph *alpā* pl *alpē)* 1000
ܪܒܘ	*rebbō* pl *rebbwān* 10,000, myriad

In compound numbers, the higher number generally comes first and lower numbers are joined by the conjunction *w(a)-*, e.g.

ܐܪܒܥܡܐܐ ܘܬܡܢܝܢ ܘܬܠܬܐ	*arba^cmā wa-tmānin wa-tlātā*	four hundred eighty-three

ܫܒܥܐ ܐܠܦܝܢ	*šab^cā alpin wa-tlātmā*	seven thousand,
ܘܬܠܬܡܐܐ ܘܫܒܥܐ	*w-šab^cā*	three hundred and seven

The number object usually stands in the absolute plural following the number, e.g.

ܬܠܬܐ ܝܘܡܝܢ	*tlātā yawmin*	three days
ܐܪܒܥ ܫܥܝܢ	*arba^c šā^cin*	four hours
ܫܒܥ ܫܢܝܢ	*šba^c šnin*	seven years

The emphatic plural also occurs after the numbers for the definite sense, e.g.

ܬܠܬܐ ܡܓܘܫܐ	*tlātā mgušē*	the three magi
ܬܠܬܐ ܝܘܡܬܐ	*tlātā yawmātā*	the three days
ܫܒܥ ܬܘܪܬܐ ܛܒܬܐ	*šba^c tawrātā ṭābātā*	The seven good kine
ܫܒܥ ܐܢܝܢ ܫܢܝܢ	*šba^c-ennēn šnin wa-*	are seven years;
ܘܫܒܥ ܫܒܠܐ ܛܒܬܐ	*šba^c šebblē ṭābātā*	and the seven
ܫܒܥ ܫܢܝܢ	*šba^c šnin*	good ears, seven years.

The numbered object may also precede the number in the emphatic state, e.g.

ܝܪܚܐ ܚܡܫܐ	*yarḥē ḥammšē*	five months
ܡܠܟܐ ܬܡܢܬܥܣܪ	*malkē tmānta^csar*	eighteen kings

For 'both,' the number 'two' forms a construct with the pronouns, e.g.

ܬܪܝܗܘܢ	*trayhon*	both of them (m)
ܬܪܬܝܗܝܢ	*tartayhēn*	both of them (f)

For 'the three of them' &c., the pronouns are attached to construct forms of the numbers, e.g.

ܬܠܬܝܗܘܢ	*tlātayhon*	the three of them (m)
ܐܪܒܥܬܝܗܝܢ	*arb^cātayhēn*	the four of them (f)

§ 13.3 Ordinals. The adjectival ordinal numbers, which function as ordinary adjecives, are as follows:

	MASCULINE		FEMININE	
1st	ܩܕܡܝܐ	*qadmāyā*	ܩܕܡܝܬܐ	*qadmāytā*
2nd	ܬܪܝܢܐ	*trayyānā*	ܬܪܝܢܝܬܐ	*trayyānitā*
3rd	ܬܠܝܬܝܐ	*tlitāyā*	ܬܠܝܬܝܬܐ	*tlitāytā*
4th	ܪܒܝܥܝܐ	*rbi*^{c}*āyā*	ܪܒܝܥܝܬܐ	*rbi*^{c}*āytā*
5th	ܚܡܝܫܝܐ	*ḥmišāyā*	ܚܡܝܫܝܬܐ	*ḥmišāytā*
6th	ܫܬܝܬܝܐ	*štitāyā*	ܫܬܝܬܝܬܐ	*štitāytā*
7th	ܫܒܝܥܝܐ	*šbi*^{c}*āyā*	ܫܒܝܥܝܬܐ	*šbi*^{c}*āytā*
8th	ܬܡܝܢܝܐ	*tmināyā*	ܬܡܝܢܝܬܐ	*tmināytā*
9th	ܬܫܝܥܝܐ	*tši*^{c}*āyā*	ܬܫܝܥܝܬܐ	*tši*^{c}*āytā*
10th	ܥܣܝܪܝܐ	^{c}*sirāyā*	ܥܣܝܪܝܬܐ	^{c}*sirāytā*

The ordinal for 'first' is a suppletion form that has no relation to the number 'one.' 'Second' is an exceptional form. The rest of the ordinals, from 'third' through 'tenth' are formed on the pattern *CCiCāyā* (m), *CCiCāytā* (f)

A secondary ordinal construction is noun modified by *d-* + numeral, as in ܪܫܐ ܕܬܠܬܐ *rêšā da-tlātā* 'chapter three' (as opposed to ܪܫܐ ܬܠܝܬܝܐ *rêšā tlitāyā* 'the third chapter'[1]).

§ 13.4 The Infinitive: G-Verbs. The infinitives of all sound G-form verbs are made on the pattern *meCCaC,* e.g. ܩܛܠ *qṭal* > ܡܩܛܠ *meqṭal,* ܫܠܚ *šlaḥ* > ܡܫܠܚ *mešlaḥ* and ܟܬܒ *ktab* > ܡܟܬܒ *mektab.*

Note the patterns for the infinitives of the following verb types:

(1) The *n* of I-*n* verbs assimilates to the second radical, as ܢܦܠ *npal* > ܡܦܠ *meppal* and ܢܛܪ *nṭar* > ܡܛܪ *meṭṭar.*

(2) I-*ālap* verbs

[1] I.e. the third in any series, as in "the third chapter we have studied this week," which is not necessarily chapter number three.

(a) with imperfects (see §14.3) in *-o-* are like ܐܟܠ *ekal* > ܡܐܟܠ *mekal.*

(b) with imperfects in *-a-* are like ܐܡܪ *emar* > ܡܐܡܪ *mê-mar.*

(3) III-weak verbs follow the pattern of ܒܢܐ *bnā* > ܡܒܢܐ *mebnā,* but when *mebnā* is followed by pronominal enclitics it becomes *mebny-*.

(4) hollow verbs assume the pattern of ܩܡ *qām* > ܡܩܡ *mqām.*

The infinitive is generally used with *l-* to indicate purpose, e.g.

ܐܬܝܢ ܠܡܣܓܕ ܠܗ.	*etayn l-mesgad leh.*	We have come to worship him.

and in complementary constructions with adjectives and verbs like *meškaḥ* 'able,' *ṣbā* 'to want' and others, as in the following:

ܠܐ ܡܫܟܚ ܐܝܠܢܐ ܛܒܐ ܦܐܪܐ ܒܝܫܐ ܠܡܥܒܕ.	*lā meškaḥ ilānā ṭābā pêrē bišē l-meᶜbad.*	A good tree cannot make bad fruit.
ܨܒܐ ܐܢܐ ܠܡܩܡ.	*ṣābe-nā la-mqām.*	I want to get up.
ܠܐ ܬܕܚܠ ܠܡܣܒ ܠܡܪܝܡ ܐܢܬܬܟ.	*lā tedḥal l-messab l-maryam atttāk.*	Do not fear to take Mary as your wife.

§ 13.5 Infinitives with Pronominal Objects. Pronominal objects are suffixed directly to infinitives; the pronominal enclitics I are used as infinitival objects. Suffixation of vowel-initial enclitics results in the reduction of the infinitival stem from *meCCaC* to *meCCC-;* with the 2nd-person plural enclitics *(-kon, -kēn),* the stem remains *meC-CaC-*, e.g., from *qṭal:*

+ 3 m	ܡܩܛܠܗ	*meqṭleh*	ܡܩܛܠ ܐܢܘܢ	*meqṭal-ennon*
+ 3 f	ܡܩܛܠܗ̇	*meqṭlāh*	ܡܩܛܠ ܐܢܝܢ	*meqṭal-ennēn*
+ 2 m	ܡܩܛܠܟ	*meqṭlāk*	ܡܩܛܠܟܘܢ	*meqṭalkon*

+ 2 f	ܡܩܛܠܟܝ	*meqṭlek*	ܡܩܛܠܟܝܢ	*meqtalkēn*
+ 1 c	ܡܩܛܠܢ	*meqṭlan*	ܡܩܛܠܢ	*meqṭlan*

The infinitive of III-weak roots changes from *meCCā* to *meCCy-* before the vowel-initial enclitics; it remains *meCCā* with the 2nd-person plural enclitics, e.g., from *ḥzā:*

+ 3 m	ܡܚܙܝܗ	*meḥzyeh*	ܡܚܙܐ ܐܢܘܢ	*meḥzā-ennon*
+ 3 f	ܡܚܙܝܗ̇	*meḥzyāh*	ܡܚܙܐ ܐܢܝܢ	*meḥzā-ennēn*
+ 2 m	ܡܚܙܝܟ	*meḥzyāk*	ܡܚܙܟܘܢ	*meḥzākon*
+ 2 f	ܡܚܙܝܟܝ	*meḥzyek*	ܡܚܙܟܝܢ	*meḥzākēn*
+ 1 c	ܡܚܙܝܢ	*meḥzyan*	ܡܚܙܝܢ	*meḥzyan*

Vocabulary 13

NOUNS

ܐܘܪܚܐ *urḥā* (abs *uraḥ)* pl *-ātā* (f) way, road

ܐܢܫܐ *nāšā* (abs *nāš,* abs pl *nāšin)* human being, person[1]; kinsfolk, people (with pron. encl. II for the plural, *nāšēh da-mdittā* 'the people/inhabitants of the city'); the abs. *nāš* and the negative *lā nāš* are used for 'somebody' and 'nobody'; the abs. pl. *nāšin* is used for 'some people'

ܒܝܬ ܩܒܘܪܐ *bēt-qburā* sepulchre

ܚܕܒܫܒܐ *ḥad-bšabbā* Sunday

ܚܝ̈ܐ *ḥayyē* (pl) life

ܟܐܦܐ *kêpā* (f) rock, stone

ܡܠܦܢܐ *mallpānā* pl *-ē* teacher

ܫܠܡܐ *šlāmā* peace

ܫܪܪܐ *šrārā* truth

ADJECTIVES

ܡܫܟܚ *meškaḥ* able (*l-* + infinitive, 'able to'), possible

ܩܕܡܝ *qadmāy* first, former

[1]Usually *bar-nāšā* in the meaning of 'person.'

VERBS

ܦܫ *pāš* to remain
ܨܒܐ *ṣbā* to want (*l-* + infinitive, 'to want to')
ܩܕܡ *qdam* to precede
ܫܠܡ *šlem* to be finished, over, concluded
ܫܩܠ *šqal* to lift, take up, remove

OTHERS

ܐܟܚܕܐ *akḥdā* together
ܐܠܐ ܐܢ *ellā en* unless, except that
ܐܠܘ *ellu* if (introduces impossible, contrafactual conditionals)
ܐܢ *en* if (introduces possible conditionals)
ܗܫܐ *hāšā* now
ܡܕܥ *medda*ᶜ (infinitive of *ida*ᶜ*)* knowing, to know
ܬܘܒ *tub* again, once more

PROPER NAMES

ܝܘܣܦ *yōsep* Joseph
ܡܪܝܡ *maryam* Mary
ܡܓܕܠܝܐ *magdlāyā* (m) *magdlāytā* (f) Magdalene
ܬܐܘܡܐ *tōmā* Thomas

Exercise 13

Read and translate:

1 ܠܡܢܐ ܨܒܐ ܐܢܬ ܠܡܫܩܠ ܐܢܘܢ؟

2 ܫܠܡܐ ܫܒܩ ܐܢܐ ܠܟܘܢ. ܫܠܡܐ ܕܝܠܝ ܝܗܒ ܐܢܐ ܠܟܘܢ.
ܠܐ ܗ̄ܘܐ ܐܝܟܢܐ ܕܝܗܒ ܥܠܡܐ ܐܢܐ ܝܗܒ ܐܢܐ ܠܟܘܢ.

3 ܠܐ ܡܫܟܚ ܐܢܐ ܠܡܐܬܐ ܠܘܬܟ.

4 ܨܒܝܢ ܐܢܚܢ ܠܡܐܙܠ ܠܝܡܐ.

5 ܠܐ ܡܫܟܚ ܐܢܬܘܢ ܠܡܐܡܪ ܫܪܪܐ.

6 ܐܬܝܬ ܠܡܫܐܠܟ ܥܠ ܗܕܐ.

7 ܪܚܡܐ ܐܢܐ ܠܡܫܝܚܐ.

8 ܘܠܐܝܟܐ ܕܐܙܠ ܐܢܐ ܝܕܥܝܢ ܐܢܬܘܢ. ܘܐܘܪܚܐ ܝܕܥܝܢ ܐܢܬܘܢ.
ܐܡܪ ܠܗ ܬܐܘܡܐ: ܡܪܢ ܠܐ ܝܕܥܝܢ ܚܢܢ ܠܐܝܟܐ ܐܙܠ ܐܢܬ.
ܘܐܝܟܢܐ ܡܫܟܚܝܢ ܚܢܢ ܐܘܪܚܐ ܠܡܕܥ؟ ܐܡܪ ܠܗ ܝܫܘܥ:
ܐܢܐ ܐܢܐ ܐܘܪܚܐ ܘܫܪܪܐ ܘܚܝܐ. ܠܐ ܐܢܫ ܐܬܐ ܠܘܬ ܐܒܝ
ܐܠܐ ܒܝ. ܐܠܘ ܠܝ ܝܕܥܝܢ ܗ̄ܘܝܬܘܢ ܐܦ ܠܐܒܝ ܝܕܥܝܢ
ܗ̄ܘܝܬܘܢ. ܘܡܢ ܗܫܐ ܝܕܥܝܢ ܐܢܬܘܢ ܠܗ. ܘܚܙܝܬܘܢܝܗܝ ※

9 ܒܚܕܒܫܒܐ ܕܝܢ ܐܬܬ ܡܪܝܡ ܡܓܕܠܝܬܐ ܒܨܦܪܐ ܠܒܝܬ ܩܒܘܪܐ
ܘܚܙܬ ܠܟܐܦܐ ܕܫܩܝܠܐ ܡܢ ܩܒܪܐ. ܘܪܗܛܬ ܐܬܬ ܠܘܬ ܫܡܥܘܢ
ܟܐܦܐ ... ܘܐܡܪܐ ܠܗܘܢ ܕܫܩܠܘܗܝ ܠܡܪܢ ܡܢ ܗܘ ܒܝܬ ܩܒܘܪܐ.
ܘܠܐ ܝܕܥܐ ܐܢܐ ܐܝܟܐ ܣܡܘܗܝ. ܘܢܦܩ ܫܡܥܘܢ ܘܗܘ ܬܠܡܝܕܐ ܐܚܪܢܐ.
ܘܐܬܝܢ ܗ̄ܘܘ ܠܒܝܬ ܩܒܘܪܐ ܘܪܗܛܝܢ ܗ̄ܘܘ ܬܪܝܗܘܢ ܐܟܚܕܐ. ܗܘ ܕܝܢ
ܬܠܡܝܕܐ ܪܗܛ ܩܕܡܘܗܝ ܠܫܡܥܘܢ ܘܐܬܐ ܩܕܡܝܐ ܠܒܝܬ ܩܒܘܪܐ ※

10 ܟܕ ܫܠܡܘ ܝܘܡܬܐ ܗܦܟܘ ܠܗܘܢ. ܝܫܘܥ ܕܝܢ ܛܠܝܐ ܦܫ ܠܗ
ܒܐܘܪܫܠܡ ܘܝܘܣܦ ܘܐܡܗ ܠܐ ܝܕܥܘ ... ܘܟܕ ܠܐ ܐܫܟܚܘܗܝ ܗܦܟܘ
ܠܗܘܢ ܠܐܘܪܫܠܡ ... ܘܡܢ ܒܬܪ ܬܠܬܐ ܝܘܡܝܢ ܐܫܟܚܘܗܝ ܒܗܝܟܠܐ ܟܕ
ܝܬܒ ܡܨܥܬ ܡܠܦܢܐ ܘܫܡܥ ܡܢܗܘܢ ※

Translate into Syriac:

1. After three days, on Sunday, she went to the tomb and found the rock removed.

2. Some people put a fire in the middle of the courtyard and sat around it.

3. A young woman looked at the man who had come into their midst and knew that he was of Jesus' disciples.

4. There is no abode for the poor in the wilderness.

5. After a little while they went together to lift the stone from its place.

6. If I had seen you I would have recognized (known) you.

ܪܝܫܐ ܕܐܪܒܥܬܥܣܪ
Lesson Fourteen

§ 14.1 The Imperfect and Imperative of G-Verbs: Sound Roots. Verbs with sound roots are inflected in the imperfect with a combination of pre- and post-formatives. The imperfect also has a stem vowel between the second and third radicals, but this stem vowel is reduced to schwa in those persons that have post-formatives. Most transitive verbs have *-o-* as the stem vowel of the imperfect, giving an imperfect stem of - *CCoC-*. A model imperfect inflection of *ktab* follows. Note that *syāmē* dots are put on the feminine plural forms only.

3 m	ܢܟܬܘܒ	*nek̲tob̲*	ܢܟܬܒܘܢ	*nek̲tb̲un*
f	ܬܟܬܘܒ	*tek̲tob̲*	ܢܟܬ̈ܒܢ	*nek̲tb̲ān*
2 m	ܬܟܬܘܒ	*tek̲tob̲*	ܬܟܬܒܘܢ	*tek̲tb̲un*
f	ܬܟܬܒܝܢ	*tek̲tb̲in*	ܬܟܬ̈ܒܢ	*tek̲tb̲ān*
1 c	ܐܟܬܘܒ	*ek̲tob̲*	ܢܟܬܘܒ	*nek̲tob̲*

Imperative forms are made from this same stem by dropping the preformatives and restoring the stem vowel if it has been reduced:

masc.	ܟܬܘܒ	*kt̲ob̲*	ܟܬܘܒܘ(ܢ)	*kt̲ob̲(un)*
fem.	ܟܬܘܒܝ	*kt̲ob̲*	ܟܬܘܒ(̈ܝܢ)	*kt̲ob̲(ēn)*

Most intransitive and III-guttural verbs have *-a-* as the stem vowel of the imperfect, and a very few have *-e-* as the stem vowel. The inflection is unaffected, e.g., *qreb,* imperfect *neqrab:*

3 m	ܢܩܪܒ	*neqrab̲*	ܢܩܪܒܘܢ	*neqrb̲un*
f	ܬܩܪܒ	*teqrab̲*	ܢܩܪ̈ܒܢ	*neqrb̲ān,* &c.

The imperative is regularly formed from the imperfect:

masc.	ܩܪܒ *qrab̲*	ܩܪܒܘ(ܢ) *qrab̲(un)*
fem.	ܩܪܒܝ *qrab̲*	ܩܪܒ(ܝ̈ܢ) *qrab̲(ēn)*

Most intransitive verbs that do not fall into one of the special categories below (§§14.2–14.8) have imperfects with *-o-* as the characteristic vowel, e.g.,

ܢܗܦܘܟ < ܗܦܟ *hp̲ak̲ > nehpok̲*	ܢܩܕܘܡ < ܩܕܡ *qd̲am > neqdom*
ܢܟܬܘܒ < ܟܬܒ *kt̲ab̲ > nek̲tob̲*	ܢܩܛܘܠ < ܩܛܠ *qṭal > neqṭol*
ܢܥܪܘܩ < ܥܪܩ *^{c}raq > ne^{c}roq*	ܢܪܕܘܦ < ܪܕܦ *rd̲ap̲ > nerdop̲*
ܢܦܩܘܕ < ܦܩܕ *pqad̲ > nep̲qod̲*	ܢܫܒܘܩ < ܫܒܩ *šb̲aq > nešboq*
ܢܦܪܘܣ < ܦܪܣ *pras > nep̲ros*	ܢܫܩܘܠ < ܫܩܠ *šqal > nešqol*

Most intransitive, as well as II- and III-guttural verbs have *-a-* as the imperfect vowel, e.g.

ܢܫܟܚ < ܐܫܟܚ *eškaḥ > neškaḥ*	ܢܥܡܪ < ܥܡܪ *^{c}mar > ne^{c}mar*
ܢܕܒܪ < ܕܒܪ *db̲ar > ned̲bar*	ܢܩܪܒ < ܩܪܒ *qreb̲ > neqrab̲*
ܢܕܡܟ < ܕܡܟ *dmek̲ > ned̲mak̲*	ܢܪܗܛ < ܪܗܛ *rheṭ > nerhaṭ*[2]
ܢܟܦܪ < ܟܦܪ *kp̲ar > nek̲par*	ܢܪܚܡ < ܪܚܡ *rḥem > nerḥam*
ܢܢܗܪ < ܢܗܪ *nhar > nenhar*	ܢܫܐܠ < ܫܐܠ *šel > nešal*
ܢܣܩ < ܣܠܩ *sleq > nessaq*[1]	ܢܫܠܚ < ܫܠܚ *šlaḥ > nešlaḥ*
ܢܥܒܪ < ܥܒܪ *^{c}b̲ar > ne^{c}bar*	ܢܫܠܡ < ܫܠܡ *šlem > nešlam*
ܢܥܕܪ < ܥܕܪ *^{c}d̲ar > ne^{c}dar*	ܢܫܡܥ < ܫܡܥ *šma^c > nešma^c*

A very few verbs have *-e-* as the imperfect vowel, e.g.

ܢܥܒܕ < ܥܒܕ *^{c}b̲ad̲ > ne^{c}bed̲*

§ 14.2 The Imperfect Inflection of I-*n* Verbs. Verbs with *n* as first radical show a regular assimilation of the *n* to the second radical in the imperfect, as *npaq > ne**pp**oq*. Thereafter the inflection is

[1]Note that the *l* assimilates to the *s*, just as the *l* of *ezal* assimilates to the *z* in certain forms, but the *l* is dropped in orthography in this form.

[2]The imperative of ܪܗܛ *rheṭ* is irregular: ܗܪܛ *harṭ*.

regular.

3 m	ܢܦܘܩ	*neppoq*	ܢܦܩܘܢ	*neppqun*
f	ܬܦܘܩ	*teppoq*	ܢܦܩܢ	*neppqān*
2 m	ܬܦܘܩ	*teppoq*	ܬܦܩܘܢ	*teppqun*
f	ܬܦܩܝܢ	*teppqin*	ܬܦܩܢ	*teppqān*
1 c	ܐܦܘܩ	*eppoq*	ܢܦܘܩ	*neppoq*

The imperative is a form, derived from the imperfect, that has lost the first radical altogether:

masc.	ܦܘܩ	*poq*	ܦܘܩܘ(ܢ)	*poq(un)*
fem.	ܦܘܩܝ	*poq*	ܦܘܩ(ܝܢ)	*poq(ēn)*

Almost all I-*n* verbs, as well as a few other irregular verbs like *ida*ᶜ and *iteb*, form their imperfects in this manner, e.g.:

ܢܛܪ < ܢܛܪ *nṭar* > *neṭṭar*		ܢܣܒ < ܢܣܒ *nsab* > *nessab*
ܢܚܘܬ < ܢܚܬ *nḥet* > *neḥḥot*		ܢܕܥ < ܝܕܥ *ida*ᶜ > *nedda*ᶜ
ܢܦܠ < ܢܦܠ *npal* > *neppel*		ܢܬܒ < ܝܬܒ *iteb* > *netteb*
ܢܦܘܩ < ܢܦܩ *npaq* > *neppoq*		

The notable exception, given above, is *nhar* 'to shine,' with imperfect *nenhar* without assimilation.

Also to this category belongs ܢܬܠ *nettel* (cf. Hebr. נתן), the suppletionary verb that serves as the imperfect of ܝܗܒ *y(h)ab* 'to give' (imperative ܗܒ *hab*).

§ 14.3 The Imperfect of I-*Âlap* Verbs. I-*âlap* verbs fall into two categories in the imperfect:

(1) If the imperfect vowel is *o*, the vowel of the personal prefixes is *-e-*, as expected from the paradigm given in §14.1. The *ālap* of the first radical is retained as a historical spelling, except in the imperative, where the *ālap* has the vowel *a*. Examples are ܐܟܠ *ekal* > ܢܐܟܘܠ *nekol*, inf ܡܐܟܠ *mekal*, impt ܐܟܘܠ *akol*, and ܐܚܕ *eḥad* > ܢܐܚܘܕ *neḥod*, inf ܡܐܚܕ *meḥad*, impt ܐܚܘܕ *aḥod*.

(2) If the imperfect vowel is *-a-*, the vowel of the personal prefixes is *-ê-;* the infinitive is similarly formed as *mêCaC*. The initial vowel in the imperative is *e*. Examples are ܐܒܕ *ebad* > ܢܐܒܕ *nêbad*, inf ܡܐܒܕ *mêbad,* impt ܐܒܕ *ebad,* and ܐܡܪ *emar* > ܢܐܡܪ *nêmar,* inf ܡܐܡܪ *mêmar,* impt ܐܡܪ *emar.*

Note the anomalous imperative of ܐܙܠ *ezal* > ܢܐܙܠ *nêzal*, inf ܡܐܙܠ *mêzal,* impt ܙܠ ***zel***.

§ 14.4 The Imperfect of I-*y* Verbs. I-*y* verbs normally form the imperfect exactly as though they were I-*âlap*—the imperfects are even written with an *ālap* as the first radical. The only difference lies in the imperative, which reverts to *y*-initial.

Examples are ܝܠܕ *iled* > ܢܐܠܕ *nêlad,* inf ܡܐܠܕ *mêlad,* impt ܝܠܕ *ilad,* and ܝܩܕ *iqed* > ܢܐܩܕ *nêqad,* inf ܡܐܩܕ *mêqad,* impt ܝܩܕ *iqad.*

Exceptional in this category are ܝܬܒ *iteb* 'to sit' and ܝܕܥ *ida*^{c} 'to know,' which form their imperfects are though they were I-*n,* ܢܬܒ *netteb* and ܢܕܥ *nedda*^{c} (see above, §14.2). Other forms derived from the imperfect are predictable, inf ܡܬܒ *mettab* and ܡܕܥ *medda*^{c}, impt ܬܒ *teb* and ܕܥ *da*^{c}.

§ 14.5 The Imperfect of III-Weak Verbs. All verbs with a weak third radical are inflected in the imperfect on the following model from *bnā* 'to build':

3 m	ܢܒܢܐ	*nebnē*	ܢܒܢܘܢ	*nebnōn*
f	ܬܒܢܐ	*tebnē*	ܢܒܢܝ̈ܢ	*nebnyān*
2 m	ܬܒܢܐ	*tebnē*	ܬܒܢܘܢ	*tebnōn*
f	ܬܒܢܝܢ	*tebneyn*	ܬܒܢܝ̈ܢ	*tebnyān*
1 c	ܐܒܢܐ	*ebnē*	ܢܒܢܐ	*nebnē*

The imperatives are as follows:

masc.	ܒܢܝ	*bni*	ܒܢܘ	*bnaw*
fem.	ܒܢܝ	*bnāy*	ܒܢܝ̈ܢ	*bnāyēn*

III-weak verbs introduced so far are:

ܢܐܬܐ < ܐܬܐ	*etā > nêtē*		ܢܚܕܐ < ܚܕܝ	*ḥdi > neḥdē*
ܢܒܢܐ < ܒܢܐ	*bnā > nebnē*		ܢܚܙܐ < ܚܙܐ	*ḥzā > neḥzē*
ܢܒܥܐ < ܒܥܐ	*b^{c}ā > neb^{c}ē*		ܢܚܐ < ܚܝܐ	*ḥyā > neḥḥē*
ܢܗܘܐ < ܗܘܐ	*hwā > nehwē*		ܢܪܥܐ < ܪܥܐ	*r^{c}ā > ner^{c}ē*

Note that the imperfect of *etā* is made according to the second category of I-*ālap*s *(nêtē)*. The imperatives of *etā* are irregular, however:

masc.	ܬܐ	*tā*	ܬܘ	*taw*
fem.	ܬܝ	*tāy*	ܬܝܢ	*tāyēn*

The true imperative of *hwā* is not used; instead, the perfect inflection serves also as the imperative, as *hwayt yāda^c d-...* 'know that...' (lit., 'be knowing that...').

Note also the anomalous imperfect of *ḥyā, neḥḥē,* formed as though it were a I-*n* verb.

§ 14.6 The Imperfect of Hollow Verbs. Hollow verbs are inflected in the imperfect with the characteristic vowel *-u-* instead of *-o-*. Thus, from *qām* we have the following inflection:

3 m	ܢܩܘܡ	*nqum*	ܢܩܘܡܘܢ	*nqumun*
f	ܬܩܘܡ	*tqum*	ܢܩܘܡܢ	*nqumān*
2 m	ܬܩܘܡ	*tqum*	ܬܩܘܡܘܢ	*tqumun*
f	ܬܩܘܡܝܢ	*tqumin*	ܬܩܘܡܢ	*tqumān*
1 c	ܐܩܘܡ	*equm*	ܢܩܘܡ	*nqum*

Note that there is no reduction in the long stem vowel of hollow verbs.

Imperatives are regularly formed, e.g.

masc.	ܩܘܡ	*qum*	ܩܘܡܘ(ܢ)	*qum(un)*
fem.	ܩܘܡܝ	*qum*	ܩܘܡ(ܝܢ)	*qum(ēn)*

Alone of all hollow verbs is *sām,* which forms its imperfect with the stem vowel *i* instead of *u;* otherwise the inflection is exactly like the model above.

3 m	ܢܣܝܡ	*nsim*	ܢܣܝܡܘܢ	*nsimun*

f	ܬܣܝܡ	*tsim*	ܢܣܝܡܢ	*nsimān,* &c.

Following are the hollow verbs introduced so far:

ܢܩܘܡ < ܩܡ	*qām > nqum*		ܢܡܘܬ < ܡܝܬ	*mit > nmut*
ܢܣܝܡ < ܣܡ	*sām > nsim*		ܢܦܘܫ < ܦܫ	*pāš > npuš*
ܢܚܘܪ < ܚܪ	*ḥār > nḥur*			

§ 14.7 The Imperfect of Geminate Verbs. Geminate verbs are inflected in the imperfect as though they were I-*n,* doubling the first radical (see §14.2). Like the I-*n* verbs, geminate verbs also show reduction of the imperfect stem vowel with those persons that have suffixes. Thus, from *^{c}al:*

3 m	ܢܥܘܠ	*ne^{cc}ol*	ܢܥܠܘܢ	*ne^{cc}lun*
f	ܬܥܘܠ	*te^{cc}ol*	ܢܥܠܢ	*ne^{cc}lān*
2 m	ܬܥܘܠ	*te^{cc}ol*	ܬܥܠܘܢ	*te^{cc}lun*
f	ܬܥܠܝܢ	*te^{cc}lin*	ܬܥܠܢ	*te^{cc}lān*
1 c	ܐܥܘܠ	*e^{cc}ol*	ܢܥܘܠ	*ne^{cc}ol*

Imperatives are formed from the 2nd persons—again in the manner of I-*n* verbs:

masc.	ܥܘܠ	*^{c}ol*	ܥܘܠ(ܘܢ)	*^{c}ol(un)*
fem.	ܥܘܠ	*^{c}ol*	ܥܘܠ(ܝܢ)	*^{c}ol(ēn)*

§ 14.8 Imperfect of II-*âlap* Verbs. II-*ālap* verbs are regularly inflected in the imperfect with *-a-* as the characteristic stem-vowel (e.g., **neš'al → nešal);* in the persons with postformatives *(-in, -un, -ān),* where stem reduction would have resulted in an original glottal stop with schwa preceded by an unvocalized consonant *(*neš'lun),* a compensatory *-e-* appears *(nešelun,* see Preliminary Matters, V).

3 m	ܢܫܐܠ	*nešal*	ܢܫܐܠܘܢ	*nešelun*
f	ܬܫܐܠ	*tešal*	ܢܫܐܠܢ	*nešelān* &c.

Vocabulary 14

NOUNS

ܝܪܚܐ *yarḥā* pl *-ē* (abs ܝܪܚ *iraḥ* pl ܝܪܚܝܢ *yarḥin)* month
ܠܠܝܐ *lêlyā* pl ܠܠܝ̈ܐ *laylē/* ܠܠܝܘ̈ܬܐ *laylawwātā* night
ܫܒܬܐ *šabtā* and ܫܒܐ *šabbā* pl *-ē* week; Sabbath, Saturday
ܫܥܬܐ *šā^{c}tā* pl ܫ̈ܥܐ *šā^{c}ē* (f., abs ܫܥܐ *šā^{c}ā* pl ܫܥܝܢ *šā^{c}in)* hour
ܫܢܬܐ *šattā* pl ܫܢ̈ܝܐ *šnayyā* (f., abs ܫܢܐ *šnā* pl ܫܢܝܢ *šnin)* year

ADJECTIVES

ܐܚܪܝ *ḥrāy* last
ܙܕܝܩ *zaddiq* righteous

VERBS

ܕܚܠ *dḥel/nedḥal* to be afraid, fear
ܢܬܠ *nettel* (imperfect only) to give

MONTHS OF THE YEAR

ܬܫܪܝܢ ܩܕܝܡ *tišri(n) qdēm* October
ܬܫܪܝܢ ܐܚܪܝܐ *tišri(n) ḥrāyā* November
ܟܢܘܢ ܩܕܡܝܐ *kānun qadmāyā* December
ܟܢܘܢ ܬܪܝܢܐ *kānun trayyānā* January
ܫܒܛ *šbāṭ* February
ܐܕܪ *ādār* March
ܢܝܣܢ *nisān* April
ܐܝܪ *êyār* May
ܚܙܝܪܢ *ḥzirān* June
ܬܡܘܙ *tammuz* July
ܐܒ *āb* August
ܐܝܠܘܠ *êlul* September

DAYS OF THE WEEK

ܫܒܬܐ *šabtā* Saturday
ܚܕܒܫܒܐ *ḥadbšabbā* Sunday
ܬܪܝܢܒܫܒܐ *trēnbšabbā* Monday
ܬܠܬܒܫܒܐ *tlātbšabbā* Tuesday
ܐܪܒܥܐܒܫܒܐ *arb^{c}ābšabbā* Wednesday
ܚܡܫܒܫܒܐ *ḥammešbšabbā* Thursday
ܥܪܘܒܬܐ *^{c}rubtā* Friday

Exercise 14

Identify the following imperfect forms (for translational value use the present or future tense):

1	ܢܐܙܠܘܢ	20	ܬܦܪܘܩ	39	ܬܫܐܠܝܢ
2	ܬܦܘܩ	21	ܢܕܝ̈ܢ	40	ܬܣܡ
3	ܐܚܘܕ	22	ܬܐܬܘܢ	41	ܢܚܙܐ
4	ܢܚܕܪ̈ܢ	23	ܬܒܥܐ	42	ܢܪܕܘܦ
5	ܢܕܒܪ̈ܢ	24	ܢܗܘܐ	43	ܐܥܘܠ
6	ܬܥܒܕܘܢ	25	ܢܚܙ̈ܝܢ	44	ܢܚܡ
7	ܢܚܘܢ	26	ܬܒܕܪܘܢ	45	ܬܫܡ̈ܥܢ
8	ܬܦܠܝܢ	27	ܬܫܒܘܩ	46	ܢܥܒܕܘܢ
9	ܬܚܘܬ	28	ܬܩ̈ܛܠܢ	47	ܬܕܒܪܝܢ
10	ܢܪܗܛܘܢ	29	ܬܐܡܪ	48	ܢܦܩ̈ܢ
11	ܢܐܒܕܘܢ	30	ܬܕܒܪܝܢ	49	ܬܩܪܒܘܢ
12	ܬܫܠ̈ܡܢ	31	ܐܬܒ	50	ܐܥܘܠ
13	ܢܐܬܐ	32	ܢܒܪܘܩ	51	ܬܘ
14	ܐܛܪ	33	ܬܒܠܘܢ	52	ܐܬܠ
15	ܬܬܒܘܢ	34	ܬܩܘܡ	53	ܢܦܫܘܢ
16	ܬܐܡܪ	35	ܢܡܘܬ	54	ܬܡܘܬ
17	ܐܚܐ	36	ܬܣܝ̈ܡܢ	55	ܐܚܙܐ
18	ܬܬܚܒܝܢ	37	ܬܚܘܪ	56	ܢܕܒܘܢ
19	ܢܗܦܘܟ	38	ܢܒܥܘܢ	57	ܐܕܚܠ

Give English equivalents for the following:

1. three months
2. ten years
3. eight days
4. three hours
5. seven men
6. nine women
7. the second month
8. the fourth house
9. the fifth teacher
10. the first good word

Read and translate the following:

1 ܙܒܢܐ ܗ̄ܘܐ ܠܡܣܩ.

2 ܠܐ ܡܫܟܚ ܐܢܐ ܠܡܦܫ.

3 ܨܒܝܢ ܗ̄ܘܘ ܠܡܚܪ ܒܗ.

4 ܡܫܟܚ ܗ̄ܘܬ ܠܡܚܙܝܗ.

5 ܨܒܐ ܒܝܬܐ ܠܡܒܢܐ.

6 ܠܐ ܡܫܟܚ ܗ̄ܘ ܠܡܕܝܢܬܐ ܠܡܐܙܠ.

7 ܠܐ ܨܒܐ ܠܡܐܒܕ.

8 ܨܒܝܐ ܐܢܬܝ ܢܡܘܣܐ ܠܡܛܪ.

9 ܠܐ ܨܒܐ ܠܝ ܠܡܬܠܗ.

10 ܠܐ ܨܒܐ ܐܢܐ ܠܡܬܠܟ.

Give the Syriac for the following:

1. I give
2. they (m) fear
3. she sleeps
4. you (m s) build
5. he falls
6. you (f pl) go
7. they (f) take
8. you (f s) know
9. we go down
10. you (f pl)
11. she goes up
12. he rises
13. they (m) put
14. I come
15. you (m s) rejoice
16. I see
17. come! (m s)
18. they (m) will not die
19. you (f s) remain
20. you (f pl) ask
21. she seeks
22. they (m) will be
23. she looks
24. you (f s) eat

ܪܫܐ ܕܚܡܫܬܥܣܪ
Lesson Fifteen

§ 15.1 Uses of the Imperfect.

(1) As a general or habitual present tense, e.g.

ܢܥܪܩܘܢ ܥܘܠܐ ܟܕ ܠܝܬ ܕܪܕܦ ܠܗܘܢ.	*ne^{c}rqun ^{c}awwālē kad layt d-rādep l-hon.*	The wicked flee when there is no one pursuing them.
ܬܒܥܘܢܢܝ ܘܠܐ ܬܫܟܚܘܢܢܝ.	*teb^{c}ōnān w-lā teškḥunān.*	You seek me and do not find me.

(2) As a future, e.g.

ܢܐܬܐ ܠܘܬܟܘܢ.	*nêtē lwātkon.*	He will come to you.
ܫܡܝܐ ܘܐܪܥܐ ܢܥܒܪܢ ܘܡܠܝ ܠܐ ܢܥܒܪܢ.	*šmayyā w-ar^{c}ā ne^c-brān w-mellay lā ne^{c}brān.*	The heavens and earth will pass away, but my words will not.

(3) As an optative, e.g.

ܬܐܬܐ ܡܠܟܘܬܟ.	*têtē malkutāk.*	Thy kingdom come.
ܢܗܘܐ ܨܒܝܢܟ.	*nehwē ṣebyānāk.*	Thy will be done.
ܘܐܡܪ ܐܠܗܐ ܢܗܘܐ ܢܘܗܪܐ ܘܗܘܐ ܢܘܗܪܐ.	*w-emar alāhā nehwē nuhrā wa-hwā nuhrā.*	And God said, Let there be light: and there was light.

(4) With *lā* and the 2nd persons as negative imperative, e.g.

ܠܐ ܬܩܛܘܠ.	*lā teqṭol!*	Do not kill.
ܠܐ ܬܒܥܘܢ.	*lā tebʿōn.*	Seek you not.

(5) In all dependent and complementary verbal clauses and in purpose clauses with *d-* or *l-*, e.g.

ܐܢ ܒܪܗ ܐܢܬ ܕܐܠܗܐ ܐܡܪ ܕܗܠܝܢ ܟܐܦܐ ܢܗܘܝ̈ܢ ܠܠܚܡܐ.	*en breh att d-alāhā,* *emar d-hālēn kêpē* *nehwyān laḥmā.*	If you are the son of God, say that these rocks be bread.
ܦܩܘܕ ܠܗ ܠܢܣܒ ܥܡܗ ܢܘܢܐ ܕܡܠܝܚ.	*pqod leh l-nessab* *ʿammeh nunā da-mliḥ.*	Order him to take with him a fish that has been salted.
ܠܐ ܨܒܐ ܐܢܐ ܕܐܩܘܡ.	*lā ṣābē-nā d-equm.*	I don't want to get up.
ܐܢܬܘܢ ܠܐ ܬܒܥܘܢ ܡܢܐ ܬܐܟܠܘܢ ܘܡܢܐ ܬܫܬܘܢ.	*atton lā tebʿōn mānā* *teklun w-mānā* *teštōn.*	Seek not what you should eat or what you should drink.
ܡܢ ܕܨܒܐ ܕܢܗܘܐ ܩܕܡܝܐ ܢܗܘܐ ܐܚܪܝܐ.	*man d-ṣābē d-nehwē* *qadmāyā nehwē* *ḥrāyā.*	He who wishes to be first shall be last.

§ 15.2 The Imperfect with Enclitic Objects. The objective pronominals are attached to the imperfect as follows. Note that many persons have more than one alternative form, the first of which is usually simply the imperfect with reduced stem plus the unaugmented object enclitic.

	3RD MASC. SING. & 1ST COM. PL.	3RD FEM. SING. & 2ND MASC. SING.
	ܢܪܕܘܦ *NERDOP*	ܬܪܕܘܦ *TERDOP*
+ 3 m s	ܢܪܕܦܗ *nerdpeh* ܢܪܕܦܝܘܗܝ *nerdpiw*	ܬܪܕܦܗ *terdpeh* ܬܪܕܦܝܘܗܝ *terdpiw*

			ܬܪܕܘܦܝܗܝ	*terdopiw*
+ 3 f s	ܢܪܕܦܝܗ	*nerdpih*	ܬܪܕܦܝܗ	*terdpih*
			ܬܪܕܘܦܝܗ	*terdopēh*
+ 2 m s	ܢܪܕܦܟ	*nerdpāk*	ܬܪܕܦܟ	*terdpāk*
+ 2 f m	ܢܪܕܦܟܝ	*nerdpek*	ܬܪܕܦܟܝ	*terdpek*
+ 1 c s	ܢܪܕܦܢܝ	*nerdpan*	ܬܪܕܦܢܝ	*terdpan*
			ܬܪܕܘܦܢܝ	*terdopayn*
+ 3 m pl	ܢܪܕܘܦ ܐܢܘܢ	*nerdop-ennon*	ܬܪܕܘܦ ܐܢܘܢ	*terdop-ennon*
+ 2 m pl	ܢܪܕܘܦܟܘܢ	*nerdopkon*	ܬܪܕܘܦܟܘܢ	*terdopkon*
+ 1 c pl	ܢܪܕܦܢ	*nerdpan*	ܬܪܕܦܢ	*terdpan*
			ܬܪܕܘܦܢ	*terdopayn*

All imperfect forms that end in *-in, -un* and *-ān* take the objective enclitics of the 3rd masc. pl. example:

ܢܪܕܦܘܢ *NERDPUN*

+ 3 m s	ܢܪܕܦܘܢܗ	*nerdpuneh* or
	ܢܪܕܦܘܢܗܝ	*nerdpunāy*
+ 3 f s	ܢܪܕܦܘܢܗ	*nerdpunāh*
+ 2 m s	ܢܪܕܦܘܢܟ	*nerdpunāk*
+ 2 f s	ܢܪܕܦܘܢܟܝ	*nerdpunek*
+ 1 c s	ܢܪܕܦܘܢܢܝ	*nerdpunān*

§ 15.3 Suffix Pronouns with III-Weak Imperfect Verbs. The imperfect inflectional pattern of III-weak verbs is the only type to produce an ending different from that of sound verbs. With pronominal objects, the *-ē* termination of the III-weak verb is as follows:

+ 3 m s	ܢܒܥܝܘܗܝ	*neb^{c}ēw*	+ 3 m pl	ܢܒܥܐ ܐܢܘܢ	*neb^{c}ē-ennon*
+ 3 f s	ܢܒܥܝܗ	*neb^{c}ēh*	+ 3 f pl	ܢܒܥܐ ܐܢܝܢ	*neb^{c}ē-ennēn*
+ 2 m s	ܢܒܥܝܟ	*neb^{c}ēk*	+ 2 m pl	ܢܒܥܝܟܘܢ	*neb^{c}ēkon*
+ 2 f s	ܢܒܥܝܟܝ	*neb^{c}ēk*	+ 2 f pl	ܢܒܥܝܟܝܢ	*neb^{c}ēkēn*
+ 1 c s	ܢܒܥܝܢܝ	*neb^{c}ēn*	+ 1 c pl	ܢܒܥܝܢ	*neb^{c}ēn*

§ 15.4 Imperatives with Suffix Pronouns. Imperative forms with enclitic pronominal objects are as follows. Note especially the vocalic shift of the masc. pl. imperative from *CCoC(un)/CCaC(un)* to *CuCCu(n)-:*

	MASC. SING.		FEM. SING.	
+ 3 m s	ܩܛܘܠܝܗܝ	*qṭolāy*	ܩܛܘܠܝܘܗܝ	*qṭoliw*
+ 3 f s	ܩܛܘܠܝܗ	*qṭolēh*	ܩܛܘܠܝܗ	*qṭolih*
+ 1 c s	ܩܛܘܠܝܢܝ	*qṭolayn*	ܩܛܘܠܝܢܝ	*qṭolin*
+ 1 c pl	ܩܛܘܠܢ	*qṭolayn*	ܩܛܘܠܢ	*qṭolin*

	MASC. PL.		FEM. PL.	
+ 3 m s	ܩܘܛܠܘܗܝ	*quṭlu*	ܩܛܘ̈ܠܝܗܝ	*qṭolāy*
	ܩܘܛܠܘܢܗܝ	*quṭlunāy*	ܩܛܘ̈ܠܝܢܗܝ	*qṭolēnāy*
+ 3 f s	ܩܘܛܠܘܗ	*quṭluh*	ܩܛܘ̈ܠܝܗ	*qṭolāh*
	ܩܘܛܠܘܢܗ	*quṭlunāh*	ܩܛܘ̈ܠܝܢܗ	*qṭolēnāh*
+ 1 c s	ܩܘܛܠܘܢܝ	*quṭlun*	ܩܛܘ̈ܠܝܢܝ	*qṭolān*
	ܩܘܛܠܘܢܢܝ	*quṭlunān*	ܩܛܘ̈ܠܝܢܢܝ	*qṭolēnān*
+ 1 c pl	ܩܘܛܠܘܢ	*quṭlun*	ܩܛܘ̈ܠܢ	*qṭolān*
	ܩܘܛܠܘܢܢ	*quṭlunān*	ܩܛܘ̈ܠܝܢܢ	*qṭolēnān*

§ 15.5 Imperatives of III-Weak Roots with Suffix Pronouns. The suffixation of enclitic pronominal objects to the imperatives of III-weak verbs is basically similar to that of sound verbs. The masculine singular imperative, which ends in *-i,* takes the same enclitic forms as the feminine singular of sound verbs *(qṭoliw, qṭolih,* &c).

The fem. sing. base form changes from *CCāy* to *CCā'i-*, written with *ālap.*

The masc. pl. base form changes from *CCaw* to *CCa'u-,* again spelled with *ālap* for the intervocalic glottal stop. The fem. pl. imperative shows reduction from *CCāyēn* to *CCāyen-*.

	MASC. SING.		FEM. SING.	
+ 3 m s	ܩܪܝܘܗܝ	*qriw*	ܩܪܐܝܘܗܝ	*qrā'iw*

+ 3 f s	ܩܪܝܗ̇	*qrih*	ܩܪܐܝܗ̇	*qrā'ih*
+ 1 c s	ܩܪܝܢܝ	*qrin*	ܩܪܐܝܢܝ	*qrā'in*
+ 1 c pl	ܩܪܝܢ	*qrin*	ܩܪܐܝܢ	*qrā'in*

	MASC. PL.		FEM. PL.	
+ 3 m s	ܩܪܐܘܗܝ	*qra'u*	ܩܪܐܝ̈ܢܗܝ	*qrāyenāy*
+ 3 f s	ܩܪܐܘܗ̇	*qra'uh*	ܩܪܐܝ̈ܢܗ̇	*qrāyenāh*
+ 1 c s	ܩܪܐܘܢܝ	*qra'un*	ܩܪܐܝ̈ܢܢܝ	*qrāyenān*
+ 1 c pl	ܩܪܐܘܢ	*qra'un*	ܩܪܐܝ̈ܢܢ	*qrāyenān*

§ 15.6 Nouns in *-u* and *-i*. Nouns with absolute singulars in *-u* have the following inflection:

	SINGULAR		PLURAL	
abs.	ܨܒܘ	*ṣbu*	ܨܒ̈ܘܢ	*ṣebwān*
emph.	ܨܒܘܬܐ	*ṣbutā*	ܨܒ̈ܘܬܐ	*ṣebwātā*
const.	ܨܒܘܬ	*ṣbut-*	ܨܒ̈ܘܬ	*ṣebwāt-*

This important class includes the infinitives of all increased verbal forms (to be introduced in the following lessons) as well as abstract nouns like ܡܠܟܘܬܐ *malkutā* 'kingdom' and ܛܠܝܘܬܐ *ṭalyutā* 'childhood.'

Similar are nouns with absolute singulars in *-i:*

abs.	ܡܪܕܝ	*mardi*	ܡܪܕܝܢ	*mardyān*
emph.	ܡܪܕܝܬܐ	*marditā*	ܡܪܕܝ̈ܬܐ	*mardyātā-*
const.	ܡܪܕܝܬ	*mardit-*	ܡܪܕܝ̈ܬ	*mardyāt-*

Vocabulary 15

NOUNS

ܕܒܚܐ *debḥā* sacrifice
ܕܒܪܐ *dabrā* wilderness
ܕܡܐ *dmā* (const/abs *dem)* blood
ܙܒܢܐ *zabnā* (const/abs *zban)* time
ܚܕܘܬܐ *ḥadutā* joy, gladness
ܚܛܝܐ *ḥaṭṭāyā* pl *-ē* sinner

ܟܬܦܐ *katpā* pl *-ē/-ātā* (f) shoulder
ܡܓܕܠܐ *magdlā* pl *-ē* tower
ܡܬܠܐ *matlā* parable
ܥܪܒܐ *ʿerbā* a sheep, lamb
ܫܒܒܐ *šbābā* pl *-ē* neighbor
ܬܝܒܘܬܐ *tyābutā* repentance

VERBS

ܚܠܛ *ḥlaṭ/neḥloṭ* to mix, mingle
ܣܒܪ *sbar/nesbar* to think, imagine
ܥܢܐ *ʿnā/neʿnē* to reply, answer
ܩܪܐ *qrā/neqrē* to call, summon, invite
ܬܒ *tāb/ntub* to repent

ADJECTIVES

ܝܬܝܪ *yattir* more (*men* than)
ܡܬܒܥܐ *metbʿē* (m) *metbaʿyā* (f) necessary, needed[1]

OTHERS

ܐܘ *aw* or; more than
ܐܟܘܬ *akwāt* like
ܡܐ ܕ *mā d-* when, as soon as

PROPER NAME

ܫܝܠܘܚܐ *šilōḥā* Siloam, Siloah

[1]In impersonal constructions like 'it is necessary' and 'it is possible' the adjective is usually fem. sing. *(metbaʿyā)* followed by *l-* and then *d-* and the imperfect, as ܡܬܒܥܝܐ ܠܝ ܕܐܙܠ *metbaʿyā li d-êzal* 'it is necessary for me to go, I must go,' and the past: ܡܬܒܥܝܐ ܗܘܬ ܠܗܘܢ ܕܢܐܙܠܘܢ *metbaʿyā-wāt lhon d-nêzlun* 'it was necessary for them to go, they had to go.'

Exercise 15

Read and give English equivalents for the following:

ܢܒܝܘܗܝ	1	ܬܐܬܟܠܘܢܗܝ	11	ܬܫܒܩܘܢ	21
ܬܐܘܕܪܘܣ	2	ܢܒܕܪܢ	12	ܢܒܢܘܢ	22
ܐܦܣܩܘܦܘܢ	3	ܬܒܕܪܢܗܝ	13	ܢܕܦܩܘܗܝ	23
ܢܦܪܣܘܢ	4	ܢܪܫܡܘܢ	14	ܬܬܟܬܒܘܢ	24
ܬܫܒܩܘܢܢ	5	ܢܣܡܟܢܗܝ	15	ܬܐܬܟܠܘܗܝ	25
ܬܫܠܡܢ	6	ܐܟܒܘܗܝ	16	ܐܩܛܠܢ	26
ܐܠܦܘܗܝ	7	ܚܙܘܢܢ	17	ܬܫܒܩܢܗܝ	27
ܢܐܡܪܘܢ	8	ܬܒܢܘܢ	18	ܢܩܛܠ	28
ܢܐܟܠܘܗܝ	9	ܐܚܙܢ	19	ܬܫܒܩܘܢܗܝ	29
ܐܕܒܢ	10	ܢܦܪܣܘܢܗܝ	20	ܐܒܕܪܗ	30

Reading Exercise 15

1 ܘܐܡܪ ܠܗܘܢ ܡܬܠܐ ܗܢܐ: ܡܢܘ ܡܢܟܘܢ ܓܒܪܐ ܕܐܝܬ ܠܗ
ܡܐܐ ܥܪܒܝܢ. ܘܐܢ ܢܐܒܕ ܚܕ ܡܢܗܘܢ. ܠܐ ܫܒܩ ܬܫܥܝܢ
ܘܬܫܥܐ ܒܡܕܒܪܐ. ܘܐܙܠ ܒܥܐ ܠܗܘ ܕܐܒܕ ܥܕܡܐ
ܕܢܫܟܚܝܘܗܝ. ܘܡܐ ܕܐܫܟܚܗ ܚܕܐ. ܘܡܩܒܠ ܠܗ ܥܠ
ܟܬܦܬܗ. ܘܐܬܐ ܠܒܝܬܗ. ܘܩܪܐ ܠܪܚܡܘܗܝ ܘܠܫܒܒܘܗܝ.
ܘܐܡܪ ܠܗܘܢ: ܚܕܘ ܥܡܝ ܕܐܫܟܚܬ ܥܪܒܝ ܕܐܒܝܕ ܗܘܐ.
ܐܡܪ ܐܢܐ ܠܟܘܢ: ܕܗܟܢܐ ܬܗܘܐ ܚܕܘܬܐ ܒܫܡܝܐ ܥܠ ܚܕ
ܚܛܝܐ ܕܬܐܒ ܐܘ ܥܠ ܬܫܥܝܢ ܘܬܫܥܐ ܙܕܝܩܝܢ ܕܠܐ
ܡܬܒܥܐ ܠܗܘܢ ܬܝܒܘܬܐ.

2 ܒܗܘ ܕܝܢ ܙܒܢܐ: ܐܬܘ ܐܢܫܝܢ ܐܡܪܘ ܠܗ ܥܠ ܓܠܝܠܝܐ ܗܢܘܢ
ܕܦܝܠܛܘܣ ܚܠܛ ܕܡܗܘܢ ܥܡ ܕܒܚܝܗܘܢ. ܘܥܢܐ ܝܫܘܥ
ܘܐܡܪ ܠܗܘܢ: ܡܣܒܪܝܢ ܐܢܬܘܢ ܕܗܠܝܢ ܓܠܝܠܝܐ ܚܛܝܢ ܗܘܘ
ܝܬܝܪ ܡܢ ܟܠܗܘܢ ܓܠܝܠܝܐ. ܕܗܟܢܐ ܗܘܐ ܠܗܘܢ. ܠܐ. ܐܡܪ
ܐܢܐ ܠܟܘܢ ܕܝܢ: ܕܐܦ ܟܠܟܘܢ ܐܢ ܠܐ ܬܬܘܒܘܢ. ܗܟܢܐ
ܬܐܒܕܘܢ. ܐܘ ܗܢܘܢ ܬܡܢܬܥܣܪ ܕܢܦܠ ܥܠܝܗܘܢ ܡܓܕܠܐ
ܒܫܝܠܘܚܐ ܘܩܛܠܗ ܐܢܘܢ. ܡܣܒܪܝܢ ܐܢܬܘܢ ܕܚܛܝܢ ܗܘܘ
ܝܬܝܪ ܡܢ ܟܠܗܘܢ ܒܢܝܢܫܐ ܕܥܡܪܝܢ ܒܐܘܪܫܠܡ. ܠܐ. ܐܡܪ

ܐܡܪ ܠܗܘܢ: ܕܐܢ ܠܐ ܬܬܘܒܘܢ. ܟܠܟܘܢ ܐܟܘܬܗܘܢ ܬܐܒܕܘܢ

Translate into Syriac:

1. This month will be over after five days.
2. Let us return to Jerusalem and search for the child who remained there.
3. She doesn't know where to put the lamb that she picked up on her shoulders.
4. It is not necessary for me to (that I) answer.
5. How can we know the road by which you are going?
6. I will remain here for six months.
7. If you seek me you can find me in my father's house.
8. If you had sought me, you could have found me in my brother's house.
9. I cannot give you everything you want.

Give the Syriac for the following, perfect and imperfect:

1. I wrote/write it (m)
2. you (m s) ordered/order me
3. we spread them
4. she killed/kills him
5. he persecuted/persecutes her
6. you (f) left/leave us
7. they took/take you (f s)
8. they found/find you (m pl)
9. you (pl) asked/ask me
10. we keep/kept you (m s)
11. she ate/eats it (f)
12. I built/build it (m)
13. you (m s) sought/seek us
14. he saw/sees you (m s)
15. you (pl) put it (f)
16. you (f s) saw/see me

ܪܫܐ ܕܫܬܬܥܣܪ
Lesson Sixteen

§ 16.1 The Pael Conjugation. All verbs that have been dealt with systematically so far belong to the Peal *(p^{c}al)* conjugation, i.e. they belong to the unaugmented base paradigm, the basic pattern for which is *CCaC* (including the variant *CCeC),* like *ktab, šqal, sleq,* and weak verbs like *qām, ḥzā, etā,* &c. The conjugations that will now be introduced are augmented, or derived, conjugations.

The Pael *(pa^{cc}el)* conjugation is characterized by a doubling of the second radical consonant, hence its Semitic designation as D ("doubled").[1] The basic vocalic pattern of the perfect is *CaCCeC,* as *qabbel* 'to receive' (from √*QBL)* and *mallel* 'to speak' (from √*MLL).*

The Pael conjugation serves (1) as a factitive/transitivizing form for intransitive G-form verbs, e.g., *šlem* 'to be finished, come to an end' (intransitive) > Pael *šallem* 'to finish, bring to an end' (transitive), (2) as an intensifier for transitive G-form verbs, e.g., *qṭal* 'to kill' > Pael *qaṭṭel* 'to kill in great numbers, to massacre,' and (3) as a primary verbal form for denominative roots (roots derived from nouns and for which no G-form verb exists), e.g., *melltā* 'word, speech' > *mallel* 'to speak.'

The perfect inflection of a Pael verb like *qabbel* is regular, with predictable reduction of the second stem vowel to schwa in the 3rd

---

[1]The Syriac Pael conjugation corresponds to the Piel (פִּעֵל) of Hebrew and the second form (فَعَّلَ) of Arabic.

fem. sing. and 1st sing.

3 m	ܩܒܠ	*qabbel*	ܩܒܠܘ(ܢ)	*qabbel(un)*
f	ܩܒܠܬ	*qabblat*	ܩܒܠ(ܝ̈)	*qabbel(ēn)*
2 m	ܩܒܠܬ	*qabbelt*	ܩܒܠܬܘܢ	*qabbelton*
f	ܩܒܠܬܝ	*qabbelt*	ܩܒܠܬܝܢ	*qabbeltēn*
1 c	ܩܒܠܬ	*qabblet*	ܩܒܠܢ	*qabbeln(an)*

The imperfect inflection of the Pael conjugation is exactly like that of the G-verb; the preformatives have no vowel, however, except the 1st sing., which remains *e*-. The expected stem-vowel reduction occurs in all forms with postformatives. For enclitic objects with these forms, see Appendix C (p. 145).

3 m	ܢܩܒܠ	*nqabbel*	ܢܩܒܠܘܢ	*nqabblun*
f	ܬܩܒܠ	*tqabbel*	ܢܩܒ̈ܠܢ	*nqabblān*
2 m	ܬܩܒܠ	*tqabbel*	ܬܩܒܠܘܢ	*tqabblun*
f	ܬܩܒܠܝܢ	*tqabblin*	ܬܩܒ̈ܠܢ	*tqabblān*
1 c	ܐܩܒܠ	*eqabbel*	ܢܩܒܠ	*nqabbel*

The Pael conjugation produces two participles, active on the pattern *mCaCCeC* and passive on the pattern *mCaCCaC,* e.g., ܡܩܒܠ *mqabbel* 'receiving' and *mqabbal* 'received,' ܡܡܠܠ *mmallel* 'speaking' and *mmallal* 'spoken.' Feminines and plurals are formed with predictable vocalic reduction: ܡܩܒܠܐ *mqabblā* (fem. sing. abs.), ܡܩܒܠܝܢ *mqabblin* (masc. pl. abs.), ܡܩܒ̈ܠܢ *mqabblān* (fem. pl. abs.). The distinction between the active and passive participles is obscured in these forms, as it is in III-guttural verbs (see below).

The infinitive of the Pael conjugation is on the pattern *mCaCCāCu,* e.g., ܡܩܒܠܘ *mqabbālu* 'receiving (gerund), to receive' and ܡܡܠܠܘ *mmallālu* 'speaking (gerund), to speak.'

§ 16.2 Pael Conjugation: Various Verb Types. To the basic patterns of the Pael conjugation adjustments are made with the following types:

(1) III-guttural: the *e* between the second and third radicals is changed to *a* wherever it occurs, thus *šaddar/nšaddar* 'to send' (act.

and pass. part. *mšaddar* 'sending' and 'sent,' where the difference between the active and passive is obscured) and *šabbaḥ/nšabbaḥ* 'to praise.'

(2) III-weak: all roots with weak third radicals conform to one pattern in the Pael conjugation. Perfect inflection for *dakki* 'to purify' is like the perfect inflection of *ḥdi* (see §7.1):

3 m	ܕܟܝ	*dakki*	ܕܟܝܘ	*dakki*
f	ܕܟܝܬ	*dakkyat*	ܕܟܝ	*dakki*
2 m	ܕܟܝܬ	*dakkiyt*	ܕܟܝܬܘܢ	*dakkiyton*
f	ܕܟܝܬܝ	*dakkiyt*	ܕܟܝܬܝܢ	*dakkiytēn*
1 c	ܕܟܝܬ	*dakkit*	ܕܟܝܢ	*dakkiyn(an)*

The imperfect inflection follows the model of *nebnē* (§14.3):

3 m	ܢܕܟܐ	*ndakkē*	ܢܕܟܘܢ	*ndakkōn*
f	ܬܕܟܐ	*tdakkē*	ܢܕܟܝ̈ܢ	*ndakkyān,* &c.

The masc. sing. imperative differs from that of *bnā,* however; the other imperatives are similar to those of *bnā:*

masc.	ܕܟܐ	*dakkā*	ܕܟܘ	*dakkaw*
fem.	ܕܟܝ	*dakkāy*	ܕܟܝ̈ܢ	*dakkāyēn*

Active participles are formed exactly like those of *bnā:*

masc.	ܡܕܟܐ	*mdakkē*	ܡܕܟܝܢ	*mdakkeyn*
fem.	ܡܕܟܝܐ	*mdakkyā*	ܡܕܟܝ̈ܢ	*mdakkyān*

The masc. sing. passive participle differs in formation from the active; the other participles are identical to the active.

masc.	ܡܕܟܝ	*mdakkay*	ܡܕܟܝܢ	*mdakkeyn*
fem.	ܡܕܟܝܐ	*mdakkyā*	ܡܕܟܝ̈ܢ	*mdakkyān*

The infinitive has *y* for the third radical, ܡܕܟܝܘ *mdakkāyu.*

The following root types produce no "irregularity" in the Pael conjugation

(3) hollow: most weak second radicals appear as *-yy-* in Pael,

e.g., *ṭayyeb* 'to prepare' *(√ṬWB):*

perf.	ܛܝܒ	*ṭayyeb*	part.	ܡܛܝܒ	*mṭayyeb*
impf.	ܢܛܝܒ	*nṭayyeb*	inf.	ܡܛܝܒܘ	*mṭayyābu*

(4) I-*y* verbs are regularly formed throughout, as *yaqqar* 'to honor' *(√YQR):*

perf.	ܝܩܪ	*yaqqar*	part.	ܡܝܩܪ	*myaqqar*
impf.	ܢܝܩܪ	*nyaqqar*	inf.	ܡܝܩܪܘ	*myaqqāru*

(5) I-*ālap* verbs are regularly formed; the vowel of the first radical, however, falls back to the preformatives, as *allep* 'to teach' *(√'LP):*

perf.	ܐܠܦ	*allep*	part.	ܡܠܦ	*mallep*
impf.	(ܢܐܠܦ) ܢܠܦ	*nallep*	inf.	ܡܠܦܘ	*mallāpu*

By convention the *ālap* of this and a few other I-*ālap* verbs is dropped in all forms that have preformatives; the 1st sing. of the imperfect is *allep.*

(6) II-*ālap* verbs are regularly formed with doubled glottal stop, e.g., *ša''el* 'to ask questions':

perf.	ܫܐܠ	*ša''el*	part.	ܡܫܐܠ	*mša''el*
impf.	ܢܫܐܠ	*nša''el*	inf.	ܡܫܐܠܘ	*mša''ālu*

(7) geminate verbs are regularly formed throughout, as *mallel* 'to speak':

perf.	ܡܠܠ	*mallel*	part.	ܡܡܠܠ	*mmallel*
impf.	ܢܡܠܠ	*nmallel*	inf.	ܡܡܠܠܘ	*mmallālu*

Vocabulary 16

NOUNS

ܕܘܟܬܐ *dukktā* pl ܕܘܟܝܬܐ *dukkyātā*/ܕܘܟܘܬܐ *dukkawwātā* place
ܟܢܫܐ *kenšā* crowd, multitude
ܣܦܝܢܬܐ *spittā* pl *spinē*/*spinātā* ship, boat
ܣܦܪܐ *sāprā* pl *-ē* scribe

ܨܒܝܢܐ *ṣebyānā* will
ܫܡܐ *šmā* (abs *šem)* name
ܬܘܢܐ *tawwānā* pl *-ē* inner room, closet
ܬܪܥܐ *tar*ᶜ*ā* pl *-ē* door, gate

VERBS

ܐܠܦ *allep* to teach
ܒܪܟ *barrek* to bless
ܙܩܦ *zqap/nezqop* to crucify
ܚܫܟ *ḥšek/neḥšak* to get dark (used impersonally in the 3rd fem. sing.: *ḥeškat* 'it got dark')
ܟܢܫ *kanneš/nkanneš* to assemble, gather (trs.)
ܡܠܠ *mallel* to speak
ܢܓܕ *nagged* to beat, scourge
ܦܪܥ *pra*ᶜ*/nepro*ᶜ to reward
ܨܠܝ *ṣalli* to pray *(*ᶜ*al* for)
ܩܕܫ *qaddeš/nqaddeš* to bless, make holy
ܩܨܐ *qṣā/neqṣē* to break (bread)
ܫܪܝ *šarri* to begin (+ *l-* & inf., *šarri l-mallāpu,* or + act. part., *šarri mallep* 'he began to teach')

OTHERS

ܐܝܟ *ak* like (prep.); *ak d-* so (much so) that
ܐܡܬܝ *emat* when?, *emat d-* when (conj.)
ܒܓܠܝܐ *b-gelyā* openly, publicly
ܒܟܣܝܐ *b-kesyā* secretly, privately
ܡܛܠ *meṭṭul* for, on account of (note irregular spelling)
ܡܛܠ ܕ *meṭṭul d-* since, because, inasmuch as
ܥܠ ܝܕ ᶜ*al yad* near, beside

IDIOM

ܐܚܕ ܬܪܥܐ *eḥad tar*ᶜ*ā* to shut, fasten a door, gate

Exercise 16

Identify, read, and translate the following Pael verb forms:

1 ܟܢܫ ܐܢܘܢ
2 ܫܪܝܬ ܠܡܠܦܘ
3 ܐܨܠܐ
4 ܡܠܦ ܗܘܐ

5 ܢܡܠܠܘܢ
6 ܡܫܒ̈ܚܢ
7 ܡܠܟܢ
8 ܡܫܒܚܘ
9 ܢܠܟܬ ܟܠܗ̈ܘܢ
10 ܫܪܝ ܠܡܦܩܗ ܠܠܫܢܐ
11 ܫܪܝܬ ܠܡܫܒܚܢ
12 ܢܪܕܘ
13 ܢܪܚܡܘ̈ܗܝ ܠܥܡܗ
14 ܢܐܠܦܘܢ
15 ܫܪܘ ܡܢܕܝܢ ܠܗܘܢ
16 ܫܪܝܬ ܠܡܡܠܠܘ
17 ܠܐ ܒܪܟܬ ܐܢܬ
18 ܠܐ ܬܕܢܝܢ

Reading Exercise 16

1 ܐܢܬ ܕܝܢ ܐܡܬܝ ܕܡܨܠܐ ܐܢܬ. ܥܘܠ ܠܬܘܢܟ. ܘܐܚܘܕ ܬܪܥܟ.
ܘܨܠܐ ܠܐܒܘܟ ܕܒܟܣܝܐ. ܘܐܒܘܟ ܕܚܙܐ ܒܟܣܝܐ ܢܦܪܥܟ
ܒܓܠܝܐ ※

2 ܘܗܘܐ ܕܟܕ ܗܘ̣ ܡܨܠܐ ܒܕܘܟܬܐ ܚܕܐ. ܟܕ ܫܠܡ. ܐܡ̣ܪ ܠܗ
ܚܕ ܡܢ ܬܠܡܝܕ̈ܘܗܝ: ܡܪܢ ܐܠܦܝܢ ܠܡܨܠܝܘ ܐܝܟܢܐ ܕܐܦ
ܝܘܚܢܢ ܐܠܦ ܠܬܠܡܝܕ̈ܘܗܝ. ܐܡ̇ܪ ܠܗܘܢ ܝܫܘܥ: ܐܡܬܝ
ܕܡܨܠܝܢ ܐܢܬܘܢ ܗܟܢܐ ܗܘܝܬܘܢ ܐܡܪܝܢ: ܐܒܘܢ ܕܒܫܡܝܐ
ܢܬܩܕܫ[1] ܫܡܟ. ܬܐܬܐ ܡܠܟܘܬܟ. ܢܗܘܐ ܨܒܝܢܟ ܐܝܟܢܐ
ܕܒܫܡܝܐ ܐܦ ܒܐܪܥܐ ※

3 ܫܩܠ ܝܫܘܥ ܠܚܡܐ. ܘܒܪܟ ܘܩܨܐ. ܘܝܗ̣ܒ ܠܬܠܡܝܕ̈ܘܗܝ.
ܘܐܡܪ: ܣܒܘ ܐܟܘܠܘ. ܗܢܘ ܦܓܪܝ ※

4 ܡܛܠ ܗܢܐ ܗܐ ܐܢܐ ܡܫܕܪ ܐܢܐ ܠܘܬܟܘܢ ܢܒܝ̈ܐ ܘܚܟܝ̈ܡܐ ܘܣܦܪ̈ܐ.
ܡܢܗܘܢ ܩܛܠܝܢ ܐܢܬܘܢ ܘܙܩܦܝܢ ܐܢܬܘܢ. ܘܡܢܗܘܢ ܡܢܓܕܝܢ ܐܢܬܘܢ
ܒܟܢܘܫܬܟܘܢ. ܘܬܪܕܦܘܢ ܐܢܘܢ ܡܢ ܡܕܝܢܐ ܠܡܕܝܢܐ ※

5 ܬܘܒ ܕܝܢ ܫܪܝ. ܗܘܐ ܡܠܦ ܥܠ ܝܕ ܝܡܐ. ܘܐܬܟܢܫܘ[2] ܠܘܬܗ ܟܢܫܐ
ܣܓܝܐܐ. ܐܝܟ ܕܢܣܩ ܢܬܒ ܠܗ ܒܣܦܝܢܬܐ ܒܝܡܐ. ܘܟܠܗ ܟܢܫܐ ܩܐܡ
ܗܘܐ ܥܠ ܐܪܥܐ ܥܠ ܝܕ ܝܡܐ ※

---

[1]*netqaddaš* 'may it be blessed'; the pattern of this verb and of *etkannaš* below will be introduced in §19.1.

[2]*etkannaš* 'was gathered, assembled.'

ܪܫܐ ܕܫܒܥܬܥܣܪ
Lesson Seventeen

§ 17.1 The Aphel Conjugation. The Aphel conjugation is characterized in the perfect by a preformative *a-* and in the imperfect by the vowel *a* on the preformatives. The basic pattern of the perfect is *aC-CeC;* and of the imperfect, *naCCeC,* e.g. *(√ŠLM) ašlem/našlem* 'to hand over.'[1]

Although there are many exceptions, the Aphel conjugation functions primarily as a factitive/causative, e.g., *šlaḥ* 'to send' > *ašlaḥ* 'to cause (something) to be sent, to have (something) sent' and *ida*ᶜ 'to know' > *awda*ᶜ 'to make (something) known' or 'to make (someone) know (something).'

The inflection of the perfect is regularly formed:

3 m	ܐܫܠܡ	*ašlem*	ܐܫܠܡ(ܘܢ)	*ašlem(un)*
f	ܐܫܠܡܬ	*ašlmat*	ܐܫܠܡ(ܝ̈)	*ašlem(ēn)*
2 m	ܐܫܠܡܬ	*ašlemt*	ܐܫܠܡܬܘܢ	*ašlemton*
f	ܐܫܠܡܬܝ	*ašlemt*	ܐܫܠܡܬܝܢ	*ašlemtēn*
1 c	ܐܫܠܡܬ	*ašlmet*	ܐܫܠܡܢ	*ašlemn(an)*

The imperfect inflection has the vowel *a* on all the preformatives and the vowel *e* in the stem (reduced to schwa with the vowel-initial postformatives):

[1]The Syriac Aphel corresponds to the Hiphil (הפעיל) of Hebrew and the fourth form (افعل) of Arabic.

3 m	ܢܫܠܡ	*našlem*	ܢܫܠܡܘܢ	*našlmun*
f	ܬܫܠܡ	*tašlem*	ܢܫܠܡ̈ܢ	*našlmān*
2 m	ܬܫܠܡ	*tašlem*	ܬܫܠܡܘܢ	*tašlmun*
f	ܬܫܠܡܝܢ	*tašlmin*	ܬܫܠܡ̈ܢ	*tašlmān*
1 c	ܐܫܠܡ	*ašlem*	ܢܫܠܡ	*našlem*

The imperative is regularly formed from the imperfect with preformative *a-:*

masc.	ܐܫܠܡ	*ašlem*	ܐܫܠܡܘ(ܢ)	*ašlem(un)*
fem.	ܐܫܠܡܝ	*ašlem*	ܐܫܠܡ(ܝ̈ܢ)	*ašlem(ēn)*

Like the Pael conjugation, Aphel produces both active and passive participles, active on the pattern *maCCeC* and passive on the pattern *maCCaC.* The distinction is obscured everywhere except in the masc. sing. absolute.

masc.	ܡܫܠܡ	*mašle/am*	ܡܫܠܡܝܢ	*mašlmin*
fem.	ܡܫܠܡܐ	*mašlmā*	ܡܫܠܡ̈ܢ	*mašlmān*

The infinitive of Aphel is on the pattern *maCCāCu,* e.g. ܡܫܠܡܘ *mašlāmu.*

§ 17.2 Aphel Conjugation: Various Verb Types.

(1) III-guttural roots replace the vowel *e* of the pattern wherever it occurs with *a*, as in ܫܠܚ *šlaḥ* > ܐܫܠܚ *ašlaḥ* and ܥܕܪ *^{c}dar* > ܐܥܕܪ *a^{c}dar.* As in the participles of Pael III-gutturals, the distinction between the active and passive participles is obscured everywhere.

PERF.	ܐܫܠܚ	*ašlaḥ*	ܐܥܕܪ	*a^{c}dar*
IMPERF.	ܢܫܠܚ	*našlaḥ*	ܢܥܕܪ	*na^{c}dar*
ACT. PART.	ܡܫܠܚ	*mašlaḥ*	ܡܥܕܪ	*ma^{c}dar*
PASS. PART.	ܡܫܠܚ	*mašlaḥ*	ܡܥܕܪ	*ma^{c}dar*
INF.	ܡܫܠܚܘ	*mašlāḥu*	ܡܥܕܪܘ	*ma^{c}dāru*

(2) I-*n* roots show regular assimilation of the *n* to the second radical in all forms of the Aphel conjugation, as ܢܦܩ *npaq* > ܐܦܩ *appeq* 'make (someone) go out, send/bring out' and ܢܚܬ *nḥet* > ܐܚܬ *aḥḥet* 'to make (someone) go down, send/bring down.'

PERF.	ܐܦܩ	*appeq*	ܐܚܬ	*aḥḥet*
IMPERF.	ܢܦܩ	*nappeq*	ܢܚܬ	*naḥḥet*
ACT. PART.	ܡܦܩ	*mappeq*	ܡܚܬ	*maḥḥet*
PASS. PART.	ܡܦܩ	*mappaq*	ܡܚܬ	*maḥḥat*
INF.	ܡܦܩܘ	*mappāqu*	ܡܚܬܘ	*maḥḥātu*

(3) III-weak roots in Aphel conform to the vocalic patterns of Pael, see §16.2(2), as ܚܕܝ *ḥdi* 'rejoice' > ܐܚܕܝ *aḥdi* 'cause (someone) to rejoice'

PERF.	ܐܚܕܝ	*aḥdi*
IMPERF.	ܢܚܕܐ	*naḥdē*
ACT. PART.	ܡܚܕܐ	*maḥdē*
PASS. PART.	ܡܚܕܝ	*maḥday*
INF.	ܡܚܕܝܘ	*maḥdāyu*

(4) Hollow roots in Aphel all conform to the pattern of ܩܡ *qām* > ܐܩܝܡ *aqim* 'set up, place,' and ܡܝܬ *mit* > ܐܡܝܬ *amit* 'cause to die, put to death'

PERF.	ܐܩܝܡ	*aqim*	ܐܡܝܬ	*amit*
IMPERF.	ܢܩܝܡ	*nqim*	ܢܡܝܬ	*nmit*
ACT. PART.	ܡܩܝܡ	*mqim*	ܡܡܝܬ	*mmit*
PASS. PART.	ܡܩܡ	*mqām*	ܡܡܬ	*mmāt*
INF.	ܡܩܡܘ	*mqāmu*	ܡܡܬܘ	*mmātu*

(5) Most I-*y* and I-*ālap* roots show *w* for the first radical in Aphel, as ܝܕܥ *ida*^{c} 'know' > ܐܘܕܥ *awda*^{c} 'make known,' ܝܪܬ *iret* 'inherit' > ܐܘܪܬ *awret* 'make inherit' and ܐܒܕ *ebad* 'perish' > ܐܘܒܕ *awbed* 'make perish.' There are, however, exceptions, notably ܐܬܐ *etā* 'come' > ܐܝܬܝ *ayti* 'bring,' which shows a *y* for the first radical.

PERF.	ܐܘܕܥ	*awda*^{c}	ܐܘܪܬ	*awret*	ܐܝܬܝ	*ayti*
IMPERF.	ܢܘܕܥ	*nawda*^{c}	ܢܘܪܬ	*nawret*	ܢܝܬܐ	*naytē*
ACT. PART.	ܡܘܕܥ	*mawda*^{c}	ܡܘܪܬ	*mawret*	ܡܝܬܐ	*maytē*
PASS. PART.	ܡܘܕܥ	*mawda*^{c}	ܡܘܪܬ	*mawrat*	ܡܝܬܝ	*maytay*
INF.	ܡܘܕܥܘ	*mawdā*^{c}*u*	ܡܘܪܬܘ	*mawrātu*	ܡܝܬܝܘ	*maytāyu*

(6) II-*ālap* roots are predictably formed, as ܫܐܠ *šel* 'to ask' >

ܐܫܐܠ *ašel* 'to lend.'

PERF.	ܐܫܐܠ	*ašel*
IMPERF.	ܢܫܐܠ	*našel*
ACT. PART.	ܡܫܐܠ	*mašel*
PASS. PART.	ܡܫܐܠ	*mašal*
INF.	ܡܫܐܠܘ	*mašālu*

(7) Geminate roots form Aphel on the pattern of I-*n* roots. A spurious *ālap* occasionally appears in the imperfect and participles, as ܡܟ *mak* 'be humble' *(√MKK)* > ܐܡܟ *ammek* 'make humble.'

PERF.	ܐܡܟ	*ammek*
IMPERF.	ܢܐܡܟ	*nammek*
ACT. PART.	ܡܐܡܟ	*mammek*
PASS. PART.	ܡܐܡܟ	*mammak*
INF.	ܡܡܟܘ	*mammāku*

Vocabulary 17

NOUNS

ܓܘ *gaww, l-gaww* inside

ܓܪܝܣܬܐ *griṣtā* loaf (of bread)

ܗܝܡܢܘܬܐ *haymānutā* faith

ܚܫܘܟܐ *ḥeššokā* darkness

ܡܕܡ *meddem* thing, anything, something

ܥܪܣܐ *ᶜarsā* bed

ܦܠܓܘܬ ܠܠܝܐ *pelgut-lêlyā* middle of the night, midnight

ADJECTIVE

ܝܚܝܕܝ *iḥidāy* only, sole

VERBS

ܐܕܪܟ *adrek* to overtake, comprehend

ܐܗܪ *ahhar (√HRR)* to bother

ܐܘܚܪ *awḥar (√'ḤR)* to tarry, delay

ܐܚܒ *aḥḥeb (√ḤBB)* to love

ܐܚܬ *aḥḥet (√NḤT)* to send down

ܐܫܐܠ *ašel* to lend

ܐܚܝ *aḥḥi* to give life to, revivify
ܕܢ *dān/ndun* to judge
ܗܝܡܢ *haymen/nhaymen* to believe *(b-* in); act. part. *mhaymen* believing, faithful (in the religious sense)
ܗܠܟ *hallek* to walk

OTHER

ܗܟܢܐ...ܐܝܟܢܐ ܕ *hākannā...aykannā d-* so much so...that, enough to

Exercise 17

Identify, read, and translate the following Aphel forms:

1 ܐܫܐܠܝܢ ܡܢܟ
2 ܐܕܪܟܬ ܚܟܡܬܐ
3 ܐܚܝܒ
4 ܬܚܝܒܢ
5 ܬܚܝܒܝܢ
6 ܐܕܪܟܘܗܝ
7 ܥܒܪ ܠܡܥܡܪܘ ܠܟ
8 ܐܚܝܒܬܢ
9 ܚܬܡܘܗܝ
10 ܢܚܡܘܢ

Reading Exercise 17

1 ܘܐܡܪ ܠܗܘܢ: ܡܢܘ ܡܢܟܘܢ ܕܐܝܬ ܠܗ ܪܚܡܐ ܘܢܐܙܠ ܠܘܬܗ ܒܦܠܓܘܬ ܠܠܝܐ. ܘܢܐܡܪ ܠܗ: ܪܚܡܝ ܐܫܐܠܝܢܝ ܬܠܬ ܓܪ̈ܝܨܢ. ܡܛܠ ܕܪܚܡܐ ܐܬܐ ܠܘܬܝ ܡܢ ܐܘܪܚܐ. ܘܠܝܬ ܠܝ ܡܕܡ ܕܐܣܝܡ ܠܗ. ܘܗܘ ܪܚܡܗ ܡܢ ܠܓܘ ܢܥܢܐ ܘܢܐܡܪ ܠܗ: ܠܐ ܬܗܪܢܢܝ. ܕܗܐ ܬܪܥܐ ܐܚܝܕ ܗ̄ܘ. ܘܒܢ̈ܝ ܥܡܝ ܒܥܪܣܐ. ܠܐ ܡܫܟܚ ܐܢܐ ܕܐܩܘܡ ܘܐܬܠ ܠܟ ※

2 ܗܟܢܐ ܓܝܪ ܐܚܒ ܐܠܗܐ ܠܥܠܡܐ. ܐܝܟܢܐ ܕܠܒܪܗ ܝܚܝܕܝܐ ܢܬܠ. ܕܟܠ ܕܡܗܝܡܢ ܒܗ ܠܐ ܢܐܒܕ. ܐܠܐ ܢܗܘܘܢ ܠܗ ܚ̈ܝܐ ܕܠܥܠܡ. ܠܐ ܓܝܪ ܫܕܪ ܐܠܗܐ ܠܒܪܗ ܠܥܠܡܐ ܕܢܕܘܢܝܗ̄ ܠܥܠܡܐ. ܐܠܐ ܕܢܚܐ ܥܠܡܐ ܒܐܝܕܗ ※

3 ܐܡܪ ܠܗܘܢ ܝܫܘܥ: ܥܠܡ ܙܥܘܪ ܬܘܒ ܢܘܗܪܐ ܥܡܟܘܢ ܗ̄ܘ. ܗܠܟܘ ܥܕ ܐܝܬ ܠܟܘܢ ܢܘܗܪܐ. ܕܠܐ ܚܫܘܟܐ ܢܕܪܟܟܘܢ. ܘܡܢ ܕܡܗܠܟ

ܒܚܫܘܟܐ. ܠܐ ܝܕܥ ܠܐܝܟܐ ܐܙܠ. ܥܕ ܐܝܬ ܠܟܘܢ ܢܘܗܪܐ. ܗܝܡܢܘ
ܒܢܘܗܪܐ. ܕܒܢ̈ܘܗܝ ܕܢܘܗܪܐ ܬܗܘܘܢ: ܗܠܝܢ ܡܠܠ ܝܫܘܥ. ܘܐܙܠ
ܐܛܫܝ ܡܢܗܘܢ ※

4 ܡܢ ܕܫܡܥ ܡ̈ܠܝ ܘܠܐ ܢܛܪ ܠܗܝܢ. ܐܢܐ ܠܐ ܕܐܢ ܐܢܐ ܠܗ.[1] ܠܐ ܓܝܪ
ܐܬܝܬ ܕܐܕܘܢ ܠܥܠܡܐ. ܐܠܐ ܕܐܚܐ ܠܥܠܡܐ ※

[1] A good example of the topic-comment sentence in Syriac. This sentence type, which is fairly common in Semitic languages in general, consists of a topic that is not the logical subject of the comment part of the sentence; a referent pronoun in the comment part indicates the relationship of the topic to the comment: ***man*** *d-šāma*^{c}*...: enā lā dā'en-nā* ***leh:*** '**he** who hears...: I do not judge **him**.' Here the topic is *man d...* (with the clause that follows), and the comment is *enā lā dā'en-nā leh,* where *leh* marks the syntactical relationship between the topic and comment. Such sentences are often best translated by rearranging and putting the topic into its logical position in the comment: 'I do not judge him who hears...' In this instance the Syriac follows the Greek syntax closely: *ἐάν τίς μου ἀκούσῃ τῶν ῥημάτων καὶ μὴ φυλάξῃ, ἐγὼ οὐ κρίνω αὐτόν* (si quis audierit verba mea, et non custodierit: ego non iudico eum, John 12:47).

ܪܫܐ ܕܬܡܢܬܥܣܪܗ
Lesson Eighteen

§ 18.1 Medio-Passive Verbs: Ethpeel, Ethpaal & Attaphal Conjugations. Syriac has no true passive verbs. However, for each of the active/transitive conjugations (Peal, Pael, Aphel), there exists a corresponding reflexive/medio-passive conjugation. From the Peal conjugation the Ethpeel (basic pattern *etCCeC, etp*^{c}*el)* is made; from the Pael conjugation the Ethpaal (basic pattern *etCaCCaC, etpa*^{cc}*al)* is made; and from the Aphel conjugation is made the Ettaphal (basic pattern *ettaCCaC, ettap*^{c}*al).*

BASE PATTERN		MEDIO-PASSIVE
ܩܛܠ *qṭal* 'kill'	>	ܐܬܩܛܠ *etqṭel* 'get killed'
ܩܒܠ *qabbel* 'receive'	>	ܐܬܩܒܠ *etqabbal* 'be received'
ܐܫܠܡ *ašlem* 'betray'	>	ܐܬܬܫܠܡ *ettašlam* 'be betrayed'

§ 18.2 The Ethpeel Conjugation. The underlying pattern from which all actually occurring forms of the Ethpeel can be predicted is *etCaCeC/netCaCeC*. In forms with zero or consonant-initial postformatives, the *a* is reduced. In forms with vowel-initial postformatives, the *e* is reduced. An example is *etdḥeq* 'be driven away' < *dḥaq* 'drive away.'[1]

---

[1]Not in terms of formation, but in terms of meaning and function the Syriac Ethpeel corresponds to the Niphal (נפעל) of Hebrew and the seventh form (انفعل) of Arabic. It also bears an affinity in both formation and meaning with the eighth form (افتعل) of Arabic.

3 m	ܐܬܕܚܩ	*etdḥeq*	ܐܬܕܚܩܘ(ܢ)	*etdḥeq(un)*
f	ܐܬܕܚܩܬ	*etdaḥqat*	ܐܬܕܚܩ(ܝ̈)	*etdḥeq(ēn)*
2 m	ܐܬܕܚܩܬ	*etdḥeqt*	ܐܬܕܚܩܬܘܢ	*etdḥeqton*
f	ܐܬܕܚܩܬܝ	*etdḥeqt*	ܐܬܕܚܩܬ̈ܝܢ	*etdḥeqtēn*
1 c	ܐܬܕܚܩܬ	*etdaḥqet*	ܐܬܕܚܩܢ	*etdḥeqn(an)*

The imperfect is also regularly inflected, with an *a* appearing after the first radical with the vowel-initial postformatives.

3 m	ܢܬܕܚܩ	*netdḥeq*	ܢܬܕܚܩܘܢ	*netdaḥqun*
f	ܬܬܕܚܩ	*tetdḥeq*	ܢܬܕܚܩ̈ܢ	*netdaḥqān*
2 m	ܬܬܕܚܩ	*tetdḥeq*	ܬܬܕܚܩܘܢ	*tetdaḥqun*
f	ܬܬܕܚܩܝܢ	*tetdaḥqin*	ܬܬܕܚܩ̈ܢ	*tetdaḥqān*
1 c	ܐܬܕܚܩ	*etdḥeq*	ܢܬܕܚܩ	*netdḥeq*

The same *a* appears in variant forms of the imperative:

masc.	ܐܬܕܚܩ	*etdḥeq* *etdaḥq*	ܐܬܕܚܩܘ(ܢ)	*etdaḥq(un)*
fem.	ܐܬܕܚܩܝ	*etdḥeq* *etdaḥq*	ܐܬܕܚܩ(ܝ̈)	*etdaḥq(ēn)*

The participles are predictably formed:

masc.	ܡܬܕܚܩ	*metdḥeq*	ܡܬܕܚܩܝܢ	*metdaḥqin*
	ܡܬܕܚܩܐ	*metdaḥqā*	ܡܬܕܚܩ̈ܢ	*metdaḥqān*

And the infinitive is formed on familiar lines, ܡܬܕܚܩܘ *metdḥāqu.*

§ 18.3 Metathesis in Ethpeel. Verbs whose first radical is a sibilant *(s, z, ṣ, š)* show a regular metathesis with the *t* prefix of Ethpeel.

With *s* and *š,* simple metathesis occurs: ܣܡܟ *smak* 'lean' > ܐܣܬܡܟ *estmek* 'recline' and ܫܚܩ *šḥaq* 'break' > ܐܫܬܚܩ *eštḥeq* 'get broken.'

If the first radical is *ṣ,* metathesis occurs and the *t* is velarized to *ṭ,* as ܨܠܒ *ṣlab* 'crucify' > ܐܨܛܠܒ *esṭleb* 'be crucified.'

If the first radical is *z,* metathesis occurs and the *t* is voiced to *d,* as ܙܒܢ *zban* 'buy' > ܐܙܕܒܢ *ezdben* 'be bought' and ܙܩܦ *zqap* 'raise up' > ܐܙܕܩܦ *ezdqep* 'get raised up.'

§ 18.4 Ethpeel with Various Verb Types. Alterations are made in the Ethpeel conjugation with the following root types (3rd masc. and 3rd fem. sing. forms are given for the perfect; 3rd masc. sing. and 3rd masc. pl. are given for the imperfect; masc. and fem. active participles are given; from these forms all others can be predicted).

(1) I-*ālap:* forms are regularly produced with the glottal stop, which is subsequently dropped. Resulting forms are immune to vocalic reduction. An example is ܐܟܠ *ekal* 'eat' > ܐܬܐܟܠ *etekel* (for **et'kel)* 'to be eaten.' The Ethpeel of *eḥad* and a few other I-*ālap* verbs shows assimilation of the initial glottal stop to the *t* of the form, giving ܐܬܬܚܕ *etthed,* and so on throughout the conjugation.

PERF. 3MS	ܐܬܐܟܠ	*etekel*	ܐܬܬܚܕ	*etthed*
PERF. 3FS	ܐܬܐܟܠܬ	*etaklat*	ܐܬܬܚܕܬ	*ettaḥdat*
IMPERF. 3MS	ܢܬܐܟܠ	*netekel*	ܢܬܬܚܕ	*netthed*
IMPERF. 3MP	ܢܬܐܟܠܘܢ	*netaklun*	ܢܬܬܚܕܘܢ	*nettaḥdun*
IMPERATIVE	ܐܬܐܟܠ	*etekel/etakl*	ܐܬܬܚܕ	*etthed/ettaḥd*
MASC.PART.	ܡܬܐܟܠ	*metekel*	ܡܬܬܚܕ	*metthed*
FEM. PART.	ܡܬܐܟܠܐ	*metaklā*	ܡܬܬܚܕܐ	*mettaḥdā*
INF.	ܡܬܐܟܠܘ	*metekālu*	ܡܬܬܚܕܘ	*metthādu*

(2) II-*ālap:* like the I-*ālap,* forms are regularly produced with the glottal stop, which is subsequently dropped. Resulting forms are immune to vocalic reduction. An example is ܫܐܠ *šel* 'ask' > ܐܫܬܐܠ *eštel* (for **ešt'el)* 'be asked'

PERF. 3M/FS	ܐܫܬܐܠ	*eštel*	ܐܫܬܐܠܬ	*eštalat*
IMPERF. 3MS/P	ܢܫܬܐܠ	*neštel*	ܢܫܬܐܠܘܢ	*neštalun*
IMPERATIVE	ܐܫܬܐܠ	*eštel/eštal*		
PART. M/F	ܡܫܬܐܠ	*meštel*	ܡܫܬܐܠܐ	*meštalā*
INF.	ܡܫܬܐܠܘ	*meštālu*		

(3) I-*y:* where the *y* of the root would have a schwa, it is pro-

nounced *i;* and all resulting forms are immune to vocalic reduction. In all other respects the conjugation is regular. An example is ܝܠܕ *iled* 'give birth' > ܐܬܝܠܕ *etiled* (for **etyled)* 'be born'

PERF. 3M/FS	ܐܬܝܠܕ	*etiled*	ܐܬܝܠܕܬ	*etyaldat*
IMPERF. 3MS/P	ܢܬܝܠܕ	*netiled*	ܢܬܝܠܕܘܢ	*netyaldun*
IMPERATIVE	ܐܬܝܠܕ	*etiled/elyald*		
PART. M/F	ܡܬܝܠܕ	*metiled*	ܡܬܝܠܕܐ	*metyaldā*
INF.	ܡܬܝܠܕܘ	*metilādu*		

(4) hollow: the hollow Ethpeel is entirely replaced by the Ettaphal (see §20.1, below).

(5) III-guttural: all *e*'s occurring before the third radical consonant are changed to *a* by the guttural. An example is ܩܒܥ *qba*^{c} 'to set up' > ܐܬܩܒܥ *etqba*^{c} 'be/get set up'

PERF. 3M/FS	ܐܬܩܒܥ	*etqba*^{c}	ܐܬܩܒܥܬ	*etqab*^{c}*at*
IMPERF. 3MS/P	ܢܬܩܒܥ	*netqba*^{c}	ܢܬܩܒܥܘܢ	*netqab*^{c}*un*
IMPERATIVE	ܐܬܩܒܥ	*etqba*^{c}*/etqab*^{c}		
PART. M/F	ܡܬܩܒܥ	*metqba*^{c}	ܡܬܩܒܥܐ	*metqab*^{c}*ā*
INF.	ܡܬܩܒܥܘ	*metqbā*^{c}*u*		

(6) III-weak: conjugation follows the patterns of *dakki* as given in §16.2(2): *qrā* 'call' > ܐܬܩܪܝ *etqri* 'be called.'

PERF. 3M/FS	ܐܬܩܪܝ	*etqri*	ܐܬܩܪܝܬ	*etqaryat*
IMPERF. 3MS/P	ܢܬܩܪܐ	*netqrē*	ܢܬܩܪܘܢ	*netqrōn*
IMPERF. 3FS/P	ܬܬܩܪܐ	*tetqrē*	ܢܬܩܪܝܢ	*netqaryān*
IMPERATIVE	ܐܬܩܪܝ	*etqray/etqary*		
PART. M/F	ܡܬܩܪܐ	*metqrē*	ܡܬܩܪܝܐ	*metqaryā*
INF.	ܡܬܩܪܝܘ	*metqrāyu*		

Vocabulary 18

NOUNS

ܐܘܪܥܐ *ur*^{c}*ā* (abs *ura*^{c}*)* meeting
ܒܬܘܠܬܐ *btultā* pl *-ātā* virgin

ܚܠܘܠܐ *ḥlōlā* marriage
ܚܬܢܐ *ḥatnā* bridegroom, son-in-law, brother-in-law (any male connection by marriage)
ܟܐܢܐ *kênā* just (person)
ܟܠܬܐ *kalltā* bride
ܠܡܦܐܕܐ *lampêdā* lamp
ܡܐܢܐ *mānā* vessel
ܡܛܪܐ *meṭrā* rain
ܡܫܚܐ *mešḥā* oil
ܥܘܠܐ *^{c}awwālā* unjust
ܩܥܬܐ *q^{c}ātā* outcry
ܫܡܫܐ *šemšā* (abs *šmeš,* usually masc.) sun
ܩܛܝܪܐ *qṭirā* force, compulsion

VERBS

ܐܬܐܡܪ *etemar* (for **et'emar)* to be said
ܐܬܩܪܝ *etqri* to be called
ܕܢܚ *dnaḥ/nednaḥ* to rise (of the sun); Aphel *(adnaḥ)* to make (the sun) rise
ܕܡܐ *dmā/nedmē l-* to be like, resemble; Ethpeel *(etdmi)* to be like; Pael *(dammi)* to make (something) like *(l-)*
ܕܥܟ *d^{c}ek/ned^{c}ak* to go out (light, lamp)
ܙܒܢ *zban/nezben* to buy; Ethpeel *(ezdben)* to be/get bought; Pael *(zabben)* to sell
ܛܝܒ *ṭayyeb* to prepare
ܠܛ *lāṭ/nluṭ* to curse
ܢܡ *nām/nnum* to slumber, sleep
ܢܩܫ *nqaš/neqqoš* to knock, strike
ܣܢܐ *snā/nesnē* to hate
ܣܦܩ *spaq/nespaq* to suffice, be sufficient
ܦܬܚ *ptaḥ/neptaḥ* to open; Ethpeel *(etptaḥ)* to be open, get opened
ܬܩܢ *taqqen* to make right, get ready

ADJECTIVE

ܣܟܠ *skal/skel* (emph *saklā)* foolish

OTHERS

ܐܝܢܐ *aynā* (m), ܐܝܕܐ *aydā* (f), ܐܝܠܝܢ *aylēn* (pl) which?

(interrogative adj.), (+ *d*-) he/she/they who (relative pronoun)

ܐܡܝܢ *āmên* verily, truly

ܒܚܪܬܐ *b-ḥartā* finally, in the end

ܗܝܕܝܢ *haydēn* then, at that time

ܠܡܐ *l-mā* lest

Exercise 18

Identify, read, and translate the following Ethpeel forms:

1 ܐܢܬܬ ܕܡܬܩܪܐ ܡܪܝܡ

2 ܡܪܝܡ ܕܡܬܩܪܐ ܡܫܝܚܐ

3 ܗܘ ܕܐܬܐܡܪ ܠ

4 ܡܠܟܘܬܐ ܕܫܡ̈ܝܐ ܕܡܬܕܡܝܐ ܠܥܣܪ ܒܬܘ̈ܠܢ

5 ܡܬܒܥܝܐ ܗ̄ܝ ܕܠܐ ܢܬܐܡܪ ܗܢܐ

6 ܡܐ̈ܢܐ ܕܡܙܕܒܢܝܢ

7 ܡ̈ܠܐ ܕܡܬܐܡܪ̈ܢ

8 ܓܒ̈ܪܐ ܕܡܬܩܪܝܢ ܟܐܢܝܢ

9 ܬܪܥܐ ܕܠܐ ܡܬܦܬܚ

10 ܓܒ̈ܪܐ ܕܐܙܕܩܦܘ

Reading Exercise 18

1 ܐܦ ܐܢܐ ܐܡ̈ܪ ܐܢܐ ܠܟܘܢ: ܫܐܠܘ ܘܢܬܝܗܒ ܠܟܘܢ. ܒܥܘ
ܘܬܫܟܚܘܢ. ܩܘܫܘ ܘܢܬܦܬܚ ܠܟܘܢ. ܟܠ ܓܝܪ ܕܫܐܠ ܢܣܒ.
ܘܕܒܥܐ ܡܫܟܚ. ܘܕܢܩܫ ܡܬܦܬܚ ܠܗ ※

2 ܬܘܒ ܫܡܥܬܘܢ ܕܐܬܐܡܪ ܕܬܪܚܡ ܠܩܪܝܒܟ. ܘܬܣܢܐ ܠܒܥܠܕܒܒܟ. ܐܢܐ ܕܝܢ ܐܡܪ ܐܢܐ ܠܟܘܢ: ܐܚܒܘ ܠܒܥܠܕܒܒܝܟܘܢ. ܘܒܪܟܘ ܠܡܢ ܕܠܐܛ ܠܟܘܢ. ܘܥܒܕܘ ܕܫܦܝܪ ܠܡܢ ܕܣܢܐ ܠܟܘܢ. ܘܨܠܘ ܥܠ ܐܝܠܝܢ ܕܕܒܪܝܢ ܠܟܘܢ ܒܩܛܝܪܐ ܘܪܕܦܝܢ ܠܟܘܢ. ܐܝܟܢܐ ܕܬܗܘܘܢ ܒܢܘ̈ܗܝ ܕܐܒܘܟܘܢ ܕܒܫܡܝܐ. ܗܘ ܕܡܕܢܚ ܫܡܫܗ ܥܠ ܛܒ̈ܐ ܘܥܠ ܒܝܫ̈ܐ: ܘܡܚܬ ܡܛܪܗ ܥܠ ܟܐܢ̈ܐ ܘܥܠ ܥܘܠ̈ܐ ※

3 ܗܝܕܝܢ ܬܕܡܐ ܡܠܟܘܬܐ ܕܫܡܝ̈ܐ ܠܥܣܪ ܒܬܘ̈ܠܢ. ܗܢܝܢ ܕܢܣܒ ܠܡܫܪ̈ܓܝܗܝܢ ܘܢܦܩ ܠܐܘܪܥ ܚܬܢܐ ܘܟܠܬܐ. ܚܡܫ ܕܝܢ ܡܢܗܝܢ ܚܟܝ̈ܡܢ ܗܘ̈ܝ. ܘܚܡܫ ܣܟ̈ܠܢ. ܘܗܢܝܢ ܣܟܠܬܐ ܢܣܒ ܠܡܫܪ̈ܓܝܗܝܢ. ܘܠܐ ܢܣܒ ܥܡܗܝܢ ܡܫܚܐ. ܗܢܝܢ ܕܝܢ ܚܟܝܡܬܐ ܢܣܒ ܡܫܚܐ ܒܡܐ̈ܢܐ ܥܡ ܠܡܫܪ̈ܓܝܗܝܢ. ܟܕ ܐܘܚܪ ܕܝܢ ܚܬܢܐ. ܢܡ ܟܠܗܝܢ ܘܕܡܟ̈ܝ ܘܒܦܠܓܗ ܕܠܠܝܐ ܗܘܬ ܩܥܬܐ: ܗܐ ܚܬܢܐ ܐܬܐ. ܦܘܩܘ ܠܐܘܪܥܗ. ܗܝܕܝܢ ܩܡ ܟܠܗܝܢ ܒܬܘ̈ܠܬܐ ܗܠܝܢ. ܘܬܩܢ ܠܡܫܪ̈ܓܝܗܝܢ. ܐܡܪ̈ܝ ܕܝܢ ܗܢܝܢ ܣܟܠܬܐ ܠܚܟܝܡܬܐ: ܗܒܝܢ ܠܢ ܡܢ ܡܫܚܟܝܢ. ܕܗܐ ܕܥܟܘ ܠܗܘܢ ܠܡܫܪ̈ܓܝܢ. ܥܢ̈ܝ ܗܢܝܢ ܚܟܝܡܬܐ ܘܐܡܪ̈ܝ: ܠܡܐ ܠܐ ܢܣܦܩ ܠܢ ܘܠܟܝܢ. ܐܙܠܝܢ ܠܘܬ ܐܝܠܝܢ ܕܡܙܒܢܝܢ ܘܙܒ̈ܢܝܢ ܠܟܝܢ. ܘܟܕ ܐܙ̈ܠ ܠܡܙܒܢ. ܐܬܐ ܚܬܢܐ. ܘܐܝܠܝܢ ܕܡܛܝܒ̈ܢ ܗܘ̈ܝ ܥܠ ܥܡܗ ܠܒܝܬ ܚܠܘܠܐ. ܘܐܬܬܚܕ ܬܪܥܐ. ܒܚܪܬܐ ܕܝܢ ܐܬ̈ܝ ܐܦ ܗܢܝܢ ܒܬܘ̈ܠܬܐ ܐܚܪ̈ܢܝܬܐ ܘܐܡܪ̈ܝ ܡܪܢ ܡܪܢ. ܦܬܚ ܠܢ. ܗܘ ܕܝܢ ܥܢܐ ܘܐܡܪ ܠܗܝܢ: ܐܡܝܢ ܐܡܪ ܐܢܐ ܠܟܝܢ. ܕܠܐ ܝܕܥܢܐ ܠܟܝܢ ※

ܪܫܐ ܕܬܫܥܬܥܣܪ

Lesson Nineteen

§ 19.1 The Ethpaal Conjugation. The Ethpaal conjugation, the medio-passive of the Pael, is regularly inflected in the perfect, with predictable reduction before vowel-initial postformatives. The example is *etqabbal* 'be received' < Pael *qabbel* 'receive.' Note particularly that the *e* vowel of the Pael becomes *a* throughout the conjugation, both perfect and imperfect, of the Ethpaal.[1]

3 m	ܐܬܩܒܠ	*etqabbal*	ܐܬܩܒܠ(ܘܢ)	*etqabbal(un)*
f	ܐܬܩܒܠܬ	*etqabblat*	ܐܬܩܒܠ(ܝ̈)	*etqabbal(ēn)*
2 m	ܐܬܩܒܠܬ	*etqabbalt*	ܐܬܩܒܠܬܘܢ	*etqabbalton*
f	ܐܬܩܒܠܬܝ	*etqabbalt*	ܐܬܩܒܠܬܝܢ	*etqabbaltēn*
1 c	ܐܬܩܒܠܬ	*etqabblet*	ܐܬܩܒܠܢ	*etqabbaln(an)*

The imperfect is also regularly inflected, with predictable reductions:

3 m	ܢܬܩܒܠ	*netqabbal*	ܢܬܩܒܠܘܢ	*netqabblun*
f	ܬܬܩܒܠ	*tetqabbal*	ܢܬܩܒ̈ܠܢ	*netqabblān*
2 m	ܬܬܩܒܠ	*tetqabbal*	ܬܬܩܒܠܘܢ	*tetqabblun*
f	ܬܬܩܒܠܝܢ	*tetqabblin*	ܬܬܩܒ̈ܠܢ	*tetqabblān*
1 c	ܐܬܩܒܠ	*etqabbal*	ܢܬܩܒܠ	*netqabbal*

The participles, of which there are only active forms (although with middle/passive meanings), are predictable:

masc.	ܡܬܩܒܠ	*metqabbal*	ܡܬܩܒܠܝܢ	*metqabblin*

[1]The Syriac Ethpaal conjugation corresponds to the Pual (פֻּעַל) of Hebrew and the fifth form (تفعّل) of Arabic.

fem.	ܡܬܩܒܠܐ	*metqabblā*	ܡܬܩܒ̈ܠܢ	*metqabblān*

The infinitive is regularly and familiarly formed, ܡܬܩܒܠܘ *metqabbālu.*

§ 19.2 Metathesis in Ethpaal. The same metatheses that affect Ethpeel are also found in Ethpaal, e.g., I-*s:* ܣܠܩ *salleq* > ܐܣܛܠܩ *estallaq* 'be lifted up,' I-*š:* ܫܚܩ *šaḥḥeq* > ܐܫܬܚܩ *eštaḥḥaq* 'be smashed,' I-*ṣ:* ܨܠܚ *ṣallaḥ* > ܐܨܛܠܚ *eṣṭallaḥ* 'be ripped open,' and I-*z:* ܙܒܢ *zabben* > ܐܙܕܒܢ *ezdabban* 'be sold.'

PERF. 3M/FS	ܐܣܛܠܩ	*estallaq*	ܐܣܛܠܩܬ	*estallqat*
IMPERF. 3MS/P	ܢܣܛܠܩ	*nestallaq*	ܢܣܛܠܩܘܢ	*nestallqun*
IMPERATIVE	ܐܣܛܠܩ	*estallaq*		
PART. M/F	ܡܣܛܠܩ	*mestallaq*	ܡܣܛܠܩܐ	*mestallqā*
INF.	ܡܣܛܠܩܘ	*mestallāqu*		

§ 19.3 III-Weak Verbs in Ethpaal. The Ethpaal of III-weak verbs does not differ from the Pael of III-weak verbs given in §16.2(2). An example is ܕܟܝ *dakki* 'purify' > ܐܬܕܟܝ *etdakki* 'be purified'

PERF. 3M/FS	ܐܬܕܟܝ	*etdakki*	ܐܬܕܟܝܬ	*etdakkyat*
IMPERF. 3MS/P	ܢܬܕܟܐ	*netdakkē*	ܢܬܕܟܘܢ	*netdakkōn*
IMPERF. 3FS/P	ܬܬܕܟܐ	*tetdakkē*	ܢܬܕܟ̈ܝܢ	*netdakkyān*
IMPT. M/F	ܐܬܕܟܐ	*etdakkā*	ܐܬܕܟܝ	*etdakkāy*
PART. M/F	ܡܬܕܟܐ	*metdakkē*	ܡܬܕܟܝܐ	*metdakkyā*
INF.	ܡܬܕܟܝܘ	*metdakkāyu*		

The inflection of all other root types in Ethpaal is either completely regular or predictable from the Pael.

(1) I-*ālap:* ܐܠܨ *alleṣ* 'compel' > ܐܬܐܠܨ *etallaṣ* 'be compelled'

PERF. 3M/FS	ܐܬܐܠܨ	*etallaṣ*	ܐܬܐܠܨܬ	*etallṣat*
IMPERF. 3MS/P	ܢܬܐܠܨ	*netallaṣ*	ܢܬܐܠܨܘܢ	*netallṣun*
IMPERATIVE	ܐܬܐܠܨ	*etallaṣ*		
PART. M/F	ܡܬܐܠܨ	*metallaṣ*	ܡܬܐܠܨܐ	*metallṣā*
INF.	ܡܬܐܠܨܘ	*metallāṣu*		

(2) II-*ālap:* ܫܐܠ *ša''el* 'ask questions' > ܐܫܬܐܠ *ešta''al* 'be asked questions'

PERF. 3M/FS	ܐܫܬܐܠ	*ešta''al*	ܐܫܬܐܠܬ	*ešta''lat*
IMPERF. 3MS/P	ܢܫܬܐܠ	*nešta''al*	ܢܫܬܐܠܘܢ	*nešta''lun*
IMPERATIVE	ܐܫܬܐܠ	*ešta''al*		
PART. M/F	ܡܫܬܐܠ	*mešta''al*	ܡܫܬܐܠܐ	*mešta''lā*
INF.	ܡܐܫܬܐܠܘ	*meša''ālu*		

(3) I-*y:* ܝܩܪ *yaqqar* 'honor' > ܐܬܝܩܪ *etyaqqar* 'be honored'

PERF. 3M/FS	ܐܬܝܩܪ	*etyaqqar*	ܐܬܝܩܪܬ	*etyaqqrat*
IMPERF. 3MS/P	ܢܬܝܩܪ	*netyaqqar*	ܢܬܝܩܪܘܢ	*netyaqqrun*
IMPERATIVE	ܐܬܝܩܪ	*etyaqqar*		
PART. M/F	ܡܬܝܩܪ	*metyaqqar*	ܡܐܬܝܩܪܐ	*metyaqqrā*
INF.	ܡܬܝܩܪܘ	*metyaqqāru*		

(4) hollow: ܛܝܒ *ṭayyeb* 'prepare' > ܐܬܛܝܒ *etṭayyab* 'be prepared'

PERF. 3M/FS	ܐܬܛܝܒ	*etṭayyab*	ܐܬܛܝܒܬ	*etṭayybat*
IMPERF. 3MS/P	ܢܬܛܝܒ	*netṭayyab*	ܢܬܛܝܒܘܢ	*netṭayybun*
IMPERATIVE	ܐܬܛܝܒ	*etṭayyab*		
PART. M/F	ܡܬܛܝܒ	*metṭayyab*	ܡܬܛܝܒܐ	*metṭayybā*
INF.	ܡܬܛܝܒܘ	*metṭayyābu*		

Vocabulary 19

NOUNS

ܐܓܪܐ *eggārā* rooftop
ܐܕܢܐ *ednā* (f) ear
ܐܬܐ *ātā* pl *atwātā* sign, token
ܕܝܘܐ *daywā* evil spirit, devil
ܚܡܝܪܐ *ḥmirā* leaven
ܦܪܝܫܐ *prišā* Pharisee
ܩܢܘܡܐ *qnomā* self (reflexive pronoun)
ܫܐܕܐ *šêdā* demon, devil

VERBS

ܐܙܕܗܪ *ezdahhar* to beware

ܐܟܪܙ *akrez* to proclaim, announce; Ethpeel *(etkrez)* to be broadcast

ܐܫܬܠܡ *eštallam* to be completed, finished

ܐܬܕܡܪ *etdammar* to be astonished

ܐܬܝܕܥ *etida*ᶜ to be known

ܓܠܐ *glā/neglē* to reveal; Ethpeel *(etgli)* to be revealed

ܕܫ *dāš/nduš* to tread; Pael *(dayyeš)* to trample

ܚܪܒ *ḥreb/neḥrab* to be laid waste, be ruined

ܛܫܝ *ṭašši* to hide, conceal; Ethpaal *(etṭašši)* to hide oneself, be concealed

ܟܣܐ *ksā/neksē* to cover, clothe

ܠܚܫ *laḥḥeš* to whisper

ܡܠܝ *malli* to fill, fulfill, accomplish; Ethpaal *(etmalli)* to be filled, fulfilled, accomplished

ܢܣܝ *nassi* to try, test, ask (*l-* someone) for (something) as proof

ܦܠܓ *palleg* to divide; Ethpaal *(etpallag)* to be divided

ADJECTIVES

ܚܪܫ *ḥreš/ḥaršā* dumb, mute

ܢܗܝܪ *nahhir* light, full of light

ܨܗܐ *ṣhē* (fem *ṣahyā)* thirsty

OTHERS

ܠܘܩܕܡ *luqdam* first of all

ܡܢ ܒܬܪܟܢ *men bātarken* afterwards (adv.)

ܢܣܒ ܒܐܦܐ *nsab b-appē* to be hypocritical

PROPER NAME

ܒܥܠܙܒܘܒ *b*ᶜ*elzbob* Beelzebub

ܣܛܢܐ *sāṭānā* Satan

Exercise 19

Identify, read, and translate the following Ettaphal forms:

1 ܒܢ̈ܝܐ ܣܓ̈ܝܐܐ ܕܡܬܬܒܥܝܢ

2 ܠܡܦ̈ܩܢܝܗܝܢ ܕܡܬܩ̈ܠܬܐ ܡܫ̈ܬܠܛܐ ܠܐ ܡܬܬܟܣܝܢ ܗ̄ܘܘ

3 ܒܠܡܕ̈ܝܢܟ ܡܬܛܠܒ ܗ̄ܘܐ

4 ܐܬܦܠܓܘ ܬܢ̈ܐ ܠܡܘܫܐ

5 ܠܐ ܐܙܕܗܪܬ

6 ܐܬܛܥܝܘ ܒܫ̈ܢܝܐ ܒܒܬ̈ܝܗܘܢ

7 ܡܬܒܥܝܐ ܗ̄ܝ ܕܢܫܬܠܡܘܢ ܗܠܝܢ

8 ܢܒܥܐ ܕܠܐ ܡܬܕܗܪ

9 ܠܐ ܡܫܟܚ ܕܢܬܡܠܐ ܗܢܐ

10 ܢܫ̈ܐ ܕܡܬܛܥ̈ܝܢ ܒܓܘ ܒܬ̈ܝܗܝܢ

Reading Exercise 19

1 ܝܫܘܥ ܕܝܢ ܚܙܗ̇ ܠܐܡܗ ܘܠܬܠܡܝܕܐ ܗܘ ܕܪܚܡ ܗ̄ܘܐ
ܕܩܐܡ. ܘܐܡܪ ܠܐܡܗ: ܐܢܬܬܐ. ܗܐ ܒܪܟܝ. ܘܐܡܪ
ܠܬܠܡܝܕܐ ܗܘ: ܗܐ ܐܡܟ. ܘܡܢ ܗܝ ܫܥܬܐ ܕܒܪܗ̇
ܬܠܡܝܕܐ ܗܘ ܠܘܬܗ. ܒܬܪ ܗܠܝܢ ܝܕܥ ܝܫܘܥ ܕܟܠ ܡܕܡ
ܐܫܬܠܡ. ܘܕܢܬܡܠܐ ܟܬܒܐ. ܐܡܪ: ܨܗܐ ܐܢܐ ※

2 ܘܟܕ ܐܬܟܢܫܘ ܪ̈ܒܘܬܐ ܕܟܢ̈ܫܐ ܐܝܟ ܕܢܕܫܘܢ ܚܕ ܠܚܕ ܫܪܝ
ܝܫܘܥ ܠܡܐܡܪ ܠܬܠܡܝ̈ܕܘܗܝ: ܠܘܩܕܡ ܐܙܕܗܪܘ ܒܢܦܫܟܘܢ ܡܢ ܚܡܝܪܐ
ܕܦܪ̈ܝܫܐ. ܕܐܝܬܘܗ̄ܝ ܢܣܒ ܒܐܦ̈ܐ. ܠܝܬ ܓܝܪ ܡܕܡ ܕܟܣܐ ܕܠܐ
ܢܬܓܠܐ. ܘܠܐ ܕܡܛܫܝ ܕܠܐ ܢܬܝܕܥ. ܟܠ ܓܝܪ ܕܒܚܫܘܟܐ ܐܡܪܬܘܢ
ܒܢܘܗܪܐ ܢܫܬܡܥ. ܘܡܕܡ ܕܒܐܕ̈ܢܐ ܒܬܘ̈ܢܐ ܠܚܫܬܘܢ. ܥܠ ܐܓܪ̈ܐ
ܢܬܟܪܙ. ܐܡܪ ܐܢܐ ܠܟܘܢ ܕܝܢ ܠܪ̈ܚܡܝ: ܠܐ ܬܕܚܠܘܢ ܡܢ ܐܝܠܝܢ ܕܩܛܠܝܢ
ܦܓܪܐ. ܘܡܢ ܒܬܪܟܢ ܠܝܬ ܠܗܘܢ ܡܕܡ ܝܬܝܪ ܠܡܥܒܕ ※

3 ܘܟܕ ܣܦܩ ܚܡܪܐ. ܕܐܬܘܗ̄ܝ ܫܢܝܐ. ܗܘܐ ܕܝܢ ܢܓܗ ܗܘ ܚܡܪܐ. ܡܠܠܐ

ܗ̇ܘ ܚܪܫܐ. ܘܐܬܕܡܪܘ ܟܢ̈ܫܐ. ܐܢܫܐ ܕܝܢ ܡܢܗܘܢ ܐܡܪܘ. ܒܒܥܠܙܒܘܒ ܪܫܐ
ܕܕܝܘ̈ܐ ܡܦܩ ܗܢܐ ܕܝܘ̈ܐ. ܐܚܪ̈ܢܐ ܕܝܢ ܟܕ ܡܢܣܝܢ ܠܗ ܐܬܐ ܡܢ ܫܡܝܐ ܫܐܠܝܢ
ܗ̄ܘܘ ܠܗ. ܝܫܘܥ ܕܝܢ ܕܝܕܥ ܗ̄ܘܐ ܡܚܫܒ̈ܬܗܘܢ[1]. ܐܡܪ ܠܗܘܢ. ܟܠ ܡܠܟܘ
ܕܬܬܦܠܓ ܥܠ ܢܦܫܗ ܬܚܪܒ. ܘܒܝܬܐ ܕܥܠ ܩܢܘܡܗ ܡܬܦܠܓ. ܢܦܠ. ܘܐܢ
ܣܛܢܐ ܥܠ ܢܦܫܗ ܐܬܦܠܓ. ܐܝܟܢܐ ܬܩܘܡ ܡܠܟܘܬܗ ※

[1] *maḥšbātā* thoughts.

ܪܫܐ ܕܥܣܪܝܢ
Lesson Twenty

§ 20.1 The Ettaphal Conjugation. The Ettaphal conjugation, the medio-passive of the Aphel, is regularly formed. All its forms are quite regular and entirely predictable.[1] The *-tt-* of this conjugation results from assimilation of the initial glottal stop of the Aphel (**et'ap^{c}al > ettap^{c}al).*

Perfect:

3 m	ܐܬܬܡܠܟ *ettamlak*	ܐܬܬܡܠܟܘ(ܢ) *ettamlak(un)*
f	ܐܬܬܡܠܟܬ *ettamlkat*	ܐܬܬܡܠܟ(ܝ̈) *ettamlak(ēn)*
2 m	ܐܬܬܡܠܟܬ *ettamlakt*	ܐܬܬܡܠܟܬܘܢ *ettamlakton*
f	ܐܬܬܡܠܟܬܝ *ettamlakt*	ܐܬܬܡܠܟܬܝܢ *ettamlaktēn*
1 c	ܐܬܬܡܠܟܬ *ettamlket*	ܐܬܬܡܠܟܢ *ettamlakn(an)*

Imperfect:

3 m	ܢܬܬܡܠܟ *nettamlak*	ܢܬܬܡܠܟܘܢ *nettamlkun*
f	ܬܬܬܡܠܟ *tettamlak*	ܢܬܬܡܠܟ̈ܢ *nettamlkān*
2 m	ܬܬܬܡܠܟ *tettamlak*	ܬܬܬܡܠܟܘܢ *tettamlkun*
f	ܬܬܬܡܠܟܝܢ *tettamlkin*	ܬܬܬܡܠܟ̈ܢ *tettamlkān*
1 c	ܐܬܬܡܠܟ *ettamlak*	ܢܬܬܡܠܟ *nettamlak*

Participles (like the Ethpaal participle, active in form but medio-passive in sense):

[1] The Syriac Ettaphal conjugation corresponds to the Hophal (הפעל) of Hebrew and the tenth form (استفعل) of Arabic.

masc.	ܡܬܬܡܠܟ	*mettamlak*	ܡܬܬܡܠܟܝܢ	*mettamlkin*
fem.	ܡܬܬܡܠܟܐ	*mettamlkā*	ܡܬܬܡܠܟ̈ܢ	*mettamlkān*

Infinitive: ܡܬܬܡܠܟܘ *mettamlāku.*

The only variant form that needs to be dealt with in the Ettaphal is the hollow root, for the Ettaphal replaces the Ethpeel of all hollow types: as ܣܡ *sām* 'to place' > *ettsim* 'to be placed': perf. ܐܬܬܣܝܡ *ettsim/ettsimat,* impf. ܢܬܬܣܝܡ *nettsim/nettsimun,* impt. ܐܬܬܣܝܡ *ettsim,* part. ܡܬܬܣܝܡ *mettsim/mettsimā,* inf. ܡܬܬܣܡܘ *mettsāmu.*

The Ettaphal of all other types is completely predictable from the Aphel: I-*n:* ܐܦܩ *appeq* 'cast out' > ܐܬܬܦܩ *ettappaq* 'be cast out'; III-weak: ܐܫܩܝ *ašqi* 'give to drink, water' > ܐܬܬܫܩܝ *ettašqi* 'be made to drink, watered'; I-*y:* ܐܘܕܥ *awda*^{c} 'make known' > ܐܬܬܘܕܥ *ettawda*^{c} 'be made known'; geminate: ܐܥܠ *a*^{cc}*el* 'bring in' > ܐܬܬܥܠ *etta*^{cc}*al* 'be brought in.'

§ 20.2 Adjectives/Nouns in *-ânâ.* Substantives that end in the suffix *-ānā* in the emphatic masc. sing. make the fem. sing. in *-ānitā,* e.g. ܛܘܒܢܐ ܦܘܠܘܣ *ṭubānā pawlos* 'Blessed Paul' but ܛܘܒܢܝܬܐ ܡܪܝܡ *ṭubānitā maryam* 'Blessed Mary.'

Plurals are regularly formed, masc. in *-ānē,* fem. in *-ānyātā;* absolute singulars end in *-ān* and *-āni* (see §15.6).

§ 20.3 Substantivization of Participles. Participles of the G-form assume substantive (adjective/noun) status in the emphatic form, e.g., ܣܗܕ *shed* 'to witness' > ܣܳܗܶܕ *sāhed* 'witnessing' > ܣܗܕܐ *sāhdā* 'witness, martyr' and ܦܪܚ *praḥ* 'to fly' > ܦܳܪܰܚ *pāraḥ* 'flying' > ܦܪܚܬܐ *pāraḥtā* 'bird.'

The emphatic participles of III-weak G-verbs are regularly formed on the pattern *CāCyā,* with *y* almost always representing the weak third consonant. The emphatic masc. pl. of these substantivized participles is *-ayyā,* e.g., ܪܥܐ *r*^{c}*ā* 'to tend (flocks)' > act. part. ܪ̈ܥܐ *rā*^{c}*ē* > emph. ܪܥܝܐ *rā*^{c}*yā* 'shepherd' pl ܪ̈ܥܝܐ *rā*^{c}*ayyā* (and, in this and other cases, ܪܥܘܬܐ *rā*^{c}*awwātā).*

Participles of the increased forms, i.e., those that begin with *m,* are substantivized by adding the suffix *-ānā* (fem. *-ānitā,* absolute *-āni* [§15.4]), e.g.:

ܡܪܚܡ *mraḥḥem* 'having mercy' > ܡܪܚܡܢܐ *mraḥḥmānā* 'merciful'
ܡܩܒܠ *mqabbel* 'receiving' > ܡܩܒܠܢܐ *mqabblānā* 'recipient'
ܡܠܦ *mallep* 'teaching' > ܡܠܦܢܐ *mallpānā* 'teacher'
ܡܦܨܐ *mpaṣṣē* 'saving' > ܡܦܨܝܢܐ *mpaṣṣyānā* 'savior'
ܡܫܠܡ *mašlem* 'betraying' > ܡܫܠܡܢܐ *mašlmānā* 'traitor'
ܡܬܓܫܡ *metgšem* 'embodied' > ܡܬܓܫܡܢܐ *metgašmānā* 'corporeal'
ܡܫܬܬܐ *meštte* 'being drunk' > ܡܫܬܬܝܢܐ *meštatyānā* 'drinkable'
ܡܬܟܪܟ *metkarrak* 'wandering' > ܡܬܟܪܟܢܐ *metkarrkānā* 'mendicant'
ܡܬܬܢܝܚ *mettniḥ* 'resting' > ܡܬܬܢܝܚܢܐ *mettniḥānā* 'at rest, restful'

§ 20.4 Abstraction of Substantivized Participles. All substantivized participles may be abstracted by adding the suffix *-utā* (absolute *-u,* see §15.6), e.g.:

sāhdā 'witness, martyr' > ܣܗܕܘܬܐ *sāhdutā* 'testimony, martyrdom'
mraḥḥmānā 'merciful' > ܡܪܚܡܢܘܬܐ *mraḥḥmānutā* 'mercy'
mqabblānā 'recipient' > ܡܩܒܠܢܘܬܐ *mqabblānutā* 'receptivity'
mallpānā 'teacher' > ܡܠܦܢܘܬܐ *mallpānutā* 'teaching, doctrine'
mpaṣṣyānā 'savior' > ܡܦܨܝܢܘܬܐ *mpaṣṣyānutā* 'deliverance'
mašlmānā 'traitor' > ܡܫܠܡܢܘܬܐ *mašlmānutā* 'treachery, betrayal'
metgašmānā 'corporeal' > ܡܬܓܫܡܢܘܬܐ *metgašmānutā* 'incarnation'
meštatyānā 'drinkable' > ܡܫܬܬܝܢܘܬܐ *meštatyānutā* 'potability'
metkarrkānā 'mendicant' > ܡܬܟܪܟܢܘܬܐ *metkarrkānutā* 'mendicancy'
mettniḥānā 'restful' > ܡܬܬܢܝܚܢܘܬܐ *mettniḥānutā* 'restfulness'

§ 20.5 Other Verbal Patterns. The secondary verbal patterns given below are found with a number of roots. Their occurrence, however, cannot be predicted.

(1) PALPEL *(palpel),* the vocalic patterning of all forms of which is exactly like that of Pael. Verbs of the Palpel pattern are of three types:

(a) quadriliteral, or roots consisting of four distinct consonants, e.g., ܬܪܓܡ *targem* 'to translate' (impf. ܢܬܪܓܡ *ntargem,* act. part. ܡܬܪܓܡ *mtargem,* pass. part. ܡܬܪܓܡ *mtargam,* inf. ܡܬܪܓܡܘ *mtargāmu).*

(b) biliteral roots reduplicated, often for onomatopoeic verbs, e.g., ܥܪܥܪ *^{c}ar^{c}ar* 'to gargle' and ܡܪܡܪ *marmar* 'to make bitter.'

(c) triliteral with third radical reduplicated, e.g., ܥܒܕܕ *^{c}abded* 'to reduce to servitude.'

(2) ETHPALPAL *(etpalpal),* the medio-passive of Palpel, as ܐܬܬܪܓܡ *ettargam* 'to be/get translated,' ܐܬܡܪܡܪ *etmarmar* 'to be/get embittered, enraged,' and ܐܬܥܒܕܕ *et^{c}abdad* 'to be reduced to servitude.'

(3) PALI *(pa^{c}li).* This pattern serves as the Palpel for roots with a weak fourth radical and for triliteral roots to which a weak fourth radical has been added, e.g., ܢܟܪܝ *nakri/nnakrē)* 'to alienate' and ܬܚܬܝ *taḥti/ ntaḥtē)* 'to bring down.'

(4) ETHPALI *(etpa^{c}li),* the medio-passive of Pali, e.g., ܐܬܢܟܪܝ *et-nakri/ netnakrē* 'to be estranged' and ܐܬܬܚܬܝ *ettaḥti/nettaḥtē* 'to be brought down.'

(5) SHAPHEL *(šap^{c}el),* a secondary factitive form, usually with a different shade of meaning from Pael and Aphel, as ܫܥܒܕ *ša^{c}bed/ nša^{c}bed* 'to enslave' (cf. Aphel *a^{c}bed* 'to put to work, cause to work') and ܫܘܕܥ *šawda^c/nšawda^c* 'to make clear, explain (cf. Aphel *awda^c* 'to inform, make known').

(6) ESHTAPHAL *(eštap^{c}al),* the medio-passive of Shaphel, as ܐܫܬܥܒܕ *ešta^{c}bad/nešta^{c}bad* 'to be enslaved' and ܐܫܬܘܕܥ *eštawda^c/ neštawda^c* 'to perceive, see.'

(7) PAHLI *(pahli),* a factitive form in which an extra consonant is inserted between the first and second radicals of a III-weak root, e.g., ܫܢܐ *šnā* 'to be altered' > ܫܓܢܝ *šagni/nšagnē* 'to alter.'

(8) ETHPAHLI *(etpahli),* the medio-passive of Pahli, as ܐܫܬܓܢܝ

eštagni/neštagnē to be displaced, different.'

(9) PAIEL *(pay^{c}el),* a secondary factitive/transitivizing pattern, e.g., ܫܚܢ *šḥen* 'to grow warm' > ܫܝܚܢ *šayḥen* 'to enrage' (cf. Pael *šaḥḥen* 'to make warm, heat up' and Aphel *ašḥen* 'to give warmth').

(10) ETHPAIAL *(etpay^{c}al),* the medio-passive of Paiel, e.g., ܐܫܬܝܚܢ *eštayḥan* 'to rage, rave.'

(11) PAUEL *(paw^{c}el),* a secondary factitive/transitivizing pattern, e.g., ܦܘܫܫܐ *pušāšā* 'evaporation' > ܦܘܫܫ *pawšeš* 'to dissipate.'

(12) ETHPAUAL *(etpaw^{c}al),* the medio-passive of Pauel, e.g., ܐܬܦܘܫܫ *etpawšaš* 'to waste away.'

§ 20.6 Miscellaneous Noun Patterns. Following are noun patterns that are fairly frequent in occurrence and predictable in meaning:

(1) PAOLA *(pā^{c}ōlā),* a pattern indicating intensive, habitual or 'professional' activity in the root meaning, as ܥܒܘܕܐ *^{c}ābōdā* 'maker' (< *^{c}bad* 'to make'), *sāgōdā* 'worshipper' (< *sged* 'to worship'), ܝܕܘܥܐ *yādo^{c}ā* 'expert' (< *ida^c* 'to know') and ܡܠܘܟܐ *mālokā* 'advisor' (< *mlak* 'to advise').

(2) PUALA *(pu^{c}ālā),* an abstract noun derived from the root meaning, as ܫܘܪܝܐ *šurāyā* 'beginning' (< *šarri* 'to begin'), ܫܘܠܡܐ *šulāmā* 'end' (< *šlem* 'to be finished'), ܚܘܠܡܐ *ḥulāmā* 'health' (< *ḥlim* 'well, hail') and ܣܘܠܩܐ *sulāqā* 'ascension' (< *sleq* 'to ascend').

(3) MAPHAL (abs *map^{c}al,* emph *map^{c}lā),* a noun of place, as ܡܕܒܪܐ *madbrā* 'wilderness' (< *dbar* 'to lead a flock to pasture in the wilderness'), ܡܕܒܚܐ *madbḥā* 'altar' (< *dbaḥ* 'to slaughter, sacrifice'), ܡܕܢܚܐ *madnḥā* 'the east' (< *dnaḥ* 'for the sun to rise'), and ܡܥܪܒܐ *ma^{c}rbā* 'the west' (< *^{c}reb* 'for the sun to set').

Vocabulary 20

NOUNS

ܐܣܝܘܬܐ *āsyutā* pl *-swātā* healing, cure

ܓܡܠܐ *gamlā* camel
ܓܦܐ *geppā* wing
ܚܪܘܪܐ *ḥrōrā* opening, eye (of a needle)
ܛܠܝܘܬܐ *ṭalyutā* childhood
ܟܣܐ *kāsā* cup
ܡܚܛܐ *mḥaṭṭā* needle
ܢܟܣܐ *neksā* (usually in the pl) riches, wealth
ܢܣܝܘܢܐ *nesyonā* temptation
ܣܝܡܬܐ *simtā* treasure
ܥܝܢܐ ^{c}*aynā* (f) eye; spring
ܦܪܘܓܐ *parrugā* chick
ܪܫܢܐ *rêšānā* nobleman, prince
ܫܘܩܪܐ *šuqrā* falsehood
ܬܥܠܐ *ta*^{c}*lā* fox
ܬܪܢܓܘܠܬܐ *tarnāgultā* hen
ܬܪܢܓܠܐ *tarnāglā* (abs *tarnāgul)* cock

ADJECTIVES

ܒܪܝܟ *brik* blessed
ܕܠܝܠ *dlil* easy
ܚܣܝܪ *ḥassir* lacking, missing
ܚܪܒ *ḥreb/ḥarbā* desolate, laid waste
ܝܩܝܪ *yaqqir* heavy; honored, noble
ܟܪܝܗ *krih* sick, infirm
ܥܛܠ ^{c}*ṭel/*^{c}*aṭlā* hard, difficult

VERBS

ܐܣܗܕ *ashed/nashed* to bear witness, testify
ܐܫܬܒܩ *eštbeq/neštbeq* (Ethpeel of *šbaq)* to be abandoned, forsaken
ܐܫܬܝ *ešti/neštē* to drink
ܐܫܬܠܡ *eštlem* to be given up, handed over
ܐܬܟܡܪ *etkmar* to be sad
ܐܬܬܢܝܚ *ettniḥ* to rest
ܐܬܬܥܝܩ *ett*^{c}*iq* ($\sqrt{}$^{c}*WQ)* to be wearied
ܐܬܬܥܝܪ *ett*^{c}*ir* to wake up
ܓܢܒ *gnab/negnob* to steal
ܓܪ *gār/ngur* to commit adultery

ܘܠܐ *wālē l-* it is necessary for (only the act. part. of the defective verb is used)
ܝܩܪ *yaqqar/nyaqqar* to honor
ܝܪܬ *iret/nêrat* to inherit
ܟܢܫ *knaš/neknoš* to gather, collect; Pael *(kanneš)* assemble, bring togather
ܟܪܝ *kri/nekrē l-* to be sad (used impersonally in the 3rd fem. sing., as *keryat li* 'I became sad')
ܡܛܐ *mṭā/nemṭē* to arrive
ܦܪܩ *praq/neproq* to depart, go away, withdraw
ܣܥܪ *sʿar/nesʿor* (1) to do, perform; (2) to visit
ܩܘܝ *qawwi* to remain, stay
ܪܓܡ *rgam/nergom* to stone
ܫܗܪ *šhar/nešhar* to stay awake, keep vigil
ܫܡܠܝ *šamli/nšamlē* (Shaphel of *mlā)* to do thoroughly, complete, finish; Eshtaphal *(eštamli/ neštamlē)* to be at an end, be finished

OTHERS

ܒܪܡ *bram* nonetheless, however
ܝܘܡܢܐ *yawmānā* today
ܟܡܐ *kmā* (+ abs. pl.) how many?
ܠܒܪ ܡܢ *l-bar men* outside of
ܡܚܪ *mḥār* tomorrow
ܡܟܐ *mekkā* from here, hence
ܡܟܝܠ *mekkêl* henceforth, later; then, therefore
ܬܚܝܬ *tḥēt* beneath, under (prep.)

Reading Exercise 20

1 ܘܫܐܠܗ ܚܕ ܡܢ ܪ̈ܫܢܐ ܘܐܡܪ ܠܗ: ܡܠܦܢܐ ܛܒܐ. ܡܢܐ
ܐܥܒܕ ܕܐܝܪܬ ܚ̈ܝܐ ܕܠܥܠܡ. ܐܡܪ ܠܗ ܝܫܘܥ: ܡܢܐ ܩܪܐ
ܐܢܬ ܠܝ ܛܒܐ. ܠܝܬ ܛܒܐ ܐܠܐ ܐܢ ܚܕ ܐܠܗܐ. ܦܘܩܕ̈ܢܐ
ܝܕܥ ܐܢܬ. ܠܐ ܬܩܛܘܠ. ܘܠܐ ܬܓܘܪ. ܘܠܐ ܬܓܢܘܒ ܘܠܐ
ܬܣܗܕ ܣܗܕܘܬܐ ܕܕܓܠܘܬܐ. ܝܩܪ ܠܐܒܘܟ ܘܠܐܡܟ. ܐܡܪ
ܠܗ: ܗܠܝܢ ܟܠܗܝܢ ܢܛܪܬ ܐܢܝܢ ܡܢ ܛܠܝܘܬܝ. ܟܕ ܫܡܥ ܕܝܢ

ܝܫܘܥ: ܐܡܪ ܠܗ: ܚܕܐ ܚܣܝܪܐ ܠܟ. ܙܒܢ ܟܠܡܕܡ ܕܐܝܬ
ܠܟ. ܘܗܒ ܠܡܣ̈ܟܢܐ. ܘܬܗܘܐ ܠܟ ܣܝܡܬܐ ܒܫܡ̈ܝܐ. ܘܬܐ
ܒܬܪܝ.. ܗܘ̇ ܕܝܢ ܟܕ ܫܡܥ ܗܠܝܢ. ܟܪܝܬ ܠܗ. ܥܬܝܪ ܗ̄ܘܐ
ܓܝܪ ܛܒ. ܘܚܙܐ ܝܫܘܥ ܕܟܪܝܬ ܠܗ. ܐܡܪ: ܐܝܟܢܐ ܥܛܠܐ
ܠܐܝܠܝܢ ܕܐܝܬ ܠܗܘܢ ܢܟ̈ܣܐ. ܕܢܥܠܘܢ ܠܡܠܟܘܬܗ ܕܐܠܗܐ.
ܕܠܝܠܐ ܗ̄ܘ ܠܓܡܠܐ ܕܒܚܪܘܪܐ ܕܡܚܛܐ ܢܥܘܠ. ܐܘ ܥܬܝܪܐ
ܠܡܠܟܘܬܗ ܕܐܠܗܐ. ܐܡܪܝܢ ܠܗ ܐܝܠܝܢ ܕܫܡܥܘ: ܘܡܢܘ
ܡܫܟܚ ܠܡܚܐ. ܝܫܘܥ ܕܝܢ ܐܡܪ: ܐܝܠܝܢ ܕܠܘܬ ܒܢ̈ܝܢܫܐ ܠܐ
ܡܫܟܚܢ. ܠܘܬ ܐܠܗܐ ܡܫܟܚܢ ܠܡܗܘܐ ※

2 ܒܗ ܒܗܘ ܝܘܡܐ ܩܪܒܘ ܐܢܫܐ ܡܢ ܦܪ̈ܝܫܐ. ܘܐܡܪܝܢ ܠܗ: ܦܘܩ ܙܠ
ܠܟ ܡܟܐ. ܡܛܠ ܕܗܪܘܕܣ ܨܒܐ ܠܡܩܛܠܟ. ܐܡܪ ܠܗܘܢ ܝܫܘܥ: ܙܠܘ
ܐܡܪܘ ܠܬܥܠܐ ܗܢܐ. ܕܗܐ ܡܦܩ ܐܢܐ ܫܐܕ̈ܐ ܘܐܣܘܬܐ ܥܒܕ ܐܢܐ
ܝܘܡܢܐ ܘܡܚܪ. ܘܠܝܘܡܐ ܕܬܠܬܐ ܡܫܬܡܠܐ ܐܢܐ. ܒܪܡ ܘܠܐ ܠܝ
ܕܝܘܡܢܐ ܘܡܚܪ ܘܠܝܘܡܐ ܐܚܪܢܐ ܐܙܠ. ܡܛܠ ܕܠܐ ܡܫܟܚܐ
ܕܢܒܝܐ ܢܐܒܕ ܠܒܪ ܡܢ ܐܘܪܫܠܡ. ܐܘܪܫܠܡ ܩܛܠܬ ܢܒ̈ܝܐ
ܘܪܓܡܬ ܠܐܝܠܝܢ ܕܫܠܝܚܝܢ ܠܘܬܗ̇. ܟܡܐ ܙܒܢܝܢ ܨܒܝܬ ܠܡܟܢܫܘ ܒܢ̈ܝܟܝ
ܐܝܟ ܬܪܢܓܘܠܬܐ ܕܟܢܫܐ ܦܪ̈ܘܓܝܗ̇ ܬܚܝܬ ܓܦ̈ܝܗ̇. ܘܠܐ ܨܒܝܬܘܢ. ܗܐ
ܡܫܬܒܩ ܠܟܘܢ ܒܝܬܟܘܢ ܚܪܒܐ. ܐܡܪ ܐܢܐ ܠܟܘܢ ܓܝܪ. ܕܠܐ ܬܚܙܘܢܢܝ
ܥܕܡܐ ܕܬܐܡܪܘܢ: ܒܪܝܟ ܗ̄ܘ ܕܐܬܐ ܒܫܡܗ ܕܡܪܝܐ ※

3 ܗܝܕܝܢ ܐܬܐ ܥܡܗܘܢ ܝܫܘܥ ܠܕܘܟܬܐ ܕܡܬܩܪܝܐ ܓܕܣܡܢ. ܘܐܡܪ ܠܬܠܡܝ̈ܕܘܗ̄ܝ.
ܬܒܘ ܗܪܟܐ. ܥܕ ܐܙܠ ܐܨܠܐ. ܘܕܒܪ ܠܟܐܦܐ ܘܠܬܪ̈ܝܗܘܢ ܒܢ̈ܝ ܙܒܕܝ. ܘܫܪܝ
ܠܡܬܟܪܝܘ ܘܠܡܬܥܩܘ. ܘܐܡܪ ܠܗܘܢ. ܟܪܝܐ ܗ̄ܝ ܠܗ̇ ܠܢܦܫܝ ܥܕܡܐ
ܠܡܘܬܐ. ܩܘܘ ܠܝ ܗܪܟܐ ܘܐܬܥܝܪܘ ܥܡܝ. ܘܩܪܒ ܩܠܝܠ ܘܢܦܠ ܥܠ
ܐܦ̈ܘܗܝ. ܘܡܨܠܐ ܗ̄ܘܐ ܘܐܡܪ. ܐܒܝ. ܐܢ ܡܫܟܚܐ. ܢܥܒܪ ܟܤܐ ܗܢܐ.
ܡܢܝ ܒܪܡ ܠܐ ܐܝܟ ܕܐܢܐ ܨܒܐ ܐܢܐ. ܐܠܐ ܐܝܟ ܕܐܢܬ. ܘܐܬܐ ܠܘܬ ܬܠܡܝ̈ܕܘܗܝ.
ܘܐܫܟܚ ܐܢܘܢ ܟܕ ܕܡܟܝܢ. ܘܐܡܪ ܠܟܐܦܐ. ܗܟܢܐ ܠܐ ܐܫܟܚܬܘܢ ܚܕܐ ܫܥܐ
ܠܡܬܬܥܝܪܘ ܥܡܝ. ܐܬܬܥܝܪܘ ܘܨܠܘ. ܕܠܐ ܬܥܠܘܢ ܠܢܤܝܘܢܐ. ܪܘܚܐ ܡܛܝܒܐ.
ܦܓܪܐ ܕܝܢ ܟܪܝܗ. ܬܘܒ ܐܙܠ ܕܬܪܬܝܢ ܙܒܢܝܢ. ܨܠܝ ܘܐܡܪ. ܐܒܝ. ܐܢ ܠܐ
ܡܫܟܚ ܗܘܐ ܟܤܐ ܕܢܥܒܪ ܐܠܐ ܐܢ ܐܫܬܝܬܗ. ܢܗܘܐ ܨܒܝܢܟ. ܘܐܬܐ
ܬܘܒ. ܐܫܟܚ ܐܢܘܢ ܟܕ ܕܡܟܝܢ. ܥܝ̈ܢܝܗܘܢ ܓܝܪ ܝܩܝ̈ܪܢ ܗ̄ܘ̈ܝ. ܘܫܒܩ ܐܢܘܢ

ܘܐܙܠ ܬܘܒ ܨܠܝ ܕܬܠܬ ܙܒ̈ܢܝܢ. ܘܠܗ̇ ܠܡܠܬܐ ܐܡܪ. ܗܝܕܝܢ ܐܬܐ ܠܘܬ
ܬܠܡܝ̈ܕܘܗܝ.. ܘܐܡܪ ܠܗܘܢ. ܕܡܟܘ ܡܟܝܠ ܘܐܬܬܢܝܚܘ. ܗܐ ܩܪܒܬ ܫܥܬܐ.
ܘܒܪܗ ܕܐܢܫܐ ܡܫܬܠܡ ܒܐܝ̈ܕܝܗܘܢ ܕܚ̈ܛܝܐ. ܩܘܡܘ ܢܐܙܠ ܗܐ ܡܛܐ ܗܘ
ܕܡܫܠܡ ܠܝ ※

Appendix A

VERBAL INFLECTIONS

In the following inflections, the model root is inflected in all possible conjugations, regardless of whether or not those forms actually exist in that root. Spirantization is marked for √*KTB* only.

(1) SOUND ROOT, model √*KTB*

Perfect

	PEAL	PAEL	APHEL	ETHPEEL	ETHPAAL	ETTAPHAL
3 m sing	*kṯaḇ*	*katteḇ*	*aḵteḇ*	*eṯkṯeḇ*	*eṯkattaḇ*	*ettaḵtaḇ*
3 f sing	*keṯbaṯ*	*kattḇaṯ*	*aḵtḇaṯ*	*eṯkaṯbaṯ*	*eṯkattḇaṯ*	*ettaḵtḇaṯ*
2 sing	*kṯaḇt*	*katteḇt*	*aḵteḇt*	*eṯkṯeḇt*	*eṯkattaḇt*	*ettaḵtaḇt*
1 c sing	*keṯbeṯ*	*kattḇeṯ*	*aḵtḇeṯ*	*eṯkaṯbeṯ*	*eṯkattḇeṯ*	*ettaḵtḇeṯ*
3 m pl	*kṯaḇ(un)*	*katteḇ(un)*	*aḵteḇ(un)*	*eṯkṯeḇ(un)*	*eṯkattaḇ(un)*	*ettaḵtaḇ(un)*
3 f pl	*kṯaḇ(ēn)*	*katteḇ(ēn)*	*aḵteḇ(ēn)*	*eṯkṯeḇ(ēn)*	*eṯkattaḇ(ēn)*	*ettaḵtaḇ(ēn)*
2 m pl	*kṯaḇton*	*katteḇton*	*aḵteḇton*	*eṯkṯeḇton*	*eṯkattaḇton*	*ettaḵtaḇton*
2 f pl	*kṯaḇtēn*	*katteḇtēn*	*aḵteḇtēn*	*eṯkṯeḇtēn*	*eṯkattaḇtēn*	*ettaḵtaḇtēn*
1 c pl	*kṯaḇn(an)*	*katteḇn(an)*	*aḵteḇn(an)*	*eṯkṯeḇn(an)*	*eṯkattaḇn(an)*	*ettaḵtaḇn(an)*

Imperfect

3 m sing	*neḵtoḇ*	*nḵatteḇ*	*naḵteḇ*	*neṯkṯeḇ*	*neṯkattaḇ*	*nettaḵtaḇ*
3 f sing	*teḵtoḇ*	*tḵatteḇ*	*taḵteḇ*	*teṯkṯeḇ*	*teṯkattaḇ*	*tettaḵtaḇ*
2 m sing	*teḵtoḇ*	*tḵatteḇ*	*taḵteḇ*	*teṯkṯeḇ*	*teṯkattaḇ*	*tettaḵtaḇ*
2 f sing	*teḵtḇin*	*tḵattḇin*	*taḵtḇin*	*teṯkaṯbin*	*teṯkattḇin*	*tettaḵtḇin*
1 c sing	*eḵtoḇ*	*eḵatteḇ*	*aḵteḇ*	*eṯkṯeḇ*	*eṯkattaḇ*	*ettaḵtaḇ*
3 m pl	*neḵtḇun*	*nḵattḇun*	*naḵtḇun*	*neṯkaṯbun*	*neṯkattḇun*	*nettaḵtḇun*
3 f pl	*neḵtḇān*	*nḵattḇān*	*naḵtḇān*	*neṯkaṯbān*	*neṯkattḇān*	*nettaḵtḇān*
2 m pl	*teḵtḇun*	*tḵattḇun*	*taḵtḇun*	*teṯkaṯbun*	*teṯkattḇun*	*tettaḵtḇun*
2 f pl	*teḵtḇān*	*tḵattḇān*	*taḵtḇān*	*teṯkaṯbān*	*teṯkattḇān*	*tettaḵtḇān*
1 c pl	*neḵtoḇ*	*nḵatteḇ*	*naḵteḇ*	*neṯkṯeḇ*	*neṯkattaḇ*	*nettaḵtaḇ*

Imperative

sing	*kṯoḇ*	*katteḇ*	*aḵteḇ*	*eṯkṯeḇ/eṯkaṯb*	*eṯkattaḇ*	*ettaḵtaḇ*
m pl	*kṯoḇ(un)*	*katteḇ(un)*	*aḵteḇ(un)*	*eṯkṯeḇ(un)*	*eṯkattaḇ(un)*	*ettaḵtaḇ(un)*
f pl	*kṯoḇ(ēn)*	*katteḇ(ēn)*	*aḵteḇ(ēn)*	*eṯkṯeḇ(ēn)*	*eṯkattaḇ(ēn)*	*ettaḵtaḇ(ēn)*

Active Participle Absolute

masc sing	*kāṯeḇ*	*mḵatteḇ*	*maḵteḇ*	*meṯkṯeḇ*	*meṯkattaḇ*	*mettaḵtaḇ*
fem sing	*kāṯḇā*	*mḵattḇā*	*maḵtḇā*	*meṯkaṯbā*	*meṯkattḇā*	*mettaḵtḇā*

masc pl	*kāṯḇin*	*mḵattḇin*	*maḵtḇin*	*meṯkaṯḇin*	*meṯkattḇin*	*mettaḵtḇin*
fem pl	*kāṯḇān*	*mḵattḇān*	*maḵtḇān*	*meṯkaṯḇān*	*meṯkattḇān*	*mettaḵtḇān*

Passive Participle Absolute

	kṯiḇ	*mḵattaḇ*	*maḵtaḇ*	—	—	—

Infinitive

	meḵtaḇ	*mḵattāḇu*	*maḵtāḇu*	*meṯkṯāḇu*	*meṯkattāḇu*	*mettaḵtāḇu*

(2) III-WEAK ROOT, model √*GLY*

Perfect

3 m sing	*glā*	*galli*	*agli*	*etgli*	*etgalli*	*ettagli*
3 f sing	*glāt*	*gallyat*	*aglyat*	*etgalyat*	*etgallyat*	*ettaglyat*
2 sing	*glayt*	*galliyt*	*agliyt*	*etgliyt*	*etgalliyt*	*ettagliyt*
1 c sing	*glêt*	*gallit*	*aglit*	*etglit*	*etgallit*	*ettaglit*
3 m pl	*glaw*	*galli*	*agli*	*etgli*	*etgalli*	*ettagli*
3 f pl	*glay*	*galli*	*agli*	*etgli*	*etgalli*	*ettagli*
2 m pl	*glayton*	*galliyton*	*agliyton*	*etgliyton*	*etgalliyton*	*ettagliyton*
2 f pl	*glaytēn*	*galliytēn*	*agliytēn*	*etgliytēn*	*etgalliytēn*	*ettagliytēn*
1 c pl	*glayn(an)*	*galliyn(an)*	*agliyn(an)*	*etgliyn(an)*	*etgalliyn(an)*	*ettagliyn(an)*

Imperfect

3 m sing	*neglē*	*ngallē*	*naglē*	*netglē*	*netgallē*	*nettaglē*
3 f sing	*teglē*	*tgallē*	*taglē*	*tetglē*	*tetgallē*	*tettaglē*
2 m sing	*teglē*	*tgallē*	*taglē*	*tetglē*	*tetgallē*	*tettaglē*
2 f sing	*tegleyn*	*tgalleyn*	*tagleyn*	*tetgleyn*	*tetgalleyn*	*tettagleyn*
1 c sing	*eglē*	*egallē*	*aglē*	*etglē*	*etgallē*	*ettaglē*
3 m pl	*neglōn*	*ngallōn*	*naglōn*	*netglōn*	*netgallōn*	*nettaglōn*
3 f pl	*neglyān*	*ngallyān*	*naglyān*	*netgalyān*	*netgallyān*	*nettaglyān*
2 m pl	*teglōn*	*tgallōn*	*taglōn*	*tetglōn*	*tetgallōn*	*tettaglōn*
2 f pl	*teglyān*	*tgallyān*	*taglyān*	*tetgalyān*	*tetgallyān*	*tettaglyān*
1 c pl	*neglē*	*ngallē*	*naglē*	*netglē*	*netgallē*	*nettaglē*

Imperative

m sing	*gli*	*gallā*	*aglā*	*etglay*	*etgallā*	*ettaglā*
f sing	*glāy*	*gallāy*	*aglāy*	*etglāy*	*etgallāy*	*ettaglāy*
m pl	*glaw*	*gallaw*	*aglaw*	*etglaw*	*etgallaw*	*ettaglaw*
f pl	*glāyēn*	*gallāyēn*	*aglāyēn*	*etglāyēn*	*etgallāyēn*	*ettaglāyēn*

Active Participle Absolute

m sing	*gālē*	*mgallē*	*maglē*	*metglē*	*metgallē*	*mettaglē*

f sing	*gālyā*	*mgallyā*	*maglyā*	*metgalyā*	*metgallyā*	*mettaglyā*
m pl	*gāleyn*	*mgalleyn*	*magleyn*	*metgleyn*	*metgalleyn*	*mettagleyn*
f pl	*gālyān*	*mgallyān*	*maglyān*	*metgalyān*	*metgallyān*	*mettaglyān*

Passive Participle Absolute

m sing	*glē*	*mgallay*	*maglay*	—	—	—
f sing	*galyā*	*mgallyā*	*maglyā*	—	—	—
m pl	*gleyn*	*mgallyin*	*maglyin*	—	—	—
f pl	*galyān*	*mgallyān*	*maglyān*			

Infinitives

	meglā	*mgallāyu*	*maglāyu*	*metglāyu*	*metgallāyu*	*mettaglāyu*

(3) HOLLOW ROOT, model √*NWM*

Perfect

3 m sing	*nām*	*nawwem*	*anim*	The Ethpeel of	*etnawwam*	*ettnim*
3 f sing	*nāmat*	*nawwmat*	*animat*	all hollow roots	*etnawwmat*	*ettnimat*
2 sing	*nāmt*	*nawwemt*	*animt*	is replaced by	*etnawwamt*	*ettnimt*
1 c sing	*nāmet*	*nawwmet*	*animet*	the Ettaphal	*etnawwmet*	*ettnimet*

3 m pl	*nām(un)*	*nawwem(un)*	*anim(un)*	*etnawwam(un)*	*ettnim(un)*
3 f pl	*nām(ēn)*	*nawwem(ēn)*	*anim(ēn)*	*etnawwam(ēn)*	*ettnim(ēn)*
2 m pl	*nāmton*	*nawwemton*	*animton*	*etnawwamton*	*ettnimton*
2 f pl	*nāmtēn*	*nawwemtēn*	*animtēn*	*etnawwamtēn*	*ettnimtēn*
1 c pl	*nāmn(an)*	*nawwemn(an)*	*animn(an)*	*etnawwemn(an)*	*ettnimn(an)*

Imperfect

3 m sing	*nnum*	*nnawwem*	*nnim*	*netnawwam*	*nettnim*
3 f sing	*tnum*	*tnawwem*	*tnim*	*tetnawwam*	*tettnim*
2 m sing	*tnum*	*tnawwem*	*tnim*	*tetnawwam*	*tettnim*
2 f sing	*tnumin*	*tnawwmin*	*tnimin*	*tetnawwmin*	*tettnimin*
1 c sing	*num*	*enawwem*	*nim*	*etnawwam*	*ettnim*
3 m pl	*nnumun*	*nnawwmun*	*nnimun*	*netnawwmun*	*nettnimun*
3 f pl	*nnumān*	*nnawwmān*	*nnimān*	*netnawwmān*	*nettnimān*
2 m pl	*tnumun*	*tnawwmun*	*tnimun*	*tetnawwmun*	*tettnimun*
2 f pl	*tnumān*	*tnawwmān*	*tnimān*	*tetnawwmān*	*tettnimān*
1 c pl	*nnum*	*nnawwem*	*nnim*	*netnawwam*	*nettnim*

Imperative

sing	*num*	*nawwem*	*nim*	*tnawwam*	*ettnim*
m pl	*num(un)*	*nawwem(un)*	*nim(un)*	*tnawwam(un)*	*ettnim(un)*

f pl	*num(ēn)*	*nawwem(ēn)*	*nim(ēn)*		*tnawwam(ēn)*	*ettnim(ēn)*

Active Participle Absolute

m sing	*nā'em*	*mnawwem*	*mnim*		*metnawwam*	*mettnim*
f sing	*nāymā*	*mnawwmā*	*mnimā*		*metnawwmā*	*mettnimā*
m pl	*nāymin*	*mnawwmin*	*mnimin*		*metnawwmin*	*mettnimin*
f pl	*nāymān*	*mnawwmān*	*mnimān*		*metnawwmān*	*mettnimān*

Passive Participle Absolute

m sing	*nim*	*mnawwam*	*mnām*		—	—
f sing	*nimā*	*mnawwmā*	*mnāmā*			

Infinitives

	mnām	*mnawwāmu*	*mnāmu*		*metnawwāmu*	*mettnāmu*

(4) I-*y* ROOT, model √*YLD*

Perfect

3 m sing	*iled*	*yalled*	*awled*	*etiled*	*etyallad*	*ettawlad*
3 f sing	*yeldat*	*yalldat*	*awldat*	*etyaldat*	*etyalldat*	*ettawldat*

2 sing	*iledt*	*yalledt*	*awledt*	*etiledt*	*etyalladt*	*ettawladt*
1 c sing	*yeldet*	*yalldet*	*awldet*	*etyaldet*	*etyalldet*	*ettawldet*
3 m pl	*iled(un)*	*yalled(un)*	*awled(un)*	*etiled(un)*	*etyallad(un)*	*ettawlad(un)*
3 f pl	*iled(ēn)*	*yalled(ēn)*	*awled(ēn)*	*etiled(ēn)*	*etyallad(ēn)*	*ettawlad(ēn)*
2 m pl	*iledton*	*yalledton*	*awledton*	*etiledton*	*etyalladton*	*ettawladton*
2 f pl	*iledtēn*	*yalledtēn*	*awledtēn*	*etiledtēn*	*etyalladtēn*	*ettawladtēn*
1 c pl	*iledn(an)*	*yalledn(an)*	*awledn(an)*	*etiledn(an)*	*etyalladn(an)*	*ettawladn(an)*

Imperfect

3 m sing	*nêlad*	*nyalled*	*nawled*	*netiled*	*netyallad*	*nettawlad*
3 f sing	*têlad*	*tyalled*	*tawled*	*tetiled*	*tetyallad*	*tettawlad*
2 m sing	*têlad*	*tyalled*	*tawled*	*tetiled*	*tetyallad*	*tettawlad*
2 f sing	*têldin*	*tyalldin*	*tawldin*	*tetyaldin*	*tetyalldin*	*tettawldin*
1 c sing	*êlad*	*eyalled*	*awled*	*etiled*	*etyallad*	*ettawlad*
3 m pl	*nêldun*	*nyalldun*	*nawldun*	*netyaldun*	*netyalldun*	*nettawldun*
3 f pl	*nêldān*	*nyalldān*	*nawldān*	*netyaldān*	*netyalldān*	*nettawldān*
2 m pl	*têldun*	*tyalldun*	*tawldun*	*tetyaldun*	*tetyalldun*	*tettawldun*
2 f pl	*têldān*	*tyalldān*	*tawldān*	*tetyaldān*	*tetyalldān*	*tettawldān*
1 c pl	*nêlad*	*nyalled*	*nawled*	*netiled*	*netyallad*	*nettawlad*

Imperative

sing	*ilad*	*yalled*	*awled*	*etiled/etyald*	*etyallad*	*ettawlad*
m pl	*ilad(un)*	*yalled(un)*	*awled(un)*	*etiled(un)* *etyald(un)*	*etyallad(un)*	*ettawlad(un)*

Active Participle Absolute

m sing	*yāled*	*myalled*	*mawled*	*metiled*	*metyallad*	*mettawlad*
f sing	*yāldā*	*myalldā*	*mawldā*	*metyaldā*	*metyalldā*	*mettawldā*
m pl	*yāldin*	*myalldin*	*mawldin*	*metyaldin*	*metyalldin*	*mettawldin*
f pl	*yāldān*	*myalldān*	*mawldān*	*metyaldān*	*metyalldān*	*mettawldān*

Passive Participle Absolute

m sing	*ilid*	*myallad*	*mawlad*	—	—	—
f sing	*ilidā*	*myalldā*	*mawldā*	—	—	—
m pl	*ilidin*	*myalldin*	*mawldin*	—	—	—
f pl	*ilidān*	*myalldān*	*mawldān*	—	—	—

Infinitives

	mêlad	*myallādu*	*mawlādu*	*metilādu*	*metyallādu*	*mettawlādu*

(5) GEMINATE ROOT, model √*NDD*

Perfect

3 m sing	*nad*	*nadded*	*anned*	*etnded*	*etnaddad*	*ettannad*
3 f sing	*naddat*	*nadddat*	*anndat*	*etnaddat*	*etnadddat*	*ettanndat*
2 sing	*nadt*	*naddedt*	*annedt*	*etndedt*	*etnaddadt*	*ettannadt*
1 c sing	*naddet*	*nadddet*	*anndet*	*etnaddet*	*etnadddet*	*ettanndet*
3 m pl	*nad(un)*	*nadded(un)*	*anned(un)*	*etnded(un)*	*etnaddad(un)*	*ettannad(un)*
3 f pl	*nad(ēn)*	*nadded(ēn)*	*anned(ēn)*	*etnded(ēn)*	*etnaddad(ēn)*	*ettannad(ēn)*
2 m pl	*nadton*	*naddedton*	*annedton*	*etndedton*	*etnaddadton*	*ettannadton*
2 f pl	*nadtēn*	*naddedtēn*	*annedtēn*	*etndedtēn*	*etnaddadtēn*	*ettannadtēn*
1 c pl	*nadn(an)*	*naddedn(an)*	*annedn(an)*	*etndedn(an)*	*etnaddadn(an)*	*ettannadn(an)*

Imperfect

3 m sing	*nennad*	*nnadded*	*nanned*	*netnded*	*netnaddad*	*nettannad*
3 f sing	*tennad*	*tnadded*	*tanned*	*tetnded*	*tetnaddad*	*tettannad*
2 m sing	*tennad*	*tnadded*	*tanned*	*tetnded*	*tetnaddad*	*tettannad*
2 f sing	*tenndin*	*tnadddin*	*tanndin*	*tetnaddin*	*tetnadddin*	*tettanndin*
1 c sing	*ennad*	*enadded*	*anned*	*etnded*	*etnaddad*	*ettannad*
3 m pl	*nenndun*	*nnadddun*	*nanndun*	*netnaddun*	*netnadddun*	*nettanndun*

3 f pl	*nenndān*	*nnadddān*	*nanndān*	*netnaddān*	*netnadddān*	*nettanndān*
2 m pl	*tenndun*	*tnadddun*	*tanndun*	*tetnaddun*	*tetnadddun*	*tettanndun*
2 f pl	*tenndān*	*tnadddān*	*tanndān*	*tetnaddān*	*tetnadddān*	*tettanndān*
1 c pl	*nennad*	*nnadded*	*nanned*	*netnded*	*netnaddad*	*nettannad*

Imperative

sing	*nad*	*nadded*	*anned*	*etnded/etnadd*	*etnaddad*	*ettannad*
m pl	*nad(un)*	*nadded(un)*	*anned(un)*	*etnded(un)* *etnadd(un)*	*etnaddad(un)*	*ettannad(un)*

Active Participle Absolute

m sing	*nā'ed*	*mnadded*	*manned*	*metnded*	*metnaddad*	*mettannad*
f sing	*nāddā*	*mnadddā*	*manndā*	*metnaddā*	*metnadddā*	*mettanndā*
m pl	*nāddin*	*mnadddin*	*manndin*	*metnaddin*	*metnadddin*	*mettanndin*
f pl	*nāddān*	*mnadddān*	*manndān*	*metnaddān*	*metnadddān*	*mettanndān*

Passive Participle Absolute

m sing	*ndid*	*mnaddad*	*mannad*	—	—	—
f sing	*ndidā*	*mnadddā*	*manndā*	—	—	—
m pl	*ndidin*	*mnadddin*	*manndin*	—	—	—
f pl	*ndidān*	*mnadddān*	*manndān*	—	—	—

Infinitives

	mennad	*mnaddādu*	*mannādu*	*metndādu*	*metnaddādu*	*mettannādu*

(6) I-*n* and III-GUTTURAL ROOT, model √*NṬR*

3 m sing	*nṭar*	*naṭṭar*	*aṭṭar*	*etnṭar*	*etnaṭṭar*	*ettaṭṭar*
3 f sing	*neṭrat*	*naṭṭrat*	*aṭṭrat*	*etnaṭrat*	*etnaṭṭrat*	*ettaṭṭrat*
2 sing	*nṭart*	*naṭṭart*	*aṭṭart*	*etnṭart*	*etnaṭṭart*	*ettaṭṭart*
1 c sing	*neṭret*	*naṭṭret*	*aṭṭret*	*etnaṭret*	*etnaṭṭret*	*ettaṭṭret*
3 m pl	*nṭar(un)*	*naṭṭar(un)*	*aṭṭar(un)*	*etnṭar(un)*	*etnaṭṭar(un)*	*ettaṭṭar(un)*
3 f sing	*nṭar(ēn)*	*naṭṭar(ēn)*	*aṭṭar(ēn)*	*etnṭar(ēn)*	*etnaṭṭar(ēn)*	*ettaṭṭar(ēn)*
2 m pl	*nṭarton*	*naṭṭarton*	*aṭṭarton*	*etnṭarton*	*etnaṭṭarton*	*ettaṭṭarton*
2 f pl	*nṭartēn*	*naṭṭartēn*	*aṭṭartēn*	*etnṭartēn*	*etnaṭṭartēn*	*ettaṭṭartēn*
1 c pl	*nṭarn(an)*	*naṭṭarn(an)*	*aṭṭarn(an)*	*etnṭarn(an)*	*etnaṭṭarn(an)*	*ettaṭṭarn(an)*

Imperfect

3 m sing	*neṭṭar*	*nnaṭṭar*	*naṭṭar*	*netnṭar*	*netnaṭṭar*	*nettaṭṭar*
3 f sing	*teṭṭar*	*tnaṭṭar*	*taṭṭar*	*tetnṭar*	*tetnaṭṭar*	*tettaṭṭar*
2 m sing	*teṭṭar*	*tnaṭṭar*	*taṭṭar*	*tetnṭar*	*tetnaṭṭar*	*tettaṭṭar*
2 f sing	*teṭṭrin*	*tnaṭṭrin*	*taṭṭrin*	*tetnaṭrin*	*tetnaṭṭrin*	*tettaṭṭrin*
1 c sing	*eṭṭar*	*enaṭṭar*	*aṭṭar*	*etnṭar*	*etnaṭṭar*	*ettaṭṭar*

3 m pl	*neṭṭrun*	*nnaṭṭrun*	*naṭṭrun*	*netnaṭrun*	*netnaṭṭrun*	*nettaṭṭrun*
3 f pl	*neṭṭrān*	*nnaṭṭrān*	*naṭṭrān*	*netnaṭrān*	*netnaṭṭrān*	*nettaṭṭrān*
2 m pl	*teṭṭrun*	*tnaṭṭrun*	*taṭṭrun*	*tetnaṭrun*	*tetnaṭṭrun*	*tettaṭṭrun*
2 f pl	*teṭṭrān*	*tnaṭṭrān*	*taṭṭrān*	*tetnaṭrān*	*tetnaṭṭrān*	*tettaṭṭrān*
1 c pl	*neṭṭar*	*nnaṭṭar*	*naṭṭar*	*netnṭar*	*netnaṭṭar*	*nettaṭṭar*

Imperative

sing	*ṭar*	*naṭṭar*	*aṭṭar*	*etnṭar*	*etnaṭṭar*	*ettaṭṭar*

Active Participle Absolute

m sing	*nāṭar*	*mnaṭṭar*	*maṭṭar*	*metnṭar*	*metnaṭṭar*	*mettaṭṭar*
f sing	*nāṭrā*	*mnaṭṭrā*	*maṭṭrā*	*metnaṭrā*	*metnaṭṭrā*	*mettaṭṭrā*
m pl	*nāṭrin*	*mnaṭṭrin*	*maṭṭrin*	*metnaṭrin*	*metnaṭṭrin*	*mettaṭṭrin*
f pl	*nāṭrān*	*mnaṭṭrān*	*maṭṭrān*	*metnaṭrān*	*metnaṭṭrān*	*mettaṭṭrān*

Passive Participle Absolute

m sing	*nṭir*	*mnaṭṭar*	*maṭṭar*	—	—	—
f sing	*nṭirā*	*mnaṭṭrā*	*maṭṭrā*	—	—	—
m pl	*nṭirin*	*mnaṭṭrin*	*maṭṭrin*	—	—	—
f pl	*nṭirān*	*mnaṭṭrān*	*maṭṭrān*	—	—	—

Infinitives

meṭṭar	*mnaṭṭāru*	*maṭṭāru*	*metnṭāru*	*metnaṭṭāru*	*mettaṭṭāru*

Appendix B

STATES OF SUBSTANTIVES

	ORDINARY SUBSTANTIVES	ENDING IN *-ū(tā)*	ENDING IN *-ān(ā)/-āni(tā)*	ACT. PART. III-WEAK (G)	PASS. PART. III-WEAK (G)
ABSOLUTE					
masc. sing.	*mlek*	—	*mallpān*	*bānē*	*dkē*
fem. sing.	*malkā*	*malku*	*mallpāni*	*bānyā*	*dakyā*
masc. pl.	*malkin*	—	*mallpānin*	*bāneyn*	*dkeyn*
fem. pl.	*malkān*	*malkwān*	*mallpānyān*	*bānyān*	*dakyān*
EMPHATIC					
masc. sing.	*malkā*	—	*mallpānā*	*bānyā*	*dakyā*
fem. sing.	*malktā*	*malkutā*	*mallpānitā*	*bānitā*	*dkitā*
masc. pl.	*malkē*	—	*mallpānē*	*bānayyā*	*dkayyā*
fem. pl.	*malkātā*	*malkwātā*	*mallpānyātā*	*bānyātā*	*dakyātā*

CONSTRUCT

masc. sing.	*mlek-*	—	*mallpān-*	*bānē-*	*dkē-*
fem. sing.	*malkat-*	*malkut-*	*mallpānit-*	*bānit-*	*dkit-*
masc. pl.	*malkay-*	—	*mallpānay-*	*bānay-*	*dkay-*
fem. pl.	*malkāt-*	*malkwāt-*	*mallpānyāt-*	*bānyāt-*	*dakyāt-*

Appendix C

Verbs with Enclitic Objects

BASE	+ HIM	+ HER	+ YOU (M)	+ YOU (F)	+ ME/US[1]	+ YOU (M PL)
Perfect						
PEAL, SOUND ROOT						
rḏap̱	*raḏp̱eh*	*raḏp̱āh*	*raḏp̱āḵ*	*raḏp̱eḵ*	*raḏp̱an*	*rḏap̱ḵon*
reḏpaṯ	*rḏap̱teh*	*rḏap̱tāh*	*rḏap̱tāḵ*	*rḏap̱teḵ*	*rḏap̱tan*	*reḏpaṯḵon*
rḏap̱t	*rḏap̱tāy*	*rḏap̱tāh*	—	—	*rḏap̱tān*	—
rḏap̱t(y)	*rḏap̱tiw*	*rḏap̱tih*	—	—	*rḏap̱tin*	—
reḏpeṯ	*rḏap̱teh*	*rḏap̱tāh*	*rḏap̱tāḵ*	*rḏap̱teḵ*	*rḏap̱tan*	*reḏpeṯḵon*
rḏap̱(w)	*raḏp̱u*	*raḏp̱uh*	*raḏp̱uḵ*	*raḏp̱uḵ*	*raḏp̱un*	*raḏp̱uḵon*
rḏap̱(y)	*raḏp̱āy*	*raḏp̱āh*	*raḏp̱āḵ*	*raḏp̱eḵ*	*raḏp̱ān*	*rḏap̱ḵon*
rḏap̱ton[2]	*rḏap̱tonāy*	*rḏap̱tonāh*	—	—	*rḏap̱tonān*	—
rḏap̱n	*rḏap̱nāy*	*rḏap̱nāh*	*rḏap̱nāḵ*	*rḏap̱nāḵ*	—	*rḏap̱nāḵon*

[1]The first-person plural enclitic object is pronounced everywhere like the first-person singular; it is spelled ܢ instead of ܢܝ.

[2]Enclitic objects added to feminine plural forms ending in *-tēn* are exactly like those added to forms in *-ton.*

PEAL, III-WEAK ROOT

ḥzā	*ḥzāy*	*ḥzāh*	*ḥzāḵ*	*ḥzāḵ*	*ḥzān*	*ḥzāḵon*
ḥzāṯ	*ḥzāṯeh*	*ḥzāṯāh*	*ḥzāṯāḵ*	*ḥzāṯeḵ*	*ḥzāṯan*	*ḥzāṯḵon*
ḥzayt	*ḥzaytāy*	*ḥzaytāh*	—	—	*ḥzaytān*	—
ḥzayt(y)	*ḥzaytiw*	*ḥzaytih*	—	—	*ḥzaytin*	—
ḥzêṯ	*ḥzêṯeh*	*ḥzêṯāh*	*ḥzêṯāḵ*	*ḥzêṯeḵ*	—	*ḥzêṯḵon*
ḥzaw	*ḥza'u*	*ḥza'uh*	*ḥza'uḵ*	*ḥza'uḵ*	*ḥza'un*	*ḥza'uḵon*
ḥzay	*ḥzayāy*	*ḥzayāh*	*ḥzayāḵ*	*ḥzayeḵ*	*ḥzayān*	*ḥzayāḵon*
ḥzayton	*ḥzaytonāy*	*ḥzaytonāh*	—	—	*ḥzaytonān*	—
ḥzayn	*ḥzaynāy*	*ḥzaynāh*	*ḥzaynāḵ*	*ḥzaynāḵ*	—	*ḥzaynāḵon*

PAEL, SOUND ROOT

qabbel	*qabbleh*	*qabblāh*	*qabblāḵ*	*qabbleḵ*	*qabblan*	*qabbelḵon*
qabblaṯ	*qabblāṯeh*	*qabblāṯāh*	*qabblāṯāḵ*	*qabblāṯeḵ*	*qabblāṯan*	*qabblaṯḵon*
qabbelt	*qabbeltāy*	*qabbeltāh*	—	—	*qabbeltān*	—
qabbleṯ	*qabbelṯeh*	*qabbelṯāh*	*qabbelṯāḵ*	*qabbelṯeḵ*	—	*qabbleṯḵon*
qabbel(w)	*qabblu*	*qabbluh*	*qabbluḵ*	*qabbluḵ*	*qabblun*	*qabbluḵon*
qabbel(y)	*qabblāy*	*qabblāh*	*qabblāḵ*	*qabbleḵ*	*qabblān*	*qabbelḵon*
qabbelton	*qabbeltonāy*	*qabbeltonāh*	—	—	*qabbeltonān*	—
qabbeln	*qabbelnāy*	*qabbelnāh*	*qabbelnāḵ*	*qabbelnāḵ*	—	*qabbelnāḵon*

BASE	+ HIM	+ HER	+ YOU (M)	+ YOU (F)	+ ME/US	+ YOU (M PL)
PAEL, III-WEAK ROOT						
dakki	*dakkyeh*	*dakkyāh*	*dakkyāḵ*	*dakkyeḵ*	*dakkyan*	*dakkiḵon*
dakkyaṯ	*dakkyāṯeh*	*dakkyāṯāh*	*dakkyāṯāḵ*	*dakkyāṯeḵ*	*dakkyāṯan*	*dakkyatḵon*
dakkiyt	*dakkiytāy*	*dakkiytāh*	—	—	*dakkiytān*	—
dakkiṯ	*dakkiṯeh*	*dakkiṯāh*	*dakkiṯāḵ*	*dakkiṯeḵ*	—	*dakkitḵon*
dakki(w)	*dakkyu*	*dakkyuh*	*dakkyuḵ*	*dakkyuḵ*	*dakkyun*	*dakkyuḵon*
dakki (f pl)	*dakkyāy*	*dakkyāh*	*dakkyāḵ*	*dakkyāḵ*	*dakkyān*	*dakkiḵon*
APHEL, SOUND ROOT						
aḏreḵ	*aḏrḵeh*	*aḏrḵāh*	*aḏrḵāḵ*	*aḏrḵeḵ*	*aḏrḵan*	*aḏreḵḵon*
aḏrḵat	*aḏrḵāṯeh*	*aḏrḵāṯāh*	*aḏrḵāṯāḵ*	*aḏrḵāṯeḵ*	*aḏrḵāṯan*	*aḏrḵatḵon*
aḏreḵt	*aḏreḵtāy*	*aḏreḵtāh*	—	—	*aḏreḵtān*	—
aḏrḵeṯ	*aḏreḵteh*	*aḏreḵtāh*	*aḏreḵtāḵ*	*aḏreḵteḵ*	—	*aḏrḵetḵon*
aḏreḵ(w)	*aḏrḵu*	*aḏrḵuh*	*aḏrḵuḵ*	*aḏrḵuḵ*	*aḏrḵun*	*aḏrḵuḵon*
aḏreḵ(y)	*aḏrḵāy*	*aḏrḵāh*	*aḏrḵāḵ*	*aḏrḵeḵ*	*aḏrḵān*	*aḏreḵḵon*
APHEL, III-WEAK ROOT						
ayti	*aytyeh*	*aytyāh*	*aytyāḵ*	*aytyeḵ*	*aytyan*	*aytiḵon*
aytyaṯ	*aytyāṯeh*	*aytyāṯāh*	*aytyāṯāḵ*	*aytyāṯeḵ*	*aytyāṯan*	*aytyatḵon*
aytiyt	*aytiytāy*	*aytiytāh*	—	—	*aytiytan*	—
aytiṯ	*aytiṯeh*	*aytiṯāh*	*aytiṯāḵ*	*aytiṯeḵ*	—	*aytitḵon*

Imperfect

PEAL, SOUND ROOT

nerdop̱	*nerdp̱iw*	*nerdp̱ih*	*nerdp̱āḵ*	*nerdp̱eḵ*	*nerdp̱an*	*nerdop̱ḵon*
terdop̱	*terdp̱iw*	*terdp̱ih*	*terdp̱āḵ*	*terdp̱eḵ*	*terdp̱an*	*terdop̱ḵon*
terdp̱in	*terdp̱ināy*	*terdp̱ināh*	—	—	*terdp̱inān*	—
erdop̱	*erdp̱iw*	*erdp̱ih*	*erdp̱āḵ*	*erdp̱eḵ*	*erdp̱an*	*erdop̱ḵon*
nerdp̱un	*nerdp̱unāy*	*nerdp̱unāh*	*nerdp̱unāḵ*	*nerdp̱uneḵ*	*nerdp̱unān*	*nerdp̱unāḵon*
nerdp̱ān	*nerdp̱ānāy*	*nerdp̱ānāh*	*nerdp̱ānāḵ*	*nerdp̱āneḵ*	*nerdp̱ānān*	*nerdp̱ānāḵon*
terdp̱un	*terdp̱unāy*	*terdp̱unāh*	—	—	*terdp̱unān*	—
terdp̱ān	*terdp̱ānāy*	*terdp̱ānāh*	—	—	*terdp̱ānān*	—
nerdop̱	*nerdp̱iw*	*nerdp̱ih*	*nerdp̱āḵ*	*nerdp̱eḵ*	—	*nerdop̱ḵon*

PEAL, III-WEAK ROOT

neḥzē	*neḥzēw*	*neḥzēh*	*neḥzēḵ*	*neḥzēḵ*	*neḥzēn*	*neḥzēḵon*
neḥzōn	*neḥzōnāy*	*neḥzōnāh*	*neḥzōnāḵ*	*neḥzōneḵ*	*neḥzōnān*	*neḥzōnāḵon*

PAEL, SOUND ROOT

nqabbel	*nqabbliw*	*nqabblih*	*nqabblāḵ*	*nqabbleḵ*	*nqabblan*	*nqabbelḵon*
tqabblin	*tqabblināy*	*tqabblināh*	—	—	*tqabblinān*	—

PAEL, III-WEAK ROOT

nḏakkē	*nḏakkēw*	*nḏakkēh*	*nḏakkēḵ*	*nḏakkēḵ*	*nḏakkēn*	*nḏakkēḵon*
nḏakkōn	*nḏakkōnāy*	*nḏakkōnāh*	*nḏakkōnāḵ*	*nḏakkōneḵ*	*nḏakkōnān*	*nḏakkōnāḵon*

BASE	+ HIM	+ HER	+ YOU (M)	+ YOU (F)	+ ME/US	+ YOU (M PL)
APHEL, SOUND ROOT						
naḏreḵ	*naḏrḵiw*	*naḏrḵih*	*naḏrḵāḵ*	*naḏrḵeḵ*	*naḏrḵan*	*naḏreḵḵon*
naḏrḵun	*naḏrḵunāy*	*naḏrḵunāh*	*naḏrḵunāḵ*	*naḏrḵuneḵ*	*naḏrḵunān*	*naḏrḵunāḵon*
APHEL, III-WEAK ROOT						
naytē	*naytēw*	*naytēh*	*naytēḵ*	*naytēḵ*	*naytēn*	*naytēḵon*
naytōn	*naytōnāy*	*naytōnāh*	*naytōnāḵ*	*naytōneḵ*	*naytōnān*	*naytōnāḵon*
Imperative						
PEAL, SOUND ROOT						
rḏop̱	*rḏop̱āy*	*rḏop̱ēh*	—	—	*rḏop̱ayn*	—
rḏop̱(y)	*rḏop̱iw*	*rḏop̱ih*	—	—	*rḏop̱in*	—
rḏop̱(un)	*ruḏp̱u*	*ruḏp̱uh*	—	—	*ruḏp̱un*	—
	ruḏp̱unāy	*ruḏp̱unāh*	—	—	*ruḏp̱unān*	—
rḏop̱(ēn)	*ruḏp̱āy*	*rḏop̱āh*	—	—	*rḏop̱ān*	—
	ruḏp̱ēnāy	*ruḏp̱ēnāh*	—	—	*rḏop̱ēnān*	—
PEAL, III-WEAK ROOT						
qri	*qriw*	*qrih*	—	—	*qrin*	—
qrāy	*qrā'iw*	*qrā'ih*	—	—	*qrā'in*	—
qraw	*qra'u*	*qra'uh*	—	—	*qra'un*	—
qrāyēn	*qrāyenāy*	*qrāyenāh*	—	—	*qrāyenān*	—

PAEL, III-WEAK ROOT						
dakkā	*dakkāy*	*dakkāh*	—	—	*dakkān*	—
dakkāy	*dakkāyiw*	*dakkāyih*	—	—	*dakkāyin*	—
dakkaw	*dakka'u*	*dakka'uh*	—	—	*dakka'un*	—
dakkāyēn	*dakkāyenāy*	*dakkāyenāh*	—	—	*dakkāyenān*	—
APHEL, SOUND ROOT						
aḏreḵ	*aḏrḵāy*	*aḏrḵēh*	—	—	*aḏrḵayn*	—
aḏreḵ(y)	*aḏrḵiw*	*aḏrḵih*	—	—	*aḏrḵin*	—
aḏreḵ(w)	*aḏrḵu*	*aḏrḵuh*	—	—	*aḏrḵun*	—
aḏreḵ (f pl)	*aḏrḵāy*	*aḏrḵāh*	—	—	*aḏrḵān*	—
APHEL, III-WEAK ROOT						
aytā	*aytāy*	*aytāh*	—	—	*aytān*	—
aytāy	*aytāyiw*	*aytāyih*	—	—	*aytāyin*	—
aytaw	*ayta'u*	*ayta'uh*	—	—	*ayta'un*	—
aytāyēn	*aytāyenāy*	*aytāyenāh*	—	—	*aytāyenān*	—

For further reference:

Brockelmann, Carl. *Syrische Grammatik.* Leipzig: Veb Verlag Enzyklopädie, 1968. Also contains extensive bibliography of Syriac literature.

Duval, Rubens. *Traité de grammaire syriaque.* Paris: F. Vieweg, 1881.

Muraoka, Takamitsu. *Classical Syriac for Hebraists.* Wiesbaden: Otto Harrassowitz, 1987.

Nöldeke, Theodor. *Kurzgefasste syrische Grammatik.* Leipzig: Chr. Herm. Tauchnitz, 1898. Translated by J. A. Crichton as *Compendious Syriac Grammar.* London: Williams & Norgate, 1904.

Dictionaries:

Brockelmann, Carl. *Lexicon syriacum.* Berlin: Reuther & Reichard & Edinburgh: T. & T. Clark, 1895 (Syriac–Latin).

Costaz, L. *Dictionnaire syriaque–française: Syriac–English Dictionary: Qāmūs suryānī–ᶜarabī.* Beirut: Imprimerie Catholique, 1963.

Ibn al-Bahlūl, Abū'l-Ḥasan. *Lexicon syriacum.* Edited by Rubens Duval. 3 vols. Paris, 1902. Reprint: Amsterdam: Philo Press, 1970 (Syriac–Syriac with Arabic glosses).

Margoliouth, J. Payne Smith. *A Compendious Syriac Dictionary.* Oxford, 1903. Reprint, Oxford: Clarendon Press, 1976 (Syriac–English).

__________. *Supplement to the Thesaurus Syriacus.* Oxford: Clarendon Press, 1927.

Qardāḥī, Jibrā'īl, al-. *al-Lobab; seu, Dictionarium Syro-Arabicum.* 2 vols. Beirut, 1887–91 (Syriac–Arabic). Reprint, Aleppo: Dar Mardin, 1994.

Smith, R. Payne, ed. *Thesaurus Syriacus.* Oxford: Clarendon Press, 1879–1901.

Concordances:

Concordance to the Peshitta Version of the Aramaic New Testament. New Knoxville, Ohio: American Christian Press, 1985.

Strothmann, Werner. *Konkordanz zur syrischen Bibel der Pentateuch.* 4 vols. Wiesbaden: Otto Harrassowitz, 1986

Readings

From the *Pšiṭtā*

ܡܢ ܦܫܝܛܬܐ

ܟܪܘܙܘܬܐ ܕܡܬܝ. ܝܐ: ܟܚ - ܠ

ܬܘ ܠܘܬܝ ܟܠܟܘܢ ܠܐܝ̈ܢܐ ܘܫܩܝ̈ܠܝ ܡܘܒ̈ܠܐ. ܘܐܢܐ ܐܢܝܚܟܘܢ.
ܫܩܘܠܘ ܢܝܪܝ ܥܠܝܟܘܢ. ܘܝܠܦܘ ܡܢܝ. ܕܢܝܚ ܐܢܐ ܘܡܟܝܟ ܐܢܐ
ܒܠܒܝ. ܘܡܫܟܚܝܢ ܐܢܬܘܢ ܢܝܚܐ ܠܢܦ̈ܫܬܟܘܢ. ܢܝܪܝ ܓܝܪ ܒܣܝܡ
ܗ̄ܘ. ܘܡܘܒܠܝ ܩܠܝܠ ܗ̄ܘ ※

ܟܪܘܙܘܬܐ ܕܡܬܝ. ܙ: ܟܕ - ܟܙ

ܟܠ ܡܢ ܗܟܝܠ ܕܫܡܥ ܡ̈ܠܝ ܗܠܝܢ ܘܥܒܕ ܠܗܝܢ. ܢܬܕܡܐ ܠܓܒܪܐ
ܚܟܝܡܐ ܗܘ ܕܒܢܐ ܒܝܬܗ ܥܠ ܫܘܥܐ. ܘܢܚܬ ܡܛܪܐ. ܘܐܬܘ
ܢܗܪ̈ܘܬܐ. ܘܢܫܒ ܪ̈ܘܚܐ. ܘܐܬܛܪܝܘ ܒܗ ܒܒܝܬܐ ܗܘ. ܘܠܐ
ܢܦܠ. ܫܬܐܣܘ̈ܗܝ ܓܝܪ ܥܠ ܫܘܥܐ ܣܝܡܢ ܗ̈ܘܝ. ܘܟܠ ܡܢ
ܕܫܡܥ ܡ̈ܠܝ ܗܠܝܢ ܘܠܐ ܥܒܕ ܠܗܝܢ. ܢܬܕܡܐ ܠܓܒܪܐ ܣܟܠܐ
ܕܒܢܐ ܒܝܬܗ ܥܠ ܚܠܐ. ܘܢܚܬ ܡܛܪܐ. ܘܐܬܘ ܢܗܪ̈ܘܬܐ.
ܘܢܫܒ ܪ̈ܘܚܐ. ܘܐܬܛܪܝܘ ܒܒܝܬܐ ܗܘ. ܘܢܦܠ. ܘܗܘܬ
ܡܦܘܠܬܗ ܪܒܐ ※

ܟܪܘܙܘܬܐ ܕܡܬܝ. ܟ: ܐ - ܝܘ

ܕܡܝܐ ܓܝܪ ܡܠܟܘܬܐ ܕܫܡܝܐ ܠܓܒܪܐ ܡܪܐ ܒܝܬܐ ܕܢܦܩ ܒܨܦܪܐ. ܕܢܐܓܘܪ ܦ̈ܥܠܐ ܠܟܪܡܗ. ܦܣܩ ܕܝܢ ܥܡ ܦ̈ܥܠܐ ܡܢ ܕܝܢܪܐ ܒܝܘܡܐ. ܘܫܕܪ ܐܢܘܢ ܠܟܪܡܗ. ܘܢܦܩ ܒܬܠܬ ܫ̈ܥܝܢ. ܘܚܙܐ ܐܚܪ̈ܢܐ ܕܩܝܡܝܢ ܒܫܘܩܐ ܘܒܛܝܠܝܢ. ܘܐܡܪ ܠܗܘܢ: ܙܠܘ ܐܦ ܐܢܬܘܢ ܠܟܪܡܐ. ܘܡܕܡ ܕܘܠܐ ܝܗܒ ܐܢܐ ܠܟܘܢ. ܗܢܘܢ ܕܝܢ ܐܙܠܘ. ܘܢܦܩ ܬܘܒ ܒܫܬ ܘܒܬܫܥ ܫ̈ܥܝܢ. ܘܥܒܕ ܗܟܘܬ. ܘܠܐܦ ܚܕܥܣܪ̈ܐ ܫ̈ܥܝܢ. ܢܦܩ ܘܐܫܟܚ ܐܚܪ̈ܢܐ ܕܩܝܡܝܢ ܘܒܛܝܠܝܢ. ܘܐܡܪ ܠܗܘܢ: ܡܢܐ ܩܝܡܝܢ ܐܢܬܘܢ ܝܘܡܐ ܟܠܗ ܘܒܛܝܠܝܢ. ܐܡܪܝܢ ܠܗ: ܕܠܐ ܐ̱ܢܫ ܐܓܪܢ. ܐܡܪ ܠܗܘܢ. ܙܠܘ ܐܦ ܐܢܬܘܢ ܠܟܪܡܐ. ܘܡܕܡ ܕܘܠܐ ܢܣܒܝܢ ܐܢܬܘܢ. ܟܕ ܗܘܐ ܕܝܢ ܪܡܫܐ. ܐܡܪ ܡܪܐ ܟܪܡܐ ܠܪܒ ܒܝܬܗ: ܩܪܝ ܦ̈ܥܠܐ ܘܗܒ ܠܗܘܢ ܐܓܪܗܘܢ. ܘܫܪܝ ܡܢ ܐܚܪ̈ܝܐ ܘܥܕܡܐ ܠܩܕ̈ܡܝܐ. ܘܐܬܘ ܗܢܘܢ ܕܚܕܥܣܪ̈ܐ ܫ̈ܥܝܢ. ܢܣܒܘ ܕܝܢܪ ܕܝܢܪ. ܘܟܕ ܫܩܠܘ. ܪܛܢܘ ܥܠ ܡܪܐ ܒܝܬܐ. ܘܐܡܪܝܢ: ܗܠܝܢ ܐܚܪ̈ܝܐ ܚܕܐ ܫܥܐ ܥܒܕܘ. ܘܐܫܘܝܬ ܐܢܘܢ ܥܡܢ ܕܫܩܠܢ ܝܘܩܪܗ ܕܝܘܡܐ ܘܚܘܡܗ. ܗܘ ܕܝܢ ܥܢܐ ܘܐܡܪ ܠܚܕ ܡܢܗܘܢ: ܚܒܪܝ ܠܐ ܡܥܘܠ ܐ̱ܢܐ ܒܟ. ܠܐ ܗ̄ܘܐ ܒܕܝܢܪܐ ܦܣܩܬ ܥܡܝ. ܫܩܘܠ ܕܝܠܟ ܘܙܠ. ܨܒܐ ܐ̱ܢܐ ܕܝܢ ܕܠܗܢܐ ܐܚܪܝܐ ܐܬܠ ܐܝܟ ܕܠܟ. ܐܘ ܠܐ ܫܠܝܛ ܠܝ ܡܕܡ ܕܨܒܐ ܐ̱ܢܐ ܐܥܒܕ ܒܕܝܠܝ. ܐܘ ܥܝܢܟ ܒܝܫܐ ܕܐܢܐ ܛܒ ܐ̱ܢܐ. ܗܟܢܐ ܢܗܘܘܢ ܐܚܪ̈ܝܐ ܩܕ̈ܡܝܐ. ܘܩܕ̈ܡܝܐ ܐܚܪ̈ܝܐ. ܣܓܝܐܝܢ ܐܢܘܢ ܓܝܪ ܩܪ̈ܝܐ ܘܙܥܘܪܝܢ ܓܒ̈ܝܐ ※

ܡܢ ܟܪܘܙܘܬܐ ܕܠܘܩܐ ܒ: ܐ - ܟ

(ܐ) ܗܘܐ ܕܝܢ ܒܝܘ̈ܡܬܐ ܗܢܘܢ ܘܢܦܩ ܦܘܩܕܢܐ ܡܢ ܐܓܘܣܛܘܣ ܩܣܪ. ܕܢܬܟܬܒ ܟܠܗ ܥܡܐ ܕܐܘܚܕܢܗ. (ܒ) ܗܕܐ ܡܟܬܒܢܘܬܐ ܩܕܡܝܬܐ ܗܘܬ ܒܗܓܡܘܢܘܬܐ ܕܩܘܪܝܢܘܣ

ܒܣܘܪܝܐ. (ܓ) ܘܐܙܠ ܗܘܐ ܟܠܢܫ ܕܢܬܟܬܒ ܒܡܕܝܢܬܗ. (ܕ) ܣܠܩ ܗܘܐ ܕܝܢ ܐܦ ܝܘܣܦ ܡܢ ܢܨܪܬ ܡܕܝܢܬܐ ܕܓܠܝܠܐ ܠܝܗܘܕ. ܠܡܕܝܢܬܗ ܕܕܘܝܕ ܕܡܬܩܪܝܐ ܒܝܬܠܚܡ. ܡܛܠ ܕܐܝܬܘܗܝ ܗܘܐ ܡܢ ܒܝܬܗ ܘܡܢ ܫܪܒܬܗ ܕܕܘܝܕ. (ܗ) ܥܡ ܡܪܝܡ ܡܟܝܪܬܗ ܟܕ ܒܛܢܐ ܕܬܬܟܬܒ ܬܡܢ. (ܘ) ܘܗܘܐ ܕܟܕ ܬܡܢ ܐܢܘܢ. ܐܬܡܠܝܘ ܝܘ̈ܡܝܗ ܕܬܐܠܕ. (ܙ) ܘܝܠܕܬ ܒܪܗ ܒܘܟܪܐ. ܘܟܪܟܬܗ ܒܥܙܪ̈ܘܪܐ. ܘܐܪܡܝܬܗ ܒܐܘܪܝܐ. ܡܛܠ ܕܠܝܬ ܗܘܐ ܠܗܘܢ ܕܘܟܬܐ ܐܝܟܐ ܕܫܪܝܢ ܗܘܘ. (ܚ) ܪ̈ܥܘܬܐ ܕܝܢ ܐܝܬ ܗܘܘ ܒܗ ܒܐܬܪܐ ܕܫܪܝܢ ܗܘܘ ܬܡܢ. ܘܢܛܪܝܢ ܡܛܪ̈ܬܐ ܕܠܠܝܐ ܥܠ ܡܪ̈ܥܝܬܗܘܢ. (ܛ) ܘܗܐ ܡܠܐܟܐ ܕܐܠܗܐ ܐܬܐ ܠܘܬܗܘܢ. ܘܬܫܒܘܚܬܗ ܕܡܪܝܐ ܐܙܠܓܬ ܥܠܝܗܘܢ. ܘܕܚܠܘ ܕܚܠܬܐ ܪܒܬܐ. (ܝ) ܘܐܡܪ ܠܗܘܢ ܡܠܐܟܐ: ܠܐ ܬܕܚܠܘܢ. ܗܐ ܓܝܪ ܡܣܒܪ ܐܢܐ ܠܟܘܢ ܚܕܘܬܐ ܪܒܬܐ ܕܬܗܘܐ ܠܟܠܗ ܥܠܡܐ. (ܝܐ) ܐܬܝܠܕ ܠܟܘܢ ܓܝܪ ܝܘܡܢܐ ܦܪܘܩܐ. ܕܐܝܬܘܗܝ ܡܪܝܐ ܡܫܝܚܐ. ܒܡܕܝܢܬܗ ܕܕܘܝܕ. (ܝܒ) ܘܗܕܐ ܠܟܘܢ ܐܬܐ: ܡܫܟܚܝܢ ܐܢܬܘܢ ܥܘܠܐ ܕܟܪܝܟ ܒܥܙܪ̈ܘܪܐ ܘܣܝܡ ܒܐܘܪܝܐ. (ܝܓ) ܘܡܢ ܫܠܝ ܐܬܚܙܝܘ ܥܡ ܡܠܐܟܐ ܚܝ̈ܠܘܬܐ ܣܓܝ̈ܐܐ ܕܫܡܝܐ ܟܕ ܡܫܒܚܝܢ ܠܐܠܗܐ ܘܐܡܪܝܢ: (ܝܕ) ܬܫܒܘܚܬܐ ܠܐܠܗܐ ܒܡܪ̈ܘܡܐ. ܘܥܠ ܐܪܥܐ ܫܠܡܐ. ܘܣܒܪܐ ܛܒܐ ܠܒܢܝ̈ܢܫܐ. (ܝܗ) ܘܗܘܐ ܕܟܕ ܐܙܠܘ ܡܢ ܠܘܬܗܘܢ ܡܠܐ̈ܟܐ ܠܫܡܝܐ. ܡܠܠܘ ܪ̈ܥܘܬܐ ܚܕ ܥܡ ܚܕ ܘܐܡܪܝܢ: ܢܪܕܐ ܥܕܡܐ ܠܒܝܬܠܚܡ. ܘܢܚܙܐ ܠܡܠܬܐ ܗܕܐ ܕܗܘܬ. ܐܝܟ ܕܡܪܝܐ ܐܘܕܥܢ. (ܝܘ) ܘܐܬܘ ܡܣܪܗܒܐܝܬ. ܘܐܫܟܚܘ ܠܡܪܝܡ ܘܠܝܘܣܦ. ܘܠܥܘܠܐ ܕܣܝܡ ܒܐܘܪܝܐ. (ܝܙ) ܘܟܕ ܚܙܘ. ܐܘܕܥܘ ܠܡܠܬܐ ܕܐܬܡܠܠܬ ܥܡܗܘܢ ܥܠܘܗܝ ܛܠܝܐ. (ܝܚ) ܘܟܠܗܘܢ ܕܫܡܥܘ. ܐܬܕܡܪܘ ܥܠ ܐܝܠܝܢ ܕܐܬܡܠܠ ܠܗܘܢ ܡܢ ܪ̈ܥܘܬܐ. (ܝܛ) ܡܪܝܡ ܕܝܢ ܢܛܪܐ ܗܘܬ ܟܠܗܝܢ ܡ̈ܠܐ ܗܠܝܢ. ܘܡܦܚܡܐ ܒܠܒܗ̇. (ܟ) ܘܗܦܟܘ ܪ̈ܥܘܬܐ ܟܕ ܡܫܒܚܝܢ ܘܡܗܠܠܝܢ

ܠܐܠܗܐ ܟܠ ܟܠ ܕܣܘܦ ܘܡܫܡܠܘ ܐܒܪܐ ܕܐܬܡܠܠ ܒܫܡܗ ※

From Pseudo-Callisthenes' Legend of Alexander[1]

ܡܢ ܬܫܥܝܬܐ ܕܐܠܟܣܢܕܪܘܣ ܒܪ ܦܝܠܝܦܘܣ

ܗܕܝܢ ܐܠܟܣܢܕܪܘܣ ܡܢ ܬܡܢ ܐܫܩܠ ܘܠܡܩܕܘܢܝܐ ܐܙܠ. ܘܐܬܐ ܠܬܚܘܡܐ ܕܦܪܣ. ܘܓܫܪܐ ܥܠ ܢܗܪܐ ܕܕܩܠܬ. ܘܐܠܟܣܢܕܪܘܣ ܒܐܣܛܪܛܝܘܛܐ ܠܘܬ ܕܪܝܘܫ ܐܙܠ. ܒܕܡܟܐ ܕܐܙܠ ܠܒܒܠ. ܘܐܬܐ ܦܪ̈ܣܝܐ ܘܐܘܕܥܘ ܠܕܪܝܘܫ ܡܠܟܐ. ܘܟܕ ܐܡܪܘ: ܘܕܪܝܘܫ ܟܕ ܠܐܠܟܣܢܕܪܘܣ ܚܙܐ. ܐܬܕܡܪ ܘܠܐܠܟܣܢܕܪܘܣ ܣܓܝ. ܡܛܠ ܕܣܒܪ ܗ̄ܘܐ ܕܡܝܬܪ ܐܠܗܐ ܐܝܬܘܗ̄ܝ. ܕܐܬܬܚܬ. ܘܠܒܘܕܪܝܐ ܕܦܪ̈ܣܝܐ ܐܝܬܐ. ܡܛܠ ܕܐܣܟܡܗ ܠܐܣܟܡܐ ܕܐܠܗ̈ܐ ܡܣܟܡܗ ܗ̄ܘܐ. ܡܛܠ ܕܟܠܝܠܐ ܕܪܫܗ ܐܣܝܪ ܗ̄ܘܐ ܠܘܠܟܐ ܡܣܟܡܗ. ܘܠܒܘܫܐ ܕܠܒܝܫ ܗܘܐ ܒܕܡܘܬܐ ܡܫܚܐ ܙܗܝܪ ܗ̄ܘܐ. ܘܒ̈ܝܙܢܐ ܕܕܒܪܢܘܬܗ̄ ܒܣܐܡܐ ܠܟܠ ܒܒܝܢ ܗ̄ܘܘ. ܘܡܣܡ̈ܣܡܝܗ̄ ܕܕܗܒܐ. ܘܣܡܝܪܗ ܡܢ ܡܪ̈ܓܢܝܬܐ ܘܡܪ̈ܓܢܝܬܐ ܒܒܝܢ ܗ̄ܘܐ. ܘܕܪܘܫ ܡܩܐܡ ܗ̄ܘܐ ܘܒܐܣܡܣܡܗ ܡܬܒܡܐ ܗ̄ܘܐ. ܘܒܡܣܪܐ ܐܠܦ̈ܝ ܦܪ̈ܫܐ ܢܛ̈ܪܝ. ܣܝܡܗ ܠܬܘܬܗ ܡܢܟܝܢ ܗ̄ܘܘ. ܕܢܛܘܪܐ ܕܠܒܗ ܒܒܝܢ ܗ̄ܘܘ. ܗܕܝܢ ܠܐܠܟܣܢܕܪܘܣ ܫܐܠ ܗ̄ܘܐ. ܕܐܝܬ ܡܢ ܐܢܬ. ܘܐܠܟܣܢܕܪܘܣ ܐܡܪ. ܐܝܙܓܕܐ ܐܢܐ ܕܐܠܟܣܢܕܪܘܣ. ܕܡܢ ܐܠܟܣܢܕܪܘܣ ܫܠܝܚܘܬܐ ܐܝܬܝܬ ܠܟ. ܘܡܗܝܡܢܐ ܐܡܪ: ܕܐܫܬܘܕܥܬ ܠܗ ܡܠܟܐ ܠܡܠܟܐ. ܘܡܩܕܘܢܝܐ ܐܡܪܝܢ: ܕܡܛܠ ܕܠܒܗ ܕܕܪܝܘܫ ܫܦܠ ܒܡܠܟܐ. ܥܠ ܗܕܐ ܡܛܝ ܠܡܠܟܐ ܠܡܐܬܐ. ܗܫܐ ܗܒܠ ܐܢܬ ܠܐ ܬܗܘܐ. ܐܠܐ ܥܠܘܗܝ ܠ ܕܐܡܪܬ. ܗܢܐ ܐܢܬ

[1] *The History of Alexander the Great, Being the Syriac Version of Pseudo-callisthenes,* ed. E. A. W. Budge (Cambridge, 1889; reprint: Amsterdam: APA-Philo Press, 1976).

ܠܬܬܘܥܐ ܠܡܐܬܐ. ܗܝܕܝܢ ܕܪܝܘܫ ܐܡܪ ܠܗ. ܕܠܡܢܐ ܐܢܬ ܣܘܡܟܟ ܐܠܟܣܢܕܪܘܣ ܐܢܬ ܘܠܐ ܗܘܝܬ ܐܝܙܓܕܐ. ܡܛܠ ܕܡ̈ܠܐ ܗܟܢ ܠܒܝܬܐܝܬ ܡܡܠܠ ܗܘܐ ܐܠܟܣܢܕܪܘܣ. ܘܠܐ ܡܡܠܠ ܗܘܐ ܢܣܐܝܬ ܐܝܟ ܓܒܪܐ ܐܝܙܓܕܐ. ܐܡܪ ܠܗ ܕܪܝܘܫ: ܐܢܐ ܡܢ ܡ̈ܠܝܟ ܠܐ ܡܬܦܪܫ ܐܢܐ. ܐܢܬ ܗܟܢܐ ܐܝܟ ܒܝܕܐ ܕܐܝܙܓܕܐ ܫܪܘܬܐ ܡܕܡܟ ܠܟܘ. ܡܛܠ ܕܐܦ ܐܠܟܣܢܕܪܘܣ ܒܐܝܙܓܕܐ ܕܠܟ ܗܟܢ ܟܕܒ. ܗܝܕܝܢ ܕܪܝܘܫ ܒܪܘܫܗ ܐܟܦ ܗܘܐ. ܘܣܐ̈ܘܗܝ ܘܪ̈ܘܪܒܢܘܗܝ ܡܕܡܢܘܗܝ ܐܫܬܡܥܘ. ܘܠܡܟܠܗ ܕܕܪܝܘܫ ܐܠܟܣܢܕܪܘܣ ܕܗܘ̣ܐ ܐܝܙܓܕܐ. ܘܒܫܢܬܐ ܒܠܠܗܘܢ ܬܡܝܗܝܢ ܗܘܘ ܒܗ. ܕܟܦܪܢܗ ܙܥܘܪ ܗܘܐ. ܘܡܠ̈ܘܗܝ ܚܪܝܦܝܢ ܗܘ̈ܝ. ܘܟܕ ܠܟܣܘ ܫܟܪܐ ܒܟܣܘ. ܘܐܠܟܣܢܕܪܘܣ ܟܠ ܡܐܢܐ ܕܕܗܒܐ ܕܐܘܫܛܘ ܠܗ. ܫܩܠܐ ܒܟܠ ܐܘܪܒܐ ܐܥܒܪ ܗܘܐ. ܘܡ̈ܐܢܐ ܒܥܘܒܗ ܣܐܡ ܗܘܐ. ܗܝܕܝܢ ܚܕ ܫܘ ܕܡܠܟܐ ܒܒܪ. ܠܕܪܝܘܫ ܐܘܕܥܘ ܗܘܘ. ܘܕܪܝܘܫ ܟܕ ܥܒܪ. ܡܢ ܒܪܘܫܗ ܡܒܪ. ܘܠܘܬ ܐܠܟܣܢܕܪܘܣ ܐܬܐ ܘܐܡܪ ܠܗ. ܕܐܘ ܒܪ ܢܫܐ. ܡܛܠ ܡܢܐ ܕܐܝܟ ܗܠܝܢ ܥܒܕ ܐܢܬ. ܕܟܠܗܘܢ ܡ̈ܐܢܐ ܕܡܫܬܝܐ ܒܥܘܒܟ ܣܡܬ. ܐܠܟܣܢܕܪܘܣ ܐܡܪ. ܡܛܠ ܕܒܪ ܡܢܝ. ܐܠܟܣܢܕܪܘܣ܂ ܐܡܠܬ܂ ܕܫܪܘܬܐ ܠܣܐ̈ܘܗܝ܂ ܒܢ̈ܝ ܗܘܐ. ܟܠܗܘܢ ܡ̈ܐܢ ܡܫܬܝܐ ܕܡܫܬܝܐ ܠܗܘܢ ܢܣܒ ܗܘ̣ܝܢ. ܐܦ ܐܢܐ ܣܒܪܬ ܕܐܦ ܒܗ ܒܢܝܐ ܒܒܪ ܐܢܬ. ܐܠܐ ܗܟܢܐ ܟܝ ܠܝܬ ܠܝ ܕܐܝܟ ܗܢܐ ܒܒܪܐ. ܗܘ ܡ̈ܐܢܐ ܡܫܬܝܐ ܡܕܡܢܝܢ. ܦܩܘܕ ܘܕܗܒܝܢ ܡܬܟܠܦ ܐܢܐ ܠܢ. ܗܝܕܝܢ ܕܪܝܘܫ ܐܡܪ. ܐܦ ܐܢܐ ܦܫܪܬ ܕܕܗܒܝܢ ܠܘܬܢ ܢܕܡܘܢܗ̈. ܘܦ̈ܣܩܐ ܟܠܗܘܢ ܒܐܠܟܣܢܕܪܘܣ ܚܪܝܢ ܗܘ̣ܘ. ܘܟܕ ܬܡܝܗܝܢ ܗܘܘ ܡܛܠ ܕܡ̈ܠܘܗܝ ܚܠܝ̈ܬܐ ܗܘ̈ܝ ܘܡܠ̈ܝܢ ܢܥܡܬܐ. ܚܕ ܗܟܠ ܡܢ ܡܪ̈ܘܬܐ ܚܕ. ܕܐܬܘܗܝ ܗܘܐ ܦܘܣܩ ܥܒܕܗ: ܕܡܢ ܡܒܪ ܒܐܝܙܓܕܘܬܐ ܡܢ ܕܪܝܘܫ ܠܡܩܕܘܢܝܐ ܐܫܬܕܪ ܗܘܐ ܠܘܬ ܦܝܠܝܦܘܣ ܐܒܘܗܝ ܕܐܠܟܣܢܕܪܘܣ: ܘܚܙܐ ܒܐܠܟܣܢܕܪܘܣ

ܫܬܩܬ ܐܬܒܣܡ ܢܕܒܗ ܗܘܐ. ܘܒܠܫܢܐ ܦܪܣܝܐ ܠܕܪܝܘܫ ܐܡܪ ܗܘܐ. ܐܦ ܟܕ ܠܒ̈ܢܬܗ ܕܕܪܝܘܫ ܡܠܟܐ. ܦܩܘܕ ܕܠܡܢܐ ܐܚܝܕܐ ܒܬܘܠܘܬܗ ܗܘܪܐܝܬ ܢܛܪܘܢ. ܡܛܠ ܕܗܘܝܘ ܣܘܡܟܗ ܕܐܠܟܣܢܕܪܘܣ. ܘܡܢ ܚܘܬܗ ܢܕܒ ܐܢܐ ܠܗ ܘܡܣܬܟܠ ܐܢܐ. ܗܝܕܝܢ ܟܕ ܕܪܝܘܫ ܘܫܐܪܘܗܝ ܘܪܘ̈ܪܒܢܘܗܝ ܥܡܟܘ. ܫܪܝܘ ܚܕ ܒܬܪ ܚܕ ܠܡܡܠܠܘ ܘܒܐܠܟܣܢܕܪܘܣ ܡܬܟܢܫܝܢ ܗܘܘ. ܗܝܕܝܢ ܐܠܟܣܢܕܪܘܣ ܢܚܬ. ܘܡܢ ܒܬܪ ܡܥܬܡܬܗ ܡܝܬ. ܘܠܬܪܥܐ ܕܡܠܟܐ ܥܒܪ. ܟܕ ܗܘܐ ܚܠܡܘܗܝ ܡܐܢ̈ܐ ܕܗܒܐ ܕܒܣܡܐ ܐܣܝ ܗܘܐ. ܘܟܠ ܬܪܥܐ ܕܒܝܬ ܡܠܟܐ ܢܒܪܐ ܚܕ ܢܛܘܪܐ ܐܥܡܝܚ. ܟܕ ܒܐܝܕܗ ܣܡܐ ܕܐܪܙܐ ܚܕ ܟܕ ܕܠܗ ܐܝܬ ܗܘܐ. ܘܡܛܠܠܗ ܘܫܡܟܗ ܡܢܗ. ܘܟܠ ܣܘܣܝܗ ܪܟܒ. ܘܒܡܣܟܗ ܒܒܛܠܗ. ܘܗܘ ܣܡܐ ܟܕ ܢܘܪܐ ܡܬܒܥܪܐ ܗܘܬ ܡܢ ܒܢܘܗܝ. ܕܣܡܣܡܐ ܠܒܢܝ ܗܘܐ ܘܣܡܣܡܐ ܒܗ ܒܝܘܡܐ ܕܢܘܪܐ ܒܐܬܪܚܐ ܡܣܪܗܒܐܝܬ ܪܗܛ ܗܘܐ. ܘܠܡܦܪ ܢܗܪܐ ܚܕ ܐܬܐ. ܗܝܕܝܢ ܐܬܝܕܐ ܒܬܪܗ ܢܦܩܘ ܡܠܟܐܝܬ. ܘܡܛܠ ܣܥܘܪܐ ܕܠܠܝܐ ܣܘܝܐܝܗܝ ܒܝܗ ܢܩܡܝܢ ܘܒܫܥܬܐ ܢܦܠ. ܐܠܟܣܢܕܪܘܣ ܕܝܢ ܒܚܠܐ ܕܐܠܗ̈ܐ ܠܢܗܪܐ ܗܘ ܥܒܪ. ܘܟܕ ܠܗܘ ܓܒܐ ܕܢܗܪܐ ܥܒܪ. ܘܐ̈ܬܠܘܗܝ ܡܫ̈ܚܠܦܬܐ ܕܣܘܣܝܐ ܠܒܥܠܐ ܣܡܟܢ: ܬ̈ܒܝܐ ܗܘܝ ܕܡܬܚܠܦܝܢ ܗܘܘ ܡܫܢܐ ܦܥܪܘ ܗܘܘ. ܘܐ̈ܬܠܘܗܝ ܐܣ̈ܝܪܬܐ ܕܣܘܣܝܐ ܒܝܗ ܢܗܪܐ ܣܠܩ̈ ܗܘܝ̈. ܘܐܠܟܣܢܕܪܘܣ ܡܢ ܣܘܣܝܐ ܠܒܥܠܐ ܥܒܪ. ܘܣܘܣܝܐ ܒܢܗܪܐ ܛܒܥ. ܗܝܕܝܢ ܟܕ ܐܬܝܕܐ ܠܡܦܪ ܢܗܪܐ ܐܬܬ. ܘܚܙܘ ܕܐܠܟܣܢܕܪܘܣ ܠܢܗܪܐ ܗܘ ܥܒܪ. ܘܩܝܡܘ ܕܒܥܒܪܘ ܒܬܪܗ ܠܐ ܐܫܟܚܘ. ܗܝܕܝܢ ܬܩܢܘܗ ܘܚܕ ܠܚܕ ܐܡܪܝܢ ܗܘܘ. ܕܪܟܒ ܢܒܗ ܕܐܠܟܣܢܕܪܘܣ ܕܠܢܗܪܐ ܕܗܘ ܪܒ ܡܢܒܪܬܐ ܢܦܩ ܠܗ. ܘܐܫܟܚ ܠܡܥܒܪܗ. ܘܟܕ ܦܢܘ. ܠܘܬ ܕܪܝܘܫ ܐܬܘ. ܘܐܘܕܥܘ ܠܕܪܝܘܫ ܟܠ ܦܘܠܚܢܗ ܘܡܥܒܪܢܘܬܗ ܕܐܠܟܣܢܕܪܘܣ ܕܠܢܗܪܐ. ܕܪܝܘܫ ܒܟܡܘܬܐ ܪܒܬܐ ܗܘܐ. ܘܡܢ ܥܠܬܐ ܐܬܐ ܐܬܚܙܝܬ ܠܗ. ܢܠܡܝܗ ܚܝܪ ܕܒܣܝܪܘ ܡܠܟܐ. ܗܘ

ܕܕܪܘܫ ܪܫܝܟ ܗܘܐ ܠܗ. ܒܒܝܬ ܡܫܬܘܬܐ ܟܠ ܐܣܛܘܣ ܪܓܝ
ܗܘܐ. ܘܡܢ ܥܠ ܐܬܡܦܠ ܗܘܐ ܡܢ ܐܣܛܘܣ. ܘܠܒܢܝ̈ܘܗܝ
ܕܕܪܘܫ ܟܠ ܐܪܒܐ ܢܦܠ. ܐܠܟܣܢܕܪܘܣ ܕܝܢ ܡܢ ܕܠܚܪܐ
ܓܒܪ. ܡܢ ܪܗܛܗ ܘܡܢ ܒܡܠܟܗ ܐܬܬܢܝܚ. ܘܩܒܪ ܒܬܝܠܘܗܝ
ܡܬܠܝܢ ܗܘܐ. ܘܒܝܬܗ ܗܘ ܫܥܒܐ ܕܐܠܠܝܐ ܠܐܡܦܪܘܣ ܪܫ
ܝܘܕܐ ܒܠܝܐ ܕܘܗܝ. ܢܝܐ. ܘܒܪ ܒܒܝܬܗ ܪܒܬܐ ܡܬܠܠ
ܐܠܟܣܢܕܪܘܣ ܩܐܡ ܗܘܐ ܘܟܒܫܐ. ܡܕܝܢ ܐܠܟܣܢܕܪܘܣ ܒܠܗܝܢ
ܬܠܬܐ ܕܒܒܝ̈ܬܐ. ܒܠܗܘܢ ܠܐܡܦܪܘܣ ܐܦܢܝ ܗܘܐ ※

The First Discovery of the True Cross[1]

ܫܟܝܚܘܬܐ ܕܨܠܝܒܗ

ܕܡܪܢ ܝܫܘܥ ܡܫܝܚܐ: ܕܐܝܟ ܐܫܬܟܚ ܡܩܕܡܝܬܐ

ܟܕ ܦܪܘܛܘܢܝܩܐ ܐܢܬܬܗ ܕܩܠܘܕܝܘܣ ܩܣܪ.

ܡܪܝ ܥܕܪܝܢ ܒܪ̈ܚܡܝܟ: ܐܡܝܢ.

ܡܢ ܒܬܪ ܡܣܩܬܗ ܕܡܪܢ ܝܫܘܥ ܠܫܡܝܐ: ܒܗ ܒܙܒܢܐ ܗܘ ܟܕ ܐܘܦ ܗܘܐ ܫܡܥܘܢ ܟܐܦܐ ܒܪܗܘܡܐ: ܘܐܟܪܙ ܬܡܢ ܡܠܬܐ ܕܐܠܗܐ: ܫܡܥܬ ܗܘܬ ܦܪܘܛܘܢܝܩܐ ܐܢܬܬܗ ܕܩܠܘܕܝܘܣ ܩܣܪ: ܗܘ ܕܥܒܕܗ ܛܝܒܪܝܘܣ ܬܢܝܢܐ ܒܡܠܟܘܬܗ: ܟܕ ܐܘܦ ܗܘܐ ܕܩܣܪ ܠܗܘ ܒܢܝ̈ ܐܢܫܐ ܕܡܪܕܘ ܗܘܘ ܒܠܘܗܝ: ܗܝ ܕܝܢ ܗܕܐ ܐܢܬܬܐ: ܟܕ ܐܬܘܗܝ ܗܘܐ ܫܡܥܘܢ ܒܪܗܘܡܐ: ܚܙܬ ܗܘܬ ܐܬܘܬܐ ܘܚܝ̈ܠܐ ܐܡܪ̈ܬܐ ܕܥܒܕ ܗܘܐ ܒܫܡܗ ܕܡܪܢ ܡܫܝܚܐ. ܘܟܦܪܬ ܒܚܢܦܘܬܐ ܕܐܒܗܘ̈ܗ ܕܡܠܟܐ ܗܘܬ ܒܗ: ܘܕܚܠܬ̈ܐ ܕܚܢܦܘܬܐ ܕܐܚܝܕܐ ܗܘܬ ܠܗܝܢ. ܘܗܝܡܢܬ ܡܪܢ ܡܫܝܚܐ ܗܘܬ ܘܣܓܕܐ ܗܘܬ ܠܗ: ܟܕ ܒܠܗܘܢ ܐܠܗ ܕܒܫܡܝܐ ܗܘܘ ܠܗ ܠܫܡܥܘܢ: ܘܐܚܕܐ ܗܘܬ ܠܗ ܒܐܝܩܪܐ ܪܒܐ.

---

[1]From ܥܒ̈ܕܐ ܕܣܗ̈ܕܐ ܘܕܩܕܝ̈ܫܐ : *Acta martyrum et sanctorum,* ed. Paulus Bedjan (Leipzig: Harrassowitz, 1892), III, 175–183.

ܘܡܢ ܒܬܪ ܗܟܢܐ ܨܒܝܐ ܗܘܬ ܕܐܦ ܠܐܘܪܫܠܡ ܬܚܙܐ: ܘܕܘܟܝܬܐ ܐܝܠܝܢ ܕܒܗܝܢ ܐܫܬܥܪܘ ܚܝ̈ܠܐ ܬܡܗ̈ܐ ܘܬܗܪ̈ܐ ܕܡܪܢ ܝܫܘܥ ܡܫܝܚܐ. ܘܣܥܪܬ ܗܘܬ ܚܦܝܛܐ: ܘܣܠܩܬ ܠܗ̇ ܡܢ ܪܗܘܡܐ ܠܐܘܪܫܠܡ: ܗܝ ܘܬܪܝܢ ܒܢ̈ܝܗ̇ ܥܡܗ̇ ܘܚܕܐ ܒܪܬܗ̇ ܒܬܘܠܬܐ. ܘܟܕ ܡܛܬ ܗܘܬ ܕܬܥܘܠ ܠܐܘܪܫܠܡ: ܫܡܥܬ ܘܢܦܩܬ ܟܠܗ̇ ܡܕܝܢܬܐ ܠܐܘܪܥܗ̇: ܘܩܒܠܘܗ̇ ܗܘܘ ܒܐܝܩܪܐ ܪܒܐ: ܐܝܟ ܕܠܡܠܟܬܐ ܡܪܬܗ ܕܐܬܪܐ ܕܒܝܬ ܪ̈ܗܘܡܝܐ. ܝܥܩܘܒ ܕܝܢ ܗܘ̇: ܗܘ ܕܡܩܝܡ ܗܘܐ ܡܕܒܪܢܐ ܘܦܩܘܕܐ ܕܡܕܝܢܬܐ: ܒܥܕܬܐ ܕܒܢܝܐ ܗܘܬ ܠܗ̇ ܬܡܢ ܒܐܘܪܫܠܡ.

ܘܟܕ ܫܡܥ ܕܡܠܟܬܐ ܐܬܝܐ ܗܘܬ ܠܬܡܢ: ܩܡ ܗܘܐ ܢܦܩ ܘܐܙܠ ܨܐܕܝܗ̇. ܘܥܠ ܠܘܬܗ̇ ܐܝܟܐ ܕܫܪܝܐ ܗܘܬ: ܒܦܠܛܝܢ ܪܒܐ ܕܡܠܟܘܬܐ ܕܒܗ̇ ܗܘܪܕܘܣ. ܘܟܕ ܚܙܬܗ ܗܘܬ: ܡܩܒܠܬܗ ܗܘܬ ܒܚܕܘܬܐ ܪܒܬܐ: ܐܦ ܠܗ ܐܝܟ ܕܠܫܡܥܘܢ ܟܐܦܐ. ܘܚܘܝܗ̇ ܚܝ̈ܠܐ ܕܐܬܥܒܕܘ: ܐܦ ܗܘ ܐܝܟ ܫܡܥܘܢ. ܘܐܡܪܬ ܠܗ: ܚܘܐ ܠܝ ܓܓܘܠܬܐ: ܗܝ ܕܐܨܛܠܒ ܒܗ̇ ܡܪܢ ܡܫܝܚܐ: ܘܩܝܣܐ ܕܨܠܝܒܘܬܗ ܕܐܬܬܠܝ ܗܘܐ ܒܗ ܡܢ ܝܗܘܕ̈ܝܐ: ܘܩܒܪܐ ܗܘ̇ ܕܒܗ ܐܬܬܣܝܡ. ܗܕܝܢ ܐܡܪ ܠܗ̇ ܗܘ ܝܥܩܘܒ: ܗܠܝܢ ܬܠܬܝܗܘܢ ܕܨܒܝܐ ܡܠܟܘܬܟܝ ܕܬܚܙܐ: ܬܚܬ ܐܝܕܝ ܐܢܝܢ ܕܝܗܘܕ̈ܝܐ: ܘܗܢܘܢ ܐܚܝܕܝܢ ܠܗܘܢ. ܘܠܐ ܫܒܩܝܢ ܠܝ ܕܐܙܠ ܘܐܨܠܐ ܬܡܢ ܩܕܡ ܓܓܘܠܬܐ ܘܩܒܪܐ: ܘܐܦܠܐ ܩܝܣܐ ܕܨܠܝܒܘܬܗ ܝܗܒܝܢ ܠܝ. ܘܠܐ ܗܘܐ ܗܕܐ ܒܠܚܘܕ: ܐܠܐ ܐܦ ܡܪܕܦ ܪܕܦܝܢ ܠܝ: ܕܠܐ ܢܚܘܐ ܘܢܣܒܪ ܒܫܡܗ ܕܡܫܝܚܐ: ܘܙܒܢ̈ܝܢ ܣܓܝ̈ܐܢ ܐܦ ܒܝܬ ܐܣܘܪ̈ܐ ܪܡܝܢ ܠܝ.

ܘܟܕ ܫܡܥܬ ܗܠܝܢ ܗܝ ܦܪܘܛܘܢܝܩܐ ܡܠܟܬܐ: ܒܗ̇ ܒܫܥܬܐ ܦܩܕܬ ܘܐܬܝܘ ܠܩܕܡܝܗ̇ ܠܚܢܢܝܐ ܒܪ ܚܢܢ ܟܗܢܐ: ܘܠܓܕܠܝܐ ܒܪ ܩܝܦܐ: ܘܠܝܗܘܕܐ ܒܪ ܥܒܫܠܘܡ: ܪ̈ܫܐ ܕܝܗܘܕ̈ܝܐ. ܘܐܡܪܬ ܠܗܘܢ ܡܠܟܬܐ: ܐܫܠܡܘ ܓܓܘܠܬܐ ܘܩܒܪܐ ܘܩܝܣܐ ܕܨܠܝܒܐ ܠܥܡܡܗ ܘܗܠܝܢ ܕܫܠܝܛܝܢ ܠܗ̇: ܠܐ ܐܢܫ ܢܟܠܐ ܐܢܘܢ ܡܢ ܕܢܫܡܫܘܢ ܬܡܢ ܐܝܟ ܥܝܕܐ ܕܬܫܡܫܬܗܘܢ. ܘܟܕ

ܗܟܢܐ ܦܩܕܬ ܗܘܬ ܠܟܗ̈ܢܐ: ܨܒܬ ܗܘܬ ܕܬܐܙܠ ܘܬܚܙܐ ܐܝܟ ܠܕܘܟܝ̈ܬܐ ܗܠܝܢ: ܘܐܦ ܕܬܫܟܚ ܐܬܪܐ ܗܘ ܠܩܝܣܐ ܨܠܝܒܐ ܕܡܪܢ. ܘܒܬܪܟܢ ܥܠܬ ܠܩܒܪܗ ܕܡܪܢ: ܘܐܫܟܚܬ ܗܘܬ ܒܓܘܗ ܕܩܒܪܐ ܬܠܬܐ ܙܩܝ̈ܦܐ: ܚܕ ܕܡܪܢ: ܘܬܪܝܢ ܕܗܢܘܢ ܓܝ̈ܣܐ ܕܐܙܕܩܦܘ ܗܘܘ ܥܡܗ: ܚܕ ܡܢ ܝܡܝܢܗ ܘܚܕ ܡܢ ܣܡܠܗ. ܘܒܗ ܒܥܕܢܐ ܕܥܠܬ ܗܘܬ ܠܩܒܪܐ ܗܝ ܡܠܟܬܐ ܘܒ̈ܢܝܗ̇ ܥܡܗ̇: ܒܗ̇ ܒܫܥܬܐ ܢܦܠܬ ܗܘܬ ܒܪܬܗ̇ ܒܬܘܠܬܐ ܘܡܝܬܬ ܕܠܐ ܟܐܒܐ ܘܕܠܐ ܟܘܪܗܢܐ ܘܕܠܐ ܥܠܬܐ ܡܕܡ. ܘܟܕ ܚܙܬ ܗܘܬ ܦܪܘܛܘܢܝܩܐ ܕܡܝܬܬ ܠܗ̇ ܒܪܬܗ̇ ܡܢ ܫܠܝ: ܒܪܟܬ ܗܘܬ ܒܨܠܘܬܐ: ܘܡܨܠܝܐ ܗܘܬ ܒܓܘܗ ܕܩܒܪܐ ܘܐܡܪܐ ܗܘܬ ܗܟܢܐ: ܡܫܝܚܐ ܕܝܗܒ ܢܦܫܗ ܠܡܘܬܐ ܚܠܦ ܟܠܗܘܢ ܒܢ̈ܝܢܫܐ: ܘܐܙܕܩܦ ܒܐܬܪܐ ܗܢܐ: ܘܐܬܬܩܒܪ ܒܩܒܪܐ ܗܢܐ: ܐܝܟ ܐܠܗܐ ܡܚܝܐ ܟܕ ܩܡ: ܘܐܩܝܡ ܥܡܗ ܠܣܓܝ̈ܐܐ: ܠܐ ܢܫܡܥܘܢ ܝܗ̈ܘܕܝܐ ܘܥܡ̈ܡܐ ܘܚܢܦ̈ܐ ܗܠܝܢ: ܗܢܘܢ ܕܨܥܪܬ ܒܡܩܕܫܝܗܘܢ ܘܒܟܢܘܫܝܗܘܢ ܘܒܓܒܠܬܗܘܢ ܕܣܓܕܬܐ: ܘܣܓܕܘ ܠܗ ܟܕ ܡܗܠܟܝܢ ܒܗ ܘܢܐܡܪܘܢ: ܕܟܠܗ̇ ܕܗܘܬ ܠܗ̇ ܗܕܐ: ܟܠ ܕܦܓܥܬ ܒܠܗܐ ܕܚܛܝܬܐ ܗܘܬ ܠܗܘܢ: ܘܐܘܕܝܬ ܒܡܫܝܚܐ ܕܠܐ ܚܙܬ ܗܘܬ ܠܗ: ܘܐܙܠܬ ܕܬܩܒܪ ܕܗܟܢܐ ܕܡܕܒܪܗ ܨܠܝܒܘܬܗ. ܘܐܢ ܐܢܐ ܠܐ ܫܡܥܐ ܐܢܐ ܕܐܫܬܡܥ: ܟܠ ܕܨܦܪܬ ܠܟܪܝܬܐ ܫܠܦܝ: ܚܘܣ ܐܢܬ ܡܛܠ ܥܡܟ ܗܕܐ: ܕܠܐ ܬܘܒ ܢܬܒܕܩ ܒܬܪܐ ܗܢܐ: ܐܝܟ ܕܢܒܙܚܘܢ ܥܠܝ ܨܠܝܒܘܬܟ.

ܘܟܕ ܗܠܝܢ ܒܨܠܘܬܗ̇ ܐܡܪܐ ܗܘܬ: ܩܕܡ ܐܚܝܗ̇ ܕܐܝܬ ܗܘܘ ܬܡܢ: ܩܪܒ ܠܘܬܗ̇ ܒܪܗ̇ ܡܫܒܚܐ ܘܐܡܪ ܠܗ̇: ܫܡܥܝ ܡܕܡ ܕܐܡܪ ܐܢܐ ܩܕܡ ܡܠܟܘܬܟܝ. ܐܢܐ ܗܟܢܐ ܣܒܪ ܐܢܐ ܒܪܚܡܝܢ ܘܒܡܫܒܚܬܟܝ: ܕܗܢܐ ܡܘܬܐ ܕܗܕܐ ܚܕܐ ܕܡܫܒܚ: ܠܐ ܗܘܐ ܣܪܝܩܐܝܬ ܗܘܐ: ܐܠܐ ܣܘܪܢܐ ܗܘ ܗܢܐ ܬܘܩܢܐ: ܕܐܠܗܐ ܡܫܬܒܚ ܒܗ: ܘܠܐ ܗܘܐ ܕܢܫܡܥܗ ܢܬܒܕܩ ܒܗ: ܐܝܟ ܕܫܡܥܬ ܐܢܐ ܕܫܡܥܐ ܗܕܐ. ܗܐ ܟܠܝ ܠܩܒܪܐ ܗܢܐ ܕܡܫܝܚܐ ܘܐܫܟܚܬ ܬܠܬܐ ܙܩܝ̈ܦܐ: ܘܠܐ ܝܕܥܝܢ ܐܝܢܐ ܗܘ ܡܢܗܘܢ ܙܩܝܦܐ ܗܘ ܕܐܬܬܠܝ ܒܗ ܡܫܝܚܐ. ܗܫܐ ܕܝܢ ܒܡܘܬܗ̇ ܕܗܕܐ ܚܕܐ

ܡܫܒܚܝܢ ܕܚܙܐ ܘܝܠܦ: ܕܐܝܢܘ ܙܩܝܦܗ ܕܡܫܝܚܐ: ܠܐ ܓܝܪ ܡܕܡ ܡܢ ܐܝܠܝܢ ܕܡܗܝܡܢܝܢ ܒܗ. ܡܠܟܬܐ ܕܝܢ ܦܪܘܛܘܢܝܩܐ: ܟܕ ܛܒ ܡܪܝܪܐ ܗܘܬ ܢܦܫܗ ܒܥܕܢܐ ܗܘ: ܚܪܬ ܗܘܬ ܒܒܪܬܗ ܐܝܟ ܚܟܡܬܗ: ܕܟܐܢܐܝܬ ܘܬܪܝܨܐܝܬ ܐܡܪ ܒܪܗ ܗܠܝܢ. ܘܩܪܒܬ ܡܚܕܐ ܡܫܩܠܬ ܗܘܬ ܗܝ ܒܐܝܕܝ̈ܗ ܚܕ ܡܢ ܗܠܝܢ ܙܩܝ̈ܦܐ: ܘܣܡܬܗ ܥܠ ܫܠܕܗ ܕܒܪܬܗ ܕܪܡܝܐ ܗܘܬ ܩܕܡܝܗ: ܘܐܡܪܬ ܗܘܬ ܒܨܠܘܬܗ: ܡܫܝܚܐ ܕܝܗܒ ܚܝ̈ܐ ܬܡܝ̈ܗܐ ܒܐܬܪܐ ܗܢܐ: ܐܝܟ ܕܫܡܥܝܢ ܘܡܗܝܡܢܝܢ. ܐܢ ܕܝܠܟ ܗܘ ܡܪܝ ܗܢܐ ܙܩܝ̈ܦܐ: ܘܒܗܘ ܐܬܬܠܝܬ ܐܢܫܘܬܟ ܡܢ ܩܝ̈ܣܐ: ܚܘܐ ܚܝܠܟ ܓܘܙܐ ܘܬܘܩܦܐ ܕܐܠܗܘܬܟ ܕܥܡ ܐܢܫܘܬܟ ܚܕܐ ܗܘܬ. ܘܬܚܐ ܗܕܐ ܒܪܬܝ ܘܬܩܘܡ: ܘܢܫܬܒܚ ܒܗ ܫܡܟ: ܟܕ ܦܢܝܐ ܢܦܫܗ ܠܗܘ ܦܓܪܗ: ܘܢܒܗܬܘܢ ܙܩܘܦܝ̈ܟ: ܘܢܚܕܘܢ ܣܓܘܕܝ̈ܟ. ܘܩܝܡ ܗܘܐ ܥܕܬܐ ܣܓܝܐܐ: ܡܢ ܒܬܪ ܕܐܡܪܬ ܗܠܝܢ. ܘܒܬܪܟ ܫܩܠܬܗ ܗܘܬ ܠܙܩܝܦܐ ܗܘ ܡܢ ܫܠܕܗ ܕܒܪܬܗ: ܘܣܡܬ ܗܘܬ ܗܘ ܐܚܪܢܐ. ܘܐܡܪܬ ܬܘܒ ܒܨܠܘܬܗ: ܐܠܗܐ ܗܘ ܕܒܪܡܙܗ ܩܝܡܝܢ ܟܠܗ̈ܝܢ ܒܪ̈ܝܬܐ: ܘܩܪܒܐ ܒܢ̈ܝܐ ܕܟܠܗܘܢ ܒܢܝ̈ܢܫܐ ܕܡܬܦܢܝܢ ܠܘܬܗ: ܘܠܐ ܡܕܡ ܡܢ ܒܥܘܬܐ ܕܐܝܠܝܢ ܕܒܥܝܢ ܠܗ. ܐܢ ܕܝܠܟ ܗܘ ܡܪܝ ܗܢܐ ܙܩܝ̈ܦܐ: ܚܘܐ ܚܝܠܐ ܕܢܨܚܢܝܟ ܐܝܟ ܕܡܥܒܕܬ: ܘܬܚܐ ܗܕܐ ܒܪܬܝ ܘܬܩܘܡ. ܘܢܒܗܬܘܢ ܚܢ̈ܦܐ ܣܓܘ̈ܕܝ ܠܦܬܟܪ̈ܐ ܚܠܦܝ: ܘܢܗܘܘܢ ܡܗܝܡ̈ܢܐ ܫܪܝܪ̈ܐ: ܕܡܬܦܬܚ ܦܘܡܗܘܢ ܠܡܫܝܚܘܬܟ ܩܕܡ ܐܝܠܝܢ ܕܟܦܪܝܢ ܒܟ. ܘܐܓܪܬ ܗܘܬ ܬܘܒ ܛܘܪܐ ܣܓܝܐܐ: ܘܗܝܕܝܢ ܫܩܠܬܗ ܗܘܬ ܠܙܩܝܦܐ ܗܘ ܕܬܪܝܢ ܡܢ ܒܪܬܗ: ܘܣܡܬ ܗܘ ܕܬܠܬܐ ܥܠ ܒܪܬܗ. ܘܟܕ ܒܥܝܐ ܗܘܬ ܕܬܪܝܡ ܒܢ̈ܝܗ ܠܫܡܝܐ: ܘܐܬܦܬܚ ܦܘܡܗ ܒܨܠܘܬܐ: ܒܗ ܒܫܥܬܐ ܘܒܗ ܒܙܒܢܐ: ܐܝܟ ܡܛܪܦ ܥܝܢܐ ܕܚܕܐ: ܕܩܪܒ ܗܘܐ ܙܩܝܦܐ ܗܘ ܠܫܠܕܐ ܕܒܪܬܗ: ܚܝܬ ܗܘܬ ܒܪܬܗ ܡܢ ܫܠܝܐ ܘܩܡܬ. ܘܡܫܒܚܐ ܗܘܬ ܠܡܫܝܚܐ: ܕܐܚܝܗ ܒܙܩܝܦܗ.

ܡܠܟܬܐ ܕܝܢ ܦܪܘܛܘܢܝܩܐ: ܟܕ ܚܙܬ ܗܘܬ ܕܐܝܟܢܐ ܚܝܬ ܒܪܬܗ: ܐܬܬܙܝܥܬ ܘܐܬܪܗܒܬ ܛܒ: ܘܡܫܒܚܐ ܗܘܬ ܠܡܫܝܚܐ ܕܗܝܡܢܬ ܒܗ:

ܕܒܪܗ̇ ܗܘܐ ܕܐܠܗܐ ܚܝܐ. ܐܡܪ ܠܗ̇ ܒܪܗ̇: ܚܘܝܬܝ ܡܪܬܝ: ܕܐܠܘ ܗܕܐ
ܠܐ ܗܘܬ ܡܨܝܐ: ܓܒܪܐ ܕܒܥܪܣܡ ܗܘܐ ܙܩܝܦܐ ܗܢܐ ܕܡܫܝܚܐ ܕܒܚܝܠ
ܒܗ ܚܝܬ: ܘܐܬܢܒܝ ܗܘܘ ܘܡܩܒܪܝ ܗܘܘ ܕܢܒ ܡܢ ܗܘܢ ܓܢܒܪ̈ܐ
ܡܬܘܠܐ. ܐܠܐ ܗܟܢܐ ܗܘ ܐܝܟ ܚܘܒ ܘܚܒܝܒ ܒܗܘܢܐ. ܘܐܠܗܐ ܕܒܪܗ̇ ܠܗܘܢ:
ܫܪܝܬ ܐܬܥܡܕܬ ܒܗ̇. ܘܡܛܠܬܗ̇ ܡܠܟܬܐ ܦܪܘܛܘܢܝܩܐ ܠܘܩܒܠܗ
ܕܡܫܝܚܐ: ܘܩܒܠܬܗ ܗܘܬ ܠܒܗܘܢ: ܐܝܟ ܕܢܬܚܙܐ ܒܐܬܪܐ ܪܒܐ.
ܘܦܩܕܬ ܗܘܬ ܕܢܬܒܢܐ ܒܢܝܢܐ ܪܒܐ ܡܥܒܕܐ ܥܠ ܓܓܘܠܬܐ ܘܥܠ
ܩܒܪܐ: ܐܝܟ ܕܢܬܩܪܘܢ ܕܩܒܝܬܐ ܗܠܝܢ ܕܙܩܝܦܐ ܘܕܩܒܪܐ: ܘܢܗܘܐ ܬܡܢ
ܒܗ ܘܩܒܪܐ ܠܚܘܫܒܬܐ ܕܡܫܡܫܬܐ. ܡܠܟܬܐ ܕܝܢ ܟܕ ܚܙܬ ܗܘܬ:
ܕܟܝܢܐ ܐܢܫܘܬܐ ܟܠܗ̇ ܕܡܕܝܢܬܐ ܠܚܘܬܐ ܕܗܘܝܕܐ ܗܢܐ: ܦܩܕܬ
ܕܟܠ ܐܢܫ ܐܬܐ ܕܡܠܟܘܬܐ ܐܬܪܐ ܕܐܬܚܙܝ ܗܘܬ[1] ܒܪܬܗ̇ ܢܬܒܪ ܒܠܚܘܕܬ
ܠܐܦܝܐ ܕܡܠܟܐ ܗܘ ܕܥܒܕܐ ܗܘܬ ܒܗ: ܐܝܟ ܕܢܚܙܐ ܟܠܢܫ ܘܢܥܒܕ
ܬܘܕܝܬܐ. ܢܬܒ ܕܝܢ ܕܢܗܘܒܐ ܘܕܢܩܦܐ: ܗܢܘܢ ܕܢܒܗ ܗܘܘ ܒܫܘܪܗ̇
ܕܗܕܐ: ܐܬܚܡܪܘ ܗܘܘ ܒܫܘܠܛܢܗ̇ ܕܗܕܐ. ܛܒ ܓܝܪ ܡܢܝܢ ܗܘܘ ܐܠܘ
ܠܐ ܗܘܬ ܗܕܐ: ܕܢܚ̈ܝܢ ܗܘܘ ܕܗܝܟܠܐ ܡܢܗܘܢ ܗܢܝܢܘ ܗܘܘ ܒܗ
ܒܡܫܝܚܐ. ܫܪܝܬ ܕܝܢ ܕܢܚܝܢ ܗܘܘ ܕܗܝܟܠܐ ܗܘܝ̈ ܐܬܬܘܬܐ ܘܬܕܡܪ̈ܬܐ
ܕܗܘܝ ܗܘܝ̈ ܡܢ ܒܬܪ ܫܘܠܛܢܗ: ܫܪ ܡܢ ܗܢܝܢ ܕܗܘܝ ܗܘܝ̈ ܡܢ
ܡܕܡ ܫܘܠܛܢܗ. ܘܐܦ ܬܬܒܘܬܐ ܩܢܝܢܐ ܐܘܟ ܗܘܐ ܛܒܗ ܕܫܘܪܒܐ
ܗܢܐ: ܘܐܦ ܠܥܠܡܐ ܟܠܗܘܢ ܐܠܝܢ ܕܡܫܒܚܝܢ ܗܘܘ ܠܡܫܝܚܐ. ܘܗܘܐ
ܗܘܐ ܥܠܝܐ ܒܒܝܬܐ ܕܐܘܪܫܠܡ: ܘܡܕܝܢܬܐ ܕܢܒܪܗ̇. ܘܐܠܝܢ ܕܟܠ
ܚܘܒ ܐܬܐ ܗܘܐ: ܒܢ ܐܠܝ ܕܚܘܒ: ܐܦ ܗܢܘܢ ܡܫܒܚܝܢ ܗܘܘ ܠܐܠܗܐ.

ܘܡܢ ܗܠܝܢ ܡܠܟܬܐ ܦܪܘܛܘܢܝܩܐ ܡܢ ܐܘܪܫܠܡ ܠܪܗܘܡܐ ܡܕܝܢܬܗ̇:
ܟܠ ܡܕܝܢܬܐ ܐܝܟ ܕܐܬܠܐ ܗܘܬ ܠܗ̇: ܠܚܘܬܐ ܕܒܪܬܗ̇ ܚܡܝܪ ܗܘܘ
ܐܢܫܐ ܕܚܙܘ. ܘܡܢ ܟܠܗ ܠܪܗܘܡܐ: ܐܫܬܥܝܬ ܡܕܡ ܡܠܘܒܘܗ ܩܕܡ

[1]*têzal-wāt,* imperfect + perfect, used as a modal after verbs of commanding, wanting, etc., "she ordered that she should go…"

ܥܠܘܗܝ ܗܠܝܢ ܕܐܫܬܥܝ ܗܘܐ̈ ܐܕܝ: ܕܐܝܟ ܡܫܬܬ ܒܪܬܗ ܘܒܬܪܟܢ ܣܒܠ. ܘܟܕ ܫܡܥ ܗܘܐ ܡܫܪ ܗܠܝܢ: ܦܩܕ ܗܘܐ ܕܢܦܩܘܢ ܟܠܗܘܢ ܝܗܘܕܝܐ ܡܢ ܐܘܪܗܝ ܘܡܢ ܐܬܪܐ ܕܐܝܠܝܢ. ܟܕ ܟܠܗܘܢ ܐܬܪܐ ܗܘ ܗܡܢܝܢܐ ܗܘܐ ܡܬܡܠܠ ܗܘܐ ܡܢ ܗܢܐ: ܘܡܢ ܥܡܗܘܢ ܟܐܦܐ ܐܫܬܥܝ ܗܘܬ ܗܝ ܦܪܘܩܘܬܐ ܕܡܫܝܚܐ ܗܕܐ: ܘܟܠ ܡܢ ܕܡܫܬܘ ܗܘܘ ܥܠܝܬܐ ܒܝܘܡܬܗ. ܘܡܢ ܟܠܝܘ ܡܟܬܘܒ ܗܘܘ: ܕܢܬܥܡܘܢ ܐܦ ܐܝܢ ܕܠܐ ܚܙܘ ܘܚܙܘ: ܘܢܗܘܘܢ ܐܝܟ ܕܗܠܝܢ ܦܝܫ ܘܡܫܬ ܡܢ ܚܠܦ: ܕܢܫܬܒܩ ܚܛܗ ܕܡܢ ܡܢ ܟܠܝܘ ܠܟܠ ܢܦܫ: ܐܡܝܢ ※

ܗܠܝܢ ܗܟܝܠ ܕܬܚܘܐ ܐܝܟ ܡܕܡܝܟܝܢ: ܕܬܕܡܘܢ ܘܬܬܟܣܘܢ ܕܒܡܢܐ ܪܒܐ ܗܡܝܢܘܬܗ ܕܡܫܝܚܐ: ܠܐܝܠܝܢ ܕܢܣܒܝܢ ܠܗ ܫܪܝܪܐܝܬ. ܐܦ ܢܗܘܘܢ ܕܝܢ ܡܕܟܪܢܐ ܕܕܝܢܐ ܕܐܘܪܫܠܡ: ܗܘ ܕܗܘ ܒܢܝܢܗ. ܚܘܐ ܠܗܡܢܝܢܐ ܗܢܐ: ܗܘ ܐܦ ܒܬܪܗ ܡܕܒܪܗ ܠܥܠܝܬܐ ܒܝܘܡܬܗ: ܠܡܕܝܢܬܐ ܕܐܬܐ ܗܘܐ̈ ܒܐܬܘܬܗܘܢ. ܘܐܦ ܗܢܘܢ ܥܠܝܬܐ ܒܬܪܗ ܘܐܘܕܝܘ ܠܢܗܘܪ ܟܠܡܕܡ ܕܕܝܢ ܡܫܝܚܐ ܒܐܕܢܝܗܘܢ: ܘܡܬܡܢܪܝܢ ܗܘܘ ܡܕܡ ܟܠܗ ܒܫܢܐ ܕܕܝܢܐ ܘܡܕܡ ܟܠܗ ܢܦܫܐ. ܫܠܡܬ ※

The Teaching of the Apostle Thaddeus[1]

ܡܠܦܢܘܬܐ ܕܐܕܝ ܫܠܝܚܐ

ܒܫܢܬ ܬܠܬܡܐܐ ܘܐܪܒܥܝܢ ܘܬܠܬ ܕܡܠܟܘܬܐ ܕܝܘܢܝܐ ܘܒܡܠܟܘܬܗ ܕܡܪܢ ܛܒܪܝܘܣ ܩܣܪ ܪܗܘܡܝܐ ܘܒܡܠܟܘܬܗ ܕܐܒܓܪ ܡܠܟܐ ܒܪ ܡܥܢܘ ܡܠܟܐ ܒܝܪܚ ܬܫܪܝ ܩܕܝܡ ܒܬܪܝܢ ܒܗ: ܫܕܪ ܗܘܐ ܐܒܓܪ ܐܘܟܡܐ ܠܡܪܝܗܒ ܘܠܫܡܫܓܪܡ: ܪ̈ܒܐ ܘܡܝܩܪ̈ܐ ܕܡܠܟܘܬܗ: ܘܠܚܢܢ ܬܒܘܠܪܐ ܫܪܝܪܐ ܥܡܗܘܢ:

---

[1]Labubna bar Sennak, *Mallpānutā d-Addai Šliḥā: The Doctrine of Addai, the Apostle,* ed. G. Phillips (London: Trubner, 1876).

ܠܡܕܝܢܬܐ ܐܝܕܐ ܕܡܬܩܪܝܐ ܐܠܘܬܪܘܦܘܠܝܣ ܘܐܪܡܝܬ ܕܝܢ ܒܝܬ ܓܘܒܪ̈ܝܢ: ܠܘܬ ܡܩܪܐ ܣܒܝܢܘܣ ܒܪ ܐܘܣܛܪܝܣ ܐܦܛܪܦܐ ܕܡܪܢ ܩܣܪ: ܗܘ ܕܗܘ ܫܠܝܛ ܗ̄ܘܐ ܥܠ ܣܘܪܝܐ ܘܥܠ ܦܘܢܝܩܐ ܘܥܠ ܦܠܣܛܝܢܐ ܘܥܠ ܐܬܪܐ ܟܠܗ ܕܒܝܬ ܢܗܪ̈ܝܢ. ܘܐܘܒܠܘ ܗ̄ܘܘ ܠܗ ܐܓܪ̈ܬܐ ܡܛܠ ܨܒܘ̈ܬܐ ܕܡܠܟܘܬܐ: ܘܟܕ ܐܬܘ ܗ̄ܘܘ ܠܘܬܗ ܡܩܒܠ ܗ̄ܘܐ ܐܢܘܢ ܒܚܕܘܬܐ ܘܒܐܝܩܪܐ. ܘܗܘܘ ܠܘܬܗ ܝܘ̈ܡܬܐ ܥܣܪ̈ܝܢ ܘܚܡܫܐ. ܘܟܬܒ ܗ̄ܘܐ ܠܗܘܢ ܦܢܝܬܐ ܕܐܓܪ̈ܬܐ ܘܫܕܪ ܗ̄ܘܐ ܐܢܘܢ ܠܘܬ ܐܒܓܪ ܡܠܟܐ. ܘܟܕ ܢܦܩܘ ܗ̄ܘܘ ܡܢ ܠܘܬܗ. ܗܦܟܘ ܗ̄ܘܘ ܘܐܬܘ ܒܐܘܪܚܐ ܠܩܘܒܠ ܐܘܪܫܠܡ. ܘܚܙܘ ܗ̄ܘܘ ܐܢܫܐ ܣܓܝ̈ܐܐ ܕܐܬܝܢ ܗ̄ܘܘ ܡܢ ܪܘܚܩܐ: ܕܢܚܙܘܢ ܠܡܫܝܚܐ: ܡܛܠ ܕܢܦܩ ܗ̄ܘܐ ܛܒܐ ܕܐܣܘ̈ܬܐ ܕܢܨ̈ܚܢܘܗܝ ܒܐܬܪ̈ܘܬܐ ܡܕܒܪ̈ܐ. ܘܟܕ ܚܙܘ ܒܐܢܫܐ ܗܢܘܢ ܡܪܝܗܒ ܘܫܡܫܓܪܡ ܘܚܢܢ ܛܒܘܠܪܐ: ܐܬܘ ܗ̄ܘܘ ܐܦ ܗܢܘܢ ܥܡܗܘܢ ܠܐܘܪܫܠܡ. ܘܟܕ ܥܠܘ ܗ̄ܘܘ ܠܐܘܪܫܠܡ: ܚܙܐܘܗ̄ܝ ܗ̄ܘܘ ܠܡܫܝܚܐ ܘܚܕܝܘ ܥܡ ܟܢ̈ܫܐ ܕܢܩܦܝܢ ܗ̄ܘܘ ܠܗ. ܘܚܙܘ ܗ̄ܘܘ ܐܦ ܠܝܗܘܕ̈ܝܐ: ܕܩܝܡܝܢ ܗ̄ܘܘ ܟ̈ܢܝܫܝܢ: ܘܡܬܚܫܒܝܢ ܗ̄ܘܘ ܕܡܢܐ ܢܥܒܕܘܢ ܠܗ. ܡܥܩܝܢ ܗ̄ܘܘ ܓܝܪ: ܕܚܙܝܢ ܗ̄ܘܘ ܕܣܓ̈ܝܐܐ ܕܐܢܫܘܬܐ ܕܥܡܗܘܢ ܡܘܕܝܢ ܗ̄ܘܘ ܒܗ. ܘܗܘܘ ܬܡܢ ܒܐܘܪܫܠܡ ܝܘ̈ܡܬܐ ܥܣܪܐ. ܘܟܬܒ ܗ̄ܘܐ ܚܢܢ ܛܒܘܠܪܐ ܟܠܡܕܡ ܕܚܙܐ ܗ̄ܘܐ ܕܥܒܕ ܗ̄ܘܐ ܡܫܝܚܐ: ܐܦ ܫܪܟܐ ܕܡܕܡ ܕܥܒܕ ܗ̄ܘܐ ܠܗ ܬܡܢ: ܗ̄ܘܘ ܩܕܡ ܕܢܐܬܘܢ ܠܬܡܢ: ܘܗܦܟܘ ܗ̄ܘܘ ܘܐܬܘ ܗ̄ܘܘ ܠܐܘܪܗܝ.. ܘܥܠܘ ܗ̄ܘܘ ܩܕܡ ܐܒܓܪ ܡܠܟܐ ܡܪܗܘܢ ܕܫܕܪ ܗ̄ܘܐ ܐܢܘܢ. ܘܩܪܘ ܗ̄ܘܘ ܠܗ ܦܢܝܬܐ ܕܐܓܪ̈ܬܐ ܘܐܘܒܠܘ ܗ̄ܘܘ ܥܡܗܘܢ. ܘܡܢ ܒܬܪ ܕܐܬܩܪ̈ܝ ܗ̈ܢܝ ܐܓܪ̈ܬܐ: ܫܪܝܘ ܗ̄ܘܘ ܕܢܫܬܥܘܢ ܩܕܡ ܡܠܟܐ ܟܠ ܡܕܡ ܕܚܙܘ: ܘܟܠ ܡܕܡ ܕܥܒܕ ܗ̄ܘܐ ܡܫܝܚܐ ܒܐܘܪܫܠܡ. ܘܩܪܐ ܗ̄ܘܐ ܚܢܢ ܛܒܘܠܪܐ ܩܕܡܘܗ̄ܝ. ܟܠ ܡܕܡ ܕܟܬܒ ܗ̄ܘܐ ܘܐܝܬܝ ܥܡܗ. ܘܟܕ ܫܡܥ ܗ̄ܘܐ ܐܒܓܪ ܡܠܟܐ: ܐܬܡܗ ܗ̄ܘܐ ܘܐܬܕܡܪ: ܐܦ ܪ̈ܘܪܒܢܘܗ̄ܝ ܕܩܝܡܝܢ ܗ̄ܘܘ ܩܕܡܘܗ̄ܝ.. ܘܐܡܪ ܠܗܘܢ ܐܒܓܪ. ܗܠܝܢ ܚܝ̈ܠܐ ܠܐ ܗܘܘ ܕܒܢ̈ܝ ܐܢܫܐ: ܡܛܠ ܕܠܝܬ ܕܚܝܐ ܡܝ̈ܬܐ ܐܠܐ ܐܠܗܐ ܒܠܚܘܕ. ܨܒܐ ܗ̄ܘܐ ܕܝܢ ܐܒܓܪ: ܕܗܘ ܩܢܘܡܗ ܢܥܒܪ ܗ̄ܘܐ ܘܢܐܙܠ ܠܦܠܣܛܝܢܐ ܘܢܚܙܐ ܗ̄ܘܐ ܒܥܝ̈ܢܘܗ̄ܝ. ܟܠ ܡܕܡ ܕܥܒܕ ܗ̄ܘܐ ܡܫܝܚܐ. ܘܡܛܠ ܕܠܐ ܐܫܟܚ ܕܢܥܒܪ ܒܐܬܪܐ ܕܪ̈ܗܘܡܝܐ ܕܠܘ ܕܝܠܗ ܗ̄ܘܐ: ܕܠܡܐ

ܒܠܠܝܐ ܗܘܐ ܕܠܡܐ ܬܗܘܐ[1] ܠܡܒܠܒܠܘܬܐ ܗܢܝܐ: ܟܬܒ ܗܘܐ ܐܓܪܬܐ ܘܫܕܪ ܗܘܐ ܠܡܫܝܚܐ ܒܐܝܕܗ ܕܚܢܢ ܛܒܘܠܪܐ. ܘܢܦܩ ܗܘܐ ܡܢ ܐܘܪܗܝ. ܒܐܪܒܥܣܪܐ ܒܐܕܪ. ܘܥܠ ܗܘܐ ܠܐܘܪܫܠܡ ܒܬܪܬܥܣܪܐ ܒܢܝܣܢ ܒܐܪܒܥܐ ܒܫܒܐ. ܘܐܫܟܚܗ ܗܘܐ ܠܡܫܝܚܐ ܒܝܬ ܓܡܠܝܐܝܠ ܪܒܐ ܕܝܗܘܕܝܐ. ܘܐܬܩܪܝܬ ܗܘܬ ܐܓܪܬܐ ܩܕܡܘܗܝ. ܐܝܟ ܕܟܬܝܒܐ ܗܘܬ ܗܟܢܐ. ܐܒܓܪ ܐܘܟܡܐ ܠܝܫܘܥ ܐܣܝܐ ܛܒܐ ܕܐܬܚܙܝ ܒܐܬܪܐ ܕܐܘܪܫܠܡ. ܡܪܝ ܫܠܡ. ܫܡܥܬ ܥܠܝܟ ܘܥܠ ܐܣܘܬܟ ܕܠܐ ܗܘܬ ܒܣܡ̈ܡܢܐ ܘܒܥܩܪ̈ܐ ܡܐܣܐ ܐܢܬ: ܐܠܐ ܒܡܠܬܟ ܥܘܝܪ̈ܐ ܡܦܬܚ ܐܢܬ. ܘܠܚܓܝܪ̈ܐ ܡܗܠܟ ܐܢܬ. ܘܠܓܪ̈ܒܐ ܡܕܟܐ ܐܢܬ. ܘܠܚܪ̈ܫܐ ܡܫܡܥ ܐܢܬ. ܘܠܡܚܝܠܐ ܘܠܡܫܪ̈ܝܐ ܡܩܝܡ ܐܢܬ ܘܡ̈ܟܐܒܐ ܒܗ ܒܡܠܬܟ ܡܐܣܐ ܐܢܬ. ܐܦ ܡܝ̈ܬܐ ܡܩܝܡ ܐܢܬ. ܘܟܕ ܗܠܝܢ ܬܕܡܪ̈ܬܐ ܪ̈ܘܪܒܬܐ ܫܡܥܬ ܕܥܒܕ ܐܢܬ: ܣܡܬ ܒܪܥܝܢܝ: ܕܐܘ ܐܠܗܐ ܐܢܬ ܕܢܚܬܬ ܡܢ ܫܡܝܐ ܘܥܒܕܬ ܗܠܝܢ: ܐܘ ܒܪܗ ܐܢܬ ܕܐܠܗܐ: ܕܗܠܝܢ ܟܠܗܝܢ ܥܒܕ ܐܢܬ. ܡܛܠ ܗܢܐ ܟܬܒܬ ܒܥܝܬ ܡܢܟ: ܕܬܬܠܐܐ ܠܘܬܝ. ܟܕ ܗܢܝ ܐܢܐ ܠܟ. ܘܟܐܒܐ ܡܕܡ ܕܐܝܬ ܠܝ ܬܐܣܐ ܐܝܟ ܕܗܝܡܢܬ ܒܟ. ܐܦ ܗܢܐ ܬܘܒ ܫܡܥܬ. ܕܝܗܘܕܝܐ ܪܛܢܝܢ ܥܠܝܟ ܘܪܕܦܝܢ ܠܟ: ܘܐܦ ܕܢܨܠܒܘܢܟ ܒܥܝܢ: ܘܡܬܚܫܒܝܢ ܒܟ ܒܝܫܬܐ. ܡܕܝܢܬܐ ܚܕܐ ܙܥܘܪܬܐ ܐܝܬ ܠܝ: ܘܫܦܝܪܐ ܘܠܬܪܘܝܢ ܣܦܩܐ ܠܡܥܡܪ: ܒܗ ܒܫܝܢܐ. ܘܟܕ ܡܪܢ ܗܘܐ ܩܒܠ ܠܐܓܪܬܐ ܒܝܬ ܪܒ ܟܗ̈ܢܐ ܕܝܗܘܕܝܐ: ܐܡܪ ܠܗ ܠܚܢܢ ܛܒܘܠܪܐ: ܙܠ ܘܐܡܪ ܠܗ ܠܡܪܟ ܕܫܕܪܟ ܠܘܬܝ: ܛܘܒܝܟ ܕܟܕ ܠܐ ܚܙܝܬܢܝ ܗܝܡܢܬ ܒܝ. ܟܬܝܒ ܓܝܪ ܥܠܝ: ܕܐܝܠܝܢ ܕܚܙܝܢ ܠܝ ܠܐ ܢܗܝܡܢܘܢ ܒܝ. ܘܕܟܬܒܬ ܠܝ ܕܐܬܐ ܠܘܬܟ: ܗܘ̄ ܡܕܡ ܕܐܫܬܕܪܬ ܠܗ ܟܠܗ. ܠܗܪܟܐ ܡܫܠܡ ܕܐܬܡܠܐ ܠܗ. ܘܣܠܩ ܐܢܐ ܠܝ ܠܘܬ ܐܒܝ ܕܫܕܪܢܝ: ܘܡܐ ܕܣܠܩܬ ܠܘܬܗ: ܫܕܪ ܐܢܐ ܠܟ ܚܕ ܡܢ ܬܠܡ̈ܝܕܝ: ܕܟܐܒܐ ܡܕܡ ܕܐܝܬ ܠܟ ܢܐܣܐ ܘܢܚܠܡ. ܘܠܟܠܗܘܢ ܡܢ ܕܐܝܬ ܠܘܬܟ. ܢܬܠ ܐܦ ܠܚ̈ܝܐ ܕܠܥܠܡ. ܘܠܡܕܝܢܬܟ ܢܗܘܐ ܒܪܝܟ. ܘܒܥܠܕܒܒܐ ܬܘܒ ܠܐ ܢܫܬܠܛ ܒܗ ܠܥܠܡ. ܟܕ ܕܝܢ ܚܙܐ ܗܘܐ ܚܢܢ ܛܒܘܠܪܐ: ܕܗܟܢܐ ܐܡܪ ܗܘܐ ܠܗ ܝܫܘܥ. ܘܟܕ ܕܨܝܪܐ ܗܘܐ ܕܡܠܟܐ. ܫܩܠ ܗܘܐ ܘܨܪ ܨܠܡܗ ܕܝܫܘܥ ܒܣܡ̈ܡܢܐ ܓܒ̈ܝܐ. ܘܐܬܐ ܗܘܐ ܥܡ

[1]See note 1, p. 161. The modal here occurs after *da-l-mā* 'lest.'

ܛܒܘܠܪܐ ܥܡܗ ܠܐܒܓܪ ܡܠܟܐ ܡܪܗ. ܘܟܕ ܚܙܝܗ ܗܘܐ ܐܒܓܪ ܡܠܟܐ ܠܨܠܡܐ ܗܘ ܩܒܠܗ ܗܘܐ ܒܚܕܘܬܐ ܪܒܬܐ: ܘܣܡܗ ܗܘܐ ܒܐܝܩܪܐ ܪܒܐ: ܒܚܕ ܡܢ ܒ̈ܬܐ ܕܐܦܕܢܐ ܕܝܠܗ. ܘܐܫܬܥܝ ܗܘܐ ܠܗ ܟܠܡܕܡ ܕܫܡܥ ܗܘܐ ܡܢ ܝܫܘܥ : ܟܕ ܟܬܝ̈ܒܢ ܗ̈ܘܝ ܠܗ ܡ̈ܠܘܗܝ ܒܟ̈ܬܒܐ. ܘܡܢ ܒܬܪ ܕܐܣܬܠܩ ܗܘܐ ܡܫܝܚܐ ܠܫܡܝܐ: ܫܕܪ ܗܘܐ ܝܗܘܕܐ ܬܐܘܡܐ ܠܘܬ ܐܒܓܪ ܠܐܕܝ ܫܠܝܚܐ: ܗܘ ܕܐܝܬܘܗܝ ܗܘܐ ܡܢ ܫܒܥܝܢ ܘܬܪܝܢ ܫܠܝܚ̈ܝܢ. ܘܟܕ ܐܬܐ ܐܕܝ ܠܟܪܟܐ ܕܐܘܪܗܝ. ܫܪܐ ܗܘܐ ܒܒܝܬ ܛܘܒܝܐ ܒܪ ܛܘܒܝܐ ܝܗܘܕܝܐ: ܗܘ ܕܐܝܬܘܗܝ ܗܘܐ ܡܢ ܦܠܣܛܝܢܐ. ܘܐܫܬܡܥ ܗܘܐ ܒܟܠܗ̇ ܟܪܟܐ. ܘܥܠ ܗܘܐ ܚܕ ܡܢ ܚܐܪ̈ܘܗܝ ܕܝܠܗ ܕܐܒܓܪ ܘܐܡܪ ܗܘܐ ܥܠܘܗܝ ܕܐܕܝ: ܗܘ ܕܫܡܗ ܗܘܐ ܥܒܕܘ ܒܪ ܥܒܕܘ: ܡܢ ܪ̈ܫܢܐ ܕܬ̈ܟܒ ܘܟܕܐ ܕܝܠܗ ܕܐܒܓܪ. ܘܗܐ ܐܬܐ ܐܣܝܐ ܕܫܪܐ ܗܪܟܐ: ܗܘ ܕܫܠܚ ܗܘܐ ܠܟ ܥܠܘܗܝ ܝܫܘܥ : ܕܡܫܕܪ ܐܢܐ ܠܘܬܟ ܚܕ ܡܢ ܬܠܡ̈ܝܕܝ. ܘܟܕ ܫܡܥ ܗܘܐ ܐܒܓܪ ܗܕܝܢ ܗܠܝܢ ܘܓܒܘܪ̈ܬܐ ܪ̈ܘܪܒܬܐ ܕܥܒܕ ܗܘܐ ܐܕܝ ܘܐܣܝ̈ܘܬܐ ܬܡܝ̈ܗܬܐ ܕܡܐܣܐ ܗܘܐ: ܣܒܪ ܗܘܐ ܒܪܥܝܢܗ ܘܐܡܪ: ܕܫܪܝܪܐܝܬ ܗܢܘ ܗܘ ܕܫܠܚ ܗܘܐ ܠܗ ܝܫܘܥ : ܘܡܐ ܕܣܠܩܬ ܠܫܡܝܐ: ܡܫܕܪ ܐܢܐ ܠܟ ܚܕ ܡܢ ܬܠܡ̈ܝܕܝ: ܘܟܐܒܟ ܢܐܣܐ. ܘܫܕܪ ܗܘܐ ܕܝܢ ܐܒܓܪ ܘܩܪܝܗ ܠܛܘܒܝܐ ܘܐܡܪ ܗܘܐ ܠܗ: ܫܡܥܬ ܕܓܒܪܐ ܚܕ ܚܝܠܬܢܐ ܐܬܐ ܘܫܪܐ ܒܒܝܬܟ. ܐܣܩܝܗܝ ܠܘܬܝ. ܟܒܪ ܢܫܟܚ ܠܝ ܣܒܪܐ ܫܦܝܪܐ ܘܚܘܠܡܢܐ ܡܢ ܠܘܬܗ. ܘܩܕܡ ܗܘܐ ܛܘܒܝܐ ܠܨܦܪܐ ܐܚܪܢܐ ܘܕܒܪܗ ܗܘܐ ܠܐܕܝ ܫܠܝܚܐ ܘܐܥܠܗ ܠܘܬ ܐܒܓܪ: ܟܕ ܝܕܥ ܗܘܐ ܗܘ ܐܕܝ: ܕܒܚܝܠܐ ܕܐܠܗܐ ܡܫܕܪ ܗܘܐ ܠܘܬܗ. ܘܟܕ ܣܠܩ ܗܘܐ ܐܕܝ ܘܥܠ ܗܘܐ ܠܘܬ ܐܒܓܪ: ܟܕ ܩܝܡܝܢ ܚܐܪ̈ܘܗܝ ܠܘܬܗ: ܒܗ ܒܡܥܠܢܐ ܕܠܘܬܗ ܚܙܘܐ ܬܡܝܗܐ ܐܬܚܙܝ ܗܘܐ ܠܗ ܠܐܒܓܪ ܡܢ ܦܪܨܘܦܗ ܕܐܕܝ. ܘܟܕ ܒܫܥܬܐ ܕܚܙܐ ܗܘܐ ܐܒܓܪ ܚܙܘܐ ܗܘ: ܢܦܠ ܗܘܐ ܘܣܓܕ ܗܘܐ ܠܐܕܝ. ܘܬܗܪܐ ܪܒܐ ܐܚܕ ܗܘܐ ܠܟܠܗܘܢ ܗܢܘܢ ܕܩܝܡܝܢ ܗܘܘ ܩܕܡܘܗܝ. ܗܢܘܢ ܓܝܪ ܠܐ ܚܙܘ ܠܚܙܘܐ ܗܘ ܕܐܬܚܙܝ ܗܘܐ ܠܗ ܠܐܒܓܪ. ܗܝܕܝܢ ܐܡܪ ܠܗ ܐܒܓܪ ܠܐܕܝ: ܕܫܪܝܪܐܝܬ ܬܠܡܝܕܗ ܐܢܬ ܕܝܫܘܥ ܗܘ ܓܢܒܪܐ ܚܝܠܬܢܐ ܒܪܗ ܕܐܠܗܐ: ܗܘ ܕܫܠܚ ܗܘܐ ܠܝ ܕܡܫܕܪ ܐܢܐ ܠܟ ܚܕ ܡܢ ܬܠܡ̈ܝܕܝ ܠܐܣܝܘܬܐ ܘܠܚܝ̈ܐ. ܐܡܪ ܠܗ ܐܕܝ: ܡܛܠ ܕܡܢ ܩܕܝܡ ܗܝܡܢܬ ܒܗ ܒܡ

ܕܥܒܕܘ ܠܗ: ܡܛܠ ܗܘ ܗܘ ܐܫܬܕܪܬ ܠܘܬܟ: ܘܟܕ ܬܘܒ ܬܗܝܡܢ ܒܗ: ܒܟܠ ܡܕܡ ܕܬܗܝܡܢ ܒܗ ܢܗܘܐ ܠܟ. ܐܡܪ ܠܗ ܐܒܓܪ. ܗܟܢܐ ܗܝܡܢܬ ܒܗ: ܕܠܝܗܘܕܝܐ ܗܢܘܢ ܕܙܩܦܘܗܝ. ܗܘܘ: ܒܥܝܬ ܗܘܝܬ ܕܐܕܒܪ ܠܝ ܚܝܠܐ: ܘܐܙܠ ܐܚܪܒ ܐܢܘܢ. ܘܡܛܠ ܡܠܟܘܬܐ ܗܝ ܕܪ̈ܗܘܡܝܐ ܐܬܟܠܝܬ ܒܩܝܡܐ ܕܫܝܢܐ ܕܣܝܡ ܠܝ ܥܡ ܡܪܝ ܩܣܪ ܛܝܒܪܝܣ ܐܝܟ ܐܒܗ̈ܝ. ܩܕܡ̈ܝܐ. ܐܡܪ ܠܗ ܐܕܝ. ܡܪܢ ܨܒܝܢܐ ܗܘ ܕܐܒܘܗܝ ܫܡܠܝ. ܘܟܕ ܫܠܡ ܨܒܝܢܐ ܕܐܒܘܗܝ: ܐܬܪܝܡ ܠܘܬ ܐܒܘܗܝ: ܘܝܬܒ ܥܡܗ ܒܫܘܒܚܐ: ܗܘ ܕܐܝܬܘܗܝ. ܗܘܐ ܥܡܗ ܡܢ ܥܠܡ. ܐܡܪ ܠܗ ܐܒܓܪ: ܐܦ ܐܢܐ ܡܗܝܡܢ ܐܢܐ ܒܗ ܘܒܐܒܘܗܝ. ܐܡܪ ܠܗ ܐܕܝ. ܡܛܠ ܕܗܟܢܐ ܗܝܡܢܬ: ܣܐܡ ܐܢܐ ܐܝܕܝ ܥܠܝܟ ܒܫܡܗ ܘܗܘ ܕܗܝܡܢܬ ܒܗ. ܘܒܗ ܒܫܥܬܐ ܕܣܡ ܗܘܐ ܐܝܕܗ ܥܠܘܗܝ: ܐܬܐܣܝ ܡܢ ܟܝܒܐ ܕܟܐܒܐ ܕܐܝܬ ܗܘܐ ܠܗ ܢܘܦܙܐ. ܘܐܬܕܡܪ ܗܘܐ ܐܒܓܪ ܘܐܬܕܡܪ ܕܐܝܟܢܐ ܕܫܡܥ ܗܘܐ ܠܗ ܥܠ ܝܫܘܥ: ܕܥܒܕ ܗܘܐ ܘܡܐܣܐ: ܗܟܢܐ ܐܦ ܗܘ ܐܕܝ ܕܠܐ ܣܡܐ ܡܕܡ ܡܐܣܐ ܗܘܐ ܒܫܡܗ ܕܝܫܘܥ. ܘܐܦ ܠܥܒܕܘ ܒܪ ܥܒܕܘ ܦܘܕܓܪܐ ܐܝܬ ܗܘܐ ܠܗ ܒܪ̈ܓܠܘܗܝ. ܘܐܦ ܗܘ ܩܪܒ ܗܘܐ ܠܗ ܪ̈ܓܠܘܗܝ. ܘܣܡ ܗܘܐ ܐܝܕܗ ܥܠܝܗܝܢ ܘܐܣܝܗ ܗܘܐ. ܘܬܘܒ ܠܐ ܗܘܬ ܠܗ ܦܘܕܓܪܐ ܘܐܦ ܒܡܕܝܢܬܐ ܟܠܗ ܐܣܘ̈ܬܐ ܪ̈ܘܪܒܬܐ ܡܐܣܐ ܗܘܐ. ܘܚܝܠܐ ܬܡܝܗܬܐ ܥܒܕ ܗܘܐ ܒܗ. ܐܡܪ ܠܗ ܐܒܓܪ. ܗܫܐ ܕܝܕܥ ܟܠ ܐܢܫ: ܕܒܚܝܠܗ ܕܝܫܘܥ ܡܫܝܚܐ ܗܠܝܢ ܬܕܡܪ̈ܬܐ ܥܒܕ ܐܢܬ: ܘܗܐ ܬܡܝܗܝܢ ܚܢܢ ܒܥܒ̈ܕܝܟ. ܒܥܐ ܐܢܐ ܗܟܝܠ ܡܢܟ: ܕܬܫܬܥܐ ܠܝ ܥܠ ܡܐܬܝܬܗ ܕܡܫܝܚܐ ܕܐܝܟܢܐ ܗܘܬ: ܘܥܠ ܚܝܠܗ ܫܒܝܚܐ ܘܥܠ ܬܕܡܪ̈ܬܐ ܐܝܠܝܢ ܕܫܡܥܬ ܗܘܐ ܠܝ ܕܥܒܕ ܗܘܐ. ܐܝܠܝܢ ܕܐܢܐ ܚܙܝܬ ܐܝܟ ܥܡ ܫܪܟܐ ܕܚܒܪ̈ܝܟ. ܐܡܪ ܠܗ ܐܕܝ. ܡܢ ܗܕܐ ܠܐ ܫܬܩ ܐܢܐ ܕܐܟܪܙ. ܕܡܛܠ ܗܕܐ ܗܘ ܓܝܪ ܐܫܬܕܪܬ ܠܗܪܟܐ ܕܐܡܪ ܘܐܠܦ. ܠܟܠ ܡܢ ܕܨܒܐ ܕܢܗܝܡܢ ܐܝܟܘܬܟ. ܠܡܚܪ ܟܢܘܫ ܠܝ ܟܠܗ̇ ܡܕܝܢܬܐ ܘܐܙܪܘܥ ܒܗ̇ ܡܠܬܐ ܕܚܝܐ ܒܟܪܘܙܘܬܐ ܕܡܟܪܙ ܐܢܐ ܩܕܡܝܟܘܢ. ܘܒܬܪ ܗܟܢܐ ܗܘ ܦܩܕ ܗܘܐ ܐܒܓܪ ܠܥܒܕܘ ܒܪ ܥܒܕܘ ܗܘ ܕܐܬܐܣܝ ܗܘܐ ܡܢ ܟܐܒܐ ܡܪܝܪܐ ܕܪ̈ܓܠܘܗܝ. ܕܢܥܒܕ ܗܘܐ ܟܪܘܙܐ: ܘܢܥܒܪ ܗܘܐ ܒܟܘܠܗ̇ ܡܕܝܢܬܐ: ܘܬܬܟܢܫ ܗܘܬ ܐܢܫܘܬܐ ܟܠܗ̇ ܓܒܪ̈ܐ ܘܢܫ̈ܐ ܠܕܘܟܬܐ ܗ̇ܝ ܕܡܬܩܪܝܐ ܒܝܬ ܛܘܒ̈ܝܐ:

ܠܐܬܪܐ ܙܘܚܐ ܕܟ̈ܠܗ ܒܩ̈ܪܝܐ: ܕܢܫܡܥܘܢ ܗܘܘ ܡܠܦܢܘܬܗ ܕܐܕܝ ܫܠܝܚܐ. ܘܟܕ ܐܬܟܢܫܬ ܟܠܗ̇ ܡܕܝܢܬܐ ܓܒܪ̈ܐ ܘܢܫ̈ܐ ܐܠܦ ܠܗܘܢ ܐܕܝ ܫܠܝܚܐ ܟܠ ܗܝܡܢܘܬܐ ܕܡܪܢ ܝܫܘܥ ܡܫܝܚܐ ܘܐܡܪ ܠܗܘܢ: ܐܝܟ ܕܩܒܠܘ ܡܠܬܗ ܕܡܫܝܚܐ ܢܗܘܘܢ ܙܕܝܩܝܢ: ܘܐܦ ܐܝܟ ܕܪܚܡܝܢ ܕܫܠܡܘܬܗܘܢ ܒܗ ܒܟܝܢܬܐ: ܘܟܕ ܢܐܬܘܢ ܠܒ̈ܬܝܗܘܢ. ܘܚܕܝ ܗܘܐ ܒܗܕܐ ܗܘ ܐܕܝ ܫܠܝܚܐ: ܕܚܙܐ ܗܘܐ ܕܫܦܝܪܬܐ ܕܐܢܫܘܬܐ ܕܡܕܝܢܬܐ ܦܫܛ ܠܗ ܠܘܬܗ. ܘܬܠܡܝܕܐ ܗܘܘ ܐܝܟ ܕܟܠ ܝܘܡ ܗܘܘ ܒܗܘ ܒܙܒܢܐ: ܟܕ ܐܦ ܗܢܘܢ ܗܠܝܢ ܬܠܡܝܕܐ ܒܬܪ ܦܪܘܫܬܐ ܡܠܠ ܡܠܬܐ ܗܘܘ ܠܟܠܗܘܢ. ܘܗܝܡܢܘ ܗܘܘ ܒܡܫܝܚܐ ܕܒܪܘܚܗ ܕܡܫܝܚܐ. ܘܟܕ ܚܙܐ ܗܘܐ ܐܒܓܪ ܡܠܟܐ: ܕܟܠܗ̇ ܡܕܝܢܬܐ ܚܕܝܐ ܗܘܬ ܒܡܠܦܢܘܬܗ. ܐܡܪ ܠܗ ܐܦ ܗܘ ܐܒܓܪ ܡܠܟܐ ܠܐܕܝ ܫܠܝܚܐ: ܡܛܠ ܟܠ ܐܝܟܐ ܕܪܚܐ ܐܢܬ. ܒܢܝ ܒܝܬܐ ܒܗ ܥܕܬܐ ܕܐܝܟ ܕܗܝܡܢܘ ܘܡܗܝܡܢܝܢ ܒܟܠܗܝܢ ܘܐܝܟ ܡܐ ܕܦܩܕ ܠܟ ܡܢ ܡܪܢ. ܗܘܝܬ ܡܫܡܫ ܐܢܬ ܒܟܢ̈ܫܐ ܠܐܟܠܗ̇. ܘܐܝܟ ܕܗܘܦ ܒܟܡ ܩܠܝܠܐ ܒܥܕܢܐ ܗܕܐ: ܬܫܒܘܚܬܐ ܙܥܘܪܬܐ ܡܛܠ ܐܢܐ ܕܐܬܐ ܠܗܘܢ. ܕܡܕܡ ܟܡ ܠܫܡܫܬܐ ܠܐ ܢܗܘܐ ܠܗܘܢ ܒܟܕܐ ܐܚܪܢܐ. ܘܟܠܐ ܡܕܡ ܕܡܬܒܥܐ ܠܟ ܠܢܦܩܬܗ ܕܒܝܬܐ ܐܢܐ ܝܗܒ ܐܢܐ ܠܟ ܕܟܠ ܢܗܘܐ. ܟܕ ܗܘܐ ܡܠܬܝ ܫܠܝܛܐ ܘܡܡܠܟܐ ܒܟܪܟܐ ܗܢܐ. ܘܟܠ ܐܢܫ ܐܚܪܢܐ ܗܘܬ ܥܠܠܐ ܐܝܬ ܠܗ. ܡܫܠܛܬ ܒܐܦܝܐ ܕܐܢܫܘ ܕܡܠܟܘܬܐ. ܘܟܕ ܒܥܬ ܗܘܐ ܐܒܓܪ ܡܠܟܐ. ܒܐܦܝܐ ܕܡܠܟܘܬܗ ܚܙܐ ܗܘܐ ܗܘ ܘܪܘܪܒܢܘܗܝ. ܟܡܗ ܘܟܕ ܚܙܬܐ ܕܒܟܘܢ ܡܫܟܚ ܗܘܘ ܐܦ ܝܘܡ ܒܟܠܗܘܢ: ܕܐܦܝ ܗܘܐ ܙܟܝܘܢ ܠܗܘܢ: ܟܕ ܚܙܝܢ ܗܘܘ ܒܟܘܫܬܐ ܕܦܫܛ ܗܘܘ ܒܗ: ܘܡܘܕܝܢ ܗܘܘ ܒܟܪܝܗܘܢ ܕܡܫܝܚܐ. ܘܟܕ ܓܒܐ ܗܘܐ ܐܕܝ ܒܟܬܐ: ܡܩܪܒ ܗܘܘ ܒܗ ܕܪܬܐ ܘܡܘܕܝܢ: ܝܘܡ ܘܐܫܬܐ ܕܡܕܝܢܬܐ. ܘܐܡܪ ܡܫܡܫܝܢ ܗܘܘ ܟܠܐ ܩܕܡ ܚܝܗܘܢ. ܫܘܕܝܐ ܕܝܢ ܘܡܟܒܕܝܢ ܦܠܐ ܕܒܥܬܐ ܕܒܪܬܐ ܗܝܐ: ܟܕ ܚܙܘ ܗܘܘ ܐܬܐܬܐ ܕܥܒܕ ܗܘܐ ܐܕܝ: ܙܗܝܪܐ ܗܘܘ ܘܟܡܪܘ ܗܘܘ ܒܟܠܬܐ: ܕܒܠܚܘܕ ܡܕܡ ܗܘܘ ܡܕܡ ܢܟܘ ܘܟܠܐ ܐܠܗ̈ܝܗܘܢ ܠܟܪ ܡܢ ܟܠܐ ܕܟܠܬܐ ܕܡܪܝܐ ܟܪܐ. ܘܦܟܪ ܗܘܘ ܘܐܡܪܝ. ܕܥܪܩܬ ܗܝܐ ܕܗܝ ܙܟܐ ܡܗܘܪܐ ܘܡܟܝܐ. ܕܫܟܡ ܗܘܝ ܟܠܐ ܙܟܬܐ ܕܟܪܝ ܗܘܐ ܠܐܬܪܐ ܕܦܠܛܝܐ. ܘܟܠܐ ܐܝܟ ܠܡܬܕܐ ܕܡܗܝܡܢ ܗܘܘ ܒܡܫܝܚܐ:

ܡܩܒܠ ܗܘܐ ܠܗܘܢ ܐܕܝ ܐܠܝܢ ܘܡܥܡܕ ܗܘܐ ܠܗܘܢ ܒܫܡ ܐܒܐ ܘܒܪܐ ܘܪܘܚܐ ܕܩܘܕܫܐ. ܐܦ ܝܗܘܕܝܐ ܬܓܪ̈ܐ ܠܢܡܘܣܐ ܘܢܒ̈ܝܐ ܐܠܝܢ ܕܬܓܪ̈ܐ ܡܪܒܝܢ ܗܘܘ: ܐܦ ܗܢܘܢ ܐܬܛܦܝܣܘ ܗܘܘ ܘܐܬܬܠܡܕܘ ܘܐܘܕܝܘ ܗܘܘ ܒܡܫܝܚܐ ܕܒܪܗ ܗܘ ܕܐܠܗܐ ܚܝܐ. ܟܠ ܕܝܢ ܐܒܓܪ ܡܠܟܐ ܘܟܠ ܐܕܝ ܫܠܝܚܐ ܚܙܐ ܗܘܐ ܠܐܢܫ ܕܡܗܝܪܐܝܬ ܢܗܝܡ ܗܘܐ ܒܗ ܒܡܫܝܚܐ. ܐܓܝ ܕܝܢ ܥܒܕ ܫܐܪ̈ܐ ܘܬܝ̈ܓܐ ܕܡܠܟܐ ܘܦܠܘܛ ܘܥܒܫܠܡܐ ܘܒܪܣܡܝܐ ܥܡ ܫܪܟܐ ܕܐܚ̈ܝܐ ܚܒ̈ܪܝܗܘܢ ܢܩܦܘܗ̇ ܗܘܘ ܠܐܕܝ ܫܠܝܚܐ. ܘܡܩܒܠ ܗܘܐ ܐܢܘܢ ܘܡܫܬܘܦ ܐܢܘܢ ܒܗ ܒܬܫܡܫܬܐ: ܟܕ ܩܪܝܢ ܗܘܘ ܒܕܝܬܩܐ ܥܬܝܩܬܐ ܘܚܕܬܬܐ ܘܒܢܒ̈ܝܐ ܘܒܣܦܪ̈ܝܗܘܢ ܕܫܠܝ̈ܚܐ ܒܟܠܝܘܡ ܒܗܘܢ ܡܬܗܓܝܢ ܗܘܘ ܀

ܘܡܢ ܒܬܪ ܫܢܝܐ ܕܒܢܐ ܗܘܐ ܐܕܝ ܫܠܝܚܐ ܥܕܬܐ ܒܐܘܪܗܝ. ܘܐܬܩܢܗ̇ ܗܘܐ ܒܟܠ ܡܕܡ ܕܙܕܩ ܗܘܐ ܠܗ̇: ܘܐܠܦ ܗܘܐ ܠܟܗ̈ܢܐ ܘܐܫܡܫܬܐ ܕܡܕܝܢܬܐ ܘܐܦ ܒܩܘܪ̈ܝܐ ܐܚܪ̈ܢܝܬܐ ܕܪ̈ܚܝܩ ܘܕܩܪ̈ܝܒ ܒܢܐ ܗܘܐ ܥܕ̈ܬܐ ܘܟܠܠ ܘܨܒܬ ܘܡܫܡ̈ܫܢܐ ܘܩܫ̈ܝܫܐ ܐܩܝܡ ܗܘܐ ܒܗܝܢ. ܘܕܩܪܝܢ ܗܘܘ ܒܟܬ̈ܒܐ ܐܠܦ ܗܘܐ ܒܗܝܢ. ܘܛܟ̈ܣܐ ܕܬܫܡܫܬܐ ܠܗܘܢ ܘܠܒܪ ܐܠܦ ܗܘܐ. ܒܬܪ ܗܠܝܢ ܟܠܗܝܢ ܐܬܟܪܗ ܗܘܐ ܟܘܪܗܢܐ ܕܢܦܩ ܗܘܐ ܒܗ ܡܢ ܥܠܡܐ ܗܢܐ. ܘܩܪܐ ܗܘܐ ܠܐܓܝ ܩܕܡ ܟܠܗ ܟܢܫܐ ܕܥܕܬܐ ܘܩܪܒܗ ܗܘܐ ܘܥܒܕܗ ܗܘܐ ܡܕܒܪܢܐ ܘܦܩܘܕܐ ܒܕܘܟܬܗ. ܘܠܟܠܗܝܢ ܕܡܫܡܫܢܐ ܗܘܐ. ܒܬܪܗ ܗܘܐ ܩܫܝܫܐ. ܘܠܥܒܫܠܡܐ ܕܣܦܪܐ ܗܘܐ. ܒܬܪܗ ܗܘܐ ܡܫܡܫܢܐ. ܘܡܢ ܒܬܪ ܬܠܬܐ ܝܘ̈ܡܝܢ ܐܚܪ̈ܢܝܢ ܕܫܡܠܝ ܗܘܐ ܘܡܩܒܠ ܗܘܐ ܣܗܕܘܬܐ ܕܩܛܝܠܘܬܐ ܕܒܪܘܪܘܬܗ ܡܢ ܒܢ̈ܝ ܠܫܡܫܬܗ ܡܕܡ ܚܐܪܐ ܟܠܗܘܢ ܕܩܡ ܗܘܐ ܠܗ ܗܘ ܡܢ ܥܠܡܐ ܗܢܐ. ܘܐܬܘܗ̇. ܗܘܐ ܝܘܡܐ ܚܡܫܐ ܒܫܒܐ. ܒܐܪܒܥܣܪܐ ܒܐܝܪ ܢܝܚܐ. ܘܐܒܠܐ ܪܒܐ ܘܒܚܫܐ ܡܪܝܪܐ ܗܘܬ ܒܟܠܗ̇ ܟܠܗ̇ ܡܕܝܢܬܐ. ܟܠ ܗܘܐ ܕܝܢ ܟܪ̈ܣܛܝܢܐ ܒܠܚܘܕ ܡܥܩܝܢ ܗܘܘ ܥܠܘܗܝ: ܐܠܐ ܐܦ ܝܗܘܕܝܐ ܘܚܢ̈ܦܐ ܕܐܝܬ ܗܘܘ ܒܗ̇ ܒܡܕܝܢܬܐ ܗܕܐ. ܐܒܓܪ ܕܝܢ ܡܠܟܐ ܝܬܝܪ ܡܢ ܟܠ ܐܢܫ ܡܥܩ ܗܘܐ ܥܠܘܗܝ.. ܗܘ ܘܪ̈ܘܪܒܢܐ ܕܡܠܟܘܬܗ. ܘܒܟܪܝܘܬܐ ܕܢܦܫܗ ܫܠܚ ܗܘܐ ܘܡܫܟܒܗ ܠܐܣܛܠܐ ܕܡܠܟܘܬܗ ܒܗܘ ܝܘܡܐ. ܘܒܪܡܫܐ ܚܫ̈ܝܫܬܐ ܥܒܕ ܗܘܐ ܠܗ ܥܡ ܟܠ ܐܢܫ. ܘܥܡܐ ܟܠܗ ܕܡܕܝܢܬܐ ܕܚܙܐ

ܗܘܐ ܠܗ: ܡܬܕܡܪ ܗܘܐ ܒܗ ܘܒܥܠܐ ܚܐܫ ܗܘܐ ܒܠܒܗ.. ܘܒܐܡܪܐ ܪܒܐ ܘܡܬܛܪܐ ܪܚܡ ܗܘܐ ܘܡܒܪܗ ܐܝܟ ܚܕ ܡܢ ܬ̈ܘܪܒܝܐ ܡܠ ܕܫܪܝܐ ܗܘܐ ܘܫܡܫܗ ܗܘܐ ܠܡܒܪܐ ܪܒܐ ܕܟ̈ܠܗܝܢ ܕܪ̈ܟܫܬܐ ܗܘ ܐܝܟ ܕܫܡܫ ܗܘܘ ܒܗ ܕܡܠܟ ܐܘܪܗ ܐܒܗ̈ܬܐ ܘܐܒܗܘܗܝ ܘܐܚܘ̈ܗܝ ܡܠܟܐ. ܐܝܟ ܫܡܫܗ ܗܘܐ ܫܡܫܬܐ ܒܒܪ̈ܘܬܐ ܘܒܢܝܢܬܐ ܪܒܬܐ. ܘܟܠܗ ܒܗܠܝܢ ܕܒܝܬܐ ܐܝܟܢܐ ܗܘܐ ܡܢ ܒܝܬܐ ܠܒܝܬܐ ܘܡܥܠܐ ܗܘܐ ܐܝܟ ܫܥܬܐ ܘܦܘܪܝܐ ܕܒܗܘܢܗ ܒܒܝܬ ܗܘܘ ܡܢ ܥܒܐ ܠܥܒܐ ܐܝܟ ܦܩܕܐ ܘܡܠܟܐ ܕܡܚܝܠܐ ܗܘܐ ܠܗܘܢ ܡܢ ܐܦ ܥܡܠܐ ܘܐܝܟ ܡܠܬܗ ܘܐܡܪ: ܕܒܗ ܗܘܐ ܡܕܒܪܢܐ ܘܦܩܘܕܐ ܘܕܢܬܐ ܕܒܘܪܫܗ ܡܢ ܒܬܪܗ ܒܐܝܕܐ ܕܒܘܢܝܬܐ ܕܡܚܝܠܐ ܗܘܐ ܡܢܗ ܡܕܡ ܒܠܐ ܐܢܫ ܀

The Martyrdom of St. Barbara[1]

ܣܗܕܘܬܐ ܕܩܕܝܫܬܐ ܒܪܒܪܐ

ܒܙ̈ܒܢܐ ܗܢܘܢ: ܕܒܗܘܢ ܡܫܠܛ ܗܘܐ ܡܟܣܡܝܢܘܣ ܗܘ ܪܫܝܥܐ ܘܥܘܠܐ: ܒܡܠܟܘܬܗ ܕܡܟܣܡܝܢܘܣ ܡܠܟܐ: ܗܘܐ ܪܕܘܦܝܐ ܪܒܐ ܥܠ ܟܠܗܘܢ ܟܪ̈ܣܛܝܢܐ. ܐܝܬ ܗܘܐ ܓܒܪܐ ܚܕ ܪܒܐ ܒܐܬܪܐ ܕܐܠܝܘܦܘܠܝܣ ܒܡܕܝܢܬܐ ܕܫܡܗ̇ ܓܠܝܘܢ: ܘܩܪܝܒܐ ܡܢ ܐܝܠܘܦܢܐ ܩܕܡܠ ܐܬܪܥܐ: ܘܫܡܗ ܐܝܠܘܗܝ ܗܘܐ ܕܝܘܣܩܘܪܘܣ. ܗܢܐ ܥܬܝܪ ܗܘܐ ܛܒ: ܒܢܝܢ ܕܝܢ ܐܝܠܘܗܝ ܗܘܐ ܚܕܐ. ܐܝܬ ܗܘܐ ܠܗ ܕܝܢ ܒܪܬܐ ܚܕܐ ܚܒܝܒܬܐ: ܕܫܡܗ̇ ܒܪ̈ܒܪܐ: ܘܫܦܝܪܐ ܗܘܬ ܛܒ. ܗܘ ܕܝܢ ܐܒܘܗ̇ ܚܒܝܒ ܗܘܐ ܠܗ̇ ܛܒ: ܘܒܢܐ ܠܗ̇ ܡܓܕܠܐ ܚܕ ܪܡܐ: ܘܫܒܩܗ̇ ܒܗ. ܐܝܟܢܐ ܕܠܐ ܬܬܚܙܐ ܠܒܢ̈ܝܢܫܐ: ܡܛܠ ܫܘܦܪܗ̇ ܪܒܐ: ܘܡܛܠ ܕܪܚܡܬܐ ܕܦܪܨܘܦܗ̇. ܐܬܘ ܕܝܢ ܐܢ̈ܫܐ ܡܢ ܪܘܪ̈ܒܢܐ: ܘܫܐܠܘ ܒܗ̇ ܐܒܘܗ̇ ܡܛܠܬܗ̇: ܐܝܟܢܐ

[1]From ܫܪ̈ܒܐ ܕܣܗ̈ܕܐ ܘܕܩܕ̈ܝܫܐ: *Acta martyrum et sanctorum,* ed. Paulus Bedjan (Leipzig: Harrassowitz, 1892), III, 356ff.

ܕܢܬܠܝܗ̇ ܠܓܒܪܐ. ܗܘ ܕܝܢ ܥܠ ܠܘܬܗ̇ ܘܐܡܪ ܠܗ̇: ܒܪܬܝ: ܐܢ̈ܫܐ ܡܢ ܪ̈ܘܪܒܢܐ ܡܠܠܘ ܥܡܝ ܡܛܠܬܟܝ: ܐܬܠܟܝ ܠܓܒܪܐ. ܐܝܟܢܐ ܨܒܝܐ ܐܢܬܝ: ܒܪܬܝ ܚܒܝܒܬܝ: ܐܡܪܝ ܠܝ. ܗܝ ܕܝܢ ܟܕ ܫܡܥܬ ܗܘ ܒܪܘܚܐ: ܐܪܝܡܬ ܥܝ̈ܢܝܗ̇ ܠܫܡܝܐ ܘܐܡܪܬ ܕܠܐ ܐܬܠܝܕ ܐܢܐ: ܕܗܘܝܐ ܐܫܬܘܪ. ܘܐܠܐ ܗܘܬ ܢܓܕ: ܕܐܢܐ ܢܦܫܝ ܠܡܘܬܐ ܡܫܠܡܐ ܐܢܐ. ܗܘ ܕܝܢ ܚܢܩ: ܘܢܦܩ ܡܢ ܠܘܬܗ̇. ܡܬܐܡܪ ܗܘܐ ܕܝܢ ܒܟܠܗ̇ ܕܡܕܝܢܬܐ ܒܫܡܗ̇ ܡܬܟܪܙܐ ܗܘܬ. ܐܝܬ ܗܘܐ ܕܝܢ ܒܗ̇ ܐܦܝܣܩܘܦܐ ܗܘܓܠܐ: ܐܝܟܢܐ ܕܒܢܝܐ ܘܡܠܠܬܐ ܬܫܡܫܬܐ. ܟܕ ܕܝܢ ܦܩܕ ܐܢܘܢ ܠܐܦܝܣܩܘܦܐ ܗܘ ܕܗܘܣܦܘܪܘܣ ܐܒܘܗ̇: ܕܐܝܟܢܐ ܙܕܩ ܠܗܘܢ ܕܢܥܒܕܘܢ: ܘܦܩ̄ܕ ܠܟܠܚܕ ܡܢܗܘܢ ܐܝܟܢܐ ܡܥܡܠܐ: ܥܢ ܗܘܐ ܠܬܪܥܐ ܕܣܚܪܐ: ܘܬܡܢ ܐܘܚܪ ܘܟܕ ܫܒܩܐ. ܢܬܬܝ ܕܝܢ ܗܝ ܐܡܬܗ ܕܡܫܝܚܐ ܒܪܒܪܐ: ܐܝܟܢܐ ܕܬܚܙܐ ܒܝܬܐ ܕܟܠܗ̇ ܕܟܠܝܢ. ܘܟܕ ܚܙܬ ܒܟܢܫܬܐ ܬܫܡܫܬܐ: ܘܐܬܟܢܫܬ ܕܬܪܬܝܢ ܒܥܝ̈ܢܝܗ̇ ܟܠܗܘܢ ܦܬܝܚ ܟܕ ܐܢܫܐ. ܗܢܐ ܘܐܡܪܬ ܠܗܘܢ ܠܬܪ̈ܥܝܬܐ: ܠܡܢܐ ܟܠܗܘܢ ܬܪܬܝܢ ܒܬܪ ܦܬܚܘܗܝ؟ ܗܢܘ ܘܐܡܪܘ ܠܗ̇: ܕܐܝܟܢܐ ܦܩܕ ܠܢ ܕܢܥܒܕ ܗܟܢܐ. ܘܐܡܪܬ ܠܗܘܢ ܕܝܢ ܗܘܕܝܬܗ ܕܡܫܝܚܐ ܒܪܒܪܐ: ܗܘ ܡܢܐ ܕܐܡܪܐ ܐܢܐ ܠܟܘܢ ܫܡܘܥ ܕܠܐ ܕܚܠܐ: ܘܡܚܕܐ ܒܒܢܝܢ ܘܡܠܠܬ ܐܦܝܣܩܘ ܠܗ ܗܕܪܐ ܒܗܘܬܐ ܐܚܪܬܐ. ܘܐܡܪܘ ܠܗ̇ ܗܢܝܢ: ܡܪܬܐ: ܕܫܠܝܚܐ ܘܡܢ ܕܡܫܠܡܐ ܟܕ ܢܬܐ ܐܟܡܐ ܘܣܘܐ: ܚܝ ܠܐ ܡܬܚܫܚ ܠܡܥܒܕ ܡܕܡ ܚܢܬܗ. ܐܡܪܐ ܠܗܘܢ ܐܡܬܗ ܕܐܠܗܐ ܒܪܒܪܐ: ܗܘ ܡܕܡ ܕܐܢܐ ܐܡܪܐ ܐܢܐ ܠܟܘܢ ܫܡܘܥ ܕܠܐ ܕܚܠܐ. ܘܟܕ ܢܬܐ ܐܟܡܐ. ܐܢܐ ܡܦܣܩܐ ܐܢܐ ܠܗ ܠܟܘܪܐ. ܗܝܕܝܢ ܕܝܢ ܫܡܥܘܗ̇: ܘܡܚܕܐ ܐܦ ܗܘܬ ܐܚܪܬܐ: ܐܝܟܢܐ ܕܦܩܕܬ ܠܗܘܢ.

ܟܕ ܕܝܢ ܡܫܠܬ ܗܝ ܡܕܝܢܬܐ ܘܟܠ ܡܕܡ ܠܡܕܝܢܬܐ ܕܐܘܪܗܝ ܕܡܫܝ̈ܚܝܐ: ܐܬܦܢܝܬ ܠܡܕܝܢܬܐ ܘܫܡܥܬ ܒܛܟܣܗ̇ ܟܠ ܥܣܪܐ ܦܘܩܕ̈ܢܘܗܝ ܕܓܠܝܢܐ ܒܢܫܐ. ܘܟܡ ܗܘ ܫܡܥܬܗ ܕܓܠܝܢܐ ܟܠܗܘܢ ܕܫܢܝܐ ܟܕܡܐ ܠܗܘܢܐ: ܠܬܕܡܘܪܬܐ ܕܐܠܗ̇ ܕܚܙܐ: ܘܠܬܫܒܘܚܬܐ ܕܐܠܗܐ. ܟܕ ܕܝܢ ܟܠܗ̇ ܠܟܠܗ̇ ܕܠܗ̇: ܐܦ ܕܦܩܘܬܐ ܡܕܝܢܬܐ ܕܢܫܒܬܗ̇: ܒܗ̇ ܒܐܪܥܐ ܗܝ ܐܬܓܠܝ.

ܘܡܢ ܕܘܟܬܐ ܗܝ: ܟܠܗ ܢܦܫ ܕܚܝܐ ܠܫܘܠܡܐ ܘܠܡܘܕܪܐ. ܗܕܐ ܗܝ ܡܫܝܚܘܬܐ ܕܐܬܓܠܝܬ ܠܥܘܕܪܢ: ܕܒܗ ܗܘ ܡܕܒܪ ܫܘܒܚ ܡܫܝܚܐ ܐܪܥ ܗܘܬ ܪܫܝܗ ܒܝܫܬܐ: ܘܒܟܠ ܗܘܬ ܠܥܕܐ ܡܢ ܢܘܚܝ ܟܪܘܒܗ ܘܡܬܡܕܪܢ. ܗܕܐ ܗܝ ܡܬܡܘܕܝܢܘܬܐ ܕܐܬܕܡܝܬ ܠܡܢܝܢܐ ܕܫܠܘܚܐ: ܕܒܗ ܫܡܐ ܕܡܢ ܟܪܘܙ ܐܡܘܗ ܐܟܝܕ: ܠܡܬܡܘܕܝܢܘܬܐ ܕܒܬܫܒܚܬܐ: ܕܒܗ ܡܥܪܐ ܒܟܠܬܐ ܐܬܐܦ. ܗܕܐ ܗܝ ܡܬܡܘܕܝܢܘܬܐ: ܕܐܝܬ ܒܗ ܡܢ̈ܝܐ ܚ̈ܝܐ: ܗܠܝܢ ܕܫܩܠܬ ܡܢ ܡܪܝ ܐܝܬܬܐ ܗܝ ܫܡܪܬܐ.

ܬܘܒ ܕܝܢ ܟܝܢܐ ܡܢ ܢܩܡܝ: ܟܕ ܢܦܪܐ ܗܘܬ ܕܬܐܙܠ ܠܗ ܠܟܠܝܐ ܗܝ ܫܘܕܥܗ ܕܡܫܝܚܐ ܒܪܒܪܐ: ܚܙܬ ܦܬܟܪܐ ܕܠܗܘܢ ܫܒܩ ܗܘܐ ܐܟܘܗ ܕܡܪܝܐ: ܘܐܬܬܠܝܬ ܗܘܬ ܪܘܚܐ ܕܡܘܕܥܐ: ܗܘ ܡܟܘܢܐ ܕܢܝ̈ܚܬܐ ܘܡܘܟܢܐ ܕܥܘܩ̈ܒܐ ܘܡܢܕܪܢܐ ܕܫܪ̈ܒܬܐ: ܗܝ ܗܕܐ ܫܘܕܥܗ ܕܡܫܝܚܐ: ܘܡܦܪܢܐ ܗܘܬ ܒܥܘܦܪܐ: ܕܘܟܝ ܘܕܫܟܝ ܠܟܠܡܢ̈ܐ. ܟܕ ܗܟܠ ܚܙܬ ܠܦܬܟܪܐ ܗܢܘܢ ܢܦܫܐ: ܪܫܡܬ ܒܐܦ̈ܝܗܘܢ ܟܕ ܐܡܪܐ ܠܗܘܢ: ܕܐܟܬܟܘܢ ܢܗܘܘܢ ܥܒܘܕ̈ܝܟܘܢ: ܘܐܝܟ ܕܬܬܟܠܝܢ ܢܬܟܘܢ. ܘܟܕ ܫܠܡܬ ܬܘܒ ܠܡܙܕܩܐ ܕܒܗ ܗܘ ܢܦܪܐ ܗܘܬ: ܟܝܠܘܬܐ ܕܠܘܬ ܐܠܗܐ ܟܗ ܐܡܝܢܬ ܐܝܢܐ ܗܘܬ.

ܟܕ ܕܝܢ ܐܫܬܡܥ ܟܝܢܐ ܘܐܬܬܨܝ ܕܠܗ ܕܟܠܢ: ܩܡ ܡܢ ܐܘܪܚܗ ܗܘ ܪܫܝܐ ܐܟܘܗ ܕܡܫܡܘܪܘܫ. ܘܒܠ ܗܘܐ ܠܟܠܢ ܐܟܦ ܕܝܘܢܗ: ܘܝܗܒ ܬܠܬ ܟܘ̈ܝܢ ܟܝܢܐ. ܘܝܗܒ ܘܐܡܪ ܠܐܣܝܐ: ܬܠܬ ܟܘ̈ܝܢ ܐܟܡܬܗܘܢ؟ ܐܡܪܢ ܠܗ ܐܣܝܐ: ܟܪܬܐ ܗܘ ܩܡܝܬ ܠܝ ܕܡܟܝܐ ܢܟܝܒ. ܘܐܬܦܢܝ ܠܗܬ ܟܪܬܗ ܘܐܡܪ: ܐܢܬ ܩܡܝܬ ܐܝܟ ܠܐܣܝܐ: ܕܬܠܬ ܟܘ̈ܝܢ ܢܬܐܣܘܢ؟ ܢܝܚ ܘܐܡܪܬ ܠܗ: ܐܝܢ ܐܟ: ܥܡܝܪ ܩܡܝܪܬ. ܡܛܠ ܕܬܠܬ ܐܝܢ ܟܘ̈ܝܢ ܡܢܗܘܢ ܠܟܠ ܟܪܝܗܐ ܕܐܬܐ ܠܟܠܡܐ: ܘܬܪܬܝܢ ܟܠܗܘܢ ܢܦܩܬܐ ܐܝܢ. ܘܢܫܟܚܘ ܗܘܐ ܐܟܘܗ ܘܝܗܒ ܠܟܠܢ. ܘܐܡܪܬ ܠܗ: ܟܡܐ ܗܪ ܡܢ ܬܪܬܝܢ ܡܢܗܘܢ ܢܝܚܝܢ ܗܠܝܢ ܬܠܬ. ܘܐܡܪܬ ܬܘܒ ܠܬܘܗ ܐܡܬܗ ܕܡܫܝܚܐ ܟܪܟܪܐ: ܐܬܟܝܢ ܗܫܐ ܐܟ ܘܚܕ: ܗܐ ܓܒܪ

ܐܒܐ: ܘܗܘܐ ܒܪܐ: ܘܗܘܐ ܪܘܚܐ ܩܕܝܫܐ.

ܘܟܕ ܥܒܕ ܗܠܝܢ ܐܒܘܗܝ: ܐܬܡܠܝ ܚܡܬܐ ܘܪܘܓܙܐ ܣܓܝܐܐ. ܘܥܒܕܗ ܣܦܩܐ ܕܒܠܘܗܝ ܬܠܐ ܗܘܐ: ܐܚܕܝܗ ܕܒܥܠܕܒܒܗ. ܘܡܠܟܬ ܕܝܢ ܡܕܝܢܬܐ ܒܪܒܪܐ: ܘܐܬܬܦܬܚܬ ܫܐܕܐ ܗܝ ܕܠܗ ܡܕܒܪܐ ܗܘܬ: ܘܡܫܠܡܬܗ ܒܝܘܡܗ. ܘܡܚܕܐ ܐܦܩܬܗ ܗܘܬ ܠܗܬ ܛܘܪܐ ܗܘ ܕܐܬܡܪ ܐܝܬ ܗܘܐ ܠܡܫܡܠܝܘܬܗ ܩܕܡܝܬܐ ܬܪܝܢ: ܕܪܝܫ ܗܘܘ ܒܛܘܪܐ ܗܘ: ܘܣܘܐܪܗ ܟܕ ܚܪܫܐ. ܘܟܕ ܐܬܡܢܝ ܐܒܘܗ ܠܬܗܘܢ: ܡܥܠܠ ܗܘܐ ܠܗܘܢ: ܐܝܟ ܗܘ ܕܣܘܐܪܗ ܠܒܪܬܗ. ܘܚܕ ܡܢܗܘܢ: ܡܛܠ ܕܪܝܫܐ ܗܘܐ ܕܡܫܬܘܕܥ: ܡܩܪܒܬܐ ܢܦܫܐ ܗܘܐ ܕܠܐ ܢܗܘܐ ܠܗ. ܘܗܘܐ ܐܚܪܢܐ ܕܝܢ ܦܓܪܗ ܗܘܐ ܪܕܘܗ: ܘܠܐܒܘܗ ܡܚܘܐ ܗܘܐ ܠܗ. ܟܕ ܕܝܢ ܚܙܬ ܡܕܝܢܬܐ ܡܕܡ ܕܓܕܫ: ܠܛܠܗ ܗܘܬ: ܘܡܚܕܐ ܗܘܐ ܗܘ ܡܠܟܘܬܗ ܣܥܪܢܘܬܐ. ܘܗܘܐ ܟܢܫܐ ܣܥܪܢܘܬܐ ܗܠܝܢ ܟܠ ܡܟܪܗ ܕܡܕܝܢܬܐ ܟܕܡܐ ܠܘܩܒܠ. ܘܟܕ ܫܠܡ ܗܘܐ ܐܒܘܗ ܒܬܪܗ ܠܛܘܪܐ ܗܘ: ܘܐܥܒܪܗ ܗܘܐ ܠܡܕܝܢܬܐ ܘܢܟܕܗ ܡܪܪܐܝܬ: ܘܐܣܕܗ ܒܡܥܪܬܐ ܕܪܥܝܗ ܘܩܒܪ ܗܘܐ ܠܗ. ܘܐܚܬܗ ܗܘܐ ܡܢ ܗܘ ܛܘܪܐ: ܘܐܙܠܗ ܗܘܐ ܘܣܓܕܗ ܒܒܝܬܐ ܚܕ ܥܡܛܠܐ: ܘܐܚܕ ܘܚܬܡ ܒܐܦܝܗ ܒܚܘܪܬܗ. ܘܐܡܪ ܠܟܠܗ ܢܛܘܪܐ: ܐܝܟܢܐ ܕܠܐ ܢܥܒܕ ܐܢܫ ܢܦܠ ܠܒܬܗ: ܒܟܠܐ ܕܐܘܪܚ ܘܐܘܕܥ ܠܟܠܗ ܠܡܪܚܡܢܘܬ ܗܡܢܘܢܐ: ܐܝܟܢܐ ܕܢܘܟܪܝܗ.

ܟܕ ܕܝܢ ܐܬܐ ܗܡܝܢܐ: ܦܩܕ ܕܢܬܒܢܐ ܠܗ ܡܥܠܬܐ. ܟܕ ܕܝܢ ܐܬܐ ܐܒܘܗ ܠܡ ܒܪܡܠܟܐ ܒܡܘܠܕܢܐ ܐܦܝܗ ܡܢ ܒܝܬܐ ܗܘ ܕܒܗ ܣܒܝܐ ܗܘܬ: ܘܐܫܬܘܝܗ ܠܗܡܝܢܐ: ܟܕ ܡܣܡܟ ܠܗ ܐܒܘܗ ܒܓܢܒܪܐ: ܕܒܢܝܢܐ ܡܢܐ ܢܒܢܝܗ. ܗܕܝܢ ܝܗܒ ܗܡܝܢܐ ܟܠ ܒܢܝܢ ܕܠܗ: ܘܟܕ ܚܙܐ ܒܡܦܩܢܗ ܐܡܪ ܠܗ: ܡܢܐ ܦܪܣܐ ܐܝܬܝܟ؟ ܣܘܦ ܟܠ ܢܦܫܟ: ܘܕܚܠ ܠܐܠܗܐ. ܘܐܠܐ ܬܕܚܠ: ܠܡܕܝܢܬܐ ܡܪܕܐ ܡܫܠܡ ܐܢܐ ܠܟ. ܚܙܐ ܕܝܢ ܘܐܡܪܬ ܠܗ ܗܡܝܢܘܬܗ ܕܡܫܝܚܐ: ܕܐܢܐ ܡܫܠܡ ܐܢܐ: ܕܐܢܐ ܡܗܝܡܢ ܒܥܕܬܐ ܕܬܘܕܝܬܐ ܐܡܪ ܠܐܠܗܐ ܦܪܘܩܐ ܕܟܠ: ܗܘ

ܕܟܒܒ ܫܡܫܐ ܘܐܪܥܐ ܘܟܠ ܕܒܗܘܢ. ܡܛܠ ܕܝܢ ܐܠܗܝ̈ ܥܡܡܐ ܕܥܒܝܕ ܐܡܪ: ܕܦܘܡܐ ܐܝܬ ܠܗܘܢ ܘܠܐ ܡܡܠܠܝܢ: ܥܝܢ̈ܐ ܐܝܬ ܠܗܘܢ ܘܠܐ ܚܙܝܢ: ܐܕܢ̈ܐ ܐܝܬ ܠܗܘܢ ܘܠܐ ܫܡܥܝܢ: ܐ̈ܝܕܐ ܐܝܬ ܠܗܘܢ ܘܠܐ ܡܓܫܝܢ: ܐܟܘܬܗܘܢ ܢܗܘܘܢ ܥܒܘܕ̈ܝܗܘܢ:[1] ܘܐܝܠܝܢ ܕܬܟܝܠܝܢ ܥܠܝܗܘܢ: ܗܟܢ ܗܝܡܢܘܬܐ ܐܬܡܠܟ ܫܪܪܬܐ: ܘܦܩܕ ܕܢܥܠܘܢܗ̇: ܘܠܦܬܓܡܗ̇ ܕܠܐ ܚܘܫܒ ܒܝܬܕܐ ܢܟܥܟܗܘܢ: ܘܟܬ̈ܒܐ ܕܡܪܕܐ ܢܬܚܪܡ ܡܢܗܘܬܐ ܕܟܠ ܓܡܝܪܘܬܗ̇. ܘܢܩܒܠܘܢ ܠܗ̇ ܗܝܡܢܐ: ܒܕܡܐ ܕܟܠܗ ܓܡܝܪܘܬܗ̇ ܐܬܦܠܦܠ ܒܕܡܐ. ܦܩܕ ܗ̄ܘܐ ܕܬܐܙܠ ܠܟܠܗ̇ ܡܠܟܘܬܐ: ܟܕ ܡܬܚܫܒ ܕܟܠܗܝܢ ܡܕܝܢܬܐ ܢܬܒܕܪܗ̇. ܟܦܠܓܗ ܕܝܢ ܕܠܠܝܐ: ܕܢܚ ܗ̄ܘܐ ܠܘܬܗ̇ ܢܗܘܪܐ ܪܒܐ: ܘܐܬܚܙܝ ܠܗ̇ ܦܪܨܘܦܐ ܟܕ ܐܡܪ: ܐܬܚܝܠܝ ܘܐܬܠܒܒܝ ܗܝܡܢܬܐ ܕܟܠ ܚܕܬܐ. ܗܐܕܐ ܓܒܪ ܕܡܫܬܠܛ: ܣܓܘܬܐ ܪܒܬܐ ܗܘܬ ܒܥܡܡܐ ܘܒܐܪܥܐ ܒܝܘܡܝܟܝ. ܠܐ ܬܕܚܠܝܢ ܡܢ ܠܡܣܩ̈ܘܗܝ ܕܛܪܘܢܐ ܗܢܐ: ܐܢܐ ܓܝܪ ܗ̄ܘܐ ܐܢܐ ܥܡܟܝ: ܘܐܦܪܘܩܟܝ ܡܢ ܠܡܣܩ̈ܘܗܝ. ܟܕ ܗܟܝܠ ܐܡܪ ܠܗ̇: ܐܝܟ ܠܡܠܘܬܗ̇: ܘܠܐ ܐܬܚܙܝ̈ ܡܢܗܘܢ ܟܠ ܦܓܪܗ̇. ܐܠܐ ܢܚܬܐ ܗ̄ܘܬ ܘܪܘܙܐ ܗܘ ܡܘܗܒܬܐ ܡܕܢܚܬܐ: ܠܥܠܡܐ ܕܗܘܐ ܠܗ̇ ܡܢ ܡܪܢ ※

From the Tale of Sindban the Wise[2]

ܡܢ ܬܫܥܝܬܐ ܕܣܢܕܒܢ ܚܟܝܡܐ

ܐܝܬ ܗ̄ܘܐ ܡܠܟܐ ܚܕ ܕܫܡܗ ܗ̄ܘܐ ܟܘܪܫ. ܘܡܢ ܢܫ̈ܐ ܣܘ̈ܓܐܗ̄ܝ. ܒܪܐ ܠܐ ܗܘܐ ܠܗ ܘܐܝܬ ܗ̄ܘܐ ܠܗ ܢܫ̈ܐ ܫܒܥ. ܘܨܡ ܘܨܠܝ ܘܢܕܪ ܢܕܪ̈ܐ. ܘܡܟܟ ܢܦܫܗ. ܘܒܥܐ ܐܠܗܐ. ܘܝܗܒ ܠܗ ܒܪܐ ܚܕ. ܘܪܒܐ ܛܠܝܐ ܘܡܫܘܚ ܐܝܟ ܐܪܙܐ. ܘܡܗܒܗ

[1]Ps. 115:5–8.

[2]*Sindban oder die sieben weisen Meister,* ed. Friedrich Baethgen (Leipzig: Hinrichs'sche Buchhandlung, 1879).

ܕܢܐܠܦ ܚܟܡ̈ܬܐ. ܘܗܘܐ ܬܠܬ ܫܢܝܢ ܠܘܬ ܣܦܪܘܗܝ ܘܡܕܡ ܠܐ ܝܠܦ. ܘܐܡܪ ܕܝܢ ܡܠܟܐ. ܕܗܢܐ ܛܠܝܐ ܠܐ ܢܗܘܐ ܨܝܕ ܣܦܪܘܗܝ ܪܒܘ ܥܡܝ. ܡܕܡ ܠܐ ܝܠܦ. ܐܠܐ ܐܬܠܘܗ̄ܝ ܠܣܢܕܒܢ ܚܟܝܡܐ. ܡܛܠ ܕܐܝܬܘܗ̄ܝ ܝܬܝܪ ܚܟܝܡܐ. ܘܡܝܬܪ ܡܢ ܟܠܗܘܢ ܦܝܠܣ̈ܘܦܐ. ܘܩܪܐ ܡܠܟܐ ܠܣܢܕܒܢ ܘܐܡܪ ܠܗ: ܐܝܟܢܐ ܨܒܝܬ ܕܬܐܠܦܝܘܗ̄ܝ ܠܛܠܝܐ ܐܡܪ ܠܝ. ܘܥܢܐ ܣܢܕܒܢ ܘܐܡܪ ܠܡܠܟܐ. ܡܠܦ ܐܢܐ ܠܛܠܝܐ ܒܝܪ̈ܚܐ ܐܫܬ. ܒܕܡܐ ܕܢܕܥ ܡܢ ܟܠ ܦܝܠܣܘܦ ܕܐܝܬ ܬܚܝܬ ܐܘܚܕܢܝ. ܘܐܝܟܢܐ ܕܠܐ ܡܫܡܠܐ ܐܢܐ ܡܕܡ ܕܐܡܪܬ ܢܣܒܘܢ ܚ̈ܝܝ ܡܢ ܐܪܥܐ. ܘܟܠ ܕܨܒܐ ܐܢܐ ܠܟ ܢܗܘܐ. ܠܘܬܟ ܒܪ ܕܡܠܟ̈ܐ ܐܝܟ ܢܘܪܐ ܐܬܚܡܝܘ. ܘܐܡܪܬ ܕܬܡܟܠܐ ܠܐܢܫ ܐܘܨܒܬܗ. ܐܝܟܢܐ ܠܝ ܕܡܠܦ ܐܢܐ ܠܒܪܟ ܡܢܝ. ܡܠܟܐ ܘܟܕ ܢܫܡܠܐ ܝܘܠܦܢܗ. ܬܬܠ ܠܝ ܗܘ ܡܕܡ ܕܐܬܒܥ ܡܢܟ.

ܘܐܡܪ ܡܠܟܐ ܗܘ ܕܒܥܝܬ ܐܬܠ ܠܟ. ܐܡܪ ܣܢܕܒܢ ܒܠܚܘܕ ܕܠܐ ܢܣܒ ܐܢܬ ܕܢܣܒܪܘܢ ܐܢܫ ܠܘܬܝ. ܠܐ ܬܟܣܪܘܗ̄ܝ ܠܘܬ ܐܚܪܢܐ. ܘܒܢܐ ܒܬܐ ܒܝܬܗܘܢ. ܘܗܘܐ ܣܢܕܒܢ ܒܢܝܐ ܠܡܠܟܐ. ܘܐܫܠܡ ܛܠܝܐ ܠܣܢܕܒܢ. ܘܦܩܕܗ ܘܐܡܪ ܠܗ. ܕܡܢ ܒܬܪ ܫܬܐ ܝܪ̈ܚܝܢ ܘܬܐܬܝܢ ܬܚܘܝܢ. ܢܐܬܐ ܛܠܝܐ ܠܘܬ ܐܒܘܗ̄ܝ. ܘܠܐ ܢܬܪܐ ܫܒܬܐ ܚܕܐ ܐܠܐ ܢܩܘܡ ܪܝܫܗ ܕܣܢܕܒܢ.

ܘܐܚܕ ܣܢܕܒܢ ܒܐܝܕܗ ܕܛܠܝܐ. ܘܐܘܒܠܗ ܠܒܝܬܗ ܘܒܢܐ ܠܗ ܒܝܬܐ ܪܘܚܐ. ܘܟܠܫܗ ܚܘܪܗ ܘܟܬܒ ܒܟܠ ܐܣܛ̈ܘܢܘܗ̄ܝ. ܘܟܬܒ ܣܢܕܒܝ[1] ܠܟܬܒܗ. ܘܡܠܦ ܗ̄ܘܐ ܠܗ. ܘܟܠܗ ܒܟܬܒܐ ܐܝܬ ܗ̄ܘܐ ܠܗܘܢ ܡܐܟܠܐ ܘܡܫܬܝܐ ܘܠܐ ܢܦܩ ܒܝܬܐ ܚܕ ܡܢ ܦܪܘܬܣܡܝܐ ܕܒܝܬܐ ܒܝܬܗܘܢ. ܘܒܬܪ ܫܬܐ ܝܪ̈ܚܝܢ ܝܠܦ ܛܠܝܐ

[1]For ܣܢܕܒܢ ܕܝܢ.

ܗܘ̇ ܗܕܝܢ ܕܠܐ ܡܒܓܐ ܐܝܟ ܡܢ ܒܫܢܝܐ ܕܢܐܠܦ ܐܒܘܬܗ. ܘܡܢ ܗܕܝܢ ܘܡܟܐ ܚܕ ܫܒܪ ܡܠܟܐ ܠܘܬ ܗܕܝܢ ܘܐܡܪ ܠܗ. ܡܢܐ ܐܝܬ ܠܘܬܟ ܘܦܫ ܗܘ ܘܐܡܪ ܠܗ. ܗܘ ܗܕܝܢ ܕܪܫܢ ܐܝܬ. ܠܡܚܪ ܡܫܬܐ ܐܝܟ ܠܗ ܠܛܠܝܐ ܠܘܬܟ ܒܒܕܝܐ ܕܬܪܬܝܢ ܥ̈ܕܝܢ ܠܝ ܡܪܢܐ ܣܓܝܐ. ܘܫܕܪ ܡܠܟܐ ܘܐܬܦܝܣ ܘܗܦܟ ܣܕܝܢ ܠܘܬ ܛܠܝܐ ܘܐܡܪ ܠܗ. ܣܓܝܐ ܐܝܟܐ ܕܒܗܝܐ ܠܠܝܐ. ܐܬܚܫܒ ܥܠ ܡܠܘܫܟ. ܒܗ̇ܝ ܕܒܢܝܐ ܐܝܟ ܕܐܘܒܠܟ ܠܘܬ ܐܒܘܟ.

ܘܡܢ ܒܬܪ ܕܒܪ ܒܡܠܘܫܗ ܕܛܠܝܐ. ܚܙܐ ܕܠܐ ܙܕܩ ܕܢܡܠܠ ܒܕܡܐ ܠܥܒܕܐ ܢܘܡܝܢ. ܡܛܠ ܕܕܢܠ ܗ̄ܘܐ ܒܠܘܗܝ ܕܠܐ ܢܒܘܬ. ܘܒܗ ܚܙܐ ܣܕܝܢ ܐܟܠ ܐܝ̈ܕܘܗܝ ܘܪ̈ܓܠܘܗܝ ܘܐܬܒܗܬ ܒܠܘܗܝ. ܘܚܙܐ ܛܠܝܐ ܠܪܓܠܗ ܕܐܬܬܒܗܬ ܘܐܡܪ ܠܗ. ܡܢܐ ܠܟ ܕܐܬܟܡܪ ܒܠܒܟ ܗܢܐ ܣܓܝܐܐ. ܡܛܠ ܕܠܝ ܦܩܕ ܐܝܬ ܠ ܕܠܐ ܐܡܠܠ ܢܘܣܐ ܚܕ ܟܠܗ ܐܝܟ ܐܠܐ ܦܘܡܕ ܠ ܗܘ ܗܕܝܢ ܕܪܫܢ ܐܝܬ. ܘܐܡܪ ܣܕܝܢ: ܒܗ ܐܣܡܟܬ ܡܫܟܐ ܒܟܢ ܐܒܘܟ ܕܠܡܚܪ ܢܐܬܐ ܒܪܟ ܠܘܬܟ. ܘܠܐ ܙܕܩ ܠ ܕܐܬܗܦܟ ܒܗ. ܘܠܐ ܒܪܐ ܐܝܟ ܕܐܗܘܐ ܠܘܬ ܐܒܘܟ ܕܝܠܐ. ܐܢܐ ܡܟܝܠ ܐܝܟ ܐܢܐ ܡܬܛܠܒܐ ܐܢܐ. ܚܝ ܐܝܬ ܒܪܝ ܠܐ ܬܡܠܠ ܒܕܡܐ ܕܒܢܝ̈ܢ ܥܒ̈ܕܐ ܢܘܡܝܢ. ܘܠܘܡܐ ܕܠܡܚܪ ܦܩܕ ܠܗ ܠܛܠܝܐ ܕܢܐܙܠ ܠܘܬ ܐܒܘܗ̄ܝ.

ܘܐܒܘܗ̄ܝ ܕܝܢ ܡܢ ܪܚܡܬܗ ܠܘܬ ܒܪܗ. ܚܙܐ ܠܗ ܚܒܝܒܐ ܐܝܟ ܕܬܠܬܝܢ ܗ̄ܘܘ ܒܒܗ. ܘܒܟܐ ܠܗ ܡܫܬܐ. ܗܕܝܢ ܡܪ̈ܝܗ̄ܝ ܐܒܘܗ̄ܝ ܘܡܪ̈ܒܝܗ ܠܘܬܗ ܘܢܫܩܗ. ܘܡܛܠܠ ܒܟܝܗ. ܗܘ ܠܐ ܡܛܠ ܒܟܢ ܐܒܘܗ̄ܝ. ܘܫܪܝ ܡܫܐܠ ܠܗ ܘܗܘ ܠܐ ܦܫ ܦܬܓܡܐ. ܗܕܝܢ ܐܡܪ ܡܠܟܐ ܠܐܚܝܢ ܕܣܕܪܘܗ̄ܝ. ܡܢܐ ܐܬܘܗ̄ܝ ܥܘܒܗ ܕܒܪܝ.

ܘܒܟܐ ܚܕ ܘܐܡܪ ܕܒܥܬܐ ܡܢܫ ܠܗ ܪܒܗ ܕܢܬܦܢܩ ܒܗ

ܘܠܒܫܗ ܘܡܢ ܗܘ ܒܣܪܐ ܦܓܪ ܠܒܝܫܗ. ܘܐܬܟܒܫ ܫܪܒܗ ܕܛܠܝܐ ܥܠ ܡܠܟܐ. ܘܟܕ ܚܙܐ ܡܢ ܢܟܣܘܗ̄ܝ ܕܡܠܟܐ. ܐܡܪܬ ܠܗ ܫܒܩܘܗ̄ܝ. ܐܒܐ ܕܛܠܝܐ ܐܢܐ. ܐܢܐ ܘܗܘ ܒܠܚܘܕ. ܒܪܝ ܡܘܕܐ ܠܝ ܫܪܒܗ. ܡܛܠ ܕܐܬܚܒܠ ܗ̄ܘܐ ܥܠ ܡܢ ܩܕܡ. ܘܡܘܕܝܢ ܕܐܠܗܗ ܠܐ ܡܣܘܪܐ ܗ̄ܘܐ. ܠܐ ܕܝܢ ܡܣܘܪܐ ܘܦܠܓܐ. ܡܛܠ ܕܐܡܗ ܕܛܠܝܐ ܡܒܣܡܐ ܗ̄ܘܬ ܥܠ ܫܘܩܗ. ܘܫܡܠܬܗ ܐܬܬ̈ܗ ܠܛܠܝܐ ܘܐܘܠܕܬܗ ܠܒܪܬܗ. ܘܫܪܝܬ ܬܡܠܠ ܒܡܪܗ. ܗܘ ܠܐ ܡܠܠ ܒܡܪܗ. ܘܠܐ ܦܫ ܠܗ ܦܬܓܡܐ. ܗܝܕܝܢ ܐܡܪܬ ܠܗ ܕܠܐ ܢܕܥܐ ܐܢܐ ܠܟ ܡܚܠܐ. ܘܐܦ ܠܐ ܐܢܬܝ ܡܠܟܐ. ܘܠܐ ܦܠܛ ܐܢܬ ܡܢ ܒܝܫ. ܐܡܪܐ ܐܢܐ ܠܟ ܡܘܕܝܢ. ܘܠܐ ܫܒܩܪܐ ܐܢܐ ܠܟ ܒܕܡܐ ܕܫܡܪܬ ܠܗ. ܘܐܦ ܛܠܝܐ ܐܢܬܝ. ܘܐܦ ܓܪ̈ܐ ܐܢܬ ܒܒܪ ܡܘܕܝܢ ܕܐܡܪܬ ܐܢܐ ܠܟ. ܢܕܥܐ ܐܢܐ ܕܐܒܘܟ ܗܘܐ ܘܐܬܡܣܟܢ ܘܐܬܦܪܫ ܘܐܢܐ ܡܛܠܬܐ ܐܢܐ ܠܗ ܠܐܒܘܟ. ܘܗܘܐ ܐܢܬ ܡܠܟܐ ܫܠܝܛܗ̄. ܘܫܩܠ ܐܢܬ ܠܟ ܒܢܫܐ. ܘܗܘܐ ܐܢܐ ܠܟ ܐܢܬܬܐ. ܘܡܢ ܒܬܪ ܕܐܡܪܬ ܠܛܠܝܐ ܗܠܝܢ ܐܫܬܡܥ ܫܡܥܐ ܪܒܐ. ܘܐܡܪ ܠܗ: ܕܟܕ ܕܠܐ ܡܡܠܠ ܐܢܐ ܒܟܠܗ ܘܠܐ ܒܟ ܐܝܟ ܐܚܪܢܐ ܒܕܡܐ ܕܒܢ̈ܝ ܫܢ̈ܝܐ ܢܫܡ̈ܬܗ. ܘܡܚܕܐ ܫܢ̈ܝܐ ܐܢܬ. ܦܘܫ ܦܬܓܡܐ ܡܢ ܟܠ ܬ̈ܠܡܝܕܝ. ܘܡܢ ܒܬܪ ܕܫܡܥܬ ܗܠܝܢ ܢܕܥܬ ܕܦܠܛܬ ܡܢ ܐܡܪܗ̇. ܘܕܚܠܬ ܘܐܬܚܫܒܬ. ܕܡܢܐ ܬܥܒܕ ܠܗ.

ܗܝܕܝܢ ܐܡܪܬ ܩܠܗ̇ ܠܒ. ܘܡܛܝܬ ܥܠ ܐܦ̈ܝܗ̇. ܘܬܠܝܬ ܡܐܢ̈ܝܗ̇. ܘܫܡܥ ܡܠܟܐ ܩܠܗ̇ ܘܩܪܗ̇. ܘܫܐܠܗ̇ ܘܐܡܪ ܠܗ̇ ܡܢܐ ܠܟܝ. ܗܝܕܝܢ ܐܡܪܬ ܠܗ ܐܢܐ ܐܡܪܬܐ ܗ̄ܘܝܬ ܠܒܪܟ ܕܡܠܠ ܒܟܝ. ܗܝܕܝܢ ܡܫܠܡ ܢܦܠ ܥܠ ܘܪ̈ܓܠܐ ܕܡܠܟ ܒܟ. ܘܫܪܝܬ ܐܒܝ ܠܐܦ̈ܝ ܘܒܕܐ ܗ̄ܘܬ ܕܠܒܡܘܗܝ ܡܫܡܐ ܐܢܬ ܒܗ. ܘܗܘܐ ܡܘܕܐ ܠܐ ܢܕܥܐ ܗ̄ܘܬ ܒܗ.

ܘܟܕ ܗܠܝܢ ܐܡܪܬ ܠܡܠܟܐ. ܦܩܕ ܠܛܒܬܐ ܡܢ ܒܪܗ. ܘܦܩܕ ܕܢܬܩܛܠ. ܝܕܥ ܕܝܢ ܘܐܝܬ ܗܘܐ ܠܗ ܠܡܠܟܐ ܡܠܘ̈ܟܐ ܦܝܠܘܣܘ̈ܦܐ ܠܐ ܐܝܟ ܕܒܣܘܪܗܒܐ ܥܒܕ ܗܘܐ ܡܕܡ. ܥܕܡܐ ܕܡܬܡܠܟ ܗܘܐ ܒܗܘܢ. ܘܟܕ ܫܡܥܘ ܗܠܝܢ. ܕܦܩܕ ܡܠܟܐ ܕܢܬܩܛܠ ܒܪܗ. ܘܠܐ ܐܬܡܠܟ ܒܗܘܢ. ܐܬܚܫܒܘ ܒܢܦܫܗܘܢ. ܕܗܘ ܡܕܡ ܕܦܩܕ ܡܠܟܐ ܒܚܫܘܟܐ ܒܝܕ ܕܗܝܡܢ ܠܐܢܬܬܐ. ܘܐܡܪܘ ܦܝܠܘܣܘ̈ܦܐ ܠܐ ܙܕܩ ܕܢܬܩܛܠ. ܘܠܐ ܙܕܩ ܠܡܠܟܐ ܕܢܛܠܘܡ ܠܒܪܗ. ܡܛܠ ܕܠܚܢܬܐ ܠܢܦܫܗ ܒܥܠ. ܘܠܟ ܡܪܚܡ ܡܢ ܠܘܬܗ. ܐܠܐ ܢܬܦܪܫ ܐܝܟܢܐ ܕܢܫܘܙܒ ܠܛܠܝܐ ܡܢ ܡܘܬܐ. ܗܝܕܝܢ ܐܡܪ ܚܕ ܡܢܗܘܢ ܕܚܟܝܡ ܡܢ ܣܘܡܟ. ܢܫܘܙܒ ܒܗ ܒܡܕܐ ܚܕ. ܘܐܙܠ ܗܘ ܘܥܠ ܠܘܬ ܡܠܟܐ ܘܦܝܣ ܠܗ ܘܐܡܪ ܕܠܐ ܙܕܩ ܕܢܥܒܕܘܢ ܡ̈ܠܟܐ ܡܕܡ. ܥܕܡܐ ܕܢܫܡܥܘܢ ܥܠ ܫܪܪܐ.

ܦܝܠܘܣܘܦܐ ܡܕܡܢܐ ܐܡܪ ܡܪܝ. ܡܠܟܐ ܚܕ ܕܫܡܥܬ ܠܗ: ܕܐܝܬ ܗܘܐ ܒܝܢ ܡܠܟܐ ܚܕ. ܕܠܐ ܢܣܒ ܗܘܐ ܟܠܗܘ. ܡܕܡ ܐܝܟ ܕܫܡܥܬ ܢܫ̈ܐ ܘܐܡܪ ܘܚܙܐ ܒܚܕ ܡܢ ܝܘܡܬܐ ܐܢܬܬܐ ܫܦܝܪܬܐ. ܘܥܠܬ ܪܚܡܬܗ ܒܠܒܗ ܘܐܚܒܗ̇. ܘܫܕܪ ܚܕ ܡܢ ܡܫ̈ܡܫܢܐ ܘܦܩܕܗ ܠܡܝܬܝܘܬܗ̇ ܘܐܝܬܝܗ̇ ܠܘܬܗ. ܗܝܕܝܢ ܐܙܠ ܡܠܟܐ ܠܘܬ ܐܢܬܬܐ ܗܝ. ܘܒܥܐ ܡܢܗ̇ ܕܬܐܬܐ ܠܗ. ܗܝ ܕܝܢ ܒܚܟܡܬܗ̇ ܐܡܪܬ ܠܡܠܟܐ. ܡܪܝ ܐܡܬܟ ܐܝܬܝ. ܘܥܠ ܡܐ ܕܢܓܒܐ ܐܝܬ ܒܟܕ. ܘܐܝܬ ܗܘܐ ܥܒܕܐ ܚܕ ܠܒܥܠܗ̇ ܕܡܘܩܪ ܗܘܐ ܟܠ ܝܘܡܬܐ ܦܬܪ. ܘܐܡܪܬ ܠܡܠܟܐ. ܡܪܝ ܒܗܢܐ ܥܒܕܐ. ܘܢܦܩ ܡܠܟܐ ܘܥܒܪ ܘܚܙܐ ܕܡܘܩܪ ܦܬܪ ܒܟܠ ܙܘܝܬܐ. ܗܝܕܝܢ ܦܩܕ ܡܠܟܐ ܕܢܨܠܒܘܢܗ ܘܨܠܒܘ. ܘܢܦܠܬ ܠܪܘܚܬܗ ܬܚܝܬ ܒܪܫܐ: ܘܗܘܐ ܢܦܫ ܘܐܫܬܘܕܥܬ: ܐܝܟܐ ܕܒܪܬܗ̇ ܘܬܒܥ ܟܠ ܒܪ̈ܫܐ. ܘܚܙܐ ܠܚܘܒܬܐ ܘܐܫܬܘܕܥ ܒܗ̇ ܗܘ. ܐܢܬܬܐ ܠܐ ܢܝܚܐ ܗܘܬ ܒܗ̇. ܘܐܡܪܬ ܝܕܥܐ ܒܢܦܫܗ̇: ܕܡܠܟܐ ܠܒ ܘܢܦܠ ܒܟ ܐܢܬܬܐ. ܘܙܕ ܡܢ ܡܠܟܐ. ܘܠܐ ܠܒ ܒܠܒܗ̇ ܙܒܢܐ

ܦܝܣܐܐ. ܗܝܕܝܢ ܫܕܪܬ ܐܢܬܬܐ ܠܘܬ ܐܒܘܗ̇ ܘܐܘܕܥܬܗ. ܕܒܪܬܐ ܕܝܠܗ ܐܬܢܨܚܬ ܡܢܗ. ܘܐܙܠ ܐܒܘܗ̇ ܠܘܬ ܡܠܟܐ. ܘܐܡܪ: ܐܪܒܐ ܐܝܬ ܗܘܐ ܠܝ. ܘܠܗܘܢܐ ܫܒܩܬܗ̇ ܕܢܦܠܘܚܗ̇ ܘܦܠܚ ܒܗ̇ ܙܒܢܐ. ܘܗܫܐ ܐܬܢܨܚܬ ܡܢܗ ܘܠܐ ܦܠܚ ܒܗ̇ ܘܫܒܩܗ̇ ܠܗ̇. ܐܡܪ ܡܠܟܐ ܠܓܒܪܐ ܕܐܢܬܬܐ: ܐܢܬ ܡܢܐ ܐܡܪ ܐܢܬ؟ ܘܓܒܪܐ ܗܘ ܘܐܡܪ: ܫܪܝܪܐܝܬ ܡܪܝ. ܐܪܒܐ ܝܗ̄ܒ ܠܝ. ܘܠܐ ܡܗܝܡܢ ܠܝ ܡܢ ܛܘܦܣܗ̇ ܒܡܟܐ ܕܡܟܝܬ ܫܠܐ. ܘܢܓܕ ܒܫܗ ܡܢ ܝܘܡܬ̈ܢ ܟܠܗ̇ ܠܗ̇ ܘܣܝܓܗ̇ ܒܗ̇ ܫܒܠܐ ܕܦܪܣܘܬܐ ܕܐܪܥܐ. ܘܕܝܠܗ̇ ܡܢ ܐܪܥܐ ܕܐܗܦܘܟ ܐܟܘܠ ܠܗ̇. ܐܡܪ ܡܠܟܐ ܠܓܒܪܐ: ܫܪܝܪܐܝܬ ܚܕ ܠܗ̇ ܐܠܐ ܠܐ ܩܢܛ ܒܗ̇ ܡܕܡ. ܙܠ ܚܒܘܠ ܠܐܪܥܐ. ܦܠܘܚܗ̇ ܠܓܡܝܪܘܬ ܘܠܐ ܬܕܚܠ ※

ܘܬܘܒ ܐܝܬ ܗ̄ܘܐ ܓܒܪܐ ܚܕ ܘܙܒܢ ܦܪܣܬܐ ܕܡܡܠܠܐ ܒܠܫܢܐ ܕܐܢܫܐ. ܘܣܡܗ̇ ܒܩܦܣܐ ܚܕ. ܘܬܠܗ̇ ܒܒܝܬܐ ܕܝܠܗ. ܘܦܩܕܗ̇ ܕܬܘܕܥ ܠܗ ܟܠܡܕܡ ܕܗܘܝܐ ܐܢܬܬܗ. ܘܢܦܩ ܗܘ ܘܐܙܠ ܒܐܘܪܚܐ. ܘܐܬܬܐ ܪܚܡܗ̇ ܕܗܝ ܐܢܬܬܐ ܘܥܠ ܠܒܝܬܗ̇. ܘܟܕ ܚܙܬ ܗܝ ܦܪܣܬܐ ܕܥܠ ܠܒܝܬܗ ܕܡܪܗ̇ ܗ̄ܘܐ. ܘܡܢ ܒܬܪ ܕܐܬܐ ܓܒܪܐ ܕܗܝ ܐܢܬܬܐ. ܐܘܕܥܬܗ ܠܗ ܦܪܣܬܐ ܟܠ ܡܕܡ ܕܥܒܕܬ ܐܢܬܬܗ. ܘܠܐ ܫܒܩܬ ܚܕܐ ܕܠܐ ܐܘܕܥܬܗ. ܘܢܦܩ ܡܢ ܠܘܬܗ̇ ܘܐܬܚܫܒ ܒܠܒܗ. ܘܐܡܪܬ ܐܢܬܬܗ ܒܢܦܫܗ̇ ܐܡܬܐ ܐܘܕܥܬ ܠܓܒܪܐ. ܘܐܡܪܬ ܠܐܡܬܗ̇: ܐܢܬܝ ܐܡܪܬܝ ܠܓܒܪܐ ܕܝܠܝ ܡܕܡ ܕܥܒܕܬ؟ ܘܝܡܬ ܐܡܬܐ ܕܠܐ ܐܡܪܬ ܠܗ. ܗܝܕܝܢ ܐܣܬܟܠܬ ܒܗ̇ ܦܘܪܣܐ ܕܬܥܒܕ ܠܦܪܣܬܐ ܕܝܠܬܐ. ܗܝܕܝܢ ܫܩܠܬ ܠܩܦܣܐ. ܘܣܡܬܗ ܟܠܗ ܠܠܝܐ ܠܦܪܣܬܐ. ܘܡܚܕܪܐ ܗ̄ܘܬ ܪܚܝܐ ܒܐܝܕܗ̇ ܙܒܢ ܙܒܢ. ܘܡܫܕܪܐ ܗ̄ܘܬ ܡܚܝܢܬܐ ܡܢܗ̇. ܘܐܕܠܦܬ ܡܛܪܐ ܘܙܒܢ ܡܣܚܝܐ ܗ̄ܘܬ ܠܗ ܘܙܒܢ ܡܟܣܝܐ ܗ̄ܘܬ ܠܗ. ܘܪܥܡܐ ܗ̄ܘܬ ܡܢܐ ܟܠ ܠܝܠܝܐ. ܘܡܫܚܠܦܐ ܗ̄ܘܬ ܗܟܢ ܟܠܗ ܠܠܝܐ. ܒܨܦܪܐ ܕܐܡܪܬ ܦܪܣܬܐ ܒܢܦܫܗ̇ ܒܪܡܫܐ ܕܝܢ

ܘܦ̈ܓܪܐ ܘܡܨܠܝܢܐ ܗܘܐ ܟܠܗ ܠܠܝܐ. ܘܡܢܐ ܕܐܬܬܐ ܢܗܪܐ ܒܨܦܪܐ ܐܬܬܗ ܠܦܪܨܘܦܗ̇ ܘܫܐܠܗ̇ ܕܡܢܐ ܚܙܬ ܒܗܢܐ ܠܠܝܐ ܬܬܒܥܘܢ. ܐܡܪܐ ܠܗ ܦܪܨܘܦܐ. ܕܒܪܝܐ ܘܡܨܠܝܢܐ ܘܦ̈ܓܪܐ ܠܐ ܥܡܘܕܝ ܕܐܬܢܐ ܡܕܝܢ. ܘܡܢ ܕܫܡܥ ܢܗܪܐ ܗܠܝܢ ܡܢ ܦܘܣܬ. ܢܕܪ ܥܠ ܕܐܡܪܬ ܦܘܣܬ ܥܠ ܐܢܬܬܐ. ܒܪܘܟܐ ܐܬܬܘܣܝܡ. ܡܢ ܕܡܬܠܝܪܐ ܠܐ ܗܘ̄ܐ ܟܠܗ ܠܠܝܐ ܗܢܐ. ܘܡܬܚܒܠܢܘܬܐ ܘܡܫܡܥܢܘܬܐ ܘܢܘܪܐ ܩܠܝܬܐ ܐܬܬܢܝܬ ܘܡܒܕܬܐ ܠܦܘܣܬܐ ܕܢܠܬܐ. ܘܐܦܣܘܢ ܡܢܗ ܘܩܠܠܗ ܘܪܒ ܠܐܬܬܐ ※

From *The Cave of Treasures*[1]

ܡܢ ܟܬܒܐ ܕܡܥܪܬ ܓܙ̈ܐ

ܘܐܪܡܝ ܐܠܗܐ ܫܢܬܐ ܥܠ ܐܕܡ ܘܕܡܟ: ܘܢܣܒ ܚܕܐ ܐܠܥܐ ܡܢ ܓܒܗ ܕܝܡܝܢܐ ܘܒܢܝܗ̇ ܠܚܘܐ ܡܢܗ. ܘܟܕ ܐܬܬܥܝܪ ܐܕܡ ܡܢ ܫܢܬܗ ܘܚܙܗ̇ ܠܚܘܐ ܚܕܝ ܒܗ̇ ܛܒ. ܘܗܘܘ ܐܕܡ ܘܚܘܐ ܒܓܘ ܦܪܕܝܣܐ ܠܒܝܫܝܢ ܫܘܒܚܐ ܘܡܨܦܪܝܢ ܒܬܫܒܘܚܬܐ ܬܠܬ ܫܥ̈ܝܢ: ܗܘ̇ ܕܝܢ ܗܢܐ ܦܪܕܝܣܐ ܠܥܠ ܐܬܬܣܝܡ. ܘܡܥܠܠ ܡܢ ܟܠܗܘܢ ܛܘܪ̈ܐ ܪ̈ܡܐ. ܬܠܬܝܢ ܙܪ̈ܝܢ ܒܡܫܘܚܬܐ ܕܪܘܚܐ ܕܡܬܘܫܐ ܘܚܕܪ ܠܟܠܗ̇ ܐܪܥܐ.

ܐܡܪ ܕܝܢ ܡܘܫܐ ܢܒܝܐ ܐܝܟܢܐ ܕܢܨܒ ܡܪܝܐ ܐܠܗܐ ܚܠܬܝܐ ܦܪܕܝܣܐ ܒܝܗ ܒܢ: ܘܣܡ ܬܡܢ ܠܐܕܡ ܕܓܒܠ. ܟܢ ܕܝܢ ܐܬܬܗ̇ ܠܦܘܩܕܢܐ ܕܒܫܪ̈ܪܐ ܘܒܕ̈ܬܗ̇ ܐܬܬܗ̇ ܡܪ̈ܚܡܢܘܬܗ ܕܐܠܗܐ: ܗܝ̇ ܕܒܬܪ ܗܘ̄ܐ ܐܠܗܐ ܕܢܦܪܘܩ ܟܠ

[1]*Die Schatzhöhle*, ed. Carl Bezold, Syriac and Arabic texts (Leipzig: J.C. Hinrichs'sche Buchhandlung, 1883), pp. 18ff.

ܠܟܠܗܘܢ ܒܢ̈ܝܢܫܐ: ܡܛܠ ܕܒܪ ܐܠܗܐ ܐܝܟ ܡܡܪܡܡܘܬ ܪܒܘܬܗ ܡܪܝܡ ܕܐܬܚܫܒ ܫܦܝܠܐ ܟܠ ܐܝܟ ܕܝܠܗ ܘܒܗܕܐ ܕܡܪܚܡܢܘܬܗ ܡܪܝܡ ܫܡܝܐ. ܐܝܟ ܕܡܙܡܪ ܗ̄ܘܐ ܛܘܒܢܐ ܕܘܝܕ: ܕܡܪܝܐ ܒܝܬ ܡܥܡܪܐ ܗܘܝܬ ܠܢ ܠܕܪ ܕܪ̈ܝܢ.[1] ܗܢܘ ܕܝܢ ܕܒܝܗ ܡܪܚܡܢܘܬܟ ܒܒܪܬ ܠܝ. ܘܒܪ ܡܦܩ ܠܗ ܠܐܠܗܐ ܚܠܦ ܦܘܪܩܢܐ ܕܒܢ̈ܝܢܫܐ ܐܡܪ ܐܬܒܪܬ ܒܪܬܟ ܕܡܫܚܬ ܡܢ ܡܪܝܡ. ܗܢܘ ܕܝܢ. ܠܗܢ ܡܪܚܡܢܘܬܐ ܕܒܪܬܟ ܕܬܦܪܘܩ ܟܠ ܚܛܗܝܢ ܡܚܝܠܐ.

ܟܢ ܐܬܬܢܝ ܒܒܪܬܐ ܡܫܝܚܬܐ. ܘܦܪܕܝܣܐ ܕܒܝܬ ܐܬܪܐ ܕܚܝܠܐ ܘܪܬܘܬܐ ܕܢܝܐ ܗܘ ܕܝܠܒ ܐܠܗܐ ܠܟܠܗܘܢ ܒܢ̈ܝܢܫܐ ܡܫܝܚܐ.

ܘܡܛܠ ܕܐܬܐܘܕܝ ܗ̄ܘܐ ܐܝܟ ܒܗܢܐ ܘܡܠܟܐ ܘܒܢܝܐ ܐܟܠܗ ܐܠܗܐ ܠܦܪܕܝܣܐ ܕܢܥܡܪ ܒܝܗ ܒܢ ܐܝܟ ܒܗܢܐ ܒܒܪܬܐ ܡܫܝܚܬܐ: ܐܝܟ ܕܡܫܡܫ ܠܟܠܗ̄ܘܢ ܛܘܒܢܐ ܡܘܫܐ. ܕܢܦܫܗ̄ ܠܟܢ ܠܐܠܗܐ ܒܪ ܬܫܡܫܬܐ ܒܚܝܘܬܐ ܒܬܫܒܘܚܬܐ. ܘܢܛܪܘܗ̄ܝ ܠܦܪܕܝܣܐ ܗܘ ܕܐܬܝܗܒ ܠܗ ܒܪ ܡܪܚܡܢܘܬܗ ܕܐܠܗܐ. ܘܐܡܪܝ ܐܒܘܢ ܐܠܗܐ ܠܐܕܡ ܘܚܘܐ ܒܦܪܕܝܣܐ ܘܢܛܪ ܐܠܗܐ ܐܝܠܢܐ ܕܚܝܐ ܒܡܨܥܬܗ ܕܦܪܕܝܣܐ. ܘܡܪܐ ܗܘ ܡܠܬܐ ܗܕܐ ܘܡܚܘܝܬ ܫܪܪܐ ܕܗܘܝܘ ܐܝܠܢܐ ܕܚܝܐ ܒܡܨܥܬܗ ܕܦܪܕܝܣܐ ܠܨܠܝܒ ܦܪܘܩܢܐ ܡܚܝܕܢ ܐܪܥ ܗ̄ܘܐ. ܐܬܢܨܒ ܬܡܢ ܒܡܨܥܬܗ ܕܦܪܕܝܣܐ ܘܗܘܐ ܗܘ ܕܐܬܩܒܥ ܒܡܨܥܬܗ̇ ܕܐܪܥܐ ※

[1] Psalm 90:1.

From *Kalilag and Demnag*[1]

ܡܢ ܡܬ̈ܠܐ ܕܟܠܝܠܓ ܘܕܡܢܓ

ܬܓܪܐ ܡܣܟܢܐ ܐܝܬ ܗܘܐ. ܘܐܙܠ ܒܬܓܪܘܬܗ̇ ܠܐܬܪܐ ܐܚܪܢܐ. ܘܐܝܬ ܗܘܐ ܠܗ ܡܐܐ ܡܢܝ̈ܢ ܦܪܙܠܐ. ܡܛܠ ܕܐܢܫ ܒܝܬܐ ܠܝܬ ܗܘܐ ܠܗ: ܐܫܠܡܗ ܠܚܒܪܐ ܝܕܝܥܗ ܕܡܗܝܡܢ ܒܗ ܘܣܡ. ܘܟܕ ܚܠܦ ܒܥܝܗ̄ ܠܦܪܙܠܐ ܡܢ ܝܕܝܥܗ. ܘܦܪܙܠܐ ܙܒܢܗ ܘܐܟܠܗ ܟܠ ܢܦܩܗ ܘܐܡܪ ܠܬܓܪܐ ܕܦܪܙܠܐ ܐܟܠܘܗܝ ܥܘܩܒܪ̈ܐ. ܘܬܓܪܐ ܒܗ̇ܝ ܕܠܐ ܢܣܛ ܝܕܝܥܗ ܘܒܕܝܠ ܐܡܪ ܠܗ. ܡܕܝܢ ܫܪܝܪܐ ܗ̇ܘ ܕܐܡܪܝܢ ܕܠܝܬ ܒܐܬܪ̈ܘܬܐ ܕܩܠܐ: ܘܠܐ ܒܬ̈ܪܬܝܢ: ܕܫܦܝܢ ܥܒܘܗ̈ܝ ܡܢ ܕܒܡܕܝܢܬܐ. ܐܠܐ ܒܗ̇ ܗܕܐ ܗܘܬ: ܐܬܚܙܝܬ ܕܐܝܬ ܣܠܝܩ ܐܝܬ: ܥܘܩܒܪܐ ܕܐܟܠܘ ܒܡܕܝܢܬܐ ܡܬܚܫܒܐ. ܘܗ̇ܘ ܚܕ ܒܗ̇ܝ ܕܬܓܪܐ ܠܗ ܐܬܚܫܒܘ. ܘܟܕ ܙܒܢܗ ܕܢܠܥܘ ܠܗܘܢܐ ܒܒܝܬܗ. ܘܕܒܪ ܬܓܪܐ ܠܒܪ ܝܕܝܥܗ ܘܐܙܠ ܛܫܝܗ. ܐܡܪ ܠܗ ܝܕܝܥܗ. ܟܕ ܕܒܪܬܘܗܝ ܠܒܪܝ. ܡܢܐ ܥܒܕܬ ܠܗ. ܐܡܪ ܠܗ ܬܓܪܐ ܕܐܢܐ ܒܪܟ ܠܐ ܕܒܪܬ. ܐܠܐ ܗܘ ܐܬܚܙܝ ܗܘܐ ܒܬܪܝ: ܘܚܙܝܬ ܕܢܫܪ ܒܪܟ ܘܚܛܦܗ. ܘܝܕܝܥܗ ܐܠܠ ܘܦܢܐ ܒܬܪ ܡܠܟܐ: ܒܕ ܡܣܟܢ ܪܥܡ ܘܣܢܕܗ ܘܐܡܪ. ܐܝܟܐ ܐܬܚܙܝܬ ܐܘ ܐܫܬܡܥܬ ܕܒܪ ܢܫܪܐ ܕܢܚܛܘܦ ܛܠܝܐ؟ ܘܬܓܪܐ ܐܡܪ ܠܗ. ܐܝܟܐ ܕܥܘܩܒܪ̈ܐ ܐܬܚܙܝܘ ܕܐܟܠܝܢ ܡܐܐ ܡܢܝ̈ܢ ܦܪܙܠܐ. ܡܕܝܢ ܐܦ ܒܪܝ ܕܠܘܬܟ ܚܛܦ ܠܗ ܢܫܪܐ. ܗܝܕܝܢ ܐܡܪ ܝܕܝܥܗ: ܐܚܝ: ܦܪܙܠܟ ܐܢܐ ܐܟܠܬܗ ܘܐܟܠܬ ܡܢ̈ܘܪܐ: ܛܠܝ̈ܘܗܝ ܗܒ: ܘܗܒ ܠܝ ܒܪܝ ※

---

[1] *Kalīla und Dimna*, ed. Friedrich Schulthess (Amsterdam: Apa-Philo Press, 1982), p. 48f.

From a Metrical Sermon by Ephraem Syrus[1]

ܡܢ ܡܠܟܐ ܕܟܠܐ ܡܟܣܝܘܬܐ ܘܓܠܝܘܬܐ
ܕܠܗ ܕܓܠܝܐ ܡܢ ܐܦ̈ܝܢ
ܡܢ ܪܘܡܐ ܕܢܚ ܪ̈ܚܫܐ.[2]
ܕܠܐ ܢ̄ܚܘܪ ܠܡܪܘܡܐ.
ܡܢ ܫܡܥ ܫܡܥܐ ܗ̄ܘ ܦܘܪܫܢܐ.
ܢܘܪܐ ܠܟܡ̈ ܒܫܡܝܐ.
ܒܪ̈ܡܙܐܬܗ ܐܡܪ ܕܗܘ
ܡܠܬܐ ܕܓܠܝܬܐ ܗ̄ܝ. ܒܠܒܗ:
ܕܠܬܝ ܡܢ ܐܘܢܟܠ
ܟ̈ܢ ܟܡ̈ ܒܫܡܐ.
ܘܡܟܝܢ ܢܦܫܗ ܕܐܟܘܬܗ
ܚܢ ܢܬܡܟܝ ܒܫܪܪܐ
ܐܝܟ ܟ̈ܢ ܟܒܪܐ ܕܠܗܬ
ܡ̈ܢܗܘܢ ܐܬ̈ܟܢ ܒܠܫܢ
ܕܚܙܘܢ ܐܢܘܢ ܕܒܢ̈ܝܢ
ܢܗܘܘܢ ܙܗܝܬܐ ܘܒܢ̈ܬܐ.
ܘܐܢܘܢ ܕܦܓܥܝܢ ܐܢܘܢ
ܐܦ ܟܒܪܐ ܚܒܪܐ ܢܗܘܘܢ.
ܘܐܘܫܦ ܬܘܒ ܕܗܘ ܘܪܬܡ

---

[1]"Sermo Beati Mar Ephraemi de reprehensione et oratione," *Sancti Mar Ephraemi hymni et sermones,* ed. T. J. Lamy, 4 vols. (Mechliniae: H. Dessain, 1882–1902), vol. iv, col. 125ff.

[2]Syriac poetry is based on syllable counting. The metrical syllable, unlike the normal syllable, is reckoned as one syllable per *full* vowel, and the schwa is ignored altogether. In this metrical sermon, each "line" consists of seven metrical syllables. Extra, "allowable" vowels added for metrical exigence in this passage are: *neḥur* for *nḥur* (p. 182, line 5) and *ᶜalayn* for *ᶜlayn* (p. 183, lines 14, 18 and 19).

ܦܓܪܐ ܐܝܟ ܩܒܪܐ:
ܕܐܝܟ ܥ̈ܝܢܗ ܕܐܡܬܐ ܠܘܬܗ
ܕܡܪܬܗ ܚܝܪ̈ܢ ܟܠܟܝ
ܕܐܢܗܘܘ ܕܦܪܝܫܐ ܗ̄ܘ ܡܪܟܒ
ܠܘܬ ܦܪܨܘܦܗ ܚܕܬܐ.
ܘܐܢ ܡܪܬܐ ܬܗܘܐ ܟܡܪܐ
ܐܡܬܐ ܕܢܟܠܐ ܘܡܬܟܬܫܐ
ܕܚܕܬܐ ܕܒܢ̈ܝ ܐܦܝܗ
ܡܣܬܟܪܐ ܡܢ ܟܘܟܒܬܗ.
ܗܟܢܐ ܠܡ ܐܦ ܥ̈ܝܢܢ
ܠܘܬܟ ܡܪܝܐ ܐܠܗܢ
ܕܠܐ ܡܢܐ ܬܐܬܐ ܐܡܪ ܕܘܝܕ
ܕܐܘܕܝ ܘܐܚܪܐ ܡܕܡ ܐܦܝ
ܟܕܡܐ ܕܬܐܢܚ ܟ݁ܠܝ
ܕܚܪܬ ܕܟܠܗ ܦܪܨܘܦܝ.
ܘܚܢܢ ܗ̇ܘ ܗܕܐ ܕܕܘܝܕ
ܬܫܒܚ ܢܬܐ ܘܐܡܪ:
ܪܚܡ ܟ݁ܠܝ ܐܠܗܐ
ܘܐܢܬ ܡܪܝܐ ܪܚܡ ܟ݁ܠܝ.

From *The Syriac Book of Medicines*[1]

ܪܫܐ ܕܬܠܬܐ

※ ܥܠ ܟܘܪܗܢܐ ܟܠܗܘܢ ܕܗܘܝܢ ܒܪܫܐ ※

ܘܡܣܡܟܬ ܒܟܠ ܒܢܝ̈ܐ ܘܡܕܒܪܢܘܬܐ ܬ̈ܠܝܬܝܬܐ: ܐܬܦܫܛܬ ܓܪ ܡܢ ܡܕܒܪ: ܕܟܠܗܝܢ ܡܕܒܪܢܘܬܐ ܕܦܓܪܐ: ܠܬܪܝܢ ܦܘܪ̈ܫܢܐ ܡ̈ܬܦܠܓܢ. ܠܢܦܫܢܝܬܐ ܘܠܚܝܘܬܐ ܀ ܘܗܢܝܢ ܢܦܫܢܝܬܐ: ܡ̈ܬܦܠܓܢ ܠܬ̈ܠܝܬܝܬܐ ܘܠܡܕ̈ܒܪܢܝܬܐ. ܘܐܬܬܡܪܬ ܬܘܒ ܕܢܦܫܢܝܬܐ ܗܘ ܡܘܚܐ ܡܢܗ ܠܗܝܢ. ܡܢܗܝܢ ܒܗ ܡܬܝܠܕܢܘܬܐ ܕܗܕ̈ܡܐ ܐܚܪ̈ܢܐ. ܡܢܗܝܢ ܗ̄ܘ ܡܘܚܗ ܡܢܗ ܠܗܝܢ. ܕܐܬܝܠܕܝܢ ܗܢܝܢ ܬ̈ܠܝܬܝܬܐ ܀

ܟܬܒܝܢ ܕܝܢ ܕܝܠܗ ܒܪܫܐ ܗܢܐ. ܒܟܠ ܢܟܝ̈ܢܐ ܕܡܕܒܪܝܢ ܠܡܕܒܪ̈ܢܘܬܐ ܗܢܝܢ ܬ̈ܠܝܬܝܬܐ ܀ ܗܢܘ ܕܝܢ: ܠܗܢܝܢ ܕܡܬܬܟܒܢ ܡܢ ܬܠܬܐ ܒܟܒ̈ܘܗܝ ܕܡܘܚܐ ܀ ܡܕܡܝܢܘܬܐ ܐܬܬܣܝܡ: ܗܢ: ܕܡܬܗܦܟܐ ܘܡܬܬܦܢܐ ܦܢܛܣܝܐ: ܘܕܬܪܬܝܢ ܗܢ ܕܡܬܚܫܒܢܐ ܘܡܬܬܟܝܢܐ ܡܘܡܠܐ ܀ ܘܕܬܠܬ: ܗܢ ܕܡܬܕܟܪܢܐ: ܘܡܬܥܗܕܢܘܬܐ ܒܡܕܢܚܐ ܀ ܗܘ ܕܝܢ ܡܘܚܐ: ܠܐ ܗܘܐ ܐܘܪܓܝܘܢ ܡܪܓܫܢܐ ܒܠܚܘܕ ܐܬܬܣܝܡ ܡܢ ܟܝܢܐ: ܐܠܐ ܪܓܫܐ ܕܪ̈ܓܫܐ ܗ̄ܘܐ ܡܢ ܒܪܫܐ ܬܘܒ. ܘܗܢ ܕܒܗ ܢܝ̈ܒܐ: ܗܘ ܡܘܚܐ ܡܫܒܕ ܣܠܩܐ ܡܪܓܫܢܐ ܠܟܠܗܘܢ ܗܕ̈ܡܘܗܝ ܕܦܓܪܐ: ܢܒܥܐ ܗ̄ܘ ܝܠܝܬܐ: ܡܢ ܗܢ ܕܒܗ ܢܬܦܫܛ ܢܝܒܐ ܐܝܟܐ ܕܗܘ: ܒܪ ܥܒܕܬܗ ܕܠܐ ܪܓܫܬܐ ܗܘܐ ܗܕܡܐ ܗܘ. ܒܗ ܕܡܬܟܠܐ ܠܗ ܣܠܩܐ ܗܘ ܕܝܚܬ ܗ̄ܘܐ ܠܗ: ܡܢ ܡܘܚܐ ܘܡܬܦܠܓ ܒܗ ܀ ܝܠܝܐ ܗ̄ܘ ܕܝܢ ܬܘܒ ܢܒܥܝܬ: ܘܐܦ ܡܢ ܗܢ ܕܒܥܝܢܐ. ܐܘ ܠܝܬܪ ܒܢ̈ܝܢܝܢ

[1] *The Syriac Book of Medicines,* ed. E. A. W. Budge (London, 1913; reprint: Amsterdam: APA-Philo Press, 1976), pp. 1–3.

ܪ̈ܝܥܐ: ܐܘ ܓܒ ܒܡܘܓܐܝܬ ܡܒܒܕܝܢ ܀ ܢܕܒܐ ܗ̄ܘ̇ ܗܒܠ
ܕܡܠܠ ܗ̄ܘ ܪ̈ܙܐ ܗܕܝܢ ܚܠܐ ܘܫܪܬ ܡܢ ܪܥܐ ܠܗܘ̈ܢܐ.
ܘܗܕܐ ܡܬܚܙܝܢܐ ܒܒܢܕܐ: ܒܡܫܐܝܬ ܘܠܐ ܒܡܫܐܝܬ. ܐܬܬܢܝ
ܒܡܫܘܬܗ̇ ܥܝܢܗ̇ ܠܦܘܬ ܕܡܢܕܝܢܗ̇ ܀ ܗܕܐ ܕܝܢ ܢܕܥܐ ܕܕܐܝܟ
ܗܟܢܐ ܓܝܪ ܪ̈ܙܐ ܘܫܪܬ ܐܦ ܒܡܐ ܕܐܬܝܢ ܐܦ ܥܢܝܬܗ̇
ܒܒܡܫܘܬܗ̇ ܀ ܕܡܢܐ ܗܟܝܠ ܕܒܢܝܢܐ ܟܠܗ ܕܥܒܢܬܗ̇: ܗܘ̇ܐ
ܡܚ ܚܠܐ ܗ̇ܘ ܢܦܫܐ: ܘܡܒܒܕ ܬܫܦܐܬ ܗ̇ܘ ܒܚܐ ܀
ܡܬܕܒܪܐ ܕܝܢ ܗܕܐ: ܡܢ ܗ̇ܢ ܕܡܐ ܕܐܠܐ ܚܠܐ ܗܘܐ: ܒܟ
ܕܕܡܝܢ ܒܪ ܥܒܕܗ ܡܬܚܫܠ. ܘܬܪܐܝܬ ܡܢܐ ܕܒܬܪ ܡܣܒܪܢܘܬܗ̇
ܡܡܥܚܫܬܗ̇ ܢܕܡܝܢ. ܘܡܢ ܗܪ ܠܘܒ ܕܒܝܢ ܥܝܢܗ̇: ܗܘܐ
ܦܬܪܐ ܥܦܪܢܝܬܐ ܒܟܠܗ ܦܓܪܐ. ܠܗ ܒܪܘܚܐ ܠܚܘܕ ܀ ܐܠܐ
ܕܗܫܐܝܬ ܗܕܝܢ ܡܬܬܚܫ: ܐܦ ܗܕܡܐ ܗ̇ܘ ܕܒܗ ܐܬܚܘܝ.
ܪܥܝܢ ܕܢܦܥܐ ܡܠܠܗ̇. ܠܒܐ ܓܝܪ ܡܬܚܙܝܐ ܕܡܠܠ ܡܠܠ
ܡܢܪ ܗ̄ܘܐ. ܐܝܟ ܕܠܐ ܢܫܬܫܫ ܒܢܐ ܢܦܪܐ ܠܚܫܬܗ܀ ܡܘܚܐ
ܕܝܢ ܠܗ ܡܚܝܐ: ܐܠܐ ܒܪܘܚܗ̇ ܡܒܒܕ ܒܟܠܗܝܢ. ܒܥܝܢܗ̇ ܕܝܢ
ܓܠܝܐ ܀ ܘܒܕܝܢ ܥܝܢܗ̇ ܒܡܫܘܬܗ̇ ܢܦܠܐ ܒܟܠ ܐܠܝܢ
ܕܡܬܕܪܫܝܢ ܡܢܝܐܝܬ. ܐܝܟ ܗܪܝܢ ܕܬܫܪܐܝܬ ܪ̈ܙܐ ܚܠܐ.
ܘܐܬܦܫܛ ܡܢ ܪܥܐ ܒܪ ܡܬܕܪܫܝܢ ܗ̄ܘܘ. ܡܛܠ ܡܫܦܫܐ
ܗܒܠ ܕܚܠܐ ܗ̇ܘ ܕܐܬܥܡܪ ܡܢ ܡܫܘܚܐ: ܘܡܛܠ ܠܐܘܬܗ̇
ܕܠܐܪ ܒܡܒܒܢܘܬܗ̇ ܡܫܝܐܝܬܗ̇. ܒܠ ܚܫܬܗ̇ ܡܫܚܫ ܐܚܫܕ ܒܠ
ܚܘܠܐ ܀ ܐܟܪܢܐ ܗܘܠ ܕܡܢ ܒܬܪ ܕܘܪܥܐ ܕܪ̈ܚܡܝܢ ܦܥܡܐܝܬ
ܘܒܫܡܐܝܬ. ܘܗܒܢܐ ܘܐܦ ܒܪ ܢܒܠܘܢ ܡܒܪ̈ܢܬܗ̇: ܘܐܦ ܒܠܒܐ
ܕܬܗܘܐ ܪ̈ܓܒܐ ܒܚܫܢ: ܕܐܝܟ ܗܘܒܢܐ ܕܪ̈ܚܡܝܢ ܬܢܪ ܒܢ
ܒܕܡܘܬܗ̇ ܘܐܦ ܒܪ ܢܬܒܠܘܢ ܚܡܪܐ ܬܢܝܢܐ: ܐܘ ܒܪ ܢܫܫܘܢ
ܡܫܫܘ̈ܬܗ̇ ܕܪ̈ܚܝܐ ܥܫܢܬܐ ܕܡܬܚܠܝܢ ܒܠ ܪ̈ܥܫܘܢ: ܕܡܚܝܢ
ܬܪܐܝܬ ܀ ܒܠܗܝܢ ܓܝܪ ܗܠܝܢ ܕܡܬܚܙܝܢ ܕܡܠܟܝܢ ܠܗ ܠܡܫܝܚܐ
ܕܠܝܢ ܕܗܕܐ ܡܠܝܘܬܗ̇ ܡܫܫ: ܡܢܐ ܕܒܡܒܠ ܘܡܒܒܥ
ܒܡܒܒܕܘܬܗ̇ ܡܫܝܐܝܬܗ̇. ܘܡܢ ܗܠܝܢ ܟܠܗܝܢ ܡܬܕܒܪܐ: ܕܡܫܘܚܐ

ܡܢܐ ܕܒܡܟܠ ܛܒ ܘܣܛܒܬܐ ܕܢܬܬܣܝܡ: ܗܕܝܢ ܒܢ̈ܝ ܥܢܘܬܐ ܚܣܝܘܬܐ ܘܬܘܬܐܪܬ ܐܝܗܘ ܕܣܠܩܐ ܗܘ̇ ܡܬܪܘܡܡܢܐ ܕܒܗ: ܡܬܢܓܚ ܠܗ ܪܛܒܘܬܐ ܐܘ ܡܢ ܡܪܘܬܐ ܡܫܝܚܝܬܐ ܗܢܘ. ܗܕܝܢ ܥܢܘܬܐ ܗܝ̣ ܕܛܠܝܘܬܐ ܘܡܬܟܫܦܢܘܬܐ ܗܘܝܐ. ܘܒܠܗܘܢ ܣܓܝ̈ܐ ܐܢ̈ܫܐ ܕܐܝܟ ܗܠܝܢ ܀

A Flood in Edessa

ܬܘܒ ܡܢ ܬܫܥܝܬܐ ܕܣܘܥܪܢܐ ܐܝܟ ܕܒܦܢ̈ܩܝܬܐ

ܒܫܢܬ ܫܬܡܐܐ ܘܬܠܬܥܣܪ ܒܡܠܟܘܬܗ ܕܣܘܪܘܣ ܘܒܡܠܟܘܬܗ ܕܐܒܓܪ ܡܠܟܐ ܒܪ ܡܥܢܘ ܡܠܟܐ ܒܝܪܚ ܬܫܪܝ ܐܚܪܝ ܢܒܥ ܗܘܐ ܡܥܝܢܐ ܕܡ̈ܝܐ ܕܢܦܩ ܡܢ ܐܦܕܢܐ ܪܒܐ ܕܐܒܓܪ ܡܠܟܐ ܪܒܐ ܘܒܥܐ ܘܣܠܩ ܐܝܟ ܥܝܕܗ ܡܩܕܡܐ ܘܡܠܐ ܗܘܐ ܘܫܦܥ ܠܟܠ ܓܒ̈ܝܢ. ܘܫܪܝܘ ܗܘܘ ܕܪ̈ܬܐ ܘܐܣܛܘ̈ܐ ܘܒ̈ܬܐ ܕܡܠܟܘܬܐ ܕܢܬܡܠܘܢ ܡ̈ܝܐ. ܘܟܕ ܚܙܐ ܡܢܗ ܐܒܓܪ ܡܠܟܐ. ܣܠܩ ܗܘܐ ܠܗ ܠܬܡܢܐ ܕܛܘܪܐ ܕܠܥܠ ܡܢ ܐܦܕܢܐ ܕܠܗ ܐܬܐ ܕܥܡܪܝܢ ܘܡܥܡܪܝܢ ܒܥܒ̈ܕܐ ܒܥܒܕܐ ܕܒܠܘ ܕܡܠܟܘܬܐ. ܘܟܕ ܚܟܝ̈ܡܐ ܡܬܚܫܒܝܢ ܗܘܘ: ܕܡܢܐ ܢܥܒܕܘܢ ܠܗܘܢ ܠܡ̈ܝܐ ܣܓ̈ܝܐܐ ܕܐܬܬܘܣܦܘ ܗܘܘ. ܢܦܩ ܘܗܘܐ ܡܛܪܐ ܪܒܐ ܘܣܓܝܐܐ ܒܠܠܝܐ. ܘܐܬܐ ܕܝܢ ܕܠܐ ܒܥܕܢܗ ܘܕܠܐ ܒܙܒܢܗ. ܘܐܬܘ ܡ̈ܝܐ ܣܓܝ̈ܐܐ. ܘܐܬܟܢܫܘ ܐܝܟ ܠܦܬܘ̈ܚܐ ܒܝܕ ܐܣܟܦ̈ܬܐ ܕܦܪ̈ܙܠܐ ܬܪ̈ܥܐ ܕܦܪܝܣܝܢ ܗܘܘ ܘܡܣܩ̈ܒܠܐ ܕܦܪܙܠܐ ܕܡܥܪܒܝܢ ܗܘܘ. ܘܕܠܐ ܐܫܟܚܘ ܠܗܘܢ ܡܥܠܢܐ ܠܡ̈ܝܐ. ܗܘܐ ܠܗ ܝܡܐ ܪܒܐ ܠܒܪ ܡܢ ܥܘܪ̈ܝܗ ܕܡܕܝܢܬܐ. ܘܫܪܝܘ ܗܘܘ ܡ̈ܝܐ ܢܚܬܝܢ ܡܢ ܟܘܬ ܚ̈ܠܬܐ ܕܫܘܪܐ ܠܡܕܝܢܬܐ. ܘܐܒܓܪ ܡܠܟܐ ܟܕ ܩܐܡ ܗܘܐ ܒܦܘܪܓܘܣܐ ܪܒܐ ܕܡܬܩܪܐ ܕܦܪ̈ܣܝܐ. ܚܙܐ ܗܘܐ ܒܠܡܦܐܕܐ ܕܢܘܪܐ ܠܡ̈ܝܐ. ܘܦܩܕ ܗܘܐ. ܘܐܫܬܩܠܘ ܗܘܘ ܠܐܪ̈ܬܐ ܘܡܫܬ̈ܡܗܐ ܠܐܢܫܐ ܕܥܡܪܝܢ ܡܕܝܢܬܐ ܡܢ ܐܝܟܐ ܕܢܦܩ ܢܗܪܐ. ܘܒܗ ܒܫܥܬܐ ܬܪܥܘܗ̇ ܗܘܘ ܡ̈ܝܐ ܠܫܘܪܐ ܡܥܪܒܝܐ ܘܚܪܒܘ ܠܗܝܟܠܐ ܪܒܐ ܘܫܦܝܪܐ ܕܡܕܝܢܬܐ. ܘܟܠܗ ܠܗ ܡܕܝܢܬܐ ܕܡܢ ܡܠܟܐ. ܘܡܚܘ ܗܘܘ ܟܠ ܡܕܡ ܕܐܫܟܚܘ ܗܘܐ ܩܕܡܝܗܘܢ ܒܢܝ̈ܢܐ ܫܦܝ̈ܪܐ ܘܦܐܝ̈ܐ ܕܡܕܝܢܬܐ. ܟܠ ܡܕܡ ܕܩܪܝܒ ܗܘܐ ܠܢܗܪܐ ܡܢ ܓܒܘܗܝ ܕܓܪܒܝܐ. ܘܥܒܪܘ

ܗܘܘ ܬܘܒ ܒܗܝܟܠܐ ܕܥܕܬܐ ܕܟܪ̈ܣܛܝܢܐ. ܘܡܝܬܘ ܗܘܘ ܒܗܝܐ ܒܕܐ ܝܬܝܪ ܡܢ ܬܪ̈ܝܢ ܐܠܦ̈ܝܢ ܕܒܢ̈ܝܢܫܐ. ܣܓܝ̈ܐܐ ܕܝܢ ܡܢܗܘܢ. ܟܕ ܕܡܟܝܢ ܗܘܘ ܒܠܠܝܐ. ܒܠܥ ܒܠܥܘܢ ܡܝ̈ܐ ܡܢ ܫܠܝܐ ܘܐܬܚܢܩܘ ܗܘܘ. ܟܕ ܡܠܝܐ ܗܘܬ ܡܕܝܢܬܐ ܡܠܐ ܕܬ̈ܠܠܬܐ. ܘܟܕ ܚܙܐ ܐܒܓܪ ܡܠܟܐ ܣܘܪܚܢܐ ܗܢܐ ܕܗܘܐ ܗܘܐ. ܦܩܕ ܗܘܐ ܕܟܠܗܘܢ ܐܘ̈ܡܢܐ ܕܡܕܝܢܬܐ ܢܦܩܘܢ ܗܘܘ[1] ܚܩ̈ܠܬܗܘܢ ܡܢ ܠܘܬ ܢܗܪܐ. ܘܐܢܫ ܠܘܬ ܢܗܪܐ ܠܐ ܢܒܝܬ ܠܗ ܚܘܬܐ. ܘܒܚܟܡܬܐ ܕܡܫܩ̈ܚܐ ܘܕܘܟܐ ܐܬܬܣܝܡ ܢ̈ܘܬܐ ܕܟܦܐ ܢܗܘܘܢ ܦܬܝܐ ܕܢܗܪܐ. ܘܐܬܦܣܩܘ ܗܘܘ ܟܠܗ̇ ܡܫܩܝܬܗ ܡܕܝܢܬܐ. ܐܦ ܓܝܪ ܡܝ̈ܐ ܣܓܝܐܝܢ ܗܘܘ ܘܟܒܝܫܝܢ. ܐܠܐ ܐܦ ܗܘ ܦܬܝܗ ܕܢܗܪܐ ܙܥܘܪ ܗܘܐ. ܘܡܝ̈ܐ ܕܬ̈ܠܬܐ ܒܗ̈ܝܢ ܘܢܩܫ ܡܡܟܠܐ ܗܘܐ ܒܚܫܘܬܗܘܢ ܕܡܢ ܟܠ ܓܒ̈ܝܢ. ܘܦܩܕ ܗܘܐ ܐܒܓܪ ܡܠܟܐ. ܕܟܠܗܘܢ ܗܢܘܢ ܕܝܬܒܝܢ ܒܐܣܛܘ̈ܐ ܘܦܠܚܝܢ ܠܡܡܟܠܐ ܢܗܪܐ. ܕܡܢ ܬܫܪܝ ܩܕܡ ܘܥܕܡܐ ܠܢܝܣܢ ܠܐ ܗܘܘ ܒܐܬܝܢ ܒܚܩ̈ܠܬܗܘܢ. ܐܠܐ ܒܓܢ̈ܬܐ ܕܠܣܛܪ ܡܕܝܢܬܐ. ܚܫܒܐ ܡܢܗܘܢ ܗܘܘ ܒܐܬܝܢ ܒܫܘܪܐ ܠܟܠܐ ܡܢ ܕܘܟܬܐ ܕܥܠܝܢ ܒܗ̇ ܡܝ̈ܐ ܠܡܕܝܢܬܐ ܟܠܗ̇ ܙܒܢܐ ܕܣܬܘܐ. ܘܡܐ ܕܐܬܦܫܘ ܟܠ̈ܠܐ ܘܡܫܡܟܘ ܡܠܐ ܕܡܝ̈ܐ ܢܘܒ̈ܝܐ ܕܫܪܘ ܕܢܥܠܘܢ ܠܡܕܝܢܬܐ... ܘܟܠܡ ܕܫܡܥܝܢ ܡܠܐ ܘܡܣܘܣܐ ܘܠܐ ܢܦܩ. ܗܐ ܡܝ̈ܐ ܐܬܟܒ ܡܢܗܘ ܒܚܝܠܐ ܕܥܠ ܦܘܩܕܢܗ ܕܡܠܟܐ. ܘܐܬܬܣܝܡ ܗܘܐ ܗܢܐ ܦܘܩܕܢܐ ܡܢ ܗܢܐ ܙܒܢܐ ܕܗܘܐ ܒܗ ܗܒܝܐ ܒܕܡܐ ܠܩܘܒܠ ܟܠܡܐ. ܡܢ ܕܝܢ ܐܒܓܪ ܡܠܟܐ ܦܩܕ ܗܘܐ ܘܐܬܒܢܝ ܠܗ ܒܢܝܢܐ ܠܡܥܡܪܐ ܕܡܠܟܘܬܗ ܒܬ ܣܬܘܐ ܒܬ ܬܒܪܐ. ܘܐܡܪ ܒܗܝܢ ܗܘܐ ܟܠܗ̇ ܙܒܢܐ ܕܣܬܘܐ. ܘܒܩܝܛܐ ܢܚܬ ܗܘܐ ܠܗ ܠܐܦܕܢܐ ܚܕܬܐ ܕܐܬܒܢܝ ܗܘܐ ܠܗ ܥܠ ܪܫ ܡܥܘܟܐ. ܘܐܦ ܗܢܘܢ ܚܐܪ̈ܐ ܕܠܗ ܒܢܘ ܠܗܘܢ ܒ̈ܬܐ ܠܡܥܡܪܗܘܢ ܒܫܒܒܘܬܐ ܕܗܘܐ ܒܗ ܡܠܟܐ ܒܫܘܩܐ ܪܡܐ ܕܡܬܩܪܐ ܒܝܬ ܣܬܘܝܐ. ܘܡܛܠܠܐ ܕܬܐܡܢ ܗܘܐ[2] ܫܒܩ ܕܡܕܝܢܬܐ ܡܕܡ. ܦܩܕ ܗܘܐ ܐܒܓܪ ܡܠܟܐ ܘܐܫܬܒܩ ܚܩ̈ܠܬܐ ܕܐܒܕ̈ܬܐ ܡܢ ܓܘܝ̈ܐ ܕܡܕܝܢܬܐ. ܘܡܢ ܐܝܟ ܕܟܡܪܝܢ ܒܡܩܘܪ̈ܝܐ ܘܒܠܘܪܣܐ ܘܐܬܒܠܝܬ ܐܒ̈ܠܬܐ ܡܢܗܘܢ ܚܡܫ ܫܢ̈ܝܢ. ܒܕܡܐ ܕܒܬܪ

[1]See note 1, p. 161.
[2]See note 1, p. 161.

ܩܪ̈ܝܢܬܐ ܒܦܫܝܩܬܐ ܘܡܫܘܚܬܐ ܒܚܬܝܬܘ ※

From the *Chronicon Syriacum* of Barhebræus (1226–1286)

ܡܢ ܟܬܒܐ ܕܡܟܬܒܢܘܬ ܙܒܢ̈ܐ ܕܒܪ ܥܒܪܝܐ

The Taking of Babylon (Baghdad) by Hülägü Khan[1]

ܡܛܠ ܡܫܩܠܐ ܕܒܒܠ

ܢܚܬ ܡܠܟ ܡܠܟ̈ܐ ܗܘܠܐܘܘ ܥܠ ܒܓܕܐܕ: ܘܡܫܪܝܬܐ ܐܦ ܒܐܝܕܗ ܡܢ ܟܠܗ ܬܚܘ̈ܡܐ. ܘܢܦܩܘ ܚܝ̈ܠܘܬܗ ܕܒܓܕܐ̈ܕܝܐ ܠܒܪ ܕܢܦܩܘܢ ܒܛܛܪ̈ܝܐ. ܘܐܬܬܦܣܘܢ ܘܗ̄ܘܘ ܕܡܣܟܝܢ ܒܪ̈ܫܝܗܘܢ: ܐܡܝܪܐ ܪܒܐ ܟܘܪܕܝܐ ܕܡܬܩܪܐ ܒܪ ܟܘܪܪ: ܘܕܘܝܬܕܐܪ ܒܝܘܪܐ ܒܟܒܕܐ ܕܚܠܝܦܐ. ܘܦܓܥܘ ܛܛܪ̈ܝܗܘܢ ܝܬ̈ܝܐ ܠܡܫܒܠ ܚܕܐ: ܒܗ ܠܐ ܐܪܥܘ: ܒܡܢܝܢ ܘܬܠܬܝܢ ܐܠ̈ܦܝܢ: ܡܚܕܐ ܒܝܘܡ ܐܪܒܥܐ ܬܡܢܝܐ ܒܢܝܫܐ ܡܕܡܟܐ ܕܛܝ̈ܝܐ: ܫܢܬ ܫܬܡܐܐ ܘܚܡܫܝܢ ܘܫܬ[2]: ܕܗܝ ܫܢܬ ܐܢܣܛ[3] ܕܝ̈ܘܢܝܐ: ܐܬܩܪܒ ܡܕܡܐܫܬ ܒܐܝܕܗ ܗܢܝܢ ܘܣܝ̈ܥܬܗ ܠܫܘܪܗ̇ ܕܡܕܝܢܬܐ ܡܢ ܓܒܐ ܕܡܕܢܚܐ ܕܒܓܒܐ ܡܕܝܢܬܐ ܕܒܓܕܐܕ: ܘܩܪܒܘ ܐܦ ܒܓܕܐ̈ܕܝܐ. ܘܦܩܕܘ ܒܢ̈ܕܕܐ: ܘܐܬܬܒܪܘ ܒܟܐ ܕܒܓܕܐܕ ܗܢܝܢ: ܘܐܬܚܒܫܘ ܒܥܘܡܩܗ̇ ܒܓܕܐ̈ܕܝܐ. ܘܐܬܦܬܚܘ ܗ̄ܘܐ ܐܡܝ̈ܪܐ ܘܦܘܠܡܝܢܐ ܫܐܠܗ ܟܡ ܚܝܠܐ ܕܠܗ ܥܠ ܫܘܪܐ ܕܒܓܕܐܕ.

---

[1]Gregorios Bar ʿEbrāyā (Gregorius Barhebræus), *Ktābā d-maktbānut zabnē: Gregorii Barhebraei chronicon syriacum: e codd. mss. emendatum ac punctis vocalibus adnotationibusque locupletatum* (Paris: Maisonneuve, 1890), pp. 503–6.

[2]The Hegira year 656 began on January 8, 1258.

[3]ܐܢܣܛ represents 1569: ܐ, normally 1, is 1000, and ܢ, normally 50, is 500; ܣܛ is 69 (ܣ = 60, ܛ = 9); see pp. xxiii–xxiv. This is the year 1569 of the Seleucid (Greek) era, which began in 312 B.C.

ܘܒܗ ܗܘܐ ܪܡܫܐ: ܐܡܪ ܒܪ ܒܘܙܙ ܗܢܐ ܠܡܘܬܒܐܪ ܓܠܠܐ:
ܕܫܡܫܐ ܕܐܠܗܐ ܢܣ̄ܒ ܠܝ ܙܒܢܘܬܗ̇: ܙܘܙ ܕܢܚܘܠ ܠܒܪܬܝ
ܘܬܬܚܢ: ܘܡ ܢܦܘܩ ܡܢܕܪܫ ܘܢܦܩܕ. ܗܘ̇ ܕܝܢ ܐܫܬܒܠ ܘܠܐ
ܢܓܕܐ ܕܢܚܘܠ: ܘܟܠܗ ܒܠܚܘܕ ܠܒܪ. ܘܡܛܠ ܕܒܕܘܒܬܗ̇
ܡܡܟܟܬܗ̇ ܥܒܪ ܗܘ̄ܘ ܗܘܢ ܒܕܐܪ̈ܐ: ܐܘܠܘ ܬܬܬܪ̈ܐ ܘܬܪܒܘ
ܒܠܗܘܢ ܬܘܪܒܬܗ̇ ܕܙܒܠܬܗ̇ ܪܒܬܗ̇ ܕܡܢܐ ܡܢ ܕܡܠܬܗ̇: ܘܐܬܠܝܘ
ܐܝܟ ܡܢܐ ܒܦܠܝܓܘ ܕܠܠܐ. ܘܥܒܪܘ ܒܪܚܝܡ ܡܢ ܝܘ ܡܢܐ:
ܘܬܪ̈ܐ. ܐܦ ܡܬܬܬܗܘܢ ܘܝܐܪ̈ܝܗܘܢ ܘܬܡܢܐ ܕܗܦܩܘܗܝ. ܘܒܗ
ܢܗܪ ܓܦܪܐ: ܦܘ ܒܠܚܘܕ ܬܬܪ̈ܐ ܒܢ̈ܝ ܝܒܐ ܕܗܘܠܐܒܘ. ܘܐܝܓܪ
ܡܢܟܐ ܒܕܡܐ ܠܬܥܒ ܥܒܢܝ ܕܗܘܟ ܢܣܥܐ: ܘܢܒ ܘܐܘܢܠ
ܝܒܐ ܕܝܓܕܐܪ̈ܐ: ܘܐܬܗܦܟ ܒܪ ܒܘܙܙ: ܘܒܪܘܡ ܕܗܘܬܒܐܪ ܘܒܠ
ܠܟܪܣܗ̇.

ܗܕܝܢ ܒܐܝܕܗ ܘܫܠܝܚܘܬܗ ܐܬܐ ܥܒܪܘ ܒܝܒܫܐ ܡܒܪܟܢܐ
ܕܒܝܕܐܪ. ܘܡܫܠܡܢܘ ܥܒܪܐ ܒܝܒܫܐ ܡܕܝܢܬܐ: ܒܗܘܢ ܬܘܒ
ܬܠܬܒܗܘܪ ܒܢܝܢܐ ܡܕܡܢܐ: ܘܐܡܣܟ ܡܢܟܐ ܡܥܢܐ ܒܠܝܬ
ܕܡܕܝܢܬܗ̇: ܠܗܡܒܠ ܬܝܒܐ ܕܕܪ̈ܬܗ̇ ܕܒܠܦܘܗ. ܘܒܗ ܦܘܗ ܗܒܪ̈ܐ
ܗܘ ܡܗܘܗܬܒܝܟ ܒܠܦܘܗ ܕܘܝܐ: ܡܢܐ ܠܒܪ ܒܠܗܡܒ ܘܙܪ̈ܐ
ܕܠܗ: ܘܠܝܒܟ ܐܠܗܝ ܒܒܗ ܐܠܝܢ ܒܪ ܕܪ̈ܝܗܘܦ ܘܠܡܢ. ܡܒܒܒܐ
ܡܬܘܠܗܐ: ܘܦܗܒ ܠܗܘܢ ܕܢܗܒܘܢ ܗܘܝܐܐ ܕܕܗܒܐ: ܘܡܠܠܬܗ̇
ܡܠܟܬܗ̇: ܘܬܒܥܐ ܐܬܒܗܘ: ܘܢܦܩܘܢ ܠܐܝܕܪ̈ܐ ܕܬܬܪ̈ܐ ܡܢ
ܣܘܥܝܐ: ܘܢܠܒܥܘܢ ܐܝܟ: ܘܢܬܠܘܢ ܠܗܘܢ ܡܗ̈ܘܡܢܬܗ̇ ܥܦܪ̈ܬܗ̇:
ܘܐܪܠܘܢ ܒܒܗܘܢ ܠܗܬ ܡܠܝܢ ܡܠܟܐ. ܘܢܬܒܒܘܢ ܡܠܟܬܗ̇ ܠܣܓ̈ܘܗ̄ܝ.
ܕܒܠܦܘܗ ܘܕܒܢ̈ܘܗ̄ܝ ܘܕܒܢܬ̈ܘܗ̄ܝ: ܘܢܦܩܘܢ ܙܘܣܐ: ܕܗܠܝܢ ܕܗܘ̈ܝ:
ܒܗ ܡܠܘܟ̈ܐ ܒܢ̈ܝܐ ܗܘ̈ܝ. ܘܐܦ ܚܝܝ ܡܒܝܠ ܘܢܬܠ ܠܗܘܢ
ܫܢ̈ܝܗܘܢ: ܒܒ̈ܕܐ ܗܘܦܝ ܘܡܥܒܒ̈ܕܐ ܘܢ̈ܒܒ ܡܕܐܐܬܗ̇. ܘܒܗ ܢܦܩܘ
ܗܢܘ ܗܠܝܢ ܠܗܬ ܡܠܝܢ ܡܠܟܐ: ܘܥܒܠܘ ܐܝܕܘܬܗܘܢ: ܒܒܪ
ܐܝܟ ܘܠܐ ܐܦܣ ܠܗܘܢ ܕܢܦܩܘܢ ܠܗܬ ܒܠܦܘܗ. ܘܐܬܒܥܢܗ

ܠܡܕܒܪܐ: ܘܬܪܒܘ ܬܬܪ̈ܐ ܬܘܪܒܗ̇ ܪ̈ܒܗ̇ ܒܒܘܪܟܐ ܕܒܝܬܟܐ: ܘܟܠܗ ܠܡܕܝܢܬܗ̇: ܒܝܘܡ ܪܘܒܬܗ̇ ܒܗܪܝܢ ܘܣܓܝܐܐ ܒܢܝܫܐ ܡܕܒܪܐ. ܘܐܬܟܢܫܘ ܟܠܗܘܢ ܒܢ̈ܝ ܡܕܝܢܬܐ: ܘܐܦܝܣܘ ܐܢܘܢ ܡܢܕܝܪܐ ܠܒܪ. ܘܬܘܒ ܬܘܦܣ ܬܬܪ̈ܐ: ܘܠܡܕܝܢܬܐ ܕܒܬܪܗ: ܒܐܡܬ ܒܝܘܡ ܥܒܕܗ̇: ܐܫܬܠܛܘ ܥܠ ܟܠܗܘܢ ܫܘܪ̈ܐ. ܘܒܪܘܡܘ ܒܝܬ ܐܕܪ̈ܐ: ܘܐܬܛܥܝܘ ܒܒ̈ܝܬܗ̇ ܘܣܓܝܐܐ ܕܬܘܣܦܬ ܐܪܒܐ. ܘܒܗ ܒܝܘܡ ܥܒܕܗ̇: ܢܦܩܘ ܬܪ̈ܥܝܗܘܢ ܒܢ̈ܘܗܝ ܕܟܠܗܘܢ ܠܒܪ ܡܢ: ܡܠܟ ܡܠܟ̈ܐ: ܘܒܬܪ ܥܒܕܗ̇ ܢܦܩ ܐܦ ܗܘ ܒܠܒܘܫܗ. ܘܦܩܕ ܡܠܟ ܡܠܟ̈ܐ: ܘܐܬܪܟܒܘ ܒܗ ܦܪ̈ܫܐ: ܘܗܘܘ ܟܠܗ̇. ܢܛܘܪ̈ܐ ܒܝܕܗ ܡܢ ܬܪܥܗ̇ ܫܒܥܐ ܥܕܡܢ. ܒܕܡܐ ܕܟܠ ܗܘ ܡܠܟ ܡܠܟ̈ܐ ܣܘܡܟܐܬ ܠܕܪܗ̇ ܕܟܠܗܘܢ: ܘܡܢ ܠܬܪ̈ܐ ܘܡܬܛܟܣܢܗ̇ ܘܡܫܬܡܫܢܗ̇ ܠܬܫܡܫܬܗ̇ ܘܫܪ̈ܝܬܗ̇: ܘܒܠܠ ܟܠܗܘܢ ܘܐܦܣ. ܘܡܥܛܠܘ ܡܩ̈ܒܠܐ ܡܦܩܗܘܢ: ܘܡܛܠܠ ܠܟܠܗ ܒܗܐ ܕܒܝܬܐܪ̈ܐ ܬܒܘܗ̇ ܕܒܫܒܥܐ: ܬܪܐܢܬܐ ܐܒܪ̈ܐ ܒܒܕܘ ܡܛܠܠܐ ܗܝܟܠܐ. ܘܡܫܬܠܡܘܬܐ ܒܝܫ ܠܬ̈ܗܝܠܐ ܟܠܗܘܢ ܠܕܪܗ̇ ܕܫܡܫܐ ܕܬܠܬܗ̇: ܘܬܡܢ ܢܛܪ ܐܝܟ: ܘܠܐ ܐܢܫ ܡܢ ܒܬ̈ܗܝܠܐ ܐܬܗ̇ܒ. ܐܦ ܒܬ̈ܪܐ ܕܛܝ̈ܒܐ ܗܘܝܐܐ ܕܒܫܒܬܗܘܢ ܠܗ̇ܬ ܡܬܠܡܝܢܐ ܐܬܘܗ: ܕܕܡܐ ܠܝ ܢܬܗܘܢܒܗܘܢ ܫܕܗ ܕܠܗܘܢ: ܘܟܠܗܘܢ ܐܬܡܛܠܠ.

ܒܬܪ ܕܝܢ ܕܐܬܒܣܠ ܡܠܠ ܡܠܟ ܡܠܟ̈ܐ: ܡܪܟܗ ܠܟܠܗܘܢ ܕܗܘܐ ܡܕܡܘܗ̇: ܘܕܒܗ ܘܣܒܗ ܠܡܘܬܗ̇. ܘܦܩܕ ܘܡܫܡܫܘܗ̇. ܒܡܫܐ ܘܣܛܘ ܟܠܗ̇: ܘܒܪ̈ܦܫܐ ܕܬ̈ܝܠܝܗܘܢ ܡܛܠܠܗ̇. ܒܗ̇ ܕܐܬܒܢܝ ܛܝ̈ܒܐ ܐܕܝܠܘܗ̇. ܠܡܠܟ ܡܠܟ̈ܐ ܒܗ ܐܡܪܢ: ܕܐܦ ܢܗܒ ܡܢ ܕܡܢ ܕܗܘܐ ܥܠ ܐܪܥܐ: ܠܐ ܬܘܒ ܫܢܬ ܡܛܪ̈ܐ: ܟܠܢܐ ܐܦ ܝܘܡ̈ܬܐ ܕܢܘܪܐ ܫܒܝܢ ܡܢܢ. ܘܗܘܪܒܐ ܢܗܒܬ ܫܘܠܡܐ ܡܠܟܘܬܗ̇ ܕܒܐܦܣܐ: ܐܦ ܫܪܒܐ ܕܡܠܟܘܬܗ̇ ܕܛܝ̈ܒܐ ܫܢ̈ܝ. ܠܡܕܒܪܢܘܬܗ. ܘܡܫܟܬ ܘܐܬܦܢܝܬ ܡܠܟܘܬܗ̇ ܕܡܩ̈ܒܠܐ ܒܐܬܘܪܘܬܗ̇ ܗܠܝܢ ܕܠܒܪ: ܐܝܟ ܕܐܦ ܒܐܬܘܪܘܬܗ̇ ܗܢܘܢ ܕܠܗܘ.

From the Reign of Baidu Khan[1]

ܘܡܠܟ ܕܒܝܕܐ ܗܘܐ ܥܠܝܗܘܢ ܡܗ̈ܝܡܢܐ ܪܘܪ̈ܒܢܐ ܘܕܝܪ̈ܝܐ ܒܥܠܘܬܗܘܢ ܐܡܗܪܘ: ܘܡܣܒܕܘ ܐܬܦܪܘ: ܘܒܢ̈ܩܘܫܬܐ ܘܙ̈ܓܠܘܬܐ ܕܕܝ̈ܠܢܝܢ ܠܡܫ̈ܠܡܢܐ ܠܒ ܐܬܡܗܪܘ: ܗܘ ܬܘܒ ܒܝܕܘ ܒܕ ܓܘܪ ܠܗܘܢ ܐܡܗܪܝ: ܘܣܝܡܘ ܒܗ ܠܒ ܠܒ ܥܠܝܗܘܢ ܪܘܪ̈ܒܢܐ ܕܡܠܟܘܬܗ. ܐܠܐ ܡܢ ܚܝܢ ܟܪ̈ܣܛܝܢܐ ܠܐ ܡܬܬܢܝܚܐ ܗܘܐ ܕܬܡܛܘ: ܘܕܬܬܟܠ ܥܠ ܐܚܕ ܒܢܝܢܐ ܒܥܠܝܗܘܢ ܦܘܪ̈ܣܝܐ ܕܡܠܟܘܬܐ ܗܦܝܪ ܡܢܗܘܢ ܠܐ ܡܬܕܢܝܢܐ ܗܘܐ. ܘܡܢ ܗܘܢܐ ܥܢܝ ܡܣܝܪ ܥܠ ܬܪ̈ܥܝܗܘܢ ܡܗ̈ܦܟܢܐ. ܠܟܪ̈ܣܛܝܢܐ ܢܩܫܢ ܐܡܪ ܗܘܐ ܕܟܪ̈ܣܛܝܢܐ ܗܘ: ܘܢܝܒܝܐ ܬܠܬ ܒܢܘܬܗ. ܠܟܢ̈ܫܐ ܕ ܚܢ ܡܟܣܐ ܗܘܐ ܕܡܫܠܡܢܐ ܗܘ: ܐܠܐ ܠܗ ܡܬܟܣܝܐ ܗܘܐ ܠܡܐܠܦ ܫܒܝܬܐ ܘܦܘ̈ܩܕܢܐ. ܘܟܠܗܝܢ ܕܡܬܟܪ̈ܝܢ ܗܘܘ ܠܘܬܗ ܪܫܐ ܬܘܕܝܬܗܘܢ ܘܡܝܡܝܢ ܠܫܠܘܬܐ: ܗܘ ܒܝܕܘ ܠܒܢܘܗܝ ܡܥܡܕ ܗܘܐ ܕܢܝܠܐ ܒܫܡܗܘܢ. ܘܒܡܗܝܡܢܐ ܡܥܡܕ ܗܘܐ ܬܘܕܝܬܗܘܢ: ܘܡܫܪܝ ܪܘܚܡܗܘܢ. ܒܪܡ ܠܐ ܡܬܦܫܐ ܗܘܐ ܥܠܝܗܘܢ ܕܡܫ̈ܝܚܝܐ ܕܠܦܣܬ ܟܪ̈ܣܛܝܢܐ ܬܠܐ ܡܙܠܠܐ. ܘܡܬܚܫܢܐ. ܘܡܥܒܪܢܘܬܐ ܕܥܝܪ̈ܐ ܫܡܥܐ ܒܡܗ̈ܦܟܐ ܕܐܝܟ ܗܠܝܢ ܕܒܙ ܡܠܟܘܬܗ.

[1]Gregorios Bar ʻEbrāyā, *Ktābā d-maktbānut zabnē*, pp. 593–95.

Syriac-English Vocabulary

Words used primarily as nouns are listed in the emphatic state; words used primarily as adjectives are given in the absolute; regular, predictable plurals of nouns and adjectives are not indicated (see Appendix B, p. 142). Verbs are listed by root (III-weak verbs are alphabetized with *ālap* as the third radical; hollow verbs are given with *w* as the second radical). Perfect and imperfect forms are given for G-verbs. Abbreviations: abs: absolute state; act: active; const: construct state; impf: imperfect; impt: imperative; int: intransitive, pass: passive; pl: plural; pr n: proper name; pron encl: pronominal enclitic; trs: transitive.

ܐܒܐ *abā* pl *abāhē/abāhātā* father

ܐܒܕ *ebad/nêbad* to perish; Aph *awbed* to cause to perish

ܐܒܓܪ *abgar* Abgar (pr n)

ܐܒܝܕ *abid* lost

ܐܒܝܐ *abiyā* Abijah

ܐܒܝܠ *abil* in mourning

ܐܒܠܐ *eblā* mourning

ܐܓܘܣܛܘܣ *āgusṭos* Augustus

ܐܓܘܪܣܐ *agorsā* estate, farm

ܐܓܝ *aggay* Aggai (pr n)

ܐܓܣ *agges* see ܓܣܣ

ܐܓܪ *egar/negor* to hire; *aggar* see ܢܓܪ

ܐܓܪܐ *agrā* wage; *eggārā* rooftop

ܐܓܪܬܐ *eggartā* letter, epistle

ܐܕܝ *adday* Addai (equated with Thaddaeus, one of the seventy-two disciples)

ܐܕܡ *ādām* Adam

ܐܕܢܐ *ednā* (f) ear

ܐܕܪ *ādār* March

ܐܗܠ *ahhel* see ܗܠܠ

ܐܗܪ *ahhar* see ܗܪܪ

ܐܗܪܘܢ *ahrōn* Aaron

ܐܘ *aw* or; more than; *aw...aw* either...or; *o* O (vocative)

ܐܘܒܠ *awbel* see ܝܒܠ

ܐܘܕܝ *awdi* see ܝܕܐ

ܐܘܕܥ *awda*ᶜ see ܝܕܥ

ܐܘܙܢܐ *uznā* cistern, font

ܐܘܚܕܢܐ *uḥdānā* dominion, jurisdiction

ܐܘܚܠ *awḥel* see ܚܝܠ

ܐܘܚܪ *awḥar* see ܐܚܪ
ܐܘܟܡ *ukām* black
ܐܘܡܝ *awmi* see ܝܡܐ
ܐܘܡܢܐ *umānā* craftsman
ܐܘܡܢܘܬܐ *umānutā* trade, craft
ܐܘܡܬܐ *ummtā* community, nation
ܐܘܢܐ *awwānā* abode, lodging
ܐܘܣܛܪܓܝܣ *ewsṭārgis* Eustargis (pr n)
ܐܘܣܦ *awsep* see ܝܣܦ
ܐܘܩܕ *awqed* see ܝܩܕ
ܐܘܪܓܢܘܢ *orgānon* organ
ܐܘܪܗܝ *urhāy* Edessa
ܐܘܪܚܐ *urḥā* (f) way, road
ܐܘܪܝܐ *oryā* manger
ܐܘܪܥܐ *ur^{c}ā* (abs *ura^c*) meeting, encounter
ܐܘܪܫܠܡ *orêšlem* Jerusalem
ܐܘܪܬ *awret* see ܝܪܬ
ܐܘܫܛ *awšeṭ* see ܝܫܛ
ܐܙܠ *ezal/nêzal* to go
ܐܚܐ *aḥā* brother
ܐܚܒ *aḥḥeb* see ܚܒܒ
ܐܚܕ *cḥad/ncḥod* to seize, take, shut (door); pass part *(aḥid)* has both act & pass senses, also means possessing, having, powerful; Ethpe *etthed* to be shut
ܐܚܝ *aḥḥi* see ܐܚܐ
ܐܚܡܕ *aḥmad* Ahmad (pr n)
ܐܚܪ Aph *awḥar* to delay, tarry; Eshtaph *eštawḥar* to delay, hesitate
ܐܚܪܝ *ḥrāy* last, hind
ܐܚܪܢܐ *ḥrênā/ḥrētā* pl *ḥrānē/ḥranyātā* other
ܐܝܒܪܝܐ *iberāyā* Iberian, Georgian
ܐܝܕܐ *idā* (f, const *id-/yad-,* abs *yad)* pl *idē/idayyā* hand
ܐܝܕܐ *aydā* (f) which?; *aydā d-* she who
ܐܝܙܓܕܐ *izgaddā* ambassador, envoy
ܐܝܙܓܕܘܬܐ *izgaddutā* embassy, message
ܐܝܛܠܝܐ *iṭālyā* Italy
ܐܝܟ *ak* like; *ak d-* as
ܐܝܟܐ *aykā* where?
ܐܝܟܢ *aykan* how
ܐܝܟܢܐ *aykannā* how; *aykannā d-* as
ܐܝܠܝܢ *aylēn* (pl) which?; *aylēn d-* those who
ܐܝܠܢܐ *ilānā* tree
ܐܝܡܡܐ *imāmā* by day
ܐܝܢ *ên* yes
ܐܝܢܐ *aynā* which?; *aynā d-* he who
ܐܝܢܘ *aynaw* for *aynā-(h)u* which is?
ܐܝܣܦܘܢ *iyāspōn* jasper
ܐܝܩܪܐ *iqārā* glory, honor
ܐܝܪ *êyār* May
ܐܝܬ *it* there is/are
ܐܝܬܝ *ayti* see ܐܬܐ
ܐܟܐ as in ܐܬܐܟܝ *ettakki,* see ܢܟܐ
ܐܟܘܬ *akwāt* like (prep)
ܐܟܙܢܐ *akznā* likewise
ܐܟܚܕ *akḥad* likewise
ܐܟܚܕܐ *akḥdā* together
ܐܟܠ *ekal/nekol* to eat
ܐܟܠܩܪܨܐ *ākelqarṣā* the Devil
ܐܟܡܢ *akman* for ܐܝܟ ܡܢ *ak man* like one who, like him who, as though

ܐܟܣܢܝܐ *aksnāyā* stranger, foreigner
ܐܠܐ *ellā* but; for *en lā* if...not
ܐܠܐ ܐܢ *ellā en* unless, except that
ܐܠܗܐ *alāhā* God
ܐܠܗܘܬܐ *alāhutā* divinity
ܐܠܘ *ellu* if (contrafactual)
ܐܠܘܬܪܦܘܠܝܣ *elewṯerāpolis* Eleutherapolis
ܐܠܝܐ *eliyā* Elijah
ܐܠܝܘܦܘܠܝܣ *êliopolis* Heliopolis
ܐܠܝܫܒܥ *elišba*ᶜ Elizabeth
ܐܠܟܣܢܕܪܘܣ *aleksandros* Alexander
ܐܠܥܐ *el*ᶜ*ā* (f) rib
ܐܠܦ Pa *allep* to teach
ܐܠܦܐ *alpā* (abs *ālep)* thousand
ܐܠܨ *elaṣ/neloṣ* to compel
ܐܡܐ *emmā* pl *emmhātā* mother
ܐܡܘܪܘܣ *amoros* Amoros
ܐܡܝܢ *āmên* verily, amen
ܐܡܝܢܐܝܬ *aminā'it* always, constantly
ܐܡܝܪܐ *amirā* emir
ܐܡܢ Ethpe *etemen b-* to persevere in
ܐܡܪ *emar/nêmar* to say, tell (*l-* someone, ᶜ*al* about); Ethpe *etemar* to be said
ܐܡܪܐ *emrā* lamb
ܐܡܬܐ *amtā* pl *amhātā* maidservant
ܐܡܬܝ *emat* when
ܐܢ *en* if (possible conditional)
ܐܢܐ *enā* I
ܐܢܗܘ ܕ *enhu d-* if it is/was (a fact, true) that
ܐܢܘܢ *ennon* they, them (m)
ܐܢܛܝܘܟܝܐ *anṭyokyā* Antioch
ܐܢܝܢ *ennēn* they, them (f)
ܐܢܢܩܐ *ananqê* (ἀνάγκη) it is possible
ܐܢܫܐ *nāšā* people; *nāš* anybody, somebody; *lānāš* nobody
ܐܢܫܘܬܐ *nāšutā* humanity
ܐܢܬ *att* you (m sing)
ܐܢܬܝ *att* you (f sing)
ܐܢܬܘܢ *atton* you (m pl)
ܐܢܬܝܢ *attēn* you (f pl)
ܐܢܬܬܐ *atttā* pl *neššē* woman, wife
ܐܣܐ Pa *assi/nassē* to heal; Ethpa *etassi* to be healed
ܐܣܐ *essā* wall
ܐܣܛܘܐ *esṭwā* στοά, porch, portico
ܐܣܛܠܐ *esṭlā* (f) clothing
ܐܣܝܐ *āsyā* healer
ܐܣܝܘܬܐ *āsyutā* pl *-swātā* cure, healing
ܐܣܝܪܐ *asirā* prisoner
ܐܣܟܡܐ *eskêmā* attire, appearance
ܐܣܦܢܝܐ *espānyā* Spain
ܐܣܩ *asseq* see ܣܠܩ
ܐܣܪ *esar/nesor* to bind, fasten
ܐܣܬܐ *estā* wall
ܐܥܠ *a*ᶜᶜ*el* see ܥܠܠ
ܐܦ *āp* also, so also
ܐܦܐ *appē* (pl only) face, countenance; *l-appay* around about
ܐܦܕܢܐ *āpadnā* palace
ܐܦܛܪܦܐ *epiṭrāpā* ἐπίτροπος, procurator
ܐܦܠܐ *āplā* for *āp lā*
ܐܦܢ *āp en* even if, although
ܐܦܣ *appes* see ܦܣܣ
ܐܦܩ *appeq* see ܢܦܩ
ܐܦܪܝܡ *aprim* Ephraem
ܐܪܒܝܩܘ *arābiqo* Arabian (horse)

ܐܪܒܥ *arba*^{c} (f), *arb*^{c}*ā* (m) four; *arb*^{c}*ābšabbā* Wednesday

ܐܪܕܟܠܐ *ardeklā* master builder

ܐܪܙܐ *arzā* cedar, pine

ܐܪܝܐ *aryā* pl *-yawwātā* lion

ܐܪܡܐܝܬ *ārāmā'it* in Aramaic

ܐܪܥ *era*^{c}*/nero*^{c} to meet, encounter

ܐܪܥܐ *ar*^{c}*ā* (abs *ara*^{c}) pl *ar*^{c}*ē/ar*^{c}*awwātā* earth, land

ܐܫܕ *ešad/nešod* to pour out, shed; Ethpe *etešed* to be spilled, shed

ܐܫܟܚ *eškaḥ/neškaḥ* to find; to be able (act part *meškaḥ);* Ethpe *eštkaḥ* to be found

ܐܫܪ *aššar* see ܫܪܪ

ܐܫܬܝ *ešti/neštē* to drink

ܐܬܐ *ātā* pl *ātwātā* sign, token

ܐܬܐ *etā/nêtē* to come; Aph *ayti* to bring, take, lead

ܐܬܘܬܐ pl of ܐܬܐ

ܐܬܪܐ *atrā* pl *-rē/-rawwātā* place, country

ܐܬܦܘܫܫ *etpawšaš* see ܦܫܫ

ܒ *b(a)-* (proclitic) at, in (place); on, at (time); with (instrumental)

ܒܐܓܘ *bāju* Baju (pr n)

ܒܒܠ *bābel* Babylon

ܒܕܓܘܢ *badgon* therefore, for that reason

ܒܗܠ Ethpe *etbhel* to calm down

ܒܗܬ *bhet/nebhat* to be ashamed, confused

ܒܘܟܪ *bukar* first-born

ܒܘܪܓܐ *burgā* tower, turret

ܒܘܪܟܬܐ *burktā* blessing

ܒܬ *bāt/nbut* to pass the night, spend the night

ܒܙܚ *bzaḥ/nebzoḥ* to penetrate

ܒܙ *bāz* hawk

ܒܛܝܠ *bṭil* idle; *baṭṭil* in vain, of no effect

ܒܛܠ *baṭṭāl* idle

ܒܛܢ *bṭen/nebṭan* to conceive (child)

ܒܛܢܐ *baṭnā* conception; *qabbel baṭnā* to become pregnant

ܒܝܕܘ *baydu* Baidu Khan, Ilkhan ruler, AD 1295

ܒܝܠ *bêl* Bel, supreme god of the Babylonians

ܒܝܡ *bêm* judgment seat

ܒܝܢ Ethpa *etbayyan* to regard, consider

ܒܝܢ *bayn* (+ pron encl II) among, between

ܒܝܢܬ *baynāt* (+ pron encl I) among, between

ܒܝܫ *biš* bad, evil, wicked

ܒܝܫܘܬܐ *bišutā* malice, evil

ܒܝܬ *bēt* (prep) among; see also next entry

ܒܝܬܐ *baytā* pl *bāttē* (const sing *bēt-)* house

ܒܝܬܐܣܝܪܐ *bēt-asirē* prison

ܒܝܬܓܘܒܪܝܢ *bēt-gubrin* Beit-Jubrin (pr n)

ܒܝܬܘܥܕܐ *bēt-wa*^{c}*dā* assembly hall

ܒܝܬܚܣܕܐ *bēt-ḥesdā* Bethesda

ܒܝܬܝܐ *baytāyā* household (adj)

ܒܝܬܠܚܡ *bēt-lḥem* Bethlehem

ܒܝܬܡܫܬܘܬܐ *bēt-meštutā* banquet hall

ܒܝܬܢܗܪܝܢ *bēt-nahrin* Mesopotamia

ܒܝܬܣܗܪ̈ܝܐ *bēt-saḥrāyē* Beth Sahraye (pr n)

ܒܝܬܥܘܝܕܐ *bēt-*^{c}*widā* Beth Awida

ܒܝܬܨܘܒܐ *bēt-ṣawbā* meeting house

ܒܝܬܩܒܘܪܐ *bēt-qburā* sepulchre

ܒܝܬܬܒܪܐ *bēt-tbārā* Beth T'vara

ܒܟܐ *bkā/nebkē* to weep, cry

ܒܟܬܐ *bkātā* weeping

ܒܠܚܘܕ *balḥod* alone (takes pron encl II)

ܒܠܢܝ *balanay* (f) bath

ܒܢܐ *bnā/nebnē* to build; Ethpe *etbni* to be built

ܒܢ̈ܝܐ *bnayyā* pl of *brā*

ܒܢܝܢܐ *benyānā* building, edifice

ܒܢ̈ܬܐ *bnātā* pl of *bartā*

ܒܣܐ *bsā/nebsē* to despise *(b-* or ^{c}*al)*

ܒܣܒܣ *basbes/nbasbes* to tear to pieces

ܒܣܝܡ *bassim* pleasant

ܒܣܝܢܐ *besyānā* negligence, fine for negligence

ܒܣܡܐ *besmā* aroma, spice, incense

ܒܣܬܪ *bestar* behind (pron encl I)

ܒܥܐ *b*^{c}*ā/neb*^{c}*ē* to seek, look for; Ethpe *etb*^{c}*i* to be necessary, needed

ܒܥܘܬܐ *bā*^{c}*utā* request, petition

ܒܥܛ *b*^{c}*aṭ/neb*^{c}*aṭ* to spur, urge on

ܒܥܠܐ *ba*^{c}*lā* master, husband

ܒܥܠܕܒܒܐ *b*^{c}*eldbābā* enemy

ܒܥܠܙܒܘܒ *b*^{c}*elzbob* Beelzebub

ܒܨܝ Pa *baṣṣi* to search into, find out

ܒܩܐ Ethpa *etbaqqi* to scrutinize

ܒܪ *bar (l-bar men)* outside of

ܒܪܐ *brā/nebrē* to create; Ethpe *etbri* to be created, come into existence

ܒܪܐ *brā* (constr *bar-*) pl *bnayyā* (abs *bnin)* son; ܒܪܝ *ber* my son

ܒܪܐܓܪܐ *bar-eggārā* pl *bar-eggārē* demon

ܒܪܒܪܐ *barbārā* Barbara

ܒܪܙܢܩܐ *barzanqā* type of armor

ܒܪܝܟ *brik* blessed

ܒܪܝܬܐ *britā* pl *brayyā/beryātā* creature

ܒܪܟ *brek/nebrak* to kneel; Pa *barrek* to bless; Ethpa *etbarrak* to be blessed

ܒܪ ܟܘܪܪ *bar kurār* Ibn Kurar (pr n)

ܒܪܡ *bram* nonetheless, however

ܒܪܢܫܐ *bar-nāšā* pl *bnay-nāšā* man, human, person

ܒܪ ܥܠܩܡܝ *bar* ^{c}*alqami* Ibn al-'Alqami, d. 1258, vizier to Musta'sim

ܒܪܩܐ *barqā* lightning

ܒܪܫܝܬ *b-rāšit* in the beginning

ܒܪܬܐ *bartā* (constr *bat-*) pl ܒܢ̈ܬܐ *bnātā* daughter

ܒܬܘܠܬܐ *btultā* virgin

ܒܬܪ *bātar* after

ܒܬܪܟܢ *bātarken* afterwards, then, next

ܓܐܪܐ *gêrā* arrow

ܓܒܐ *gbā/negbē* to choose; *gbē/gabyā* chosen

ܓܒܐ *gabbā* (abs *gebb)* side

ܓܒܠ *gbal/negbol* to form, fashion

ܓܒܪ *gabbār* mighty

ܓܒܪܐ *gabrā* man, husband

ܓܒܪܘܬܐ *gabrutā* pl *-rwātā* deeds of renown
ܓܒܪܐܝܠ *gabryêl* Gabriel
ܓܓܘܠܬܐ *gāgultā* Golgotha
ܓܕܐ *gaddā* luck, fortune
ܓܕܝܐ *gadyā* pl *gdayyā* goat
ܓܕܠܝܐ *gdalyā* Gedaliah (pr n)
ܓܕܦ Pa *gaddep b-/l-/^{c}al* to revile; Ethpa *etgaddap* to be reviled
ܓܕܫ *gdaš/negdaš* to happen
ܓܗܢܐ *gehhannā* Gehenna, hell
ܓܘ *gaww* inside (also *gaww men, b-gaww, l-gaww)*
ܓܘܕܐ *gudā* band, company
ܓܘܝ̈ܐ *gawwāyē* citizens
ܓܘܡܨܐ *gumāṣā* pit
ܓܘܡܪ̈ܐ *gumrē* pl of *gmurtā*
ܓܘܪ *gār/ngur* to commit adultery
ܓܘܫܡܐ *gušmā* (abs *gšum)* body
ܓܙܐ *gazzā* treasure
ܓܙܝܪܝܐ *gzirāyā* policeman
ܓܙܪ Ethpe *etgzar* to be circumcised
ܓܝܕܐ *gyādā* nerve
ܓܝܣܐ *gayyāsā* robber
ܓܝܪ *gēr* (postpositive) but, however, for, indeed
ܓܠܐ *glā/neglē* to reveal; Pa *galli* to reveal; Ethpe *etgli* to be revealed; *glē/galyā* open, revealed; *galyā'it* openly, in public
ܓܠܕ Aph *agled* to freeze
ܓܠܝܐ *gelyā, b-* openly, publicly
ܓܠܝܠܐ *glilā* Galilee
ܓܠܝܠܝܐ *glilāyā* Galilean
ܓܠܝܢܐ *gelyānā* revelation
ܓܠܝܦܐ *glipā* carving
ܓܠܦ *glap/neglop* to carve
ܓܠܦܐ *glāpā* engraving, carving
ܓܡܘܪܬܐ *gmurtā* pl *gumrē* burning coal
ܓܡܝܪ *gmir* perfected, made ready
ܓܡܠܐ *gamlā* camel
ܓܡܠܐܝܠ *gamaliel* Gamaliel (pr n)
ܓܡܪ *gmār, la-* entirely, utterly
ܓܢܐ *gennā* protection
ܓܢܒ *gnab/negnob* to steal
ܓܢܒܪ *gabbār* mighty
ܓܢܣܐ *gensā* species
ܓܣܣ Aph *agges* to recline at table
ܓܥܠ Ethpe *etg^{c}el* to be committed, entrusted *(l-* to)
ܓܦܐ *geppā* wing
ܓܪܒ *greb/garbā* leprous
ܓܪܒܝܐ *garbyā* the north; *(gabbā) garbyāyā* north side
ܓܪܝܨܬܐ *griṣtā* loaf (of bread)
ܓܪܢܛܘܣ *geranṭos* Gerontius
ܓܪܪ *gar/neggor* to scrape off, erase, wipe out; to drag

ܕ *d(a)-* of (prep); that (conj); who, which, that (rel conj)
ܕܒܚ Pa *dabbaḥ* to sacrifice
ܕܒܚܐ *debḥā* sacrifice, victim
ܕܒܪ *dbar/nedbar* to lead; Pa *dabbar* to rule, manage
ܕܒܪܐ *dabrā* wilderness
ܕܓܠ *daggāl* false, deceitful
ܕܗܒܐ *dahb̲ā* gold
ܕܘܐ *dwā/nedwē* to be wretched
ܕܘܝܕ *dāwid* David

ܕܘܝܬܕܐܪ *dāwitdār* Dawitdar (pr n)

ܕܘܟܪܢܐ *dukrānā* remembrance, memorial

ܕܘܟܬܐ *dukktā* place

ܕܘܨ *dāṣ/nduṣ* to exult

ܕܘܢ *dān/ndun* to judge

ܕܘܩ Aph *adiq* to look out (of a window, e.g.)

ܕܘܪܫܐ *durāšā* exercise

ܕܘܫ *dāš/nduš* to tread; Pa *dayyeš* to trample

ܕܚܝܚܐ *daḥḥiḥā* dust, dirt

ܕܚܝܠ *daḥḥil* afraid, fearful

ܕܚܠ *dḥel/nedḥal* to be afraid; Aph *adḥel* to make afraid

ܕܚܠܬܐ *deḥltā* fear

ܕܝܘܐ *daywā* evil spirit, devil

ܕܝܘܣܩܘܪܘܣ *diosquros* Dioscurus

ܕܝܠ *dil* (+ pron encl I) belonging to, property of

ܕܝܠܢܝ *dilānāy l-* belonging to, appropriate to

ܕܝܢ *dēn* (postpositive) for, then, however

ܕܝܢܪܐ *dênārā* dinar

ܕܝܨܢ *dayṣān* Daissan (river)

ܕܝܬܩܐ *diatêqê* *διαθήκη*, testament

ܕܟܐ *dkā/nedkē* to be pure; Pa *dakki* to heal; Ethpa *etdakki* to be healed

ܕܟܪ *dkar/nedkar* to remember (pass part *dkir* has act & pass senses); Ethpe *etdkar* to remember; Ethpa *etdakkar* to be mindful of

ܕܠܝܠ *dlil* easy; *dallil* few

ܕܠܣܘܢ *dālāson* Dalason (pr n)

ܕܠܩ *dleq/nedlaq* to be lit; Aph *adleq* to light

ܕܠܩܐ *dalqā* (abs *dleq/dlaq)* torch

ܕܡ *dam (en)* whether

ܕܡܐ *dmā/nedmē l-* to seem, be like; Ethpa *etdammi l-* to resemble

ܕܡܘܬܐ *dmutā* pl *demwātā* form, shape, image

ܕܡܟ *dmek/nedmak* to sleep

ܕܡܥܐ *dem^{c}ā* (f) tear

ܕܡܪ Ethpa *etdammar* to be astonished

ܕܢܐ Ethpe *etdni* to agree, assent

ܕܢܚ *dnaḥ/nednaḥ* to rise (sun); Aph *adnaḥ* to make (the sun) rise

ܕܥܟ *d^{c}ek/ned^{c}ak* to go out (light, lamp)

ܕܩܕܩ *daqdaq* small; *daqdqē* the common people

ܕܩܠܬ *deqlat* Tigris

ܕܪ *dār: l-dār-dārin* for ever and ever, for all generations

ܕܪܝܘܫ *daryuš* Darius

ܕܪܟ Aph *adrek* to overtake

ܕܪܢܘܣ *darnus* Darnus (pr n)

ܕܪܥܐ *drā^{c}ā* (f) arm

ܕܪܫ *draš/nedroš ^{c}am* to dispute with; Pa *darreš* to instruct; Ethpa *etdarraš* to exercise

ܕܪܬܐ *dārtā* courtyard

ܕܫܢܐ *dāšnā* gift

ܗܐ *hā* lo, behold

ܗܓܐ Ethpa *ethaggi* to meditate

ܗܓܓ Ethpa *ethaggag* to imagine

ܗܓܡܘܢܐ *hegmōna* governor

ܗܓܡܘܢܘܬܐ *hegmōnutā* governorship
ܗܓܪ Aph *ahgar* to become Muslim
ܗܕܐ *hādē* (f sing) this
ܗܕܝܪ *hdir* comely; *hdirutā* comeliness
ܗܕܡܐ *haddāmā* member, limb
ܗܘ *hu* he; *haw* (m sing) that
ܗܘܐ *hwā/nehwē* to be
ܗܘܝܘ *huyu* he is (for *hu-hu)*
ܗܘܠܟܘ *hulāku* Hülägü, Ilkhan, r. 1256–65
ܗܘܦܟܐ *hupākā* way of life
ܗܝܕܝܢ *haydēn* then, at that time
ܗܝܟܠܐ *hayklā* temple
ܗܝ *hi* she; *hay* (f sing) that
ܗܝܡܢ *haymen/nhaymen b-* to believe in
ܗܝܡܢܘܬܐ *haymānutā* faith
ܗܟܘܬ *hākwāt* likewise
ܗܟܝܠ *hākêl* thus, therefore
ܗܟܢ *hākan* thus
ܗܟܢܐ *hākannā* thus
ܗܠܝܢ *hālēn* these (pl)
ܗܠܟ Pa *hallek* to walk; to make (someone) walk
ܗܠܠ Pa *hallel* to praise; Aph *ahhel b-* to mock
ܗܡܐ Aph *ahmi men* to neglect, disregard
ܗܢܐ *hānā* (m sing) this
ܗܢܘܢ *hānon* (m pl) those
ܗܢܘܢ *hennon* (m pl) they
ܗܦܟ *hpak/nehpok* to return (int); ~ *b-* to go back on; Pa *happek* to return (trs), convert; Ethpa *ethappak* to be turned around, converted

ܗܪܘܕܣ *hêrōdes* Herod
ܗܪܘܡܐ *hêrōmā* aromatic spice
ܗܪܟܐ *hārkā* here
ܗܪܪ Aph *ahhar* to bother
ܗܫܐ *hāšā* now

ܘ For roots see initial *ālap* or *yod.*
ܘ *w(a)-* and
ܘܙܝܪܐ *wazirā* vizier
ܘܝ *wāy* woe
ܘܠܐ *wālē l-* it is necessary for
ܘܥܕܐ *wa^{c}dā* appointed place, tryst, pledge

ܙܒܢ *zban/nezben* to buy; Pa *zabben* to sell
ܙܒܢܐ *zabnā* (abs *zban)* time; *zban-zban* from time to time; *ba-zban* once upon a time
ܙܓܘܓܝܬܐ *zgōgitā* pl *-gyātā* glass
ܙܕܝܩ *zaddiq* righteous
ܙܕܩ *zādeq* meet, fit, right
ܙܗܝܪ *zhir* wary; *zhirā'it* securely
ܙܗܪ Pa *zahhar ^{c}al* to warn against; Ethpa *ezdahhar b-* to beware of, watch over
ܙܗܪܐ *zahrā* brightness (of fire, e.g.)
ܙܘܚ Pa *zayyaḥ* to solemnize, accompany in procession
ܙܘܥ *zā^c/nzu^c* to tremble; Ettaph *ettziḥ* to be terrified
ܙܟܐ *zkā/nezkē* to conquer, overthrow, overcome
ܙܟܘܬܐ *zākutā* victory
ܙܟܪܝܐ *zkaryā* Zacharias
ܙܠܝܩܐ *zalliqā* ray

ܙܡܘܪܐ *zāmōrā* psalm
ܙܡܝܪܬܐ *zmirtā* psalm
ܙܡܢ Pa *zammen* to invite
ܙܡܪ Pa *zammar* to sing psalms
ܙܡܪܓܕܐ *zmargdā* emerald
ܙܢܐ *znā* pl *znayyā* (abs *zan* pl *znin)* kind, sort; manner; *ba-znā* in a (like) manner
ܙܢܐ *znā/neznē b-* to commit adultery with
ܙܢܝܘܬܐ *zānyutā* adultery
ܙܥܘܪ *z^{c}ōr* small, little, insignificant
ܙܥܙܥ Ethpal *ezda^{c}za^c* to totter
ܙܥܝܦ *z^{c}ip* angry
ܙܥܝܦܘܬܐ *z^{c}iputā* anger
ܙܩܘܦܐ *zāqōpā* crucifier
ܙܩܝܦܐ *zqipā* cross; crucified
ܙܩܦ *zqap/nezqop* to raise up, crucify; Ethpe *ezdqep* to be crucified
ܙܩܪ *zqar/nezqor* to compose, form
ܙܪܥ *zra^c/nezro^c* to sow
ܙܪܬܐ *zartā* pl *-ē* span

ܚܐܪܐ *ḥêrā* nobleman
ܚܒ *ḥab/neḥḥob* to burn, be set on fire; Aph *aḥḥeb* to love
ܚܒܘܫܝܐ *ḥbušyā* imprisonment; *bēt-ḥbušyā* prison, jail
ܚܒܛ *ḥbaṭ/neḥboṭ* to beat; Pa *ḥabbeṭ* to keep on beating
ܚܒܝܒ *ḥabbib* beloved
ܚܒܨ *ḥbaṣ/neḥboṣ* to crowd, throng together
ܚܒܪܐ *ḥabrā* friend, companion
ܚܒܫ *ḥbaš/neḥboš* to imprison
ܚܒܫܘܫܐ *ḥabšušā* pl *-šyātā* beetle
ܚܓܝܣ *ḥgis* lame
ܚܓܝܪ *ḥgir* lame, crippled
ܚܓܪ *ḥgar/neḥgar* to be lame; Aph *aḥgar* to stumble, waiver, ~ *^{c}al qupsā* to stumble on a pebble
ܚܕ *ḥad/ḥdā* one; *ḥad ^{c}am ḥad* with one another
ܚܕܐ *ḥdi/neḥdē* to rejoice, be glad
ܚܕܒܫܒܐ *ḥadbšabbā* Sunday
ܚܕܕܐ *ḥdādā* one another
ܚܕܘܬܐ *ḥadutā* (abs *ḥadwā)* gladness
ܚܕܝܐ *ḥadyā* breast, chest
ܚܕܪ *ḥdar/neḥdor* and *neḥdar* to surround *(b-, l-); ḥdār* around (+ pron encl II)
ܚܕܬ *ḥdat/ḥadtā* (emph *ḥadtā -ē/ḥdattā ḥadtātā)* new
ܚܘܐ Pa *ḥawwi* to show
ܚܘܐ *ḥawwā* Eve
ܚܘܒ *ḥāb/nḥub* to succomb, be conquered; Pa *ḥayyeb* to find guilty, condemn
ܚܘܒܐ *ḥawbā* trespass, guilt, ill
ܚܘܒܬܐ *ḥawbtā* debt
ܚܘܕܐ *ḥawdā* tiara
ܚܘܕܪܐ *l-ḥudrā* round about, all around
ܚܘܛ *ḥāṭ/nḥuṭ* to sew, stitch
ܚܘܝܠܐ *ḥuyālā* strength
ܚܘܠܡܢܐ *ḥulmānā* health, recovery
ܚܘܠܢܐ *ḥulānā* hole in the ground
ܚܘܡܐ *ḥummā* heat
ܚܘܢܝܐ *ḥunyā* Huniah (pr n)
ܚܘܣ *ḥās/nḥus* to have pity

ܚܘܣܢܐ *ḥawsānā* pity; *dlā-ḥawsān* pitiless

ܚܘܣܪܢܐ *ḥusrānā* damage, loss

ܚܘܪ *ḥār/nḥur l-* to look, gaze at, *b-* pay heed to

ܚܘܪ *ḥewwār* white; Pa *ḥawwar* to whiten

ܚܘܫܒܢܐ *ḥušbānā* reckoning; *dlāḥušbān* without limit

ܚܙܐ *ḥzā/neḥzē* to see; Ethpe *ethzi* to be seen, appear

ܚܙܘܐ *ḥezwā* vision

ܚܙܩ *ḥzaq/neḥzoq* to travel, journey

ܚܙܬܐ *ḥzātā* sight

ܚܛܝܐ *ḥaṭṭāyā* sinner

ܚܛܦ *ḥṭap/neḥṭop* to snatch, take away

ܚܝ *ḥayy* living, alive

ܚܝܐ *ḥyā/neḥḥē* and *nêḥē* to live; Aph *aḥḥi* to give life

ܚܝ̈ܐ *ḥayyē* (pl) life

ܚܝܒܐ *ḥayyābā* evildoer, trespasser

ܚܝܘܬܐ *ḥayyutā* pl *-ywātā* animal; living things, life (collective)

ܚܝܠ Pa *ḥayyel* to confirm, strengthen, comfort; Ethpa *etḥayyal* to be strong

ܚܝܠܐ *ḥaylā* might, power

ܚܝܠܘܬܐ *ḥaylutā* pl *-lawwātā* host, company

ܚܝܠܬܢ *ḥayltān* strong, mighty; *māryā ḥayltānā* the Lord God Sabaoth

ܚܟܝܡ *ḥakkim* wise

ܚܟܡܬܐ *ḥekmtā* wisdom

ܚܠܐ *ḥālā* sand

ܚܠܘܠܐ *ḥlōlā* marriage

ܚܠܝܡ *ḥlim* sound, correct

ܚܠܡ Aph *aḥlem* to cure, make whole

ܚܠܦ *ḥlāp* (+ pron encl II) on account of, for the sake of, instead of

ܚܡܝܪܐ *ḥmirā* leaven

ܚܡܪܐ *ḥamrā* wine; *ḥmārā* donkey, ass

ܚܡܫ *ḥammeš* (f), *ḥammšā* (m) five; *ḥammšābšabbā* Thursday

ܚܡܬܐ *ḥemmtā* rage

ܚܢܐ Ethpa *etḥanni* to lean, rely

ܚܢܐ *ḥannā* lap

ܚܢܘܬܐ *ḥānutā* pl *-nwātā* shop, stall

ܚܢܝܓ *ḥnig* doleful

ܚܢܢ *ḥnan* we; *ḥannān* Hannan (pr n)

ܚܢܦܐ *ḥanpā* pagan

ܚܢܦܘܬܐ *ḥanputā* paganism

ܚܢܩ *ḥnaq/neḥnoq* to choke, smother, drown (trs); Ethpe *etḥneq* to be drowned, choked

ܚܣܕܐ *ḥesdā* shame, reproach

ܚܣܝܪ *ḥassir* lacking, missing

ܚܦܐ Ethpa *etḥappi* ^{c}*al* to be hidden from

ܚܦܝܛ *ḥpiṭ* earnest, assiduous; *ḥpiṭā'it* earnestly

ܚܨܐ *ḥaṣṣā* rear; *nāṭar-ḥaṣṣā* bodyguard

ܚܪܒ *ḥrab/neḥrob* to lay waste; *ḥreb/ḥarbā* desolate, uninhabited

ܚܪܘܪܐ *ḥrōrā* eye (of a needle)

ܚܪܛ *ḥraṭ/neḥroṭ* to scratch

ܚܪܝܦ *ḥarrip* severe, sharp
ܚܪܟ *ḥrak/neḥrok* to burn; Ethpe *ethrek* to be burned, singed
ܚܪܫ *ḥreš/neḥraš* to be silent; *ḥreš/ḥaršā* dumb, deaf mute
ܚܪܬܐ *ḥartā, b-* in the end, finally
ܚܫܐ *ḥaššā* disease, sickness; sorrow, passion
ܚܫܒ *ḥšab/neḥšob* to count, reckon; Ethpa *etḥaššab* to plan, plot, think, meditate
ܚܫܘܟܐ *heššōkā* darkness
ܚܫܟ *ḥšek/neḥšak* to grow dark (used impersonally in the 3rd fem sing)
ܚܫܟܐ *ḥeškā* darkness
ܚܫܫ *ḥaš/neḥḥaš* to be sad, sorrow, suffer
ܚܬܐ *ḥātā* pl *aḥwātā* sister
ܚܬܝܬ *ḥattit* accurate
ܚܬܡ *ḥtam/neḥtom* to seal
ܚܬܡܐ *ḥātmā* seal
ܚܬܢܐ *ḥatnā* bridegroom

ܛܒ *ṭāb* good; very
ܛܒܐ *ṭebbā* fame, report
ܛܒܘܠܪܐ *ṭabbulārā* tabularius, registrar of tribute
ܛܒܥ *ṭba*^{c}*/neṭba*^{c} to seal; to sink (int); Pa *ṭabba*^{c} to sink (trs); Ethpe *eṭṭba*^{c} to be imprinted
ܛܒܥܐ *ṭab*^{c}*ā* seal
ܛܒܬܐ *ṭābtā* good (thing, deed)
ܛܘܒ Pa *ṭayyeb* to prepare; Ethpa *eṭṭayyab* to be ready, present, at hand
ܛܘܒܢ *ṭubān/-āni* blessed, beatified
ܛܘܠܥܐ *ṭulā*^{c}*ā* heavy sleep, stupor
ܛܘܦ Aph *aṭip* to overwhelm, deluge
ܛܘܦܣܐ *ṭupsā* type, symbol, likeness
ܛܘܪܐ *ṭurā* mountain; *ṭawrā (saggi'ā)* for a long time
ܛܝܒ *ṭayyeb* see ܛܘܒ
ܛܝܒܘܬܐ *ṭaybutā* kindness, favor
ܛܝܒܪܝܣ *ṭiberis* Tiberius
ܛܝܛܝܩܘܣ *ṭiṭikos/ṭayṭikos* parrot
ܛܝܝܐ *ṭayyāyā* Arab
ܛܝܡܐ *ṭimā* (usually pl) price, value
ܛܟ *ṭāk τάχα,* perhaps
ܛܟܣܐ *ṭaksā, ṭeksā* order, rank; rite, liturgy
ܛܠܝܐ *ṭalyā/ṭlitā* pl *ṭlāyē/ṭalyātā* (abs *ṭlē* pl *ṭleyn)* child
ܛܠܝܘܬܐ *ṭalyutā* childhood
ܛܠܩ Ethpa *eṭṭallaq* to be finished, vanish
ܛܥܐ *ṭ*^{c}*ā/neṭ*^{c}*ē* to wander, go astray; *ṭ*^{c}*ē/ṭa*^{c}*yā* astray; Ethpe *eṭṭ*^{c}*i* to be forgotten, be negligible
ܛܦܣ for ܐܬܛܦܝܣ, ܡܬܛܦܝܣ &c. see ܦܝܣ
ܛܪܐ Ethpa *eṭṭarri* to dash, beat against
ܛܪܘܢܐ *ṭrunā* tyrant
ܛܫܐ Pa *ṭašši* to hide, conceal; Aph *aṭši* to store in a secret place; Ethpa *eṭṭašši* to hide oneself

ܝܒܠ Aph *awbel* to carry, take

ܝܒܫ Pa *yabbeš* to dry (trs)

ܝܒܫܐ *yabšā* dry land

ܝܕ *yad, b-yad* through, by, by means of (see *idā)*

ܝܕܐ Aph *awdi* to confess, acknowledge

ܝܕܘܥܐ *yādo*^{c}*ā* expert

ܝܕܝܥ *idi*^{c} known, evident; *idi*^{c}*ā'it* clearly, evidently

ܝܕܥ *ida*^{c}*/nedda*^{c} to know; Aph *awda*^{c} to inform, make known; Ethpe *etida*^{c} to be known; Eshtaph *eštawda*^{c} to recognize, perceive, understand

ܝܕܥܐ *yād*^{c}*ā* acquaintance

ܝܕܥܬܐ *ida*^{c}*tā* knowledge

ܝܗܒ *yab* (perf only; impf *nettel)* to give

ܝܗܘܒܐ *yāhōbā* giver

ܝܗܘܕ *ihud (-yhud)* Judaea

ܝܗܘܕܐ *ihudā/yudā* Judah, Judas

ܝܗܘܕܝܐ *yudāyā (-yhudāyā)* Jew

ܝܘܚܢܢ *yōḥannān* John

ܝܘܠܦܢܐ *yulpānā* learning, teaching, doctrine

ܝܘܡܐ *yawmā* pl *-ē/-ātā* (abs/constr *yōm)* day

ܝܘܡܢܐ *yawmānā* today

ܝܘܢܝܐ *yawnāyā* Ionian, Greek

ܝܘܣܦ *yōsep* Joseph

ܝܘܩܪܐ *yuqrā* burden

ܝܘܪܕܢܢ *yordnān* Jordan

ܝܚܝܕܝ *iḥidāy* only, sole

ܝܚܠ Aph *awḥel* to become exhausted

ܝܠܕ *iled/nêlad* to give birth to, bear, beget

ܝܠܘܕܐ *yālōdā* parent

ܝܠܠ Aph *aylel* to cry out, howl

ܝܠܠܬܐ *illtā* pl *yallātā* shout, wail, cry

ܝܠܦ *ilep/nêlap* to learn (impt *ilap)*

ܝܡܐ *imā/nêmē* to swear; Aph *awmi* to make (someone) swear, bind with an oath

ܝܡܐ *yammā* pl ܝܡܡܐ *yammē* sea

ܝܡܝܢܐ *yamminā* right (hand, side)

ܝܣܦ Aph *awsep* to add, go on (to say, e.g.); Ettaph *ettawsap* to increase

ܝܥܝܬܐ *yā*^{c}*itā* pl *yā*^{c}*yātā* battlement

ܝܥܩܘܒ *ya*^{c}*qob* Jacob

ܝܩܕ *iqed/nêqad* to burn (int), catch fire; Aph *awqed* to burn (trs)

ܝܩܝܪ *yaqqir* heavy; noble, honored

ܝܩܪ Pa *yaqqar* to honor

ܝܩܪܐ *iqārā* honor

ܝܪܚܐ *yarḥā* (abs *iraḥ)* month

ܝܪܝܥܬܐ *yāri*^{c}*tā* tent

ܝܪܬ *iret/nêrat* to inherit; Aph *awret* to bequeathe to

ܝܪܬܘܬܐ *yārtutā* inheritance

ܝܫܘܥ *išō*^{c} Jesus

ܝܫܛ Aph *awšeṭ* to hold out, offer

ܝܬܒ *iteb/netteb* to sit, stay, dwell; *yāteb-wa*^{c}*dā* page

ܝܬܝܪ *yattir men* more than; *yattirā'it* more, all the more; especially

ܝܬܪ Pa *yattar* to increase

ܟܐܒܐ *kêbā* sickness, pain
ܟܐܡܬ *kemat* that is, that is to say, id est
ܟܐܢܐ *kênā* just; *kênā'it* justly
ܟܐܢܘܬܐ *kênutā* justice
ܟܐܦܐ *kêpā* (f) stone, rock; (m) Peter
ܟܒܪ *kbar* doubtless; perchance
ܟܕ *kad* when, as (conj)
ܟܗܢ Pa *kahhen* to serve as a priest, perform priestly functions
ܟܗܢܐ *kāhnā* priest
ܟܗܢܘܬܐ *kāhnutā* priesthood
ܟܗܢܝ *kāhnāy* priestly
ܟܘܟܒܐ *kawkbā* star, heavenly body
ܟܘܠ *koll* variant spelling of ܟܠ, q.v.
ܟܘܡܪܐ *kumrā* priest
ܟܘܣܪܘ *kosraw* Chosroës
ܟܘܪܕܝܐ *kurdāyā* Kurd
ܟܘܪܗܢܐ *kurhānā* disease
ܟܘܪܣܝܐ *kursyā* pl *-sawwātā* seat, throne
ܟܘܪܫ *kureš* Cyrus
ܟܘܬܐ *kawwtā* pl *kawwē* (abs *kawwā* pl *kawwin*) (f) opening, aperture
ܟܝ *kay* truly, now, then (particle of emphasis)
ܟܝܢܐ *kyānā* nature
ܟܝܢܝ *kyānāy* pertaining to nature
ܟܠ *koll* (+ abs) every, (+ emph or pron encl) all

ܟܠܐ *klā/neklē* to forbid, withhold; Ethpe *etkli* to be withheld; *etkalyat tba*^{c}*tā mennhon* they were exempted from taxes
ܟܠܝܘܬܐ *kollāyutā* totality
ܟܠܝܠܐ *klilā* crown
ܟܠܝܦܗ *k̲ālipāh* caliph
ܟܠܠ Pa *kallel* to crown; to surround (with a wall); Ethpa *etkallal b-* to be adorned with
ܟܠܡܐ ܕ *kollmā d-* whenever
ܟܠܡܕܡ *kollmeddem* everything
ܟܠܢܫ *kollnāš* everybody
ܟܠܥܕܢ *koll*^{c}*eddān* every moment
ܟܠܫ Pa *kalleš* to plaster, whitewash
ܟܠܫܥ *kollšā*^{c} always, constantly
ܟܠܬܐ *kalltā* bride
ܟܡܐ *kmā* (+ abs pl) how, how much, how many; *kmā d-* inasmuch as, just as
ܟܡܝܘܬܐ *kmāyutā* quantity, amount
ܟܡܝܪ *kmir* sad, gloomy
ܟܡܪ Ethpe *etkmar* to be sad
ܟܢ *ken* and so, and then
ܟܢܐ Ethpa *etkanni* to be called
ܟܢܘܫܬܐ *knuštā* assembly, synagogue
ܟܢܝܫܘܬܐ *knišutā* sum, total
ܟܢܫ *knaš/neknoš* to gather; Pa *kanneš* to take in, bring together; Ethpa *etkannaš* to be gathered together
ܟܢܫܐ *kenšā* crowd, multitude
ܟܣܐ *ksā/neksē* to clothe, cover; Pa *kassi* to clothe, cover over, hide
ܟܣܝܐ *kesyā, b-* secretly

ܟܣܦܐ *kespā* money, silver

ܟܦܢ *kpen/nekpan* to hunger; *kpen/kapnā* hungry

ܟܦܪ *kpar/nekpor b-* to deny, renounce

ܟܪܐ *kri/nekrē l-* to be sad (impers 3rd fem sing, *keryat lhon* 'they grew sad'); *karyā l-* it is sad

ܟܪܗ Ethpe *etkrah* to get sick, fall ill

ܟܪܙ Aph *akrez* to proclaim, announce, preach; Ethpe *etkrez* to be broadcast

ܟܪܘܙܐ *kārōzā* announcer, proclaimer

ܟܪܘܙܘܬܐ *kārōzutā* preaching, gospel

ܟܪܝܗ *krih* sick, ill

ܟܪܝܘܬܐ *karyutā* distress

ܟܪܟ *krak/nekrok* to wrap, roll; Pa *karrek* to twist; Ethpa *etkarrak* to be turned, twisted, wander about

ܟܪܟܐ *karkā* walled city

ܟܪܡܐ *karmā* vineyard

ܟܪܣܐ *karsā* (abs/const *kres)* belly, womb

ܟܪܣܛܝܢܐ *kresṭyānā* Christian

ܟܫܐ Ethpe *etkši* to be piled up, to be burdensome

ܟܫܠ Aph *akšel* to offend

ܟܬܒ *ktab/nektob* to write; Ethpe *etkteb* to be written, inscribed, enrolled

ܟܬܒܐ *ktābā* book, scripture

ܟܬܦܐ *katpā* pl *-ē/-ātā* (f) shoulder

ܟܬܪ Pa *kattar* to tarry

ܠ *l(a)-* to, for (prep); non-obligatory direct-object marker

ܠܐܐ *lā/nêlē* to toil; *lē* pl *leyn* (emph ܠܐܝܐ *layā* pl ܠܐܝܐ *layyā)* weary, fatigued

ܠܐܘܬܐ *leutā* labor, trouble

ܠܒܐ *lebbā* heart

ܠܒܒ Ethpa *etlabbab* to take heart

ܠܒܘܫܐ *lbušā* clothing, garment

ܠܒܝܒ *lbib* audacious, bold

ܠܒܝܫ *lbiš* wearing, clothed

ܠܒܟ *lbak/nelbok* to grasp, hold

ܠܒܫ *lbeš/nelbaš* to wear, put on; Aph *albeš* to clothe

ܠܘ *law* = *lā-(h)u* is not; also as negative prefix as in *law saggi* not much, not very

ܠܘܐ *lwā/nelwē* to accompany, follow

ܠܘܒܒܐ *lubābā* encouragement

ܠܘܚܡܐ *luḥāmā* threat

ܠܘܛ *lāṭ/nluṭ* to curse

ܠܘܩܕܡ *luqdam* first of all, before, previously

ܠܘܬ *lwāt* with, in the presence of (+ pron encl I)

ܠܚܘܕ *lḥod* alone

ܠܚܡܐ *laḥmā* bread, food

ܠܚܫ Pa *laḥḥeš* to whisper

ܠܝܬ *layt* there is/are not

ܠܠܝܐ *lêlyā* pl *laylē/laylawwātā* night

ܠܡ *lam* indicates that the phrase in which it occurs is a quotation

ܠܡܐ *l-mā* lest

ܠܡܢܐ *l-mānā* why?, what for?
ܠܡܦܐܕܐ *lampêdā* lamp
ܠܡܦܝܕܐ *lampêdā* lamp
ܠܥܠ *l*^{c}*el* above; *l*^{c}*el men* over
ܠܥܣ *l*^{c}*es/nel*^{c}*as* to partake, eat
ܠܦܘܬ *lput* according to, in proportion to
ܠܫܢܐ *leššānā* tongue, language

ܡܐ *mā* what?; *l-mā* lest
ܡܐ ܕ *mā d-* when, at such time as; whatever
ܡܐܟܠܐ *meklā* food
ܡܐܡܪܐ *mêmrā* sermon, word
ܡܐܢܐ *mānā* vessel; garment
ܡܐܬܝܬܐ *metitā* coming, advent
ܡܒܘܥܐ *mabbu*^{c}*ā* spring, source
ܡܒܥܕ *mab*^{c}*ad* remote, far off
ܡܓܕܠܐ *magdlā* tower
ܡܓܕܠܝ *magdlāy* Magdalene
ܡܕܐܬܐ *madatā* tribute
ܡܕܒܚܐ *madbḥā* altar
ܡܕܒܪܐ *madbrā* wilderness
ܡܕܒܪܢܐ *mdabbrānā* leader, guardian
ܡܕܝܢܬܐ *mdittā* pl *mdinātā* city; *men mdinā la-mdinā* from city to city
ܡܕܢܚܐ *madnḥā* (abs/constr *madnaḥ)* orient, east
ܡܕܝܢ *mādēn* then, therefore
ܡܕܡ *meddem* thing, something, anything, whatever
ܡܗܝܪ *mhir* skilled, trained
ܡܗܪ Ethpa *etmahhar* to be skilled, be instructed
ܡܘܒܠܐ *mawblā* (abs/const *mawbal,* f) burden, load
ܡܘܓܠܝܐ *moglāyā* Mongol
ܡܘܗܒܬܐ *mawhabtā* gift
ܡܘܚܐ *muḥḥā* brain
ܡܘܟܠܐ *moklā* μοχλός, bar, bolt
ܡܘܠܕܐ *mawlādā* birth
ܡܘܡܐ *mumā* blemish, flaw; *mawmē* see ܡܐܐ
ܡܘܡܬܐ *mawmtā* oath
ܡܘܣܬܥܨܡ *musta*^{c}*ṣem* Musta'ṣim, last Abbasid caliph, r. 1242–58
ܡܘܫ *māš/nmuš* to touch, feel
ܡܘܫܐ *mušē* Moses
ܡܘܬ *mit/nmut* to die; Aph *amit* to put to death, cause to die
ܡܘܬܐ *mawtā* death
ܡܙܝܥܢܝ *mzi*^{c}*ānāy* pertaining to motion
ܡܚܐ *mḥā/nemḥē* ^{c}*al* to smite
ܡܚܕܐ *meḥdā* immediately
ܡܚܘܬܐ *mḥutā* pl *maḥwātā* wound
ܡܚܙܝܬܐ *meḥzitā* mirror
ܡܚܛܐ *mḥaṭṭā* needle
ܡܚܝܪ *mḥir* delaying (Aph act part, from confusion between ܚܘܪ and ܐܚܪ, q.v.)
ܡܚܠ Ethpa *etmaḥḥal* to grow feeble
ܡܚܪ *mḥār* tomorrow
ܡܚܫܒܬܐ *maḥšabtā* calculation
ܡܛܐ *mṭā/nemṭē* to arrive, befall; *mṭāy* it fell his lot (*d-* to do something); Pa *maṭṭi l-* to arrive at
ܡܛܘܠ variant spelling of *meṭṭul,* see next entry

ܡܛܠ *meṭṭul* according to, on account of, concerning, for; *meṭṭul d-* for, because

ܡܛܠܬ *meṭṭlāt-* form of *meṭṭul* when followed by enclitic pronouns I

ܡܛܪܐ *meṭrā* rain

ܡܛܪܦ *meṭrap temrā d-ᶜaynā, ak* in the twinkling of an eye

ܡܛܪܬܐ *maṭṭartā* guard, watch; *nṭar maṭṭartā* to keep watch

ܡܛܫܝ̈ܬܐ *maṭšyāta* hidden things

ܡܝ̈ܐ *mayyā* (pl) water

ܡܝܒܫ *myabbaš* dried out, desiccated

ܡܝܠܐ *milā* mile

ܡܝܩܪܐ *myaqqrā* noble, notable

ܡܝܬ *mit* dead

ܡܝܬܐ *maytē* act. part. of *ayti,* see ܐܬܐ

ܡܝܬܪ *myattar* excelling, excellent

ܡܝܬܪܐ *myattrā* honor

ܡܟܐ *mekkā* from here, hence

ܡܟܝܟ *makkik* humble

ܡܟܝܟܐ *makkikā* Makkika (pr n)

ܡܟܝܠ *mekkêl* henceforth

ܡܟܝܪ *mkir* betrothed, espoused

ܡܟܟ Pa *makkek* to humble, humiliate; Ethpa *etmakkak* to be humbled

ܡܟܣܡܝܢܘܣ *maksemyānos* Maximian

ܡܟܣܢܘܬܐ *maksānutā* reproach, admonition

ܡܟܫܘܠܐ *makšulā* offense

ܡܟܬܒܢܐ *maktbānā* author, writer

ܡܟܬܒܢܘܬܐ *maktbānutā* enrollment, census

ܡܠܐ *mlā/nemlē* to be full; *mlē/malyā* full; Pa *malli* to fill (trs); Ethpe *etmli* to be filled; Ethpa *etmalli* to be filled, fulfilled; Shaph *šamli* to do thoroughly, complete; Eshtaph *eštamli* to be finished, at an end

ܡܠܐܟܐ *malakā* angel

ܡܠܘܟܐ *mālokā* advisor

ܡܠܚܐ *melḥā* (f) salt

ܡܠܘܫܐ *malwāšā* horoscope, natal star

ܡܠܝܘܬܐ *malyutā* fullness, abundance

ܡܠܝܠ *mlil* mental

ܡܠܟ *mlak/nemlok* to advise, counsel; Aph *amlek* to make king, to rule, reign (*ᶜal* over); Ethpe *etmlek b-* to be advised by

ܡܠܟܐ *malkā* (abs *mlek)* king

ܡܠܟܘܬܐ *malkutā* pl *-kwātā* kingdom, rule

ܡܠܟܝ *malkāy* royal, regal

ܡܠܟܬܐ *malktā* queen

ܡܠܠ Pa *mallel* to speak; Ethpa *etmallal* to be spoken, told

ܡܠܦܢܐ *mallpānā* teacher

ܡܠܦܢܘܬܐ *mallpānutā* teaching, doctrine

ܡܠܬܐ *melltā* pl *mellē* (f) word; thing, event; (m) λόγος

ܡܡܟܟ *mmakkak* low-lying

ܡܡܫܚ *mmaššaḥ* moderate

ܡܢ *men* from; *mān* what?; *man* who?

ܡܢ̇ *man* μεν, introduces the topic of a sentence, usually followed by *dēn; man... dēn* μεν...δε, on the one hand...on the other hand

ܡܢܐ *mānā* what?, (for *l-mānā)* why?; *mennā* hair, strand of hair

ܡܢܕܪܫ *men d-rêš* again

ܡܢܝܚ *mnāḥ* pass part of *aniḥ,* see ܢܘܚ

ܡܢܝܐ *manyā* mina, pound, measure of weight

ܡܢܝܢܐ *menyānā* number

ܡܢܟܕܘ *menkadu* already

ܡܢܫܠ *menšel* see *šelyā*

ܡܣܚܘܬܐ *masḥutā* washing, bathing

ܡܣܟܢܐ *meskênā* poor, unfortunate

ܡܣܢܐ *msānā* sandal, shoe

ܡܣܩܬܐ *massaqtā* ascension

ܡܥܒܕܢܘܬܐ *ma*^{c}*bdānutā* function, exertion

ܡܥܒܪܬܐ *ma*^{c}*bartā* crossing, ford

ܡܥܕ *m*^{c}*ād* accustomed

ܡܥܝܢܐ *m*^{c}*inā* (f) spring, fount

ܡܥܠܢܐ *ma*^{c}*lānā* entrance

ܡܥܡܕܢܐ *m*^{c}*ammdānā* the Baptist

ܡܥܡܘܕܝܬܐ *ma*^{c}*mōditā* pool

ܡܥܡܪܐ *ma*^{c}*mrā* dwelling, abode

ܡܥܢܘ *ma*^{c}*nu* Ma'nu (pr n)

ܡܥܪܒܝ *ma*^{c}*rbāy* western

ܡܥܪܬܐ *m*^{c}*arrtā* cave

ܡܦܘܠܬܐ *mappultā* fall, collapse

ܡܨܐ *mṣā/nemṣē* to be able; pass part *mṣē/maṣyā* able; Ethpe *etmṣi* to be able

ܡܨܥܝܘܬܐ *meṣ*^{c}*āyutā* intermediary

ܡܨܥܬܐ *mṣa*^{c}*tā* (const *meṣ*^{c}*at)* middle, midst

ܡܩܕܘܢܝܐ *māqedōniyā* Macedonia; *māqedōnāyā* Macedonian

ܡܩܕܡܘܬ *mqaddmut-* pre-, fore-

ܡܪܐ *mārā* (const *mārē)* pl *mārayyā/mārawwātā* master, lord

ܡܪܓܢܝܬܐ *margānitā* pl *-nyātā* pearl

ܡܪܓܫܢ *margšān* sensory

ܡܪܕ *mrad/nemrad* to rebel

ܡܪܕܝܬܐ *marditā* journey, course

ܡܪܘܡܐ *mrawmā* height

ܡܪܚ *marrāḥ* insolent, arrogant

ܡܪܚܡܢܘܬܐ *mraḥḥmānutā* mercy, compassion

ܡܪܝܐ *māryā* the Lord

ܡܪܝܒ *māryab* Maryab (pr n)

ܡܪܝܡ *maryam* Mary

ܡܪܝܪ *marrir* bitter

ܡܪܟܠ *mārē-kol* lord of all

ܡܪܡܙ *mermaz* with gesture, by signs

ܡܪܥܝܬܐ *mar*^{c}*itā* pl *-*^{c}*yātā* flock

ܡܪܩܘܣ *marqos* Mark

ܡܪܩܝܢܘܣ *marqiānos* Marcianus

ܡܪܪܐ *mrārā* bitterness, gall, wormwood; *ekal* ~ to be galled

ܡܪܬܐ *mārtā* mistress

ܡܫܘܚܐ *māšoḥā* surveyor

ܡܫܘܚܬܐ *mšuḥtā* pl *mušḥātā* measurement

ܡܫܚ *mšaḥ/nemšaḥ* to annoint; Pa *maššaḥ* to measure (pass part *mmaššaḥ* measured, moderate)

ܡܫܝܚ *mšiḥ* annointed, messiah; *mšiḥā* the Christ

ܡܫܟܚ *meškaḥ* able (*l-* + inf or *d-* + impf, to do)

ܡܫܠܛ *mšallaṭ* authoritative, in authority

ܡܫܠܡܢܐ *mašlmānā* Muslim

ܡܫܡܫܢܐ *mšammšānā* deacon

ܡܫܪܝ *mšarray* paralyzed

ܡܫܬܘܬܐ *meštutā* pl *-twātā* banquet, feast

ܡܫܬܝܐ *meštyā* draught, drink; *maštyā* banquet

ܡܬܒܥܐ *metb*^{c}*ē/metba*^{c}*yā* necessary

ܡܬܛܥܐ *mett*^{c}*ē* negligible

ܡܬܛܦܝܣ *mettpis* for *mettpis* obedient (see √ܦܝܣ)

ܡܬܝ *mattay* Matthew

ܡܬܠܐ *matlā* parable

ܡܬܢܫܝܢܘܬܐ *metnaššyānutā* forgetfulness, senselessness

ܡܬܪܣܝܢ *mtarsyān* nutritious, nourishing

ܢܒܘ *nebō* Nebo

ܢܒܝܐ *nbiyā* prophet

ܢܒܪܫ *nabreš/nnabreš* to kindle; Ethpal *etnabraš* to flame up

ܢܓܕ Pa *nagged* to beat, scourge

ܢܓܕܐ *negdā* scourge, beating

ܢܓܝܪ *naggir* long (time)

ܢܓ̰ܡ ܐܠܕܝܢ *najm aldin* Najm al-Din (pr n)

ܢܓܪ Aph *aggar* to be lengthy, go on for a long time

ܢܕܪ *ndar/neddor* to make a vow

ܢܕܪܐ *nedrā* vow

ܢܗܪ *nhar/nenhar* to be light, bright, shine; Aph *anhar* to shine, make light

ܢܗܪܐ *nahrā* pl *-rawwātā* river, stream

ܢܗܝܪ *nahhir* light, illuminated

ܢܘܓܪܐ *nugrā* a long time

ܢܘܗܪܐ *nuhrā* light

ܢܚ *nāḥ/nnuḥ* to be at rest; Aph *aniḥ* to give rest to; Ettaph *ettniḥ* to rest

ܢܘܝܢ *noyān* Noyan (Mongolian princely title)

ܢܘܟܪܝ *nukrāy* strange, unheard-of

ܢܡ *nām/nnum* to sleep, slumber

ܢܘܪܐ *nurā* (f) fire

ܢܚܬ *nḥet/neḥḥat* to go down, descend, dismount; (+ ^{c}*l*) to go against; Aph *aḥḥet* to send/bring down

ܢܛܘܪܐ *nāṭōrā* watchman, guard

ܢܛܘܪܬܐ *nṭurtā* guard, watch

ܢܛܪ *nṭar/neṭṭar* to keep, guard; Pa *naṭṭar* to keep under watch; Ethpe *etnṭar* to be kept

ܢܛܪܚܨܐ *nāṭar-ḥaṣṣā* bodyguard

ܢܝܚ *niḥ* calm, at rest; *niḥā'it* calmly

ܢܝܚܐ *nyāḥā* rest, calm

ܢܝܚܬܐ *nyāḥtā* rest, comfort

ܢܝܣܢ *nisān* April

ܢܝܪܐ *nirā* yoke

ܢܟܐ Aph *akki* to harm; Ettaph ܐܬܬܟܝ *ettakki* to be harmed

ܢܟܝܢܐ *nekyānā* pain, disease

ܢܟܣ *nkas/nekkos* to slaughter; Ethpe *etnkes* to be slaughtered

ܢܟܣܐ *neksā* wealth (usually pl)

ܢܟܦ Ethpa *etnakkap b-* to be shamed by

ܢܟܪ Pali *nakri* to disown; Ethpali *etnakri* to be estranged

ܢܡܘܣܐ *nāmōsā* law; *dlānāmōs* lawless

ܢܣܐ Pa *nassi* to try, test, prove

ܢܣܒ *nsab/nessab* to take, receive; *nsab b-appē* to be hypocritical

ܢܣܝܘܢܐ *nesyōnā* temptation, trial

ܢܦܠ *npal/neppel* to fall; Aph *appel* to make fall

ܢܦܩ *npaq/neppoq* to go forth; Aph *appeq* to cast out, cause to leave, take out; spend (money)

ܢܦܩܬܐ *nepqtā & npaqtā* expense

ܢܦܫܐ *napšā* (f, abs *npeš*) pl *-ātā* soul, life; -self (reflexive pron)

ܢܦܫܢܝ *napšānāy* psychological, pertaining to the soul

ܢܨܒ *nṣab/neṣṣob* to plant; Ethpe *etnṣeb* to be planted

ܢܨܚ *nṣaḥ/nenṣaḥ* to shine; Ethpa *etnaṣṣaḥ* to be victorious, triumphant

ܢܨܚܢܐ *neṣḥānā* victory, triumph, exploit, adventure

ܢܨܝܚ *naṣṣiḥ* shining, brilliant

ܢܨܠ Ethpe *etnṣel* to pour over oneself

ܢܨܪܝܐ *nāṣrāyā* Nazarene

ܢܨܪܬ *nāṣrat* Nazareth

ܢܩܥܐ *neq^{c}ā* hole

ܢܩܦ *nqep/neqqap* to follow, join

ܢܩܫ *nqaš/neqqoš* to knock

ܢܫܐ *nšā/neššē* to forget; Ethpa *etnašši* to forget

ܢܫ̈ܐ *neššē* (pl) women

ܢܫܒ *nšab/neššob* to blow

ܢܫܩ *nšaq/neššoq* to kiss

ܢܫܪܐ *nešrā* eagle

ܢܬܠ *nettel* (impf only) to give

ܣܐܒ *seb/nesab* to grow old

ܣܐܡܐ *sêmā* silver

ܣܒܐ *sābā* old man

ܣܒܗ Pa *sabbah* to make like

ܣܒܪ *sbar/nesbar* to think, imagine; Pa *sabbar* to broadcast, tell abroad, spread good news, evangelize

ܣܒܪܐ *sabrā* hope, trust, expectation

ܣܒܪܬܐ *sbartā* tidings

ܣܓܕ *sged/nesgod* to worship

ܣܓܘܕܐ *sāgōdā* worshipper

ܣܓܝ *saggi* much, many, very

ܣܗܕ *shed/neshad* to witness, testify *(b-, ^{c}al* to); Pa *sahhed* to call to witness, testify; Aph *ashed* to bear witness

ܣܗܕܐ *sāhdā* martyr

ܣܗܕܘܬܐ *sāhdutā* martyrdom

ܣܘܓܐܐ *sogā* large amount, many

ܣܘܟܠܐ *sukālā* intelligence, understanding

ܣܘܠܝܡܐܢ ܫܐܗ *sulaymān šāh* Sulayman Shah (pr n)
ܣܘܠܩܐ *sulāqā* ascension
ܣܐܡ *sām/nsim* to put, place; Ettaph *ettsim* to be put, be located
ܣܘܢܩܢܐ *sunqānā* necessity, need
ܣܘܣܝܐ *susāyā* horse
ܣܘܥܪܢܐ *su*ᶜ*rānā* errand, task; act, deed
ܣܘܦܐ *sawpā* (abs *sōp)* end
ܣܘܦܩܐ *supāqā* emptying, discharge
ܣܘܪܗܒܐ *surhābā* haste
ܣܘܝܪܘܣ *seweros* Severus
ܣܘܪܚܢܐ *surḥānā* injury, harm, damage
ܣܘܪܝܐ *suryā* Syria
ܣܘܪܝܝܐ *suryāyā* Syrian
ܣܚܐ *sḥā/nesḥē* to bathe, wash
ܣܛܢܐ *sāṭānā* Satan
ܣܛܪ *sṭar men* aside from, besides
ܣܝܒܪܬܐ *saybartā* nourishment
ܣܝܡܬܐ *simtā* treasure
ܣܝܦܐ *saypā* sword
ܣܟܐ Pa *sakki* to wait for, expect
ܣܟܠ Ethpa *estakkal* to perceive, understand
ܣܟܠ *skal* and *skel/saklā* foolish
ܣܠܩ *sleq/nessaq* to go up; Aph *asseq* to raise, lift up, have (someone) come/go up
ܣܡܐ *smē/samyā* blind; *sammā* pl *sammānē* drug, medicine; pigment
ܣܡܟ *smak/nesmok* to rest against; Ethpe *estmek* to recline

ܣܡܠܐ *semmālā* left (hand)
ܣܡܡܢܐ *sammānē* pl of *sammā*
ܣܢܐ *snā/nesnē* to hate; *snē/sanyā* hateful, odious
ܣܢܕܒܢ *sindbān* Sindban (pr n)
ܣܢܝܢ *snin* pure
ܣܢܝܩ *sniq* ᶜ*al* in need of
ܣܢܝܩܘܬܐ *sniqutā* need, necessity
ܣܢܩ Ethpe *estneq* ᶜ*al* to need, be in need of
ܣܥܪ *s*ᶜ*ar/nes*ᶜ*ar* to do; to visit; Ethpe *est*ᶜ*ar* to be done
ܣܥܪܐ *sa*ᶜ*rā* hair
ܣܦܝܢܬܐ *spittā* pl *-ē/spinātā* ship, boat
ܣܦܩ *spaq/nespaq* to suffice, be sufficient; Ethpa *estappaq* to be deprived
ܣܦܪܐ *sāprā* scribe, schoolmaster; *spārā* edge, bank
ܣܩܐ *saqqā* sack
ܣܪܕ Ethpa *estarrad* to be terrified
ܣܪܕܝܘܢ *sardyon* carnelian
ܣܪܝܩ *sriq* in vain, futile; *sriqā'it* in vain
ܣܪܗܒ *sarheb/nsarheb* to hasten; *msarhbā'it* hastily
ܣܪܚ *sraḥ/nesroḥ b-* to do harm to, hurt
ܣܬܘܐ *satwā* winter
ܣܬܬ Pa *sattet* to plant firmly

ܥܒܐܣܝܐ ᶜ*abbāsāyā* Abbasid
ܥܒܕ ᶜ*bad/ne*ᶜ*bed* to make, do; Aph *a*ᶜ*bed* make work; Ettaph *etta*ᶜ*bad* to be put to work; Shaph *ša*ᶜ*bed* to reduce to servitude

ܥܒܕܐ ^{c}*abdā* servant, slave; ^{c}*bādā* labor, work, job
ܥܒܕܐܠܓܢܝ ^{c}*abd algani* Abd al-Ghani (pr n)
ܥܒܕܢܒܘ ^{c}*abdnebō* Abdnebo
ܥܒܘܕܐ ^{c}*ābōdā* maker
ܥܒܪ ^{c}*bar/ne^{c}bar* to cross, transgress *(^{c}al);* to pass, come to pass, happen
ܥܒܫܠܡܐ ^{c}*abšlāmā* Abshlama
ܥܓܠ Pa ^{c}*aggel* to roll away
ܥܓܠ ^{c}*gal, ba-* quickly, immediately
ܥܓܠܐ ^{c}*eglā* lamb
ܥܓܡܝܐ ^{c}*ajāmāyā* Persian
ܥܕ ^{c}*ad* up to, while
ܥܕܠ ^{c}*dal/ne^{c}dol* to find fault with
ܥܕܠܝܐ ^{c}*edlāyā* blame, censure; *dlā^{c}edlāy* blameless
ܥܕܡܐ ^{c}*dammā d-* until (conj); ~ *l-* until (prep)
ܥܕܢ ^{c}*den* Eden
ܥܕܢܐ ^{c}*eddānā* moment, time, season
ܥܕܪ ^{c}*dar/ne^{c}dar* to help, be of assistance
ܥܕܬܐ ^{c}*êdtā* assembly, church
ܥܗܕ Ethpa *et^{c}ahhad* to remember
ܥܘܒܐ ^{c}*ubbā* bosom; cavity
ܥܘܕܪܢܐ ^{c}*udrānā* aid, help
ܥܘܗܕܢܐ ^{c}*uhdānā* memory; memorial, commemoration
ܥܘܠ Aph *a^{c}wel b-* to do ill to, treat ill
ܥܘܠܐ ^{c}*awwālā* unjust; ^{c}*wellā* baby
ܥܘܡܩܐ ^{c}*umqā* depth
ܥܘܩ Aph *a^{c}iq* to distress; Ettaph *ett^{c}iq* to be distressed
ܥܘܩܒܪܐ ^{c}*uqbrā* mouse
ܥܘܪ ^{c}*ār/n^{c}ur* to wake, watch; Pa ^{c}*awwar* to blind; Ettaph *ett^{c}ir* to wake up
ܥܘܫܢܐ ^{c}*ušnā* strength, might
ܥܘܬܪܐ ^{c}*utrā* wealth, riches
ܥܙܝܙ ^{c}*azziz* vehement, strong
ܥܙܩܬܐ ^{c}*ezqtā* signet
ܥܙܪ̈ܘܪܐ ^{c}*azrurē* (pl) swaddling clothes
ܥܛܝܦ ^{c}*ṭip* clothed, clad
ܥܛܠ ^{c}*ṭel/^{c}aṭlā* hard, difficult
ܥܛܦ ^{c}*ṭap/ne^{c}ṭop* to return; Pa ^{c}*aṭṭep* to clothe; to give back
ܥܝܕܐ ^{c}*yādā* custom, habit
ܥܝܢܐ ^{c}*aynā* (f) eye
ܥܝܪܘܬܐ ^{c}*irutā* wakefulness, vigilance, attention
ܥܟܪ Pa ^{c}*akkar* to detain, hinder
ܥܠ ^{c}*al* (with pron encl II, ^{c}*l-*) on, against, over; ^{c}*al d-* because, inasmuch as; ^{c}*al-yad* near, beside
ܥܠܐ Pa ^{c}*alli* to exalt, raise; Shaph *ša^{c}li* to exalt; Eshtaph *ešta^{c}li* to be arrogant
ܥܠܗܕܐ ^{c}*alhādē* orthographic convention for ^{c}*al hādē*
ܥܠ̈ܘܬܐ pl of ^{c}*lātā*
ܥܠܝ ^{c}*ellāy* exalted, supreme
ܥܠܝܕ ^{c}*alyad* near, beside
ܥܠܝܡܐ ^{c}*laymā* young man, lad
ܥܠܝܡܬܐ ^{c}*laymtā* young woman, maiden

ܥܠ *ʿal/neʿʿol* to go in, enter; Aph *aʿʿel* to have enter, allow in

ܥܠ̈ܠܬܐ *ʿellātā* pl of *ʿelltā*

ܥܠܡܐ *ʿālmā* (abs *ʿālam)* world; *dalʿālam* eternal; *l-ʿālam, l-ʿālam ʿālmin* forever

ܥܠܬܐ *ʿelltā* pl ܥܠ̈ܠܬܐ *ʿellātā* reason, cause; thing, article; *ʿlātā* pl *ʿlawwātā* altar

ܥܡ *ʿam* (+ pron encl I, *ʿamm-)* with

ܥܡܐ *ʿammā* pl ܥܡ̈ܡܐ *ʿammē* people

ܥܡܕ Aph *aʿmed* to baptize

ܥܡܕܐ *ʿmādā* baptism

ܥܡܘܛ *ʿammuṭ* dark, gloomy

ܥܡܝܠ *ʿmil* weary

ܥܡܝܩ *ʿammiq* deep

ܥܡܝܩܘܬܐ *ʿammiqutā* depth

ܥܡܠ *ʿmal/neʿmal* to labor, toil, work

ܥܡܠܐ *ʿamlā* labor, task

ܥܡܪ *ʿmar/neʿmar* to live, dwell

ܥܢܐ *ʿnā/neʿnē* to reply, answer

ܥ̈ܢܐ *ʿānā* (f coll) sheep, small cattle

ܥܢܝܢܐ *ʿenyānā* conversation, society

ܥܢܢܐ *ʿnānā* (f) cloud

ܥܢܬ *ʿannāt* wicked

ܥܣܩ Ethpa *etʿassaq* to be vexed

ܥܣܩ *ʿseq/ʿasqā* difficult, hard; *ʿasqā'it* with difficulty

ܥܣܩܘܬܐ *ʿasqutā* difficulty

ܥܣܪ *ʿsar* (f), *ʿesrā* (m) ten

ܥܨܐ *ʿṣā/neʿṣē* to compel, force

ܥܩܒܐ *ʿeqbā* (f) heel

ܥܩܒܬܐ *ʿeqbtā* footprint

ܥܩܪ *ʿqar/neʿqor* to rip up, rip out

ܥܩܪܐ *ʿeqqārā* root, medicinal herb; line

ܥܩܪܬܐ *ʿqartā* barren woman

ܥܩܬܐ *ʿāqtā* distress

ܥܪܒܐ *ʿerbā* sheep

ܥܪܘܒܬܐ *ʿrubtā* Friday

ܥܪܛܠ *ʿarṭel(lāy)* naked

ܥܪܣܐ *ʿarsā* bed, couch

ܥܪܩ *ʿraq/neʿroq* to flee

ܥܫܝܢ *ʿaššin* mighty, violent

ܥܫܢ *ʿšen/neʿšan* to gain strength; Aph *aʿšen* to make violent

ܥܬܝܕ *ʿtid* ready, prepared *(d-* + impf, to do something)

ܥܬܝܩ *ʿattiq* old

ܥܬܝܪ *ʿattir* rich, wealthy

ܥܬܪ *ʿtar/neʿtar* to grow rich

ܦܐܐ *pē*/ܦܝܐܐ *payā* comely, fair

ܦܐܪܐ *pêrā* fruit

ܦܓܥ *pgaʿ/nepgaʿ* to attack

ܦܓܪܐ *pagrā* body

ܦܘܠܛܐ *pulāṭā* escape

ܦܘܡܐ *pumā* mouth

ܦܘܢܝܐ *punāyā* return; *punāy-petgāmā* answer, reply

ܦܘܢܝܩܐ *puniqē* Phoenicia

ܦܘܣ see ܦܝܣ

ܦܘܣܩ *pusāq* Pusaq (pr n)

ܦܘܩܕܢܐ *puqdānā* commandment, order

ܦܘܪܟܣܐ *purkāsā* πύργος, tower

ܦܘܪܣܐ *pursā* plan, plot

ܦܘܪܣܢܐ *pursānā* affair, management

ܦܘܪܩܢܐ *purqānā* salvation
ܦܘܪܫܢܐ *puršānā* division
ܦܘܫ *pāš/npuš* to stay, remain
ܦܚܡ Pa *paḥḥem* to compare, collate
ܦܚܡܐ *peḥmā* copy, answer to a letter
ܦܛܓܪܐ *peṭgārā* gout
ܦܝܠܐ *pyālā* pl *pyālās* vial, phial; *pilā* elephant
ܦܝܠܘܣܘܦܐ *p̲ilosopā* philosopher
ܦܝܠܝܦܘܣ *p̲ilippaws* Philip (pr n)
ܦܝܣ Aph *apis* (with nonspirantized *p*, derives from *πεισαι*) to convince, persuade; *mpis leh* he was persuaded; Ettaph *ettpis*, usually *et̲pis* to be pursuaded, instructed
ܦܟܪ *pkar/nepkor* to bind
ܦܠܓ Pa *palleg* to divide; Ethpa *etpallag* to be divided
ܦܠܓܐ *pelgā* division, half, middle
ܦܠܓܘܬܐ *pelgutā* half, middle, division; *pelgut-lêlyā* midnight
ܦܠܘܛ *palluṭ* Pallut (pr n)
ܦܠܚ *plaḥ/neploḥ* to serve, worship; to till, plow
ܦܠܛ *plaṭ/neplaṭ* to escape
ܦܠܣܛܝܢܐ *palesṭinē* Palestine
ܦܠܦܠ Ethpal *etpalpal* to welter (in blood)
ܦܢܐ *pnā/nepnē* to return, come back; Pa *panni* to reply, answer; Aph *apni* to lead back, cause to return; Ethpe *etpni* to return, revert, turn
ܦܢܛܣܝܐ *p̲anṭāsiā* *φαντασία*, imagination
ܦܢܝܬܐ *pnitā* region, direction
ܦܣܝܩܬܐ *pāsiqātā, b-* in short, briefly
ܦܣܣ Aph *appes* to allow, permit
ܦܥܠܐ *pā^{c}lā* laborer
ܦܣܩ *psaq/nepsoq* to cut off
ܦܨܐ Pa *paṣṣi* to save, deliver, set free
ܦܨܚ Ethpe *etpṣaḥ* to be glad
ܦܨܝܚ *pṣiḥ* happy, cheerful
ܦܩܕ *pqad/nepqod* to command, order
ܦܩܘܕܐ *pāqodā* commander, leader
ܦܩܚ *paqqāḥ* expedient; *paqqāḥ-wā l-* it would be better for
ܦܪܓ Aph *apreg* to shine, be radiant, rejoice
ܦܪܕܝܣܐ *pardisā, pardaysā* paradise
ܦܪܘܓܐ *parrugā* chick
ܦܪܘܛܘܢܝܩܐ *proṭoniqê* Protonice (pr n)
ܦܪܘܩܐ *pārōqā* savior
ܦܪܘܬܣܡܝܐ *protesmiā* *προθεσμία*, term, time limit
ܦܪܙܠܐ *parzlā* iron
ܦܪܚ *praḥ/nepraḥ* to fly
ܦܪܚܬܐ *pāraḥtā* pl *pārḥātā* bird
ܦܪܝܩ *parriq* distant
ܦܪܝܫܐ *prišā* Pharisee
ܦܪܣ *pras/nepros* to spread (trs & int); Ethpa *etparras* to plot
ܦܪܣ *pāres* Persia
ܦܪܣܝܐ *pārsāyā* Persian
ܦܪܣܬܐ *parstā* foot, paw, hoof
ܦܪܥ *pra^c/nepro^c* to reward

ܦܪܨܘܦܐ *parṣōpā* face, persona
ܦܪܩ *praq/neproq* to depart, go away, withdraw
ܦܪܫ Pa *parreš* to divide
ܦܪܫܐ *parrāšā* mounted soldier
ܦܫܛ *pšaṭ/nepšoṭ* to spread, stretch out; *pšaṭ ṣebʿā* to point the finger
ܦܫܝܓ *pšig* maimed
ܦܫܝܩ *pšiq* easy; *pšiqā'it* easily
ܦܫܪ *pšar/nepšar* to melt
ܦܫܪܐ *pšārā* digestion
ܦܫܫ Ethpau *etpawšaš* to waste away
ܦܬܓܡܐ *petgāmā* word, thing
ܦܬܚ *ptaḥ/neptaḥ* to open; Pa *pattaḥ* to cause to be opened; Ethpe *etptaḥ* to be open, opened
ܦܬܝܐ *ptāyā* breadth
ܦܬܟܪܐ *ptakrā* idol

ܨܘܪ *ṣār/nṣur* to depict, represent (pass part ܨܝܪ *ṣir)*
ܨܘܪܐ *ṣawrā* neck
ܨܝܕ *ṣêd* beside, next to (with pron encl II usually spelled ܨܐܕ)
ܨܝܪ *ṣir* see ܨܘܪ
ܨܝܪܐ *ṣayyārā* painter
ܨܠܐ Pa *ṣalli* to pray (ʿ*al* for); Ethpe *eṣṭli* to incline
ܨܠܒ *ṣlab/neṣlob* to crucify; Ethpe *eṣṭleb* to be crucified
ܨܠܝܒܐ *ṣlibā* cross
ܨܠܝܒܘܬܐ *ṣlibutā* crucifixion
ܨܠܘܬܐ *ṣlōtā* pl *ṣlawwātā* prayer
ܨܠܡܐ *ṣalmā* (abs *ṣlem)* image, likeness
ܨܢܝܥܘܬܐ *ṣniʿutā* cunning
ܨܦܪܐ *ṣaprā* pl *ṣaprwātā* morning

ܨܐܕ *ṣêd* next to, beside (+ pron encl II; also spelled ܨܝܕ)
ܨܐܪ *ṣā'ar* representation (see ܨܘܪ) *mqaddam-ṣā'ar* prefiguration
ܨܒܐ *ṣbā/neṣbē* to want; Ethpe *eṣṭbi* to want
ܨܒܝܢܐ *ṣebyānā* will
ܨܒܥܐ *ṣebʿā* finger
ܨܒܬ Pa *ṣabbet* to set in order
ܨܒܬܐ *ṣebtā* pl *-tē* ornament, decoration
ܨܗܐ *ṣhā (ṣhi)/neṣhē* to thirst; pass part *(ṣhē/ṣahyā)* thirsty
ܨܘܒܐ *ṣawbā* meeting place
ܨܘܡܐ *ṣawmā* fast, fasting

ܩܒܠ Pa *qabbel* to receive, get; *qabbel baṭnā* to become pregnant
ܩܒܪ *qbar/neqbor* to bury
ܩܒܪܐ *qabrā* tomb, grave
ܩܒܥ *qbaʿ/neqboʿ* to fasten, fix, set up; Ethpe *etqbaʿ* to be set up (cross, e.g.)
ܩܕܐ Pa *qaddi* to retain, keep possession of
ܩܕܝܡ *qaddim* old, ancient; *men qdim* of old, long ago, from eternity
ܩܕܝܫ *qaddiš* holy, sacred, sainted
ܩܕܡ *qdām* before, in front of (+ pron encl II)

ܩܕܡ *qdam/neqdam* to go before, do first; Pa *qaddem* to precede, go before

ܩܕܡܝ *qadmāy* first, former, fore, of old, ancient

ܩܕܡܝܬ *qadmā'it* firstly

ܩܕܫ Pa *qaddeš* to make holy, sanctify; Ethpa *etqaddaš* to be made holy, sacred

ܩܘܐ Pa *qawwi* to remain, stay, wait

ܩܘܒܠ *qubal, l-qubal* before, in front of (+ pron encl I); *qubal-ṭaybutā* thanks, gratitude

ܩܘܕܫܐ *qudšā*, as in *ruḥā d-qudšā* the Holy Spirit

ܩܘܡ *qām/nqum* to rise up, arise; Aph *aqim* to put, place; ~ *qyāmā* to make a contract; Ethpa *etqayyam* to be established

ܩܘܦܣܐ *qupsā* cube, pebble, die

ܩܘܪܒܢܐ *qurbānā* oblation

ܩܘܪܝܐ *quryā* pl of *qritā*

ܩܘܪܝܢܘܣ *qewrinos* Cyrenius

ܩܛܘܠܐ *qāṭōlā* murderer

ܩܛܝܪܐ *qṭirā* compulsion, force; *qṭirā'it* by force

ܩܛܠ *qṭal/neqṭol* to kill; Pa *qaṭṭel* to slaughter; Ethpe *etqṭel* to be killed

ܩܛܠܐ *qeṭlā* slaughter, murder

ܩܛܪܩܛܐ *qaṭaraqṭā* cataract

ܩܝܛܐ *qayṭā* summer

ܩܝܡ *qayyām* remaining, existing, standing

ܩܝܡܐ *qyāmā* contract; ~ *d-šaynā* peace treaty; *aqim* ~ to make a contract

ܩܝܣܐ *qaysā* stick, piece of wood

ܩܝܦܐ *qaypā* Caiaphas

ܩܝܬܪܐ *qitārā* harp

ܩܠܐ *qālā* voice

ܩܠܘܕܝܘܣ *qlawdios* Claudius

ܩܠܝܠ *qallil* little, little bit, insignificant; swift; *qallilā'it* swiftly

ܩܡܪܐ *qamrā/qmārā* belt

ܩܢܐ *qnā/neqnē* to acquire, purchase, redeem

ܩܢܘܡܐ *qnomā* self, person; *qnomā'it* personally

ܩܢܛ Aph *aqneṭ* to make fear, make anxious

ܩܢܛܪܘܢܐ *qenṭrōnā* centurion

ܩܣܪ *qesar* Caesar

ܩܥܬܐ *q*^{c}*ātā* outcry

ܩܦܠ Ethpe *etqpel* to be rubbed off/out

ܩܦܠܐܘܢ *qepāle'on* pl ܩܦܠܐܐ *qepāle'ā* chapter

ܩܦܣ Ethpe *etqpes men* to withdraw from

ܩܦܣܐ *qapsā* cage

ܩܨܐ *qṣā/neqṣē* to break (bread); Ethpe *etqṣi* to be broken

ܩܨܨ *qaṣ/neqqoṣ* ^{c}*am* to come to an agreement with

ܩܪܐ *qrā/neqrē* to call, summon, invite, name, read; Ethpe *etqri* to be called, be read out

ܩܪܒ *qreb/neqrab l-* to approach, draw near to; Pa *qarreb* to put near, bring near; Aph *aqreb* ^{c}*am* to do battle with; Ethpa *etqarrab l-* to approach

ܩܪܒܐ *qrābā* battle

ܩܪܘܣܛܠܠܘܣ *qrosṭelos* crystal
ܩܪܝܒ *qarrib* close, near
ܩܪܝܒܘܬܐ *qarributā d-* nearly
ܩܪܝܘܢܐ *qeryōnā* candle, taper
ܩܪܝܡ *qrim* overlayed
ܩܪܝܪ *qarrir* cool, cold
ܩܪܝܪܘܬܐ *qarrirutā* coolness, cold
ܩܪܝܬܐ *qritā* pl *qeryātā/quryā* village
ܩܪܡ *qram/neqrom* to overlay, plate
ܩܪܢܐ *qarnā* pl *-ātā* horn
ܩܪܨܐ *qarṣā: ekal qarṣā* to backbite, slander, accuse
ܩܪ *qar/neqqar* to get cold
ܩܫܐ Ethpa *etqašši ʿal* to be grievous, difficult for
ܩܫܐ *qšē/qašyā* severe, fierce
ܩܫܝܫ *qaššiš* old, elder
ܩܫܬܐ *qeštā* pl *-ē/-ātā* bow, arc
ܩܬܘܠܝܩܐ *qātoliqā* catholicos

ܪܒ *rabb* pl *rawrbin* big, great; *rabb-kāhnē* chief priest
ܪܒܐ *rbā (rbi)/nerbē* to grow up
ܪܒܐ *rabbā* master
ܪܒܘ *rebbō* (abs) myriad; *rebbō-rebbwān* tens of thousands
ܪܒܝܥܝ *rbiʿāy* fourth
ܪܓܝܓ *rgig* delightful, pleasant
ܪܓܝܫ *rgiš* aware, perceptive
ܪܓܠܐ *reglā* (f) foot, leg
ܪܓܠܬܐ *rgeltā* flood
ܪܓܡ *rgam/nergom* to stone
ܪܓܫ Aph *argeš* to feel, perceive, become aware of
ܪܓܫܐ *regšā* sense
ܪܓܫܬܐ *rgeštā* feeling
ܪܕܐ *rdā/nerdē* to proceed, emanate
ܪܕܘܦܝܐ *rdupyā ʿal* persecution of
ܪܕܦ *rdap/nerdop* to follow, drive on/out, pursue; (+ *bātar)* persecute
ܪܗܒ Ethpa *etrahhab* to be terrified
ܪܗܘܡܐ *rōmê* Rome
ܪܗܘܡܝܐ *rōmāyā* Roman
ܪܗܛ *rheṭ/nerhaṭ* (impt *harṭ)* to run
ܪܗܝܒ *rhib* timorous; *rhibā'it* hastily, timorously
ܪܘܓܙܐ *rugzā* rage
ܪܘܙ *rwaz/nerwaz* to rejoice
ܪܘܙܐ *rwāzā* rejoicing, gladness
ܪܘܚ Pa *rayyaḥ* to soften, mollify
ܪܘܚܐ *ruḥā* pl *-ē/-ātā* (f) spirit; wind
ܪܘܚܩܐ *ruḥqā* distance; *men ruḥqā* from/at a distance
ܪܘܝܚ *rawwiḥ* spacious
ܪܘܡ Aph *arim* to raise up, lift up, take away; Ettaph *ettrim* to be lifted up, taken away
ܪܘܡܐ *rawmā* height
ܪܘܪܒܝܢ *rawrbin* abs masc pl of *rabb,* q.v.
ܪܘܪܒܢܐ *rawrbānā* grandee
ܪܘܫܡܐ *rušmā* drawing, design
ܪܚܝܐ *raḥyā* mill, handmill; *raḥyā da-ḥmārā* millstone (of a gristmill turned by a donkey)
ܪܚܡ *rḥem/nerḥam* to love; Pa *raḥḥem ʿal* to have mercy on

ܪܚܡܐ *raḥmā* mercy, favor; *rāḥmā* friend

ܪܚܡܬܐ *reḥmtā* love, passion

ܪܚܝܩ *raḥḥiq* far, distant

ܪܚܩ Aph *arḥeq* to remove, put away, to move far away (int & trs)

ܪܛܝܒ *raṭṭib* moist

ܪܛܝܒܘܬܐ *raṭṭibutā* moisture

ܪܛܢ *rṭan/nerṭan* to murmur, mutter

ܪܝܫܐ see ܪܫܐ

ܪܟܒ *rkab/nerkab* to mount, ride

ܪܟܝܟ *rakkik* mild, gentle; silk

ܪܟܢ Aph *arken* to lower, bow; Ethpe *etrken* to bow down

ܪܟܫܐ *rakšā* pl *rakšā* horse

ܪܡ *rām* high, loud (for verbs see ܪܘܡ

ܪܡܐ *rmē/ramyā* fallen, prostrate, cast down; Aph *armi* to cast, lay down, lay before, offer

ܪܡܙ *rmaz/nermoz* to make gestures

ܪܡܙܐ *remzā* sign, gesture

ܪܡܫܐ *ramšā* evening

ܪܢܐ *rnā/nernē* to reflect, meditate

ܪܣܣ *ras/nerros* to sprinkle

ܪܥܐ *r^{c}ā/ner^{c}ē* to tend, keep (flocks), to rule; Pa *ra^{cc}i* to appease, placate

ܪܥܝܐ *rā^{c}yā* pl *rā^{c}ayyā/ rā^{c}awwātā* shepherd

ܪܥܝܢܐ *re^{c}yānā* mind

ܪܥܠ Aph *ar^{c}el* to make tremble

ܪܥܡܐ *ra^{c}mā* thunder

ܪܦܐ Ethpa *etrappi* to become weak

ܪܦܣܐ *repsā* stamp, kick

ܪܩܩ *raq/nerroq* to spit

ܪܫܐ *rêšā* head, heading, chapter; *rêš-malakē* archangel; *rêš-kāhnē* high priest; *men d-rêš* again

ܪܫܝܥ *raššī^c* impious

ܪܫܡ *ršam/neršom* to draw

ܪܫܢܐ *rêšānā* noble, prince

ܪܬܝܬܐ *rtêtā* fear, trembling

ܪܬܡ Pa *rattem* to say gently

ܫܐܕܐ *šêdā* demon, devil

ܫܐܠ *šel/nešal* to ask, demand; Pa *ša''el l-* to ask questions of; Aph *ašel* to lend

ܫܐܪܐ *šērā* silk

ܫܐܪܝ *šērāy* silken

ܫܒܒܐ *šbābā* neighbor

ܫܒܒܘܬܐ *šbābutā* neighborhood

ܫܒܚ Pa *šabbaḥ* to praise; Ethpa *eštabbaḥ* to be praised

ܫܒܝܠܐ *šbilā* track, path, trace

ܫܒܥ *šba^c* (f), *šab^{c}ā* (m) seven

ܫܒܩ *šbaq/nešboq* to leave, abandon; forgive; Ethpe *eštbeq* to be abandoned, forsaken; to be forgiven

ܫܒܬܐ *šabbtā* sabbath, Saturday

ܫܓܫ Ethpe *eštgeš* to be troubled, disturbed

ܫܕܐ *šdā/nešdē* to throw, cast down

ܫܕܪ Pa *šaddar* to send; Ethpa *eštaddar* to be sent, dispatched

ܫܘܐ Aph *ašwi* to equate

ܫܘܐ *šāwē* (m), *šāwyā* (f) worthy
ܫܘܒܚܐ *šubḥā* (abs *šbuḥ)* glory
ܫܘܓ Aph *ašig* to wash, wash away, purify
ܫܘܟܢܐ *šukānā* grace
ܫܘܙܒ *šawzeb/nšawzeb* to save; Eshtaph *eštawzab* to be delivered
ܫܘܛ *šāṭ/nšuṭ* to treat with contempt
ܫܘܚ *šwaḥ/nešwaḥ* to spring up
ܫܘܝܕܐ *šwidā* Shwida (pr n)
ܫܘܠܡܐ *šulāmā* end; *nsab* ~ to come to an end
ܫܘܥܐ *šō^{c}ā* firm ground, rock
ܫܘܢ Pa *šayyen* to appease
ܫܘܦܪܐ *šuprā* beauty
ܫܘܩܐ *šuqā* market
ܫܘܩܪܐ *šuqrā* falsehood
ܫܘܪ *šwar/nešwar* to leap
ܫܘܪܐ *šurā* city wall
ܫܘܪܝܐ *šurāyā* beginning
ܫܘܬܦ Ethpau *eštawtap* to share
ܫܚܝܢ *šaḥḥin* hot
ܫܚܩ Ethpa *eštaḥḥaq* to be vexed, troubled
ܫܚܩܐ *šḥāqā* adversity
ܫܝܓܬܐ *šyāgtā* ablution
ܫܝܛ *šiṭ* mean, contemptible
ܫܝܠܘܚܐ *šilōḥā* Siloam
ܫܝܢ *šayyen* see ܫܘܢ
ܫܝܢܐ *šaynā* peace; cultivation, prosperity
ܫܝܦܘܪܐ *šipōrā* trumpet, clarion
ܫܝܫܐ *šišā* marble
ܫܟܚܬܐ *škāḥtā* discovery
ܫܟܪܐ *šakrā* strong drink, liquor
ܫܠܐ *šlā/nešlē* to draw out
ܫܠܕܐ *šladdā* corpse
ܫܠܘܡ *šālōm* Salome (pr n)
ܫܠܚ *šlaḥ/nešlaḥ* to send, dispatch; to strip bare, take off (clothes); Ethpe *eštlaḥ* to be sent
ܫܠܛ Pa *šalleṭ* to put in authority; Ethpa *eštallaṭ b-* to gain dominion over
ܫܠܝܐ *šelyā, men šelyā, menšel(y)* at once, unexpectedly; *šelyā* peace, tranquility
ܫܠܝܚܐ *šliḥā* messenger, apostle
ܫܠܝܚܘܬܐ *šliḥutā* message
ܫܠܝܛ *šliṭ* permitted
ܫܠܡ *šlem/nešlam* to be finished; to follow; Pa *šallem* to finish (trs), fulfill; Aph *ašlem* to turn over, hand over, betray; Ethpa *eštallam* to be finished, fulfilled
ܫܠܡܐ *šlāmā* greetings, peace; *šālmā* follower
ܫܡܐ *šmā* (abs *šem)* pl *šmāhē* name
ܫܡܗ Ethpa *eštammah* to be named
ܫܡܛ *šmaṭ/nešmoṭ* to draw, unsheathe
ܫܡܝܐ *šmayyā* (pl) heaven
ܫܡܥ *šma^c/nešma^c* to hear; Aph *ašma^c* to make hear; Ethpe *eštma^c* to be heard
ܫܡܥܘܢ *šem^{c}ōn* Simon, Simeon
ܫܡܪ Ethpa *eštammar* to be released
ܫܡܪܝܐ *šāmrāyā* Samaritan
ܫܡܫ Pa *šammeš* to serve

ܫܡܫܐ *šemšā* (m & f) sun

ܫܡܫܓܪܡ *šmešgram* Shmeshgram (pr n)

ܫܢܐ Pa *šanni* to depart

ܫܢܐ *šennā* (f) tooth; mountain peak

ܫܢܕܐ *šendā* torture

ܫܢܩ Pa *šanneq* to inflict pain

ܫܢܬܐ *šattā* pl *šnayyā* (abs *šnā* pl *šnin,* const *šnat-)* year; *šentā* sleep

ܫܥܐ Ethpa *eštaccі* to tell, relate

ܫܥܠ *šacli* see ܥܠܐ

ܫܥܬܐ *šāctā* pl *šācē* (abs *šācā* pl *šācin)* hour; *bāh b-šāctā, bar šācteh* immediately

ܫܦܝܥ *špic* abundant

ܫܦܝܪ *šappir* beautiful

ܫܦܠ *špal* and *špel/šaplā* coward(ly)

ܫܦܥ *špac/nešpac* to overflow

ܫܦܪ *špar/nešpar l-* to seem good to

ܫܦܪܐ *šaprā* pre-dawn, early morning

ܫܩܐ Aph *ašqi* to give to drink

ܫܩܝܠ *šqil* burdened, bearing

ܫܩܠ *šqal/nešqol* to remove, take away; Aph *ašqel* to set forth, proceed; Ethpe *eštqel* to be removed

ܫܪܐ *šrā/nešrē* to stop, camp (*cal* at, near); to loosen; pass part *(šrē/šaryā)* staying, sojourning; Pa *šarri* to begin (with *l-* + inf or with impf or part); Aph *ašri* to make dwell, settle (trs)

ܫܪܒܐ *šarbā* matter, story

ܫܪܒܬܐ *šarbtā* tribe; generation

ܫܪܘܬܐ *šārutā* feast, banquet

ܫܪܝܪ *šarrir* true, trusty, faithful; *šarrirā'it* truly, verily

ܫܪܟܐ *šarkā* the rest

ܫܪܪ Pa *šarrar* to fix firmly; Aph *aššar* to confirm, keep (a promise)

ܫܪܪܐ *šrārā* truth

ܫܬ *šet* (f), *(e)štā* (m) six

ܫܬܐ *ešti/neštē* to drink

ܫܬܐܣܬܐ *šatestā* pl *šatesē* (f) foundation

ܫܬܝܩ *šattiq* mute

ܫܬܩ *šteq/neštoq* to keep silence

ܫܬܩܐ *šetqā* silence

ܬܐܘܡܐ *tōmā* Thomas

ܬܒܥ *tbac/netbac* to seek, desire, require, exact

ܬܒܥܬܐ *tbactā* impost, tax

ܬܒܪ *tbar/netbar* to break; Ethpe *ettbar* to be broken

ܬܐܓܐ *tāgā* crown

ܬܐܓܘܪܬܐ *tgurtā* trade, commerce

ܬܐܓܪܐ *tāgrā* merchant

ܬܕܡܘܪܬܐ *tedmurtā* pl *tedmrātā* wonder, marvel

ܬܗܝܪ *thir* marvelous

ܬܗܪܐ *tahrā* and *tehrā* astonishment

ܬܘ *taw* m pl impt of ܐܬܐ

ܬܘܒ *tāb/ntub* to repent

ܬܘܒ *tub* again; introduces a new section or thought

ܬܘܕܝܬܐ *tawditā* profession, confession

ܬܘܚܪܬܐ *tawḥartā* delay

ܬܘܢܐ *tawwānā* inner room, closet

ܬܘܩܢܐ *tuqānā* cultivation, working (of the land, e.g.)

ܬܘܪܥܬܐ *tur^{c}tā* breach

ܬܚܘܡܐ *tḥumā* border

ܬܚܘܬ *tḥut* (+ pron encl II) under

ܬܚܝܬ *tḥēt* below, under

ܬܚܦܝܬܐ *taḥpitā* veil

ܬܚܬ *taḥt, l-taḥt men* under, below; Pali *taḥti* to bring down, bring low; Ethpali *ettaḥti* to be brought down, sent down, brought low

ܬܝܒܘܬܐ *tyābutā* repentance

ܬܝܡܢ *tayman* south; *taymnāy* southern; *(gabbā) taymnāyā* south side

ܬܝܩܐ *tiqā* scabbard

ܬܟܝܠ *tkil ^{c}al* faithful to, trusting in; *tkilā'it* faithfully

ܬܟܠ Ethpe *ettkel ^{c}al* to trust

ܬܟܬܘܫܐ *taktōšā* contest

ܬܠܐ *tlā/netlē* to lift up, hang up; Ethpe *ettli* to be hung

ܬܠܚ *tlaḥ/netloḥ* to rend

ܬܠܝܬܝ *tlitāy* third

ܬܠܡܕ *talmed* to make a disciple (trs); Ethpal *ettalmad* to become a disciple

ܬܠܡܝܕܐ *talmidā* disciple

ܬܠܬ *tlāt* (f)/*tlātā* (m) three

ܬܡܗ *tmah/netmah* to be astonished

ܬܡܗܐ *temhā* astonishment

ܬܡܝܗ *tammih* astonished

ܬܡܢ *tammān* there

ܬܡܢܐ *tmānē* (f)/*tmānyā* (m) eight

ܬܡܪܐ *temrā d-^{c}aynā, ak meṭrap* in the twinkling of an eye

ܬܢܐ *tnā/netnē* to repeat, narrate

ܬܢܢ *tnan* here

ܬܥܠܐ *ta^{c}lā* fox

ܬܩܝܦ *taqqip* violent, weighty, intense

ܬܩܢ Pa *taqqen* to make right, get ready, prepare; Aph *atqen* to set in order; Ethpa *ettaqqan* to be constituted

ܬܩܢܐ *taqnā d-ṭurā* table land

ܬܩܦ *tqep/netqap* to grow strong, prevail

ܬܪܐ *trā (tri)/netrē* to get soaked

ܬܪܘܢܘܣ *trōnos* throne, altar

ܬܪܝܢ *trēn/tartēn* two (+ pron encl, *tray-*, as *trayhon* the two of them, both of them)

ܬܪܝܢܐ *trayyānā/trayyānitā* second

ܬܪܝܨ *triṣ* correct, right, upright, straightforward

ܬܪܡܝܬܐ *tarmyātā* (f pl) foundation

ܬܪܢܓܘܠܬܐ *tarnāgultā* hen

ܬܪܢܓܠܐ *tarnāglā* (abs *tarnāgul)* cock

ܬܪܣܝ *tarsi/ntarsē* to nourish, rear, supply

ܬܪܥ *tra^c/netro^c* to break through

ܬܪܥܐ *tar^{c}ā* (abs *tra^c)* gate, doorway; *tra^c-malkutā* court, palace

ܬܪܥܝܬܐ *tar^{c}itā* mind, opinion

ܬܪܬܝܢ *tartēn* see *trēn*

ܬܫܒܘܚܬܐ *tešboḥtā* glorification, praise; hymn

ܬܫܡܫܬܐ *tešmeštā* service, ministration

ܬܫܥ *tša*^{c} (f)/*teš*^{c}*ā* (m) nine

ܬܫܥܝܬܐ *taš*^{c}*itā* pl *taš*^{c}*yātā* story, tale

ܬܫܪܝ/ܬܫܪܝܢ *tešri(n) ḥrāy* November; *tešri(n) qdēm* October

ܬܬܪܝܐ *tātārāyā* Tatar

Preliminary exercise (p. xxv):

ܐܒܘܢ ܕܒܫܡܝܐ. ܢܬܩܕܫ ܫܡܟ. ܬܐܬܐ ܡܠܟܘܬܟ. ܢܗܘܐ
ܨܒܝܢܟ ܐܝܟܢܐ ܕܒܫܡܝܐ. ܐܦ ܒܐܪܥܐ. ܗܒ ܠܢ ܠܚܡܐ
ܕܣܘܢܩܢܢ ܝܘܡܢܐ. ܘܫܒܘܩ ܠܢ ܚܘܒܝܢ. ܐܝܟܢܐ ܕܐܦ ܚܢܢ ܫܒܩܢ
ܠܚܝܒܝܢ. ܘܠܐ ܬܥܠܢ ܠܢܣܝܘܢܐ. ܐܠܐ ܦܨܢ ܡܢ ܒܝܫܐ. ܡܛܠ ܕܕܝܠܟ
ܗܝ ܡܠܟܘܬܐ ܘܚܝܠܐ ܘܬܫܒܘܚܬܐ ܠܥܠܡ ܥܠܡܝܢ.

*a**ḇ**[1]un **d**[4]-**ḇ**[2]a-šmayyā. neṯ[1]qa**dd**[5]aš šmā**ḵ**[1]. **t**[4]êṯ[1]ē malk[4]uṯ[1]ā**ḵ**[1]. nehwē ṣe**ḇ**[1]yānā**ḵ**[1] ay**k**[4]annā **ḏ**[1]-**ḇ**[2]a-šmayyā ā**p̱**[1] **b**[4]-ar^{c}a. ha**ḇ**[1] lan laḥmā **ḏ**[1]-sunqānan yawmānā. wa-š**ḇ**[2]oq lan ḥaw**b**[4]ayn. ay**k**[4]annā **ḏ**[1]-ā**p̱**[1] ḥnan š**ḇ**[2]aqn l-ḥayyā**ḇ**[1]ayn. w-lā **ṯ**[1]a^{cc}lan l-nesyōnā. ellā **p̱**[1]aṣṣān men **b**[4]išā. meṭṭul **d**[4]-**ḏ**[2]ilā**ḵ**[1]-i mal**k**[4]**uṯ**[3]ā w-ḥaylā w-**ṯ**[2]ešb[4]oḥṯ[3]ā l-^{c}ālam-^{c}ālmin.*

[1] spirantized because preceded by a vowel
[2] spirantized because preceded by an implied schwa (see p. xiii)
[3] spirantized because the feminine ending *-tā* is always spirantized
[4] not spirantized because preceded by a consonant
[5] not spirantized because the stop is doubled

Exercise 1

1 sleq men mḏittā. 2 ^{c}erqaṯ l-ṭurā. 3 ^{c}raq men mḏittā. 4 sleqēn l-ṭurā. 5 np̱al gaḇrā. 6 keṯbaṯ atttā. 7 ^{c}raq ^{c}ammā men hārḵā. 8 kṯaḇ malkā l-^{c}ammā. 9 ^{c}raqun men tammān. 10 šem^{c}aṯ malkṯā. 11 ^{c}erqaṯ atttā men mḏittā. 12 ^{c}raq gaḇrā men malkā. 13 selqaṯ atttā men tammān. 14 np̱al gaḇrā men ṭurā. 15 lā ^{c}raq malkā men mḏittā. 16 lā selqaṯ atttā men hārḵā. 17 lā šma^{c} l-malkā. 18 selqaṯ malkṯā men ^{c}ammā. 19 lā ^{c}raq gaḇrā l-ṯammān. 20 selqaṯ atttā la-mḏittā.

Exercise 2

1 eḇaḏ gaḇrā b-ar^{c}ā. 2 l-mānā lā nṭart l-nāmōsā? 3 sleqnan b-ṣap̱rā. 4 nep̱qeṯ w-ezzeṯ l-nahrā. 5 ^{c}ḇar ^{c}al nāmōsā. 6 kṯaḇ la-ḵṯāḇā malkā. 7 b-ramšā ^{c}barn l-nahrā. 8 mānā emart l-gaḇrā attṯā? 9 ezzeṯ men mḏittā ḇ-ṣap̱rā. 10 np̱aqton men mḏittā l-ṭurā. 11 ^{c}raq ^{c}ammā men qriṯā w-ezal la-mḏittā. 12 gaḇrā qṭal l-malkā. 13 lā ^{c}barnan ^{c}al nāmōsā. 14 mān eḥaḏ gaḇrā men qriṯā? 15 sleq l-ṭurā w-ṯammān eḇaḏ. 16 mā emart l-^{c}ammā? 17 eḇdaṯ ba-qriṯa attṯā. 18 l-mānā lā qṭalt l-malkā wa-l-malkṯā? 19 lā šem^{c}eṯ l-gaḇrā. 20 eḥdeṯ kṯāḇā w-ezzeṯ l-nahrā. 21 lā ^{c}raqn men qriṯā ḇ-ramšā. 22 lā qṭal l-attṯā. 23 kṯaḇt (keṯbaṯ) l-malkā kṯāḇā. 24 ^{c}erqeṯ men tammān w-ezzeṯ l-hārḵā. 25 emreṯ l-malkā ^{c}al attṯā. 26 lā emarnan l-^{c}ammā ^{c}al malkā. 27 l-mānā lā emarton l-malkā ^{c}al nāmōsā? 28 l-malkā wa-l-malkṯā qṭaln.

Exercise 3

1 man ezal ^{c}ammḵon? 2 nḥeṯ malkā la-mḏittā ^{c}am ^{c}ammā. 3 nesbeṯ l-ḵespā mennāḵ. 4 eḵal ^{c}amman. 5 nḥeṯton ^{c}aḏ yammā. 6 ^{c}erqeṯ menneh. 7 šlaḥ lwāṯ malkā šliḥā. 8 nsaḇ gaḇrā l-p̱uqdānā mennhon. 9 ezaln ^{c}aḏ qriṯā. 10 man ^{c}ḇaḏ l-laḥmā? 11 layt l-gaḇrā ḵespā. 12 sleq lwāṯ gaḇrā da-^{c}raq men mḏittā ḏ-layt bāh mayyā. 13 layt b-ar^{c}ā nḇiyā. 14 layt lan laḥmā ḇ-ḇaytā. 15 lā nṭarnan l-p̱uqdānā da-nsaḇ nḇiyā men ṭurā. 16 neḥteṯ men ṭurā w-ezzeṯ ^{c}aḏ yammā. 17 man šlaḥ lāḵ lwāṯan? 18 attṯā d-^{c}eḇdaṯ laḥmā nep̱qaṯ w-selqaṯ ^{c}amm w-^{c}ammeh. 19 iṯ b-ar^{c}ā nahrā ḏ-iṯ bāh mayyā. 20 iṯ ba-mḏittā malkā w-malkṯā. 21 šlaḥ kespā la-mḏittā ^{c}am šliḥā. 22 mānā emarton la-šliḥā ḏa-^{c}raq men tammān? 23 layt lāh baytā ḇa-qriṯā. 24 ezal nḇiyā lwāṯ ^{c}ammā w-emar lhon l-mānā lā nṭarton l-nāmōsā? 25 ^{c}raq gaḇrā menn. 26 eḵleṯ ^{c}ammāḵ laḥmā. 27 sleq men mayyā. 28 np̱aq mennan. 29 man emar lāḵ ^{c}al kespā d-eḥaḏ malkā men ^{c}ammā? 30 neḥteṯ la-mḏittā w-nesbeṯ l-ḵespā men šliḥā.

Exercise 4

1 rḏap̱ malkā ḇāṯar b^{c}eldḇāḇeh. 2 šeḇqeṯ l-^{c}aḇdā ḏ-hayklā. 3 eḥaḏ l-ḏahḇ b^{c}eldḇāḇ wa-^{c}raq la-mḏittā. 4 layt hārḵā ḵespā ḏ-ḏilāḵ. 5 lā

^{c}ḏar lāḵ ^{c}aḇdan. 6 rḏap̱ gaḇrā l-^{c}aḇdeh. 7 rheṭ ^{c}aḇdā ḏ-hayklā bāṯar gaḇrā ḏ-eḥaḏ l-ḵespā ḏ-ḏileh. 8 ezzeṯ la-qriṯā da-nḇiyā. 9 šḇaq l-^{c}aḇdeh gaḇrā. 10 lā ^{c}ḏar li ḏahḇāḵ. 11 šlaḥ malkā la-šliḥeh lwāṯāḵ. 12 nsaḇ gaḇrā ḵespā mennhon. 13 ^{c}ḇaḏ aykannā ḏa-p̱qaḏ lhon malkā ḏa-mḏittā. 14 emreṯ lāh aykannā ḏ-emart li. 15 rehṭeṯ bāṯarhon. 16 rḏap̱ bāṯreh b^{c}eldḇāḇā ^{c}aḏ yammā w-ṯammān eḇaḏ. 17 qṭal la-ḇ^{c}eldḇāḇeh d-malkā. 18 np̱aq nḇiyā men bayteh b-ṣap̱rā wa-sleq l-ṭurā. 19 reḏpeṯ la-ḇ^{c}eldḇāḇ ba-mḏittā ḵollāh. 20 ^{c}ḏar lan ^{c}ammā ḵollhon. 21 emar li gaḇrā ḵollmeddem d-emraṯ leh attṯā. 22 šḇaq kollmeddem d-eḥaḏ men hayklā wa-^{c}raq. 23 eḥdeṯ koll-meddem d-ḏil w-ezzeṯ l-ḇayt. 24 rheṭnan bāṯar ^{c}aḇdā ḏ-gaḇrā aykannā ḏa-p̱qaḏ lan. 25 eḵalt kolleh laḥmā ḏ-^{c}eḇdaṯ lāḵ attṯāḵ? 26 l-mānā lā ^{c}eḇdaṯ kollmeddem d-p̱eqdeṯ lāh? 27 l-mānā šḇaq l-ḇaython d-ḇa-qriṯā w-ezal la-mḏittā?

Exercise 5

1 rḏap̱ malkē ḇāṯar b^{c}eldḇāḇē ^{c}aḏ mḏinaṯhon. 2 lā šḇaqnan ^{c}aḇdē ḇ-hayklē. 3 l-ḏahḇan eḥaḏ gaḇrē wa-^{c}raq la-mḏināṯā. 4 rḏap̱ l-^{c}aḇdē gaḇrē. 5 rheṭ ^{c}aḇdē ḇāṯar gaḇrē ḏ-eḥaḏ l-ḏahḇhon dilhon. 6 ezzeṯ l-quryā ḏa-nḇiyē. 7 lā šḇaq l-^{c}aḇdē. 8 lā ^{c}ḏar lāḵ dahḇē. 9 šlaḥ malkē la-šliḥē lwāṯan. 10 nsaḇ gaḇrē l-ḵespē mennan. 11 ^{c}ḇaḏ ^{c}aḇdē aykannā ḏa-p̱qaḏ lhon malkē. 12 emraṯ leh attṯā aykannā ḏ-emar lāh neššē. 13 rheṭ bāṯarhēn neššē. 14 rḏap̱ bāṯar b^{c}eldḇāḇā ^{c}aḏ yammā w-ṯammān li qṭal. 15 kaḏ qṭal l-g̱aḇrā, selqaṯ nap̱šeh la-šmayyā. 16 hā malaḵē ḏ-alāhā qreḇ leh la-nḇiyā. 17 šḇaq la-mḏittā wa-^{c}mar ba-qriṯā. 18 qreḇ l-ḇaytāh d-emmhon. 19 man qṭal b^{c}eldḇāḇhon d-malkē? 20 qerbaṯ malkuṯā ḏa-šmayyā. 21 l-mānā rḏap̱ la-nḇiyē? 22 kaḏ nḥeṯ men ṭurā, np̱aq w-ezal l-ḇayteh. 23 qṭal l-nap̱šeh. 24 lā qṭal l-nap̱šhon. 25 np̱aq nḇiyē men baytāh d-attṯā. 26 rḏap̱ ^{c}ammā kollhon la-ḇ^{c}eldḇāḇeh d-malkā. 27 ^{c}mar neššē ḇ-quryā. 28 kaḏ qreḇ b^{c}eldḇāḇā, ^{c}raq kollhon gaḇrē. 29 l-nāmosā ḏ-alāhā nṭar gaḇrā. 30 nḥeṯ malaḵē men šmayyā. 31 eḥdeṯ laḥmē ḵollhon men baytā w-selqeṯ l-ṭurā ^{c}am emm. 32 hāḵannā emar nḇiyā kaḏ nsaḇ puqdānē ḏ-alāhā.

Index

Numbers refer to paragraphs in the text.